SOCIOLOGICAL METHODOLOGY

2000

SOCIOLOGICAL METHODOLOGY 2000

VOLUME 30

EDITORS: Michael E. Sobel and Mark P. Becker

ADVISORY EDITORS: Kenneth A. Bollen
Jacques A.P. Hagenaars
Edgar Kiser
Calvin Morrill
Martina Morris
Susan A. Murphy
Trond Petersen
Elizabeth Stasny
Ross M. Stolzenberg
Kazuo Yamaguchi

MANAGING EDITOR: Carson C. Hicks

An official publication by Blackwell Publishers for

THE AMERICAN SOCIOLOGICAL ASSOCIATION

FELICE LEVINE, *Executive Officer*

Library of Congress Catalog Card Information
Sociological Methodology, 1969–85

San Francisco, Jossey-Bass. 15 v. illus. 24 cm. annual. (Jossey-Bass behavioral science series)

Editor: 1969, 1970: E. F. Borgatta; 1971, 1972, 1973–74: H. L. Costner; 1975, 1976, 1977: D. R. Heise; 1978, 1979, 1980: K. F. Schuessler; 1981, 1982, 1983–84: S. Leinhardt; 1985: N. B. Tuma

Sociological Methodology, 1986–88

Washington, DC, American Sociological Association. 3 v. illus. 24 cm. annual.

Editor: 1986: N. B. Tuma; 1987, 1988: C. C. Clogg

Sociological Methodology, 1989–1992

Oxford, Basil Blackwell. 4 v. illus. 24 cm. annual.

Editor: 1989, 1990: C. C. Clogg; 1991, 1992: P. V. Marsden

"An official publication of the American Sociological Association."

1. Sociology—Methodology—Year books. I. American Sociological Association. II. Borgatta, Edgar F., 1924– ed.

HM24.S55	301′.01′8	68-54940
	rev.	
Library of Congress	[r71h2]	

British Cataloguing in Publication Data
Sociological Methodology. Vol. 30

7 1. Sociology. Methodology
301′.01′8

ISBN 0-631-22148-4
ISSN 0081-1750

REVIEWERS

Paul D. Allison
Luc Anselin
Neal Beck
Kenneth A. Bollen
Ronald Breiger
Babette Brumback
Mitchell Duneier
Zvi Gilula
Daniel Griffith
David H. Grusky
Shelby J. Haberman
Jacques A. P. Hagenaars
David Heise
Ge Lin
Xihong Lin
Bruce Lindsay
Roderick P. McDonald
Abt Mooijaart
Calvin Morrill
Ted Mouw
Susan A. Murphy
Trond Petersen
Stanley Presser
Stephen W. Raudenbush
Mark Reiser
Norbert W. Schwarz
Michael Seltzer
Arthur L. Stinchcombe
Robert Stine
Ross M. Stolzenberg
Clem Stone
Thomas R. TenHave
Peter G. M. van der Heijden
Kazuo Yamaguchi

CONTENTS

CONTRIBUTORS

Alan Agresti, Department of Statistics, University of Florida

Carolyn J. Anderson, Department of Educational Psychology, University of Illinois

Gerhard Arminger, Department of Economics, Bergische Universität Wuppertal

William G. Axinn, Department of Sociology and Institute for Social Research, University of Michigan

Jennifer S. Barber, Institute for Social Research, University of Michigan

Peter M. Bentler, Department of Psychology, University of California at Los Angeles

James Booth, Department of Statistics, University of Florida

Brian Caffo, Department of Statistics, University of Florida

Tzuwei Cheng

Clifford C. Clogg†, Formerly of the Department of Statistics and the Department of Sociology, Pennsylvania State University

James P. Hobert, Department of Statistics, University of Florida

Jan M. Hoem, Demography Unit, Stockholm University

†Clifford C. Clogg passed away in May, 1995.

Jerry Maples, The Methodology Center and Department of Statistics, Pennsylvania State University

John Levi Martin, Department of Sociology, Rutgers University

James D. Montgomery, Interdisciplinary Institute of Management, London School of Economics

Susan A. Murphy, Department of Statistics and Institute for Social Research, University of Michigan

Jeroen K. Vermunt, Department of Methodology, Faculty of Social and Behavioral Sciences, Tilburg University

James Wiley, The Public Health Institute, Berkeley, California

Ke-Hai Yuan, Department of Psychology, University of North Texas

SUBMISSION INFORMATION FOR AUTHORS

Sociological Methodology is an annual volume on methods of research in the social sciences. Sponsored by the American Sociological Association, its mission is to disseminate material that advances empirical research in sociology and related disciplines. Chapters present original methodological contributions, expository statements on and illustrations of recently developed techniques, and critical discussions of research practice.

Sociological Methodology seeks contributions that address the full range of problems confronted by empirical work in the contemporary social sciences, including conceptualization and modeling, research design, data collection, measurement, and data analysis. Work on the methodological problems involved in any approach to empirical social science is appropriate for *Sociological Methodology*.

The content of each annual volume of *Sociological Methodology* is driven by submissions initiated by authors; the volumes do not have specific themes. Editorial decisions about manuscripts submitted are based on the advice of expert referees. Criteria include originality, breadth of interest and applicability, and expository clarity. Discussions of implications for research practice are vital, and authors are urged to include empirical illustrations of the methods they discuss.

Authors should submit five copies of manuscripts to:

Ross M. Stolzenberg, Editor
Sociological Methodology
Department of Sociology
307 Social Science Building
1126 East 59th Street
Chicago, Illinois 60637

Manuscripts should include an informative abstract of not more than one double-spaced page, and should not identify the author within the text. Submission of a manuscript for review by *Sociological Methodology* implies that it has not been published previously and that it is not under review elsewhere.

Inquiries concerning the appropriateness of material and/or other aspects of editorial policies and procedures are welcome; prospective authors should correspond with the editor by e-mail at r-stolzenberg@uchicago.edu.

IN THIS VOLUME

FOREWORD

Latent variables of one form or another have proven invaluable in many scientific disciplines. Sociology is no exception, with its long tradition of latent structure modeling. In this volume of *Sociological Methodology* the chapters by Anderson and Vermunt; Martin and Wiley; and Yuan and Bentler advance this tradition, albeit in different ways. A related but not identical line of work that is becoming increasingly important involves the incorporation of so-called random effects into regression-type models, be they linear regressions, event-history regressions, or categorical response regressions. The contributions by Agresti, Booth, Hobert, and Caffo; Arminger, Clogg, and Cheng; and Barber, Murphy, Axinn, and Maples advance this line of work. Thus six of the eight chapters in this volume are concerned with latent variables in one guise or another.

The publication of this volume also marks the conclusion of the late Clifford C. Clogg's research career. The opening chapter is the result of a long and fruitful collaboration between Cliff and his dear friend and colleague, Gerhard Arminger. We are delighted to have the opportunity to publish the results of the work that they were deeply engaged in at the time of Cliff's sudden and unexpected death in May 1995. (Please see the opening chapter of *Sociological Methodology 1996* for a tribute to Cliff's life and work.)

Contents

Chapters 1 and 2 are concerned with models and estimation procedures for categorical responses when one or more of the predictors is a latent variable or random effect. Rasch models and more general latent trait models, which arise out of psychometrics and educational testing, are well-known examples. Recently, advances in statistical computing and power have led researchers to put forth and consider broad generalizations of these models, applicable in a variety of substantively interesting and useful contexts.

Arminger, Clogg, and Cheng, building on Lindsay, Clogg, and Grego (1991), consider semiparametric estimation of Rasch models with covariates, applying their model in the context of panel data. It is important to note that minimal assumptions are made about the distribution of the random effects in the model. Thus the models should be especially attractive to empirical researchers in the usual case where it is difficult to justify on substantive grounds important assumptions about the distribution of the random effects that are invoked in order to use such methods. The authors also provide an algorithm for fitting the models that can be viewed as a compromise between unidimensional and full Newton-Raphson.

In Chapter 2, Agresti, Booth, Hobert, and Caffo give a state of the art review of the generalized linear mixed models (GLMMs) approach to random-effects modeling of categorical responses. The models are especially useful when the observed responses do not arise from independent observations, as in longitudinal studies, family studies, and other settings where observations are either clustered and/or serially correlated. Applications of this type of modeling are starting to become more common in sociology and the authors cite a number of such articles. Further, they present nine different examples to illustrate the potential utility of the models to a broad range of sociological topics. Readers will find this paper useful not only for the breadth of applications considered but also because it includes detailed discussion of practical computational tools for fitting GLMMs. In particular, relatively detailed discussion and example code for SAS Institute's PROC NLMIXED is provided in the paper, and the SAS macro %GLIMMIX is discussed as an appropriate maximum-likelihood method. Other computing programs, including EGRET, MIXOR, BUGS, HLM, and LogExact, are also discussed. Finally, the reader will benefit from relating example 5 in this chapter to the previous chapter by Arminger, Clogg, and Cheng.

In Chapter 3, Anderson and Vermunt take up a latent variable model that is directly related to association models for multivariate categorical responses. The authors start with a general model for multiple correlated latent variables, and they develop both graphical representations for the models and corresponding log-multiplicative association models. Interestingly, both this chapter and its predecessor use the now classic Coleman (1964) panel data on membership and attitude with respect to the "leading crowd," and a comparison of the two analyses will give the reader deeper insights into both sets of methodological contributions and their respective utility in substantive work.

In Chapter 4, Martin and Wiley continue the line of research they reported on in *Sociological Methodology 1999*. There they developed latent class models for sets of dichotomous items where each item measured a particular dichotomous belief. Beliefs were related through relations of precedence (which impose restrictions on the response patterns) and the statistical model was completed by imposing restrictions on the permissible patterns of measurement error. In this paper, however, the observed dichotomous items (macrobeliefs) may measure more than one latent microbelief. To illustrate the proposed procedures, the authors analyze items from the General Social Survey on beliefs regarding economic equality.

In Chapter 5, Yuan and Bentler propose a new minimum χ^2 estimator for parameters in covariance structure models when some of the data are missing. The estimator has desirable asymptotic properties when the missing data are missing completely at random; it is not assumed that the data are drawn from a multivariate normal distribution. They also compare the performance of this estimator with several other estimators appropriate for this situation, and they develop a suitable test statistic for testing the fit of the model using this estimator.

Random-effects models are also the subject of Chapter 6, in which Barber, Murphy, Axinn, and Maples discuss a discrete-time survival model where the random effects are assumed to follow a normal distribution. The authors show that standard software for "multilevel" models can be used to fit the model. To illustrate, they model the hazard for adopting contraception using the logistic model with the woman's education, number of previous children and two terms for time as covariates; the intercept and the parameters for education and number of previous children are then allowed to depend upon characteristics of the neighborhood in which the woman lives.

In Chapter 7, Hoem considers the analysis of event-history data when certain combinations of the regressors are impossible or unobserved, implying there is no exposure information for such combinations. Consider, for example, an event-history analysis of divorce including mother's parity and the age of youngest child as predictors. Should childless women be excluded from such an analysis, or are there special considerations that must be taken into account to include them in the model, and ultimately in the interpretation of the model coefficients? This is one of Hoem's examples, and it provides an excellent context for illustrating the issues and Hoem's proposed solution.

Sociologists have long noted that persons do not simply and automatically enact the norms that are bundled together into a role, implying that traditional versions of role theory are too strong. But sociologists continue to find the basic ideas underlying role theory attractive, as evidenced by attempts to relax such theories to permit more nuanced patterns of behavior. A typical way to weaken a deterministic theory that does not successfully account for the evidence is to make the theory probabilistic; thus, for example, Stryker (1980) has put forth a version of role theory that is essentially probabilistic. In Chapter 8, Montgomery approaches this problem using fuzzy sets. Whereas in classical set theory, the function that describes whether or not an element belongs to a given set is binary (say 0 for not belonging, 1 for belonging), in fuzzy set theory, this function is allowed to take on all values in the (closed) unit interval. Thus, using fuzzy set theory, a person could, for example, "nearly" hold (not hold) the role of father. Montgomery then works through some of the implications of this point of view and contrasts his work with other approaches—for example, affect control theory and rational choice.

ACKNOWLEDGMENTS

We thank the reviewers and advisory editors who so graciously and generously gave of their time to help us and the authors. The tradition of scholarly excellence for which *Sociological Methodology* is known and respected is in no small part due to the efforts of these persons and their counterparts before them. We are especially grateful to Carson Chase Hicks for her outstanding contributions, as managing editor, to the production of this volume. Likewise, we sincerely appreciate the efforts of the copy editor, Stephanie Argeros-Magean, and the help of Janet Cronin and Roberta

Spinosa-Millman of Blackwell Publishers. *Sociological Methodology* is sponsored and supported by the American Sociological Association.

REFERENCES

Coleman, James S. (1964). *Introduction to Mathematical Sociology*. Glencoe, IL. The Free Press.

Lindsay, Bruce G., Clifford C. Clogg, and John M. Grego. 1991. "Semi-Parametric Estimation in the Rasch Model and Related Exponential Response Models, Including a Simple Latent Class Model for Item Analysis." *Journal of the American Statistical Association* 86:96–107.

Stryker, Sheldon. 1980. *Symbolic Interactionism: A Social Structural Version.* Menlo Park, CA: Benjamin/Cummings.

1

REGRESSION ANALYSIS OF MULTIVARIATE BINARY RESPONSE VARIABLES USING RASCH-TYPE MODELS AND FINITE-MIXTURE METHODS

*Gerhard Arminger**
Clifford C. Clogg†
Tzuwei Cheng†

A model is considered for the regression analysis of multivariate binary data such as repeated-measures data (for example, panel data) or multiple-indicators with measures of some underlying characteristic such as attitude or ability (for example, surveys or tests). The model is related to the usual Rasch model, the usual latent-class model, and other familiar models such as logistic regression.

This paper is dedicated to Clifford C. Clogg, who died on May 7, 1995. Clogg's research was supported in part by Grant SBR-9310101 from the National Science Foundation and in part by the Population Research Institute, Pennsylvania State University, which has core support from the National Institute of Child Health and Human Development (Grant 1-HD28263-01). Previous versions of this paper were presented at the 1993 annual meetings of the Population Association of America (March 1993), the Penn State Conference on Latent Structure Models for the Analysis of Development and Change (May 1993), and the Institute for Science Education (University of Kiel) Conference, "Applications of Latent Trait and Latent Class Models in the Social Sciences," held at Akademie Sankelmark, Germany, May 15–20, 1994. We thank the editors and anonymous reviewers of *Sociological Methodology* for helpful remarks on the previous version and Alexandra Schwarz from Bergische Universität for technical help. Address correspondence to G. Arminger, Department of Economics (FB 6), Bergische Universität, D-42097 Wuppertal, Germany; arminger@wwst09.wiwi.uni-wuppertal.de.
*Bergische Universität Wuppertal
†Pennsylvania State University

In addition to a regression specification, the model includes parameters that describe heterogeneity not accounted for by the predictors. In contrast to most other approaches, a nonparametric specification of the latent mixing distribution is used, leading to a formulation based on scaled latent classes. We examine the relationship between this model and several other models, give a tractable formulation of the likelihood function and likelihood equations, present an algorithm for maximum-likelihood estimation, and analyze marginal and conditional latent structures. The approach is illustrated with longitudinal data from the German Socioeconomic Panel.

1. INTRODUCTION

A model is proposed for the regression analysis of repeated binary measurements or similar data structures featuring multiple, correlated, or clustered binary response variables. The model can be viewed as a generalization of the binary logit model (Agresti 1990), the usual latent-class model (Goodman 1974), and the usual Rasch model (with covariates) (Fischer and Ponocny 1994; Hsiao 1986). It consists of a *regression structure* relating predictors to each response variable and a *latent structure* describing unmodeled heterogeneity or intercorrelation among response variables not captured by the regression specification. For the regression structure, predictors for each response variable may be either discrete or continuous, and different predictors can be used for each response variable.

The analysis of multivariate categorical response variables, including repeated-measures data, has received much attention recently. Diggle, Liang, and Zeger (1994), Hamerle and Ronning (1995), Lindsey (1993), and Liang, Zeger, and Qaqish (1992) provide reviews and further references. Our approach integrates several perspectives. The semiparametric approach of Lindsay, Clogg, and Grego (1991) for inference in the Rasch model without covariates is a special case. This paper extends that approach to the general context of regression analysis; we concentrate on model formulation, likelihood equations, an algorithm for estimation, and the analysis of latent structure, and we give an illustrative example. In future work we hope to examine diagnostic methods and further generalizations of the model.

An important special case is the logistic regression model for longitudinal binary data when unobserved heterogeneity across individual elements (in the sense of individual regression intercepts) is assumed. If the unobserved heterogeneity is correlated with regressors in the model, the usual maximum-likelihood estimators are inconsistent for the regression parameters. Consistent estimates may be obtained using the conditional estimation procedure for the Rasch model with covariates (cf. Hamerle and Ronning 1995; Hsiao 1986). However, this is extremely cumbersome and therefore seldom used. The latent structure formulation and semiparametric estimation method developed here is feasible, and also provides more parsimonious models that lie between the simple logistic model and the Rasch model with covariates.

2. THE MODEL AND POSSIBLE DATA STRUCTURES

We assume a data structure of the following sort. For subject i, $y_{ij} \in \{0,1\}$ is the observed response associated with random variable $Y_{ij}, i = 1,\ldots,n;$ $j = 1,\ldots,J$. The J response variables may be (1) repeated measures of the same variable (J occasions of measurement as in a panel study), (2) "indicators" or ostensibly similar variables measured at the same point in time (as in educational testing or survey research), (3) a collection of binary response variables of any form (for example, labor force participation, experience of poverty, presence of children) whose joint dependence on predictor variables is to be investigated, or (4) any combination of the first three cases. For simplicity, we refer to the J measurements as "occasions" using the imagery of longitudinal data collection designs.

The predictors for the i-th subject on the j-th occasion are $\boldsymbol{x}_{ij} = \{1, x_{ij2}, \ldots, x_{ijK}\}$, with the vector of ones always included. The predictors can be categorical, continuous, or mixtures of the two types. If the number of predictors varies by occasion, K_j can be substituted for K with only slight changes in results. Note that $\boldsymbol{x}_{ij'}$ need not equal $\boldsymbol{x}_{ij''}$—that is, the predictors for occasion j' can be different from those for occasion j''. With a panel-data structure, for example, this means that predictors can be either time-fixed or time-varying.

Let W denote a discrete, scaled latent variable having $T \geq 1$ categories. The categories of W will be called "latent classes." W is characterized by (1) the unknown *latent-class proportions*, or mixing weights, $\pi_1,\ldots,\pi_T$ with $\sum_{t=1}^{T} \pi_t = 1$ and $\pi_t > 0, t = 1,\ldots,T$, and (2) the unknown *latent-class scores*, $\alpha_t, t = 1,\ldots,T$. The marginal latent distribution can be characterized in terms of these parameters. For example, the mean is $E(W) = \sum_{t=1}^{T} \pi_t \alpha_t$ and the variance is $V(W) = \sum_{t=1}^{T} \pi_t \alpha_t^2 - (E(W))^2$; both are identified even with $T = 2$ latent classes. Note that the third moment can be identified—or a skewed latent distribution allowed—even with $T = 2$ latent classes. Higher-order moments can be defined in terms of the parameters above when $T > 2$ latent classes are posited.

The model characterizes the dependence or correlation (or the conditional dependence or conditional correlation given predictor variables) among the response variables in terms of W. W can be viewed as an approximation to a continuous variable with distribution F_{α^*} and realizations α_i^*. In most applications using a continuous latent mixing distribution, F would be assumed to be a tractable distribution characterized by a small set of parameters (say, the expectation and variance if F is Gaussian). If we take the view that the heterogeneity-inducing factor is a latent random variable having an unknown distribution F, our approach gives a nonparametric representation of F. That is, a certain number of moments of F can be identified using the parameters that describe the latent variable W.

Let $\pi_{ij|t} = Pr(Y_{ij} = 1 | W = t)$, the probability of a "success" for the i-th individual at the j-th occasion, given that W takes on level t and the explanatory variables take on the value $\boldsymbol{x}_{ij}$. Our model is

$$\text{logit}(\pi_{ij|t}) = \alpha_t + \boldsymbol{x}_{ij}\boldsymbol{\beta}_j, j = 1, \ldots, J, t = 1, \ldots, T, \qquad (1)$$

where $\boldsymbol{\beta}_j' = \{\beta_{j1}, \ldots, \beta_{jK}\}$ is a vector of *regression coefficients* for the j-th occasion and α_t is the "shift" in the intercept for the t-th latent class; the intercepts are $\alpha_t + \beta_{j1}$ ($x_{ij1} = 1$ for each i, j is assumed). The regression coefficients do not vary over latent classes. The model is completed by assuming conditional independence of the responses over occasions, given $W = t$, as discussed in the next section.

3. LIKELIHOOD FUNCTION

We give a detailed account of the likelihood function for the model partly to facilitate comparison with related models. But the main objective is to exploit the special structure of the model to simplify the likelihood. The formulation presented here also simplifies the estimation problem and is used to develop the algorithmic machinery to solve the likelihood equations. The assumptions used to build the model are also clarified.

For the i-th subject at occasion j, the following expression follows from (1):

$$\pi_{ij|t} = [\exp(\alpha_t + \boldsymbol{x}_{ij}\boldsymbol{\beta}_j)]/[1 + \exp(\alpha_t + \boldsymbol{x}_{ij}\boldsymbol{\beta}_j)],$$
$$j = 1, \ldots, J, t = 1, \ldots, T. \qquad (2)$$

Now assume that within the t-th latent class, the responses to the J items are mutually independent for the i-th individual; this gives

$$P(\boldsymbol{y}_i | W = t) = \exp\left(y_{i+}\alpha_t + \sum_{j=1}^{J} y_{ij}\boldsymbol{x}_{ij}\boldsymbol{\beta}_j \right) \times \left[\prod_{j=1}^{J} (1 + \exp(\alpha_t + \boldsymbol{x}_{ij}\boldsymbol{\beta}_j)) \right]^{-1}, \qquad (3)$$

where $\boldsymbol{y}_i = \{y_{i1}, \ldots, y_{iJ}\}$ is the response pattern for the i-th individual, and $y_{i+} = \sum_{j=1}^{J} y_{ij}$. The conditional independence (or "local independence") assumption used in (3) produces the same simplification that is used in latent-structure analysis (Clogg 1995; Goodman 1974; Lazarsfeld and Henry 1968). This assumption says that the association among the response variables remaining after taking predictors into account is explained by the discrete mixing variable W.

The joint probability of $\boldsymbol{y}_i$ and $W = t$ is π_t times the expression in (3). Summing over t thus gives the log-likelihood function $\ell_i(\boldsymbol{\theta})$ for the i-th observation:

$$\ell_i(\boldsymbol{\theta}) = \log\left\{ \sum_{t=1}^{T} \pi_t \left[\exp\left(y_{i+}\alpha_t + \sum_{j=1}^{J} y_{ij}\boldsymbol{x}_{ij}\boldsymbol{\beta}_j \right) \right] \times \left[\prod_{j=1}^{J} (1 + \exp(\alpha_t + \boldsymbol{x}_{ij}\boldsymbol{\beta}_j)) \right]^{-1} \right\}, \qquad (4)$$

where $\boldsymbol{\theta} = \{\boldsymbol{\psi}, \boldsymbol{\beta}\}$, $\boldsymbol{\psi} = (\{\pi_t, \alpha_t\}, t = 1, \ldots, T)$ is the vector of latent-structure parameters, and $\boldsymbol{\beta} = \{\boldsymbol{\beta}_1, \ldots, \boldsymbol{\beta}_J\}$ is the vector of regression parameters.

4. RELATIONSHIP TO THE RASCH REGRESSION MODEL

The Rasch model with predictors for each response (Rasch regression model) replaces (2) by

$$P_{ij} = Pr(Y_{ij} = 1 | \alpha_i) = [\exp(\alpha_i + \boldsymbol{x}_{ij}\boldsymbol{\beta}_j)]/[1 + \exp(\alpha_i + \boldsymbol{x}_{ij}\boldsymbol{\beta}_j)], \qquad (5)$$

where α_i is a fixed "subject parameter" (for example, see Hamerle and Ronning 1995; Hsiao 1986). The classical Rasch model for item analysis includes no predictors besides the vector of ones, so that $\boldsymbol{x}_{ij}\boldsymbol{\beta}_j$ is replaced by $\beta_j^*, j = 1, \ldots, J$, where β_j^* is a scalar and is often interpreted as item difficulty. (For example, see Andersen 1980, 1991; Fischer 1995.) This special case is used widely in educational testing and has been advocated for item analysis in surveys by Clogg (1988) and others. However, in the Rasch regression model, the outcomes are always conditioned on the observed values of the exogenous variables.

For individual i, the log-likelihood for the Rasch regression model, which is also completed by adding the assumption of conditional independence across items, can be written as

$$\ell_i^R(\boldsymbol{\theta}^*) = y_{i+}\alpha_i + \sum_{j=1}^{J} y_{ij}\boldsymbol{x}_{ij}\boldsymbol{\beta}_j + \log\left[\prod_{j=1}^{J}(1+\exp(\alpha_i + \boldsymbol{x}_{ij}\boldsymbol{\beta}_j))\right]^{-1}, \tag{6}$$

where $\boldsymbol{\theta}^* = (\{\alpha_i\}_{i=1}^n, \{\beta_j\}_{j=1}^J)$. If the α_i are regarded fixed subject parameters, the y_{i+} are sufficient statistics for these parameters. Typically, conditional likelihood methods are used to analyze this fixed-effects Rasch regression model. This method conditions on $Y_{i+} = y_{i+}$, producing a conditional likelihood function $\Lambda_c^R(\boldsymbol{\beta})$ that is free of the nuisance parameters α_i.

The probability of response pattern $\boldsymbol{y}_i$ in the Rasch regression model is similar to (3):

$$P(\boldsymbol{y}_i) = \exp\left(y_{i+}\alpha_i + \sum_{j=1}^{J} y_{ij}\boldsymbol{x}_{ij}\boldsymbol{\beta}_j\right) \times \left[\prod_{j=1}^{J}(1+\exp(\alpha_i + \boldsymbol{x}_{ij}\boldsymbol{\beta}_j))\right]^{-1}. \tag{7}$$

The conditional log-likelihood requires the calculation of the probability that $y_{i+} = r$ for $r = 0, 1, \ldots, J$. This is equal to summing over all probabilities of the form (7) with response patterns $\boldsymbol{d}_i$ where $d_{ij} \in \{0,1\}$ and $\sum_{j=1}^{J} d_{ij} = r$. The set of these response patterns is denoted B_r:

$$P(y_{i+} = r) = \sum_{\boldsymbol{d}_i \in B_r} \exp\left(r\alpha_i + \sum_{j=1}^{J} d_{ij}\boldsymbol{x}_{ij}\boldsymbol{\beta}_j\right) \times \left[\prod_{j=1}^{J}(1+\exp(\alpha_i + \boldsymbol{x}_{ij}\boldsymbol{\beta}_j))\right]^{-1}. \tag{8}$$

To find a different representation of $P(y_{i+} = r)$, the new quantity γ_{ri} is defined:

$$\gamma_{ri} = \sum_{\boldsymbol{d}_i \in B_r} \exp\left(\sum_{j=1}^{J} d_{ij}\boldsymbol{x}_{ij}\boldsymbol{\beta}_j\right). \tag{9}$$

Hence, $P(y_{i+} = r)$ may be written as

$$P(y_{i+} = r) = \gamma_{ri} \exp(r\alpha_i) \left[\prod_{j=1}^{J} (1 + \exp(\alpha_i + \boldsymbol{x}_{ij} \boldsymbol{\beta}_j)) \right]^{-1}. \tag{10}$$

The conditional probability for response pattern $\boldsymbol{y}_i$ given that the sum $y_{i+} = r$ is therefore

$$P(\boldsymbol{y}_i | r_i) = \frac{P(\boldsymbol{y}_i)}{P(y_{i+} = r)} = \frac{\exp\left(\sum_{j=1}^{J} y_{ij} \boldsymbol{x}_{ij} \boldsymbol{\beta}_j \right)}{\sum_{\boldsymbol{d}_i \in B_r} \exp\left(\sum_{j=1}^{J} d_{ij} \boldsymbol{x}_{ij} \boldsymbol{\beta}_j \right)}$$

$$= \gamma_{ri}^{-1} \exp\left(\sum_{j=1}^{J} y_{ij} \boldsymbol{x}_{ij} \boldsymbol{\beta}_j \right). \tag{11}$$

Each individual conditional probability can therefore be expressed as a multinomial logit model with $\binom{J}{r}$ alternatives. The set of alternatives depends on the individual y_{i+} ranging from $y_{i+} = 0, 1, \ldots, J$. The conditional probabilities with $y_{i+} = 0$ and $y_{i+} = J$ are equal to 1 and therefore do not add to the conditional log-likelihood. Hence, only observations with $1 \leq y_{i+} \leq J - 1$ can be used. The conditional log-likelihood for the Rasch regression model is therefore given by

$$\log \Lambda_c^R(\boldsymbol{\beta}) = \sum_{i=1}^{n} \log P(\boldsymbol{y}_i | y_{i+} = r) = \sum_{j=1}^{J} \left(\sum_{i=1}^{n} y_{ij} \boldsymbol{x}_{ij} \right) \boldsymbol{\beta}_j - \sum_{i=1}^{n} \log \gamma_{ri}. \tag{12}$$

The practical implementation of the estimation of $\boldsymbol{\beta}$ from maximizing the conditional log-likelihood of (12) is rather cumbersome since the individual conditional probabilities correspond to multinomial logit models with individually specific sets of alternatives for which no standard software exists. This may explain the rare use of the Rasch regression model for the analysis of multivariate binary responses.

The log-likelihood of the mixture model defined as the sum of individual log-likelihood functions in (4) can be decomposed as the sum of the conditional log-likelihood function of the Rasch regression model (12) and the log-likelihood for the raw scores given the regressors. For this purpose, we extend the arguments of Formann (1995) for the classical

Rasch model and the latent-class model to the Rasch regression model and latent-class models with covariates. First, we note from (4) that the log-likelihood $\ell(\boldsymbol{\theta})$ may be written as

$$\ell(\boldsymbol{\theta}) = \sum_{i=1}^{n} \ell_i(\boldsymbol{\theta}) = \sum_{j=1}^{J}\left(\sum_{i=1}^{n} y_{ij}\boldsymbol{x}_{ij}\right)\boldsymbol{\beta}_j + \sum_{i=1}^{n} \log\left[\sum_{t=1}^{T} \pi_t \frac{\exp(y_{i+}\alpha_t)}{\prod_{j=1}^{J}(1+\exp(\alpha_t + \boldsymbol{x}_{ij}\boldsymbol{\beta}_j))}\right]. \tag{13}$$

Second, we note the probability that $y_{i+} = r$ can be written in a similar way to (8), that is

$$P(y_{i+} = r) = \sum_{\boldsymbol{d}_i \in B_r} \sum_{t=1}^{T} \pi_t \exp\left(r\alpha_t + \sum_{j=1}^{J} d_{ij}\boldsymbol{x}_{ij}\boldsymbol{\beta}_j\right) \times \left[\prod_{j=1}^{J}(1+\exp(\alpha_t + \boldsymbol{x}_{ij}\boldsymbol{\beta}_j))\right]^{-1}. \tag{14}$$

Setting again $\gamma_{ri} = \sum_{\boldsymbol{d}_i \in B_r} \exp(\sum_{j=1}^{J} d_{ij}\boldsymbol{x}_{ij}\boldsymbol{\beta}_j)$ as in (9) yields

$$P(y_{i+} = r) = \gamma_{ri} \sum_{t=1}^{T} \pi_t \frac{\exp(r\alpha_t)}{\prod_{j=1}^{J}(1+\exp(\alpha_t + \boldsymbol{x}_{ij}\boldsymbol{\beta}_j))} \tag{15}$$

and

$$\frac{P(y_{i+} = r)}{\gamma_{ri}} = \sum_{t=1}^{T} \pi_t \frac{\exp(r\alpha_t)}{\prod_{j=1}^{J}(1+\exp(\alpha_t + \boldsymbol{x}_{ij}\boldsymbol{\beta}_j))}. \tag{16}$$

Using the equality in (16), the log-likelihood (13) may be written as

$$\begin{aligned}\ell(\boldsymbol{\theta}) &= \sum_{j=1}^{J}\left(\sum_{i=1}^{n} y_{ij}\boldsymbol{x}_{ij}\right)\boldsymbol{\beta}_j + \sum_{i=1}^{n} \log \frac{P(y_{i+} = r)}{\gamma_{ri}} \\ &= \sum_{j=1}^{J}\left(\sum_{i=1}^{n} y_{ij}\boldsymbol{x}_{ij}\right)\boldsymbol{\beta}_j - \sum_{i=1}^{n} \log \gamma_{ri} + \sum_{i=1}^{n} \log P(y_{i+} = r) \\ &= \log \Lambda_c^R(\boldsymbol{\beta}) + \sum_{i=1}^{n} \log P(y_{i+} = r).\end{aligned} \tag{17}$$

The first term is identical with the conditional log-likelihood of the Rasch regression model. The second term is the log-likelihood of the raw score distribution given the regressors, which is denoted by:

$$\log \Lambda_m(\boldsymbol{\psi}, \boldsymbol{\beta}, \{y_{i+}\}) = \sum_{i=1}^{n} \log P(y_{i+}). \tag{18}$$

The conditional ML estimation of $\boldsymbol{\beta}$ from the Rasch regression model and from maximizing $\ell(\boldsymbol{\theta})$ in the finite-mixture model yields the same parameter estimates, if for a fixed value T^* of the number of latent classes, the values of

$$D_r = \sum_{i=1}^{n} \frac{z_{ir}}{P(y_{i+} = r)} \tag{19}$$

are equal for $r = 0, 1, \ldots J$. The variable z_{ir} equals 1 if the observed value of y_{i+} equals r and is 0 otherwise. The sum of the ratios of the observed frequency that y_{i+} equals r and the probability computed from the model that $y_{it} = r$ have to be the same for all $r = 0, 1, \ldots, J$.

For proof we note that for the finite mixture log-likelihood the score function for $\boldsymbol{\beta}$ is given by

$$\frac{\partial \ell(\boldsymbol{\theta})}{\partial \boldsymbol{\beta}} = \frac{\partial \log \Lambda_c^R(\boldsymbol{\beta})}{\partial \boldsymbol{\beta}} + \frac{\partial \log \Lambda_m(\boldsymbol{\psi}, \boldsymbol{\beta}, \{y_{i+}\})}{\partial \boldsymbol{\beta}}. \tag{20}$$

Hence, the score functions for $\boldsymbol{\beta}$ in the finite mixture log-likelihood and in the conditional log-likelihood for the Rasch regression model are equal only if

$$\frac{\partial \log \Lambda_m(\boldsymbol{\psi}, \boldsymbol{\beta}, \{y_{i+}\})}{\partial \boldsymbol{\beta}} = \mathbf{0}. \tag{21}$$

To find the conditions under which (21) holds, we use the following transformations:

$$\log \Lambda_m(\boldsymbol{\psi}, \boldsymbol{\beta}, \{y_{i+}\}) = \sum_{i=1}^{n} \log P(y_{i+} = r) = \sum_{i=1}^{n} \log\left[\prod_{r=0}^{J} P(y_{i+} = r)^{z_{ir}}\right]$$
$$= \sum_{i=1}^{n}\sum_{r=0}^{J} z_{ir} \log P(y_{i+} = r). \tag{22}$$

Since $P(y_{i+} = J) = 1 - \sum_{r=0}^{J-1} P(y_{i+} = r)$, the first derivative of $\log \Lambda_m(\boldsymbol{\psi}, \boldsymbol{\beta}, \{y_{i+}\})$ with respect to β_{jk} is given by

$$\frac{\partial \log \Lambda_m(\boldsymbol{\psi}, \boldsymbol{\beta}, \{y_{i+}\})}{\partial \beta_{jk}} = \sum_{r=0}^{J-1} \left[\sum_{i=1}^{n} \frac{z_{ir}}{P(y_{i+} = r)} - \sum_{i=1}^{n} \frac{z_{iJ}}{P(y_{i+} = J)} \right] \times \frac{\partial P(y_{i+} = r)}{\partial \beta_{jk}}. \tag{23}$$

This derivative is for all values of β_{jk} 0 only if D_r in (19) is equal for all $r = 0, 1, \ldots, J$.

If there are no predictors, then

$$D_r = \frac{n_r}{P(y_{i+} = r)}, \tag{24}$$

where n_r is the observed frequency of the raw score r in the sample. Equality of D_r for $r = 0, 1, \ldots J$ is the condition that the estimates from the latent-class model without predictors and T^* latent classes and the conditional ML estimates of the item difficulties in the Rasch model coincide. The upper bound for the number T^* of latent classes is $(J + 1)/2$ (cf. Formann 1995; Lindsay, Clogg and Grego 1991). There are two ways to check from the sample whether the condition that D_r is equal for all r is fulfilled. The first is to substitute $P(y_{i+} = r)$ in D_r by the estimated probability $\hat{P}(y_{i+} = r)$ for $T = 1, \ldots, (J + 1)/2$ and check for which T^* the condition is fulfilled. The second, easier way is to compute the log-likelihood values successively for $T = 1, \ldots$ and stop when the log-likelihood does not increase which will usually be at the terminal point $(J + 1)/2$ (cf. Formann 1995; Lindsay, Clogg and Grego 1991).

It is customary to estimate and analyze the Rasch regression model without estimation of the fixed subject parameters. This strategy is useful when the primary goal is to draw inferences about the regression parameters (see Cox 1958; Andersen 1980). To make inferences about the distribution of subject parameters, as in estimating the distribution of ability from educational tests, researchers often switch to a random-effects version, typically assuming that the α_i derive from a tractable parametric family (normal, logistic, etc.), leading to various marginal-likelihood estimators. Our approach places equal attention on the regression parameters and the latent distribution, but it avoids parametric assumptions about the latter. Useful inferences concerning the latent distribution can be obtained using the semiparametric approach featured here, as demonstrated in the example.

5. THREE SPECIAL CASES

Three special cases of the model follow. These can be defined in relation to either the Rasch regression model or the finite-mixture model considered in detail here. Special estimation methods are not required for the first two cases. The special cases can serve as baseline models for evaluating the fit of other models. They are useful also for determining start values in the algorithm developed later for the general model; the algorithm has been tailored so that start values can be determined easily by using solutions obtained for the special cases.

1. *Marginal independence:* H_{MI}. Set $T = 1$ (one "latent class") and $K = 1$ (no predictors other than the intercept terms). The model in (1) then asserts the mutual independence of the items, $P(\boldsymbol{y}_i) = \prod_{j=1}^{J} P_{+j}^{y_{ij}}(1 - P_{+j})^{1-y_{ij}}$ where P_{+j} is the probability that the score $y_{+j} = \sum_{i=1}^{n} y_{ij}$ occurs in the population. This quantity may be estimated from the relative frequency $\hat{P}_{+j}$ of score y_{+j} in the sample. Equivalently, H_{MI} is the main-effects-only log-linear model for the 2^J contingency table cross-classifying the J items, or the model $\text{logit}(P_{ij}) = \beta_{j1}$; it assumes a homogeneous population and no predictors other than intercepts. This model forms a natural baseline for all models.

2. *Independent logit:* H_{IL}. Set $T = 1$ (one "latent class") but include predictors (i.e., $K > 1$ predictors for each occasion). This model reduces to a set of J independent logistic regressions whose parameters can be estimated by considering each occasion separately, using conventional algorithms for binary logit models, or estimated simultaneously using the algorithm described below. While H_{MI} is a natural baseline we expect to be false, model H_{IL} can be realistic. Return to the Rasch model described by (5). If one or more predictors are included that correlate highly with the α_i, the predictors would account for a part of the heterogeneity or correlation among multiple outcomes. The same comment applies to the latent-class model. Note that because our model allows inclusion of time-varying covariates, for cases where the replicates refer to panel observations, this model is more general than might be supposed at first glance; see

Clogg, Eliason, and Grego (1990) for some of the standard possibilities based on this formulation. This model is useful for diagnosing identifiability (or estimability) questions for the regression part of the general model, and it can also be used to obtain start values for estimating the other models.

3. *Marginal Rasch:* H_{MR}. For the latent-class version of Rasch's model, set $T^* = (J+1)/2$ if J is odd, $T^* = J/2 + 1$ if J is even. (In the latter case, the parameters for latent structure ($\boldsymbol{\psi}$) will not be identified unless one restriction, such as $\pi_1 = \pi_2$, is imposed on these parameters. See Lindsay, Clogg, and Grego (1991).) Models with $T\,(1 < T < T^*)$ can also be considered. Model H_{MR} is defined with any such value of T, with all predictors except the intercepts excluded. Because H_{MR} does not include predictors, inferences about latent structure pertain to the marginal joint distribution of the Y variables, not to the latent structure based on conditional variation in Y variables given X. The latent distribution in H_{MR} is thus the unconditional (marginal) distribution of the population heterogeneity.

The general model is called the *Rasch-Type Logit Model*, H_{RL}. For this model, pick T as in the *marginal Rasch* model and include predictors. The notation $H_{RL}(T)$ is used to denote the model with T latent classes.

The nestedness of the models above deserves comment. H_{MI} is a special case of all models considered. The following nesting properties are easily verified: (1) $H_{IL} \subset H_{RL}$, (2) $H_{MR}(T) \subset H_{RL}(T)$, (3) $H_{RL}(T) \subset H_{RL}(T'), T < T'$. H_{IL} and H_{MR} are not nested. Nested models are often compared using the likelihood ratio chi-squared statistic. Note that this statistic is asymptotically chi-square distributed when both models have the same number of latent classes; otherwise, this is not the case (Titterington et al. 1985), though the likelihood ratio statistic may be useful in a qualitative sense.

6. IDENTIFIABILITY

The different models have different identifiability conditions (or estimability conditions), which are described in an intuitive way here. Standard methods can be used to examine the shape of the log-likelihood function at or near the solution, but the following discussion should be useful for both diagnostic checking and model building.

6.1. *Identifying the Regression Parameters*

There are J logit regressions in the general model. Identifiability or estimability of the regression parameters (the $\boldsymbol{\beta}_j$) can be determined using standard methods for identifiability or estimability of conventional logistic regressions. This assumes an appropriate level of variability (over subjects) in the y_{ij}. It also assumes that $\mathbf{X}_j$, the model matrix for the j-th replicate, is of full column rank. We recommend separate fitting of the usual binary logit model to check these conditions (that is, consider model H_{IL}). Note that identifiability of the regression parameters in H_{IL} is necessary but not sufficient for identifiability of these parameters in H_{RL} models. This is seen from the denominator in (3). If the variables $\boldsymbol{x}_{ij}$ are constant across j, i.e., $\boldsymbol{x}_{ij} = \boldsymbol{x}_i$ and the regression coefficients are also constant across j—i.e., $\boldsymbol{\beta}_j = \boldsymbol{\beta}$—then $\sum_{j=1}^{J} y_{ij}\boldsymbol{x}_{ij}\boldsymbol{\beta}_j = \boldsymbol{x}_i\boldsymbol{\beta}y_{i+}$. Hence, y_{i+} is not only a sufficient statistic for α_t but also for $\boldsymbol{x}_i\boldsymbol{\beta}$; this coincides with the observation found in Hamerle and Ronning (1995) who consider the Rasch regression model for panel data with time constant regression coefficients. They point out that the regression coefficients cannot be estimated with the conditional ML method if the predictors do not vary over time. Since we allow predictors that do not change over the occasions $j = 1,\ldots,J$, we assume that the regression coefficients vary across j.

6.2. *Identifying the Latent Distribution—General Considerations*

For $T > 1$, the latent distribution consists of two sets of parameters: the π_t (latent-class proportions) and the α_t (latent-class scores), for $t = 1,\ldots,T$. The proportions satisfy $\sum_{t=1}^{T} \pi_t = 1$, so at most $T - 1$ of these are nonredundant. There are T parameters α_t (for $t = 1,\ldots,T$); it is assumed that $\alpha_t \neq \alpha_{t'}, t \neq t'$. There are thus $(T - 1) + T = 2T - 1$ parameters for the latent distribution. The number of parameters for the latent distribution cannot exceed the number of nonredundant values in the set of sufficient statistics—the $\{y_{i+}, i = 1,\ldots,n\}$ for the α_i in the Rasch model (Lindsay, Clogg, and Grego 1991). These "score totals" take on values in the set $\{0,1,\ldots,J\}$, for a total of $J + 1$ values. Let n_r denote the observed frequency of score total r. At most J parameters can be used to describe (or "fit") the score distribution completely, so there can be no more than J identified parameters for the latent distribution.

6.3. *Identifying the Latent Distribution for Models H_{MR} and H_{RL}*

Consider the model with no covariates first, H_{MR}. From (1), the model is unchanged if $\alpha_t^* = \alpha_t + c, \beta_{j1}^* = \beta_{j1} - c$ for any constant c. To resolve this location problem we set $\beta_{J1} = 0$ (Andersen 1980). This suffices to identify the latent distribution if $T \leq (J+1)/2$. The mean of the latent distribution is thus arbitrary, but the variance and other central moments are identified. This identifying restriction changes the intercepts in the regression part of the model, however. Other constraints could be used, such as $\sum_t \alpha_t = 0$ (reducing the number of parameters for the latent distribution by one) or $\sum_j \beta_{j1} = 0$ (placing a different constraint on the intercepts).

7. LIKELIHOOD EQUATIONS

A detailed treatment of the likelihood equations is given for several reasons. First, it shows that the finite-mixture approach to the general model is tractable, at least more tractable than previously assumed. Second, both score functions and Hessian functions have relatively simple forms; using these, a variety of numerical methods for obtaining maximum-likelihood estimates can be devised. (The Hessian matrix is given in the appendix.) A relatively simple algorithm based on these quantities is outlined here. Third, these formulas shed light on the relationship of the general model to logistic regression, and the relationship of the general model to other models in the latent structure family. Finally, these relationships can be extended in straightforward ways to develop the necessary machinery for more general models, such as repeated polytomous measures or repeated ordinal measures (Conoway 1989).

Throughout, the identifying restriction $\beta_{J1} = 0$ is assumed when latent structure models H_{MR}, H_{RL} are considered. Alternative restrictions as discussed above can be imposed with straightforward changes in the results.

The regression function for the j-th occasion is written as $\boldsymbol{x}_{ij}\boldsymbol{\beta}_j = \sum_{k=1}^{K} x_{ijk}\beta_{jk}$. The logit transform of the latent class proportion π_t is used, $\phi_t = \log(\pi_t/\pi_T)$, with inverse $\pi_t = \exp(\phi_t)/(1 + \sum_{t=1}^{T-1} \exp(\phi_t))$, $t = 1, \ldots, T-1$.

The following quantities are used to derive the main results:

$$q = -\log\left[1 + \sum_{t=1}^{T-1} \exp(\phi_t)\right], \tag{25}$$

$$Q_{it} = \exp\left(\phi_t + y_{i+}\alpha_t - \sum_{j=1}^{J} \log[1 + \exp(\alpha_t + \boldsymbol{x}_{ij}\boldsymbol{\beta}_j)]\right), \tag{26}$$

$$Q_i = \sum_{t=1}^{T} Q_{it}, \tag{27}$$

$$U_{it} = \sum_{j=1}^{J} [1 + \exp(-\alpha_t - \boldsymbol{x}_{ij}\boldsymbol{\beta}_j)]^{-1}, \tag{28}$$

$$V_{ij} = \sum_{t=1}^{T} Q_{it}[1 + \exp(-\alpha_t - \boldsymbol{x}_{ij}\boldsymbol{\beta}_j)]^{-1}, \tag{29}$$

and

$$W_{it} = \sum_{j=1}^{J} \exp(-\alpha_t - \boldsymbol{x}_{ij}\boldsymbol{\beta}_j)/[1 + \exp(-\alpha_t - \boldsymbol{x}_{ij}\boldsymbol{\beta}_j)]^2. \tag{30}$$

Using (4) and (25)–(27) gives the log-likelihood function for the i-th observation as

$$\ell_i(\boldsymbol{\theta}) = q + \sum_{j=1}^{J} y_{ij}\boldsymbol{x}_{ij}\boldsymbol{\beta}_j + \log Q_i. \tag{31}$$

In (31) and below, $\boldsymbol{\theta}$ refers to the vector of nonredundant (identified) parameters, a collection of $p = (T-1) + T + JK - 1 = 2T + JK - 2$ parameters, corresponding respectively to the parameters $\phi_t, \alpha_t, \beta_{jk}$. Within each latent class, the log-likelihood can be written in exponential-family form. For related representations for the latent class model, see Formann (1985); for somewhat different representations, see Haberman (1988) and the references cited there.

It is easy to verify that when $T = 1$, (31) is equivalent to the log-likelihood for J independent logistic regression models, with $\alpha_1 = 0$, $Q_i = Q_{i1}, q = 0$, and $\phi_1 = 0$. Each of the special cases discussed in Section 5 leads to simplifications in the log-likelihood.

The score functions and the likelihood equations they imply are obtained as $s_i(\theta_l) = \partial \ell_i(\boldsymbol{\theta})/\partial \theta_l$ for each parameter θ_l. For the logit-transform of the latent class proportions, we obtain

$$s_i(\phi_t) = Q_{it}/Q_i - \pi_t, \quad t = 1, \ldots, T-1, \tag{32}$$

with the associated likelihood equations

$$\hat{\pi}_t = n^{-1} \sum_i \hat{Q}_{it}/\hat{Q}_i, \quad t = 1, \ldots, T-1. \tag{33}$$

If $T = 1$ (the J regression functions are independent), (33) is skipped.

For the α_t parameters,

$$s_i(\alpha_t) = (Q_{it}/Q_i)(y_{i+} - U_{it}), \quad t = 1, \ldots, T. \tag{34}$$

At the solution point this can be rewritten as $\hat{\pi}_t(y_{i+} - \hat{U}_{it})$ in view of (33). Note that if $T = 1$, (34) is not relevant.

For the regression parameters $\boldsymbol{\beta}_j = \{\beta_{jk}, j = 1, \ldots, J, k = 1, \ldots, K\}$, we obtain

$$s_i(\beta_{jk}) = x_{ijk}(y_{ij} - V_{ij}/Q_i), \quad j = 1, \ldots, J, k = 1, \ldots, K. \tag{35}$$

For $T > 1$, the equation for β_{J1} is skipped as $\beta_{J1} = 0$ is assumed. If there are no predictors other than the intercepts, the model is the latent-class version of Rasch's model (Lindsay, Clogg, and Grego 1991), and the score function reduces to $y_{ij} - V_{ij}/Q_i$.

8. AN ITERATIVE PROCEDURE

We have experimented with several algorithms and discuss here one hybrid algorithm that gives satisfactory results. Let the parameter vector with nonredundant elements be denoted $\boldsymbol{\theta} = \{\theta_1, \ldots, \theta_p\}$, with $p = 2T + JK - 2$. Factor this as $\boldsymbol{\theta} = \{\boldsymbol{\psi}, \boldsymbol{\beta}\}$ where $\boldsymbol{\psi}$ refers to the parameters for the latent distribution (i.e., $\boldsymbol{\psi} = \{\phi_t, \alpha_t\}$), with $2T - 1$ elements, and $\boldsymbol{\beta}$ refers to the regression parameters, with $JK - 1$ elements for the general model.

First consider the ordinary Newton-Raphson procedure, which uses the overall score function (say, $\boldsymbol{S} = \{S_1, \ldots, S_p\}$) and the full Hessian matrix (say, $\boldsymbol{H}$). Let $\boldsymbol{H}^r$ and $\boldsymbol{S}^r$ denote the values of these quantities at the r-th cycle. The adjustment at cycle $r+1$ is

$$\boldsymbol{\theta}^{(r+1)} = \boldsymbol{\theta}^{(r)} + (-\boldsymbol{H}^{(r)})^{-1} \boldsymbol{S}^{(r)}. \tag{36}$$

This procedure can diverge unless start values are reasonably close to the solution. For some trial datasets, the negative of the Hessian used at initial stages of the Newton-Raphson procedure was not positive definite. See Haberman (1988) for similar comments as well as a stabilized algorithm that can be used, at least for frequency (or cross-classified) data.

An algorithm based on a simple modification of the ordinary Newton-Raphson procedure is now described. Let $\boldsymbol{H}^*$ denote the block-diagonal matrix obtained from the Hessian by replacing the entries for the mixed derivatives with respect to $\boldsymbol{\psi} \times \boldsymbol{\beta}$ with zeros. Then replace the algorithm in (36) with

$$\boldsymbol{\theta}^{(r+1)} = \boldsymbol{\theta}^{(r)} + (-\boldsymbol{H}^{*(r)})^{-1}\boldsymbol{S}^{(r)}. \tag{37}$$

After each cycle, the score function and the elements of $\boldsymbol{H}^*$ are updated, but the block-diagonalized $\boldsymbol{H}^*$ is used in place of $\boldsymbol{H}$. After convergence, the full Hessian can be calculated, and the inverse of $-\boldsymbol{H}$ at the solution provides the usual estimator of the variance-covariance matrix of all parameters. (In cases where the parameters were all identifiable—i.e., when $T \leq (J+1)/2$—we found $(-\boldsymbol{H})$ was positive definite.) We found that this algorithm converges to a solution at a satisfactory rate in all models with identifiable parameters. Note, that this algorithm is a kind of compromise between a full Newton-Raphson algorithm, using the ordinary Hessian matrix, and a kind of (unidimensional) Newton (or IPF) algorithm using only a diagonal (not block diagonal) version of the Hessian matrix. A simple modification can also be suggested: use the algorithm in (37) for, say, 5 cycles, then convert to the ordinary Newton-Raphson algorithm in (36) using the full Hessian. For models with unidentifiable parameters (for the latent distribution), the algorithm in (37) converges also, although it is slower. (For such cases it is not possible to invert the full Hessian matrix unless the model is modified by imposing one or more restrictions on the latent distribution.)

As with mixture models in general and latent-class models in particular, it is not sufficient to define tolerance for convergence in terms of the score functions alone. Another criterion used in conjunction with the gradient is the average absolute change in parameter values from cycle to cycle. This or some related criterion ought to be used in addition to the gradient for models of this type.

Models H_{MI}, H_{IL}, and H_{MR}, defined earlier, can be used to obtain start values for the general model. Difficulties in selecting appropriate start values in trial work convinced us of the importance of modifying the ordinary Newton-Raphson algorithm and the utility of these special cases for the determination of start values. For H_{MI}, the only parameters are the logit-transforms of the marginal probabilities, which can be obtained without iteration as $\hat{\beta}_{j1} = \text{logit}(\hat{P}_{+j})$. With the identifying restriction $\beta_{J1} = 0$ imposed in model H_{MR}, convenient start values for the regression intercepts are $\beta^*_{j1} = \text{logit}(\hat{P}_{+j}) - \text{logit}(\hat{P}_{+J})$, for $j = 1, \ldots, J-1$. For model H_{MR} and for $T = 2$ we can use an average of the $\hat{P}_{+j}$ as a start value for π_1. Start values for the α_t parameters can be obtained using trial and error. That is, H_{MI} is used to obtain start values for models in the H_{MR} family, and once values from H_{MR} are in hand (for a specified value of T), the values from this model can be used as start values for the latent structure parameters $\boldsymbol{\psi}$ in models in the H_{RL} family.

For model H_{IL}, start values are simple to obtain (e.g., use the marginal logits for the intercept terms and zeros for the other regression coefficients). Of course, the parameters for this model can be obtained simply by estimating the J logit regressions. In (31) and below, $\boldsymbol{\theta}$ refers to the parameters of the independent logistic regression models. Finally, trial values for the $\boldsymbol{\beta}$ parameters from the H_{IL} model, and trial values for the $\boldsymbol{\psi}$ parameters from the H_{MR} model, can be used for the general model. Centering and standardizing the predictors is important for stability of calculations, and this rescaling is assumed above. The block-diagonal form of the modified Hessian matrix used in the algorithm of (37) is consistent with the "independent" selection of trial values from the H_{MR}, H_{IL} models.

9. EXAMPLE: UNEMPLOYMENT IN THE GERMAN SOCIOECONOMIC PANEL

We consider an example from the German Socioeconomic Panel (SOEP). A sample of $n = 1246$ men in the prime working ages beween 20 and 60 years in the experienced civilian labor force was observed from 1984 to 1989. The Y_{ij} variables are coded "1" for unemployed, "0" for employed, for a total of $J = 6$ occasions. The marginal distribution of the six responses (y_{+j}/n) was $\{.061, .078, .071, .077, .090, .079\}$ (that is, 1984 had the lowest unemployment risk for this group, 1988 the highest). The following sets of predictors were selected: (1) a set including total duration of unemployment in months during the 1974–1984 interval (x_2), age in years (x_3), marital status $(x_4, 1 = \text{married})$, university education $(x_5, 1 = \text{yes})$; and (2) a set including $x_6 = x_2^2/100$, frequency of unemployment during the

1974–1984 interval (x_7), age squared divided by 100 (x_8), an indicator for severely handicapped status ($x_9, 1$ = yes), an indicator of some professional education ($x_{10}, 1$ = yes), and an indicator for white-collar occupation ($x_{11}, 1$ = yes). Note that some of the variables are essentially continuous while others are binary. Several of the variables are time-varying (for example, x_4, x_5).

We consider three regression specifications: (1) the model with regression intercepts only ($K = 1$); (2) the model with $K = 5$ predictors from the first set above, for each occasion; (3) the model with $K = 11$ predictors from both sets above, for each occasion. Because $T^* = (J + 1)/2 = 3.5$, models with $T \leq 3$ latent classes will be identified, and the model with $T = 4$ latent classes will not have identified latent structure parameters without an additional restriction (but the regression parameters will be identified). The models have many parameters; for example, for the $H_{RL}(3)$ model with $T = 3$ latent classes and $K = 11$ predictors per occasion, there are five latent structure parameters and $6 \times 11 - 1 = 65$ regression parameters. Only models with unrestricted parameters are estimated—all coefficients are free to vary across occasions. The negative of the log-likelihood values are reported in Table 1.

Consider first the H_{MR} models found in column 1 of Table 1. The model with 1 latent class is the model of mutual independence (H_{MI}); because this model for the ungrouped data is equivalent to the model of

TABLE 1
Minus Log-Likelihood Values for Several Models

Number of Latent Classes	Number of Predictors per Wave (Including Intercept)		
	$K = 1$	$K = 5$	$K = 11$
$T = 1$	2008.189	1673.080	1523.272
$T = 2$	1364.206	1239.388	1171.399
$T = 3$	1323.248	1205.539	1141.004
$T = 4$	1322.334	1197.140	1126.092

Note: The minus log-likelihood value for the saturated model without predictors is 1244.036. The likelihood-ratio chi-squared statistics for the models $K = 1$ (no predictors) are 1568.30 ($df = 57$), 240.34 ($df = 55$), 158.42 ($df = 53$), and 156.59 ($df = 52$). See text for description of variables.

mutual independence for the 2^6 contingency table cross-classifying the six Y variables, this model has $64 - 1 - 6 = 57$ *df* and a likelihood-ratio chi-squared value of 1568.30. The model with $T = 4$ latent classes has a likelihood-ratio chi-squared value of 156.59 ($df = 52$), so we see that this model for the marginal joint distribution of the Y variables does not fit the data well. On the other hand, approximately 90 percent of the variation as measured with model H_{MI} is accounted for by the model $H_{MR}(T = 4)$. A variety of methods can be used to obtain the results for these models; see Lindsay, Clogg, and Grego (1991) and references cited there. Note that these four models have the following numbers of parameters for latent structure (i.e., elements of $\boldsymbol{\psi}$): 0,3,5,6; 6 is the maximal number of parameters required to fit the distribution of the score values y_{i+} with $J + 1 = 7$ distinct values.

Next consider the H_{IL} models with $T = 1$ and multiple predictors. We see that adding 10 predictors per occasion for the $K = 11$ model reduces the negative log-likelihood value substantially, but not as much as adding the parameters for latent structure in the models without predictor effects. Finally, consider the models in the second through fourth rows and the second and third columns of Table 1. These are in the H_{RL} family. Within the second row, the first comparison yields a likelihood-ratio chi-squared statistic of 249.64 ($df = 4 \times 6 = 24$), while the second gives a chi-squared statistic of 135.00 ($df = 36$). Within the third row, the first comparison gives a chi-squared value of 235.42 ($df = 24$), the second a chi-squared value of 129.07 ($df = 36$). By comparing log-likelihood values in this fashion, it is evident that the predictors are significant as sets, when judged in the usual way, and that inclusion of at least $T = 2$ and $T = 3$ latent classes leads to rather dramatic improvements in fit.

For $H_{RL}(4)$, estimates for the regression parameters and estimates of precision are equivalent to conditional likelihood estimates for the Rasch regression model; this follows by noting that the log-likelihood increases as T increases in each case (Lindsay, Clogg, and Grego 1991).

Regression parameters for the independent logit model are shown in Table 2. For illustrative purposes, only models with five predictors per occasion are considered. The coefficients are for the normalized predictors $x^*_{ijk} = (x_{ijk} - \bar{x}_{jk})/s(x_{jk})$ (excluding intercepts).

The regression coefficients for x_2 and x_3 (except for 1984, that is $j = 1$) are positive, predicting a higher probability of unemployment for men with longer duration of unemployment before 1984 and older men while the coefficients for x_4 and x_5 are negative, predicting a lower prob-

TABLE 2
Parameter Estimates for the Independent Logit Model, H_{IL}:
Five Predictors per Occasion

Predictor	$j = 1$	$j = 2$	$j = 3$	$j = 4$	$j = 5$	$j = 6$
Intercept	−3.222	−2.849	−2.814	−2.811	−2.492	−2.681
$s(\hat{\beta})$	.158	.136	.128	.131	.111	.124
x_2: Duration	.953	.915	.668	.819	.579	.515
$s(\hat{\beta})$	.095	.091	.080	.088	.076	.075
x_3: Age	−.171	.139	.062	.328	.251	.515
$s(\hat{\beta})$	.141	.123	.120	.124	.108	.119
x_4: Married	−.170	−.065	−.178	−.088	−.117	−.108
$s(\hat{\beta})$	.122	.116	.105	.112	.097	.105
x_5: University	−.057	−.341	−.131	−.135	−.150	−.151
$s(\hat{\beta})$	.156	.181	.142	.142	.126	.133

Note: Coefficients and standard errors are identical to those obtained from separate fitting of the six binary logit models. Note that intercepts are not restricted.

ability of unemployment for married men and men with a university degree. Note that the coefficients for x_5 are highly variable.

The corresponding estimates for two of the latent structure models—$H_{RL}(2)$ and $H_{RL}(3)$—appear in Table 3.

By comparing the estimates and standard errors in Tables 2 and 3, the consequences of ignoring heterogeneity are apparent (in both sets of quantities). Coefficient estimates from the independent logit specification are usually (but not always) attenuated, when compared with the coefficient estimates for the latent structure models in Table 3. The standard errors under the independent logit specification are substantially smaller as well, indicating bias (or inconsistency) in the estimation of precision.

Until now, we have considered only estimates of the regression structure. Unlike the case where the conditional likelihood approach to the Rasch model with covariates is used, we can also obtain information about the latent structure as shown in Table 4.

As an example we consider the model H_{RL} with three latent classes and five regression coefficients. The mixing probabilities are estimated as 0.056, 0.255, and 0.688 with scores 1.235, −2.287, and −6.322. Given the predictors, the population may be divided into three classes, the first one containing about 5.6 percent of the population with a very high rate of unemployment. The second class, with about 25.5 percent of the popula-

TABLE 3
Regression Parameter Estimates for Model $H_{RL}(2), H_{RL}(3)$

Predictor	$j = 1$	$j = 2$	$j = 3$	$j = 4$	$j = 5$	$j = 6$
			Model $H_{RL}(2)$			
Intercept	−.908	−.288	−.297	−.242	.304	.000*
$s(\hat{\beta})$	.256	.237	.235	.235	.234	NA
x_2: Duration	1.131	1.088	.732	.934	.592	.498
$s(\hat{\beta})$	.120	.116	.102	.114	.095	.099
x_3: Age	−.412	−.010	−.119	.408	.213	.648
$s(\hat{\beta})$	.189	.172	.174	.171	.160	.178
x_4: Married	−.141	.004	−.129	−.112	−.082	−.136
$s(\hat{\beta})$	.168	.160	.155	.154	.143	.148
x_5: University	.125	−.257	.071	−.015	−.143	−.103
$s(\hat{\beta})$	.202	.219	.187	.187	.178	.181
			Model $H_{RL}(3)$			
Intercept	−1.069	−.371	−.360	−.294	.286	.000*
$s(\hat{\beta})$	.267	.243	.240	.240	.223	NA
x_2: Duration	1.539	1.484	1.037	1.272	.867	.765
$s(\hat{\beta})$	.161	.160	.131	.148	.123	.121
x_3: Age	−.324	.123	−.014	.573	.347	.766
$s(\hat{\beta})$	.202	.186	.189	.187	.172	.183
x_4: Married	−.228	.061	−.191	−.224	−.170	−.195
$s(\hat{\beta})$	.181	.171	.170	.165	.154	.164
x_5: University	.004	−.415	−.237	−.186	−.329	−.289
$s(\hat{\beta})$	.202	.219	.195	.190	.181	.186

Note: Asterisk denotes fixed restriction for the given intercept; standard error not applicable (NA).

tion, has a somewhat higher risk than the average risk as seen by comparing the intercepts in Table 2 and the intercepts in the second panel of Table 3, where $\hat{\alpha}_2$ is added. Finally, we have a third group of men (about 68.8 percent of the population) at low risk of unemployment. Estimates of the mean, the variance and the skew of the mixing distribution are also given in Table 4, indicating that the mixing distribution is highly skewed.

APPENDIX: ELEMENTS OF THE HESSIAN MATRIX

The Hessian matrix for the i-th observation, $H_i(\theta_r, \theta_s) = \partial^2 \ell_i(\boldsymbol{\theta})/\partial\theta_r \partial\theta_s$, for $r = 1, \ldots, p, s = 1, \ldots, p$, can be obtained by direct differentiation of the

TABLE 4

Latent Structure Parameter Estimates for Some Models

Model	$\{\hat{\pi}_t\}$	$\{\hat{\phi}_t\}$	$\{\hat{\alpha}_t\}$	$\hat{E}(W)$	$\hat{V}(W)$	Skew
$H_{MR}(2)$	(.102, .898)	−2.177	(.502, −4.075)	−3.609	1.916	2.596
$H_{MR}(3)$	(.034, .098, .869)	(−3.249, −2.184)	(2.600, −.481, −4.727)	−4.065	2.883	2.736
$H_{RL}(2, K = 5)$	(.086, .914)	−2.360	(.568, −4.076)	−3.675	1.721	2.992
$H_{RL}(3, K = 5)$	(.056, .255, .688)	(−2.511, −.990)	(1.235, −2.287, −6.322)	−4.868	2.936	2.448
$H_{RL}(2, K = 11)$	(.126, .874)	−1.936	(−.215, −4.988)	−4.386	1.824	2.489
$H_{RL}(3, K = 11)$	(.049, .196, .755)	(−2.742, −1.349)	(1.125, −2.033, −6.450)	−5.216	2.973	2.393

Note: Standard errors not reported. Skew is measured as the third central moment divided by $V(W)^{3/2}$.

score functions given earlier. (The information matrix for the i-th observation is $\boldsymbol{I}_i = -\boldsymbol{H}_i$.)

Assuming $T > 1$, we obtain for the $\boldsymbol{\phi} \times \boldsymbol{\phi}$ block

$$H_i(\phi_{t'}, \phi_{t'}) = (Q_{it'}/Q_i)(1 - Q_{it'}/Q_i) - \pi_{t'}(1 - \pi_{t'}), \quad t' = 1, \ldots, T-1; \tag{A1}$$

$$H_i(\phi_{t'}, \phi_{t''}) = -(Q_{it'} Q_{it''}/Q_i) + \pi_{t'} \pi_{t''}, t' \neq t''. \tag{A2}$$

For the $\boldsymbol{\phi} \times \boldsymbol{\alpha}$ block, we obtain

$$H_i(\phi_{t'}, \alpha_{t'}) = (Q_{it'}/Q_i)(1 - Q_{it'}/Q_i)(y_{i+} - U_{i,t'}), \tag{A3}$$

$$H_i(\phi_{t'}, \alpha_{t''}) = -(Q_{it'} Q_{it''}/Q_i^2)(y_{i+} - U_{it''}), t' \neq t''. \tag{A4}$$

For the $\boldsymbol{\phi} \times \boldsymbol{\beta}$ block,

$$H_i(\phi_t, \beta_{jk}) = x_{ijk}(Q_{it}/Q_i)[V_{ij}/Q_i - 1/(1 + \exp(-\alpha_t - \boldsymbol{x}_{ij}\boldsymbol{\beta}_j)]. \tag{A5}$$

The remaining blocks involving parameters from the latent distribution are

$$H_i(\alpha_{t'}, \alpha_{t'}) = (Q_{it'}/Q_i)\{[y_{i+} - U_{i,t'}]^2[1 - Q_{it'}/Q_i] - W_{i,t'}\}; \tag{A6}$$

$$H_i(\alpha_{t'}, \alpha_{t''}) = -Q_{it'} Q_{it''}[y_{i+} - U_{it'}][y_{i+} - U_{it''}], t' \neq t''; \tag{A7}$$

$$\begin{aligned} H_i(\alpha_t, \beta_{jk}) = x_{ijk}(Q_{it}/Q_i) & \\ \times \{[y_{i+} - U_{i,t}][V_{i,j}/Q_i &- 1/(1 + \exp(-\alpha_t - \boldsymbol{x}_{ij}\boldsymbol{\beta}_j))] \\ &- \exp(-\alpha_t - \boldsymbol{x}_{ij}\boldsymbol{\beta}_j)/(1 + \exp(-\alpha_t - \boldsymbol{x}_{ij}\boldsymbol{\beta}_j))\}. \end{aligned} \tag{A8}$$

For the $\boldsymbol{\beta} \times \boldsymbol{\beta}$ block, define

$$V_{ij}^* = \sum_{t=1}^{T} Q_{it}(1 + \exp(-\alpha_t - \boldsymbol{x}_{ij}\beta_{ij}))^{-1}(1 + \exp(-\alpha_t - \boldsymbol{x}_{ij'}\boldsymbol{\beta}_{j'}))^{-1}. \tag{A9}$$

We then obtain

$$H_i(\beta_{jk}, \beta_{j'k'}) = \frac{x_{ijk} x_{ij'k'}}{Q_i} \times \left[V_{ij}^* - \frac{V_{ij} V_{ij'}}{Q_i} - z_{j,j'} \sum_{t=1}^{T} \frac{Q_{ti} \exp(-\alpha_t - \boldsymbol{x}_{ij} \beta_{ij})}{(1 + \exp(-\alpha_t - \boldsymbol{x}_{ij} \beta_{ij}))^2} \right], \tag{A10}$$

where $z_{j,j'} = 1$ if $j = j'$ and is zero otherwise. It can be verified that when $T = 1$ (J independent logistic regressions), the usual Hessian matrix is obtained for the regression parameters. This matrix takes on particularly simple forms for the other special cases of the general model.

REFERENCES

Agresti, Alain. 1990. *Categorical Data Analysis*. New York: Wiley.

———. 1992. "A Survey of Exact Inference for Contingency Tables" (with discussion). *Statistical Science* 7:131–77.

Andersen, Erling B. 1980. *Discrete Statistical Models with Social Science Applications*. Amsterdam: North-Holland.

———. 1991. *The Statistical Analysis of Categorical Data*, 2nd ed. Berlin: Springer-Verlag.

Anderson, John A. 1984. "Regression and Ordered Categorical Variables" (with discussion). *Journal of the Royal Statistical Society*, ser. B, 46:1–30.

Clogg, Clifford C. 1988. "Latent Class Models for Measuring." Pp. 173–205 in *Latent-Trait and Latent-Class Models*, edited by Rolf Langeheine and Jürgen Rost. New York: Plenum.

———. 1995. "Latent Class Models." Pp. 311–59 in *Handbook of Statistical Modeling for the Social and Behavioral Sciences*, edited by Gerhard Arminger, Clifford C. Clogg, and Michael E. Sobel. New York: Plenum.

Clogg, Clifford C., Scott R. Eliason, and John M. Grego. 1990. "Models for the Analysis of Change in Discrete Variables." Pp. 409–41 in *New Statistical Methods in Developmental Research*, vol. 2, edited by Alexander von Eye. New York: Academic Press.

Conaway, Mark R. 1989. "Analysis of Repeated Categorical Measurements with Conditional Likelihood Methods." *Journal of the American Statistical Association* 84:53–62.

Cox, David R. 1958. "Two Further Applications of a Model for Binary Regression." *Biometrika* 45:562–65.

Diggle, Peter J., Kung-Yee Liang, and Scott L. Zeger. 1994. *Analysis of Longitudinal Data*. Oxford: Oxford University Press.

Fischer, Gerhard H. 1995. "Derivations of the Rasch Model." Pp. 15–38 in *Rasch Models: Foundations, Recent Developments, and Applications*, edited by Gerhard Fischer and Ivo W. Molenaar. New York: Springer-Verlag.

Fischer, Gerhard H., and Ivo Ponocny. 1994. "An Extension of the Partial Credit Model with an Application to the Measurement of Change." *Psychometrika* 59:177–92.

Formann, Anton K. 1985. "Constrained Latent-Class Models: Theory and Applications." *British Journal of Mathematical and Statistical Psychology* 38:87–111.

———. 1995. "Linear Logistic Latent Class Analysis and the Rasch Model." Pp. 239–56 in *Rasch Models: Foundations, Recent Developments, and Applications*, edited by Gerhard Fischer and Ivo W. Molenaar. New York: Springer-Verlag.

Gilula, Zvi, and Shelby J. Haberman. 1994. "Conditional Log-Linear Models for Analyzing Categorical Panel Data." *Journal of the American Statistical Association* 89:645–56.

Goodman, Leo A. 1974. "Exploratory Latent Structure Analysis Using Both Identifiable and Unidentifiable Models." *Biometrika* 61:214–31.

Haberman, Shelby J. 1988. "A Stabilized Newton-Raphson Algorithm for Loglinear Models for Frequency Tables Derived by Indirect Observation." Pp. 193–212 in *Sociological Methodology 1988*, edited by Clifford C. Clogg. Washington: American Sociological Association.

Hamerle, Alfred. and Gerd Ronning. 1995. "Panel Analysis for Qualitative Variables." Pp. 401–51 in *Handbook of Statistical Modeling for the Social and Behavioral Sciences*, edited by Gerhard Arminger, Clifford C. Clogg, and Michael E. Sobel. New York: Plenum.

Hsiao, Cheng. 1986. *Analysis of Panel Data*. Cambridge: Cambridge University Press.

Lazarsfeld, Paul F., and Neil W. Henry. 1968. *Latent Structure Analysis*. Boston: Houghton-Mifflin.

Liang, Kung-Yee, and Scott L. Zeger. 1986. "Longitudinal Data Analysis Using Generalized Linear Models." *Biometrika* 73:13–22.

Liang, Kung-Yee, Scott L. Zeger, and Bahjat Qaqish. 1992. "Multivariate Regression Analyses for Categorical Data" (with discussion). *Journal of the Royal Statistical Society*, Series B 54:3–40.

Lindsay, Bruce, Clifford C. Clogg, and John Grego. 1991. "Semiparametric Estimation in the Rasch Model and Related Exponential Response Models, Including a Simple Latent Class Model for Item Analysis." *Journal of the American Statistical Association* 86:96–107.

Lindsey, James K. 1993. *Models for Repeated Measures*. Oxford: Oxford University Press.

Titterington, David M., Adrian F. M. Smith, and U. E. Makov. 1985. *Statistical Analysis of Finite Mixture Distributions*. New York: Wiley.

Zeger, Scott L., and M. Rezaul Karim. 1991. "Generalized Linear Models with Random Effects: A Gibbs Sampling Approach." *Journal of the American Statistical Association* 86:79–86.

Zeger, Scott L., Kung-Yee Liang, and Paul S. Albert. 1988. "Models for Longitudinal Data: A Generalized Estimating Equation Approach." *Biometrics* 44:1049–60.

2

RANDOM-EFFECTS MODELING OF CATEGORICAL RESPONSE DATA

*Alan Agresti**
*James G. Booth**
*James P. Hobert**
*Brian Caffo**

In many applications observations have some type of clustering, with observations within clusters tending to be correlated. A common instance of this occurs when each subject in the sample undergoes repeated measurement, in which case a cluster consists of the set of observations for the subject. One approach to modeling clustered data introduces cluster-level random effects into the model. The use of random effects in linear models for normal responses is well established. By contrast, random effects have only recently seen much use in models for categorical data. This chapter surveys a variety of potential social science applications of random effects modeling of categorical data. Applications discussed include repeated measurement for binary or ordinal responses, shrinkage to improve multiparameter estimation of a set of proportions or rates, multivariate latent variable modeling, hierarchically structured modeling, and cluster sampling. The models discussed belong to the class of generalized linear mixed models (GLMMs), an extension of ordinary linear models that permits nonnormal response variables and both fixed and random effects in the predictor term. The models are GLMMs for either binomial or Pois-

This work was partially supported by a grant from the National Science Foundation. The authors appreciate comments from Brent Coull, Russ Wolfinger, and two referees. They also thank Jonathan Hartzel for advice on computing and the use of his program for the nonparametric random-effects approach.

*University of Florida

son response variables, although we also present extensions to multicategory (nominal or ordinal) responses. We also summarize some of the technical issues of model-fitting that complicate the fitting of GLMMs even with existing software.

1. INTRODUCTION

Response variables in social science studies, particularly those dealing with opinions and attitudes, are often measured on categorical scales. For many years, to model such data it was common to use ordinary least-squares methods, either for the original scale or some transformation for which the variance tends to be more stable. Recently it has become more common to use models designed specifically for categorical variables, such as logistic regression for binomial responses, generalized logit models for multinomial responses, and log-linear models for Poisson responses.

In many applications, however, the dependence structure is more complex than the independent observations assumed by ordinary models for categorical or continuous variables. In particular, observations often exhibit a clustering, with observations within clusters being correlated. A common instance of this occurs with repeated measurement on each subject in the sample, in which case a cluster consists of the set of observations for a given subject and those observations are typically positively correlated.

For continuous variables, the multivariate normal distribution provides considerable flexibility for describing dependencies. For categorical variables, there is no natural analog of the multivariate normal distribution, which makes the specification of models somewhat awkward. One solution to this introduces cluster-level terms into the model. These terms are unobserved and, varying randomly among a sample of clusters, are called *random effects*. For instance, with linear models for repeated measurement, it is often effective to add a random effect u_i to the predictor of the response for cluster i. If u_i is positive, the observations within that cluster have a larger mean than otherwise, whereas if u_i is negative, the observations within that cluster have a smaller mean than otherwise. Considered over clusters, this induces a positive within-cluster association.

1.1. *Generalized Linear Mixed Models*

Parameters in ordinary linear models are said to be *fixed effects*. They apply to *all* the levels of interest (e.g., gender, race, political party affiliation), whereas random effects apply to a *sample* of all the possible clusters. The use of random effects in linear models for normal responses is well established (e.g., see Searle, Casella, and McCulloch 1992). By contrast, only recently have random effects seen much use in models for categorical responses. We survey here a variety of potential applications of random-effects modeling for social science research.

The class of *generalized linear models* (GLMs) extends ordinary regression models in two ways: (1) it allows for nonnormal responses, and (2) it allows modeling a function of the mean rather than the mean itself. This extension is important for categorical data. For such data, one assumes a binomial or Poisson distribution for the response rather than normal. Also, one usually models the logit of a probability or the logarithm of an expected count instead of the probability or expected count itself (e.g., so that predictions are necessarily on the proper scale, and so that an additive effects model is more likely to fit well). The *generalized linear mixed model*, which we denote by GLMM, is a further extension that permits both fixed and random effects in the predictor rather than only fixed effects. The models discussed here are GLMMs for either binomial (or multinomial) or Poisson response variables.

1.2. *Applications of GLMMs*

Early applications of GLMMs occurred in the psychometrics literature, in the context of *item-response models*, generalizing the *Rasch model* (Rasch 1961). For a set of subjects and test items, the Rasch model states that the probability π_{ij} that subject i makes the correct response on question j satisfies

$$\text{logit}(\pi_{ij}) = u_i + \beta_j. \tag{1}$$

In estimating $\{\beta_j\}$, Rasch promoted the fixed-effects approach of *conditional maximum likelihood*. This method eliminates $\{u_i\}$ from the analysis by conditioning on their sufficient statistics, yielding a likelihood function that depends only on $\{\beta_j\}$. Later authors used a random-effects approach with this model and the corresponding probit model by treating $\{u_i\}$ as having a normal distribution (e.g., see Bock and Aitkin 1981; Stiratelli, Laird, and Ware 1984).

As mentioned above, random effects can represent clustering in a sample. Section 3 shows several examples of this type. Often the clusters result from repeated measurement, representing a set of observations on the same subject at different times or on different components of a response variable. In Section 3.2, for instance, subjects indicate whether or not they support legalized abortion in each of three situations; in Section 3.7, subjects indicate whether government spending should increase, stay the same, or decrease, on items related to environment, health, law enforcement, and education. In other cases the clusters may result from clustering in a multistage sample, as shown in the Section 3.8 example regarding a survey about household satisfaction. Random-effects modeling is also useful when parameters such as proportions or rates for a large number of geographical areas may share some common features. In estimating the parameters with a random-effects model, one effect is shrinkage of separate sample values toward a common value, which can result in dramatically improved estimators in an overall sense. Section 3.1 illustrates this with the use of survey data to estimate simultaneously the proportion favoring a presidential candidate in each of the 50 states. We also show applications such as hierarchically structured modeling (Section 3.4), and handling effects (such as clinics, schools, hospitals) for which the data may have only a sample of the possible levels (Section 3.3). We also present extensions to multicategory (nominal or ordinal) responses.

Random effects are sometimes regarded as unobserved responses on variables. In model (1), for instance, u_i might represent the unknown "ability" of subject i in answering the test items. More generally, models that have unobserved variables of a variety of types are, in essence, random-effects models. For instance, random-effects terms have been used in models to represent omitted explanatory variables and random measurement error in the explanatory variables (e.g., Follmann and Lambert 1989). Related to this, random effects also provide a mechanism for explaining *overdispersion* (e.g., see Breslow and Clayton 1993)—the presence of greater variability in the data than the sampling model predicts. In fact, another strand of literature on random effects for count data developed as a way of handling overdispersion. This literature discussed alternative mixture models such as the *beta-binomial* as well as related *quasi-likelihood* methods that allowed greater variance than the standard sampling models but without assuming a particular parametric distribution (e.g., Williams 1982).

In recent years GLMMs have become increasingly popular in applications in fields such as education (e.g., Goldstein 1991, 1995; Bryk and Raudenbush 1992) and medicine (e.g., Daniels and Gatsonis 1999). They have also been receiving increased attention in social science research. Published work using GLMMs includes the following: Nee (1996) used GLMMs to analyze data from a multistage, multilevel nationwide social survey of households in rural China; Sampson, Raudenbush, and Earls (1997) employed these models to construct and evaluate measures of neighborhood social organization in a study of the relationship between social cohesion among neighbors and crime; Langford (1998) used a GLMM to model an individual's "willingness to pay" to prevent saline flooding in the East Anglian region of England as a function of the cost; and Murphy and Wang (1998) used a GLMM in a discrete-time hazards context to handle cluster effects of children sampled having the same mother. Other references that used a GLMM include Raudenbush, Rowan, and Kang (1991); Langford (1994); McArdle and Hamagami (1994); Congdon (1996); Murray, Moskowitz, and Dent (1996); Saunderson and Langford (1996); Jones, Gould, and Watt (1998); Hedeker, Gibbons, and Flay (1994); Gibbons and Hedeker (1994); Gibbons, Hedeker, Charle, and Frisch (1994); Enberg, Gottschalk, and Wolf (1990); Daniels and Gastonis (1997); Akin, Guilkey, and Sickles (1979); Henretta, Hill, Li, Soldo, and Wolf (1997); Montgomery, Richards, and Braun (1986); Tsutakawa (1988); Wong and Mason (1985); Albert (1992); and Anderson and Aitkin (1985). We hope that the examples shown here will stimulate further uses of random-effects modeling in the social sciences.

1.3. *Scope of This Article*

Section 2 describes the general form of GLMMs for categorical response variables, with focus on binomial or Poisson responses. Section 3 is the heart of the paper, showing a variety of applications of random-effects modeling. Maximum likelihood (ML) is used for all of the model fitting in our examples. The basic ideas underlying ML fitting and inference are given in Section 4 along with a description of some alternative (approximate) fitting methods.

In some applications the random effects part of the model is a mechanism for representing how correlation occurs between observations within a cluster, yet the main interest is in estimating fixed effects, in which case the parameters pertaining to the random effects are *nuisance parameters*. Often though, those parameters are themselves of interest, for instance to characterize the degree of heterogeneity of a population. More generally one may be interested in combinations of fixed and random effects, in order to predict responses, as illustrated in Section 3.1. Some details regarding the prediction of random effects are given in Section 4.5. The GLMM discussed in this paper leads to conditional (i.e., *subject-specific*) interpretations of the regression parameters. Section 5 presents a discussion of a related class of models for the estimation of marginal (i.e., *population-averaged*) effects.

Software for GLMMs is still limited. The results given here were obtained using PROC NLMIXED in SAS (available beginning in version 7), which uses numerical integration for approximating the likelihood function. Section 6 discusses available software and cautions one should follow in using it. Finally, our conclusions are stated in Section 7.

2. RANDOM-EFFECTS MODELS FOR CATEGORICAL DATA

We first introduce some general notation that applies to the examples presented here. Let y_{ij} denote the jth response in cluster i, $i = 1, \ldots, I$, $j = 1, \ldots, n_i$. Let $\mathbf{x}_{ij}$ denote a column vector of values of a set of explanatory variables for the jth response in cluster i, which serve as coefficients of fixed effects in the model. Let $\mathbf{z}_{ij}$ denote a corresponding vector of coefficients of random effects. Note that these sets of coefficients need not be identical for all observations in a cluster. Let $\mathbf{u}_i$ denote the vector of random effect values for cluster i. Conditional on $\mathbf{u}_i$, a GLMM resembles an ordinary GLM. Let $\mu_{ij} = E(y_{ij}|\mathbf{u}_i)$ denote the mean of the conditional distribution of y_{ij} given $\mathbf{u}_i$. Denote the variance of the conditional distribution by $\mathrm{Var}(y_{ij}|\mathbf{u}_i) = \phi_{ij} v(\mu_{ij})$, where typically $\phi_{ij} = \phi / w_{ij}$ with the w_{ij}'s being known "weights" and ϕ being an unknown dispersion parameter, and the function v is called the *variance function*.

The linear predictor for a GLMM has the form

$$g(\mu_{ij}) = \mathbf{x}_{ij}^t \boldsymbol{\beta} + \mathbf{z}_{ij}^t \mathbf{u}_i, \tag{2}$$

where $g(\cdot)$ is a link function (such as the logit for binary data and the log for count data), a t superscript denotes the transpose of a vector, and $\mathbf{u}_i$ is usually assumed to have a normal distribution. In (2), the random effect enters the model on the same scale as the predictor terms. This is convenient but also natural for the many applications in which the random effect partly represents unmodeled heterogeneity caused by not including certain important explanatory variables.

2.1. *A GLMM for Two Dependent Binomial Samples*

We illustrate this general expression for a GLMM using perhaps the simplest example of a random-effects model for categorical response data: binary matched pairs, yielding two dependent binomial samples. For cluster i, let (y_{i1}, y_{i2}) denote the two responses in the matched pair. For instance, y_{i1} might denote a binary response measured at a particular time, and y_{i2} a response on the same outcome scale at a later time, such as when a sample of subjects is asked at two dates about whether the president is doing a good job. Suppose that subject i at time j has $y_{ij} = 1$ (a "success") or 0 (a "failure"), $j = 1, 2$. Then μ_{ij} is the probability of success. For binary data, the link function g is most often the logit transform.

Table 1, from the General Social Survey of 1994, is an example of matched-pairs data. Subjects were asked "Do you think a person has the right to end his or her own life if this person has an incurable disease?" and "When a person has a disease that cannot be cured, do you think doctors should be allowed to end the patient's life by some painless means if the patient and his family request it?" The table, which refers to these variables as "suicide" and "let patient die," reports the numbers of "yes" and "no" responses for each question. The two responses for each subject form a matched pair. For these matched pairs, consider the model

$$\text{logit}(\mu_{i1}) = \alpha + u_i, \qquad \text{logit}(\mu_{i2}) = \alpha + \beta + u_i,$$

where u_i is the value of a random effect for subject i, with $E(u_i) = 0$. This model allows heterogeneity among the probabilities for each question but assumes that the logit shifts uniformly for each subject by β for the two

TABLE 1
Opinions About Suicide and Letting an Incurable Patient Die

	Let Patient Die		
Suicide	Yes	No	Total
Yes	1097	90	1187
No	203	435	638
Total	1300	525	1825

Source: General Social Survey (1994).

questions. Thus, for each subject the odds of a "yes" response on letting the patient die equal $\exp(\beta)$ times the odds of a "yes" response on suicide. This is the special case of model (2) in which $\boldsymbol{\beta}^t = (\alpha, \beta)$, $\mathbf{x}_{i1}^t = (1,0)$ and $\mathbf{x}_{i2}^t = (1,1)$ for all i and $z_{ij} = 1$ for all i and j.

The usual random-effects model assumes that $\{u_i\}$ are independent from a $N(0, \sigma^2)$ distribution, with σ unknown, and that conditionally on the $\{u_i\}$ the $\{y_{ij}\}$ are independent. Unconditionally, variability among $\{u_i\}$ reflects subject heterogeneity, whereby different subjects have different probabilities of making a particular response. This variability induces a positive association between the binomial responses that form the margins of Table 1, manifested by a nonnegative log-odds ratio for the true cell probabilities underlying Table 1. This special case of a GLMM in which a cluster's random effect affects only the intercept of the model is called a *random intercept model.*

This model with logit link provides one of the rare instances in which a closed-form ML estimate is available for the effect β. When the sample log-odds ratio in tables that have the structure of Table 1 is nonnegative, it follows from Neuhaus, Kalbfleisch, and Hauck (1994) that $\hat{\beta}$ equals the log ratio of counts falling off the main diagonal; here, $\log(203/90) = .813$. For each subject, the estimated odds of a "yes" response on letting the patient die are $\exp(.813) = 2.26$ times the estimated odds of a "yes" response on suicide.

With this analysis for the logit model, the estimate of the treatment effect and subsequent inference does not depend on the other two cell counts. Matched-pairs data usually display a positive association, with the majority of the observations falling in these two cells. In Table 1, for instance, 1532 of the 1825 observations make no contribution to the analysis. The model provides justification for McNemar's test of equality of matched proportions, which uses only the same counts as does $\hat{\beta}$ (e.g., see Agresti and Finlay 1997:231). McNemar's test is based on a normal approximation for the probability that a binomial random variable with $90 + 203 = 293$ trials and parameter .5 takes a value of at most 90 or at least 203.

2.2. *Cluster-Specific Effects for Random-Effects Models*

Note that the effect β in the model of Section 2.1 refers to the *conditional* log-odds ratio, given the random effect. Thus it has a *subject-specific* interpretation, being the change in the logit for a given subject. This is not the same as the marginal (so-called *population-averaged*) effect, because of the nonlinearity of the logit link. For instance, in the matched-pairs model,

$$E(y_{ij}) = E[E(y_{ij}|u_i)] = E\left(\frac{\exp[\mathbf{x}_{ij}^t\boldsymbol{\beta} + u_i]}{1 + \exp[\mathbf{x}_{ij}^t\boldsymbol{\beta} + u_i]}\right),$$

and this expectation does not have the form $\exp(\mathbf{x}_{ij}^t\boldsymbol{\beta})/[1 + \exp(\mathbf{x}_{ij}^t\boldsymbol{\beta})]$ except when u_i has a degenerate distribution with a variance of 0. The estimate of β from the marginal (unconditional) model is typically smaller in absolute value than the estimate from the conditional model. The discrepancy between the two increases as σ, and hence the correlation between observations within a cluster, increases. For Table 1, the estimated marginal log-odds ratio uses the sample marginal distributions, equaling $\log[(1300/525)/(1187/638)] = .286$, compared to the conditional estimate of .813. Neuhaus, Kalbfleisch, and Hauck (1991) and Zeger, Liang, and Albert (1988) provided approximate relationships between the two types of estimate.

Similar remarks apply to any GLMM of form (2). For the probit link with binary data, however, the conditional probit model with normal random effects does imply a marginal model of probit form. In the case of a univariate random intercept, the conditional model has effect equal to the marginal effect multiplied by $[1 + \sigma^2]^{1/2}$ (Searle et al. 1992:377). For count data, such as those that occur in estimating rates or expected frequencies in a contingency table, the link function g is usually the log transform. In that case, the conditional loglinear model with normal random effect also implies a marginal model of log-linear form. The marginal model has the same effect but has intercept equal to the conditional one multiplied by $\exp(\sigma^2/2)$.

2.3. *Varieties of Ways of Handling Random Effects*

In any GLMM, a possibly controversial aspect is the assumption of a particular parametric distribution for the random effect. By far the most common choice is normality. For logit random-intercept models, evidence indicates that other choices usually provide similar results for the regression effects, with skewed actual distributions for the random effects possibly having some effect on the intercept estimate (Neuhaus, Hauck, and Kalbfleisch 1992). When the random effect relates more directly to the characteristic estimated, the choice of distribution can be more crucial

(Heckman and Singer 1984). An important advantage of the normal family is its extension to models with several correlated random effects, in which case the multivariate normal family is both flexible and simple.

The research literature now has a considerable variety of ways of handling clustering of various sorts. At first, *conjugate* mixture models received most of the attention. These are models that assume a particular parametric distribution but with the parameter itself coming from a distribution such that the marginal distribution has closed form. For binary data, one assumes that given the parameter, the response has a binomial distribution, and the parameters follow a beta distribution. This leads to the *beta binomial* model (Crowder 1978). For count data, one assumes that given the parameter the responses are Poisson, and the parameters follow a gamma distribution. This leads to the *negative binomial model* (Lawless 1987; McCullagh and Nelder 1989). A disadvantage of the conjugate approach is the lack of generality and flexibility, requiring a different mixture distribution for each type of problem. In addition, the extra variability does not enter on the same scale as the ordinary predictors. Lee and Nelder (1996) generalized these models to hierarchical models of GLMM form but in which the random effect need not be normal.

Finally, there is also some work on a nonparametric random effects approach, in which instead of choosing a parametric family one uses a discrete mixture determined empirically (Heckman and Singer 1984; Aitkin 1996). We discuss this further in Section 3.5.

3. EXAMPLES OF RANDOM-EFFECTS MODELING

This section, the heart of the paper, shows examples of random-effects modeling for a variety of types of examples.

3.1. *Example 1: Shrinkage of Proportions*

This example involves estimating a large number of proportions with only small to moderate sample sizes for each proportion. A common application is *small-area estimation*, in which relatively few observations occur in each of many geographical areas. For each area, for instance, one might want to estimate the unemployment rate or the proportion of families not having health insurance coverage or the proportion of children living in single-parent families. Random effects models can serve as a mechanism for improving on the sample proportions in estimating the true area-specific proportions. In assuming that those true proportions vary according to some distribution, one can use information from all the areas to estimate the proportion in any given area (Ghosh and Rao 1994).

Let π_i denote the true proportion in area i, $i = 1,\ldots,I$. Let $\{Y_i\}$ denote independent binomial variates with sample size indices $\{n_i\}$ and parameters $\{\pi_i\}$; that is, $Y_i = \sum_{j=1}^{n_i} y_{ij}$, where $\{y_{ij},\ j = 1,\ldots,n_i\}$ are independent with $P(y_{ij} = 1) = \pi_i$ and $P(y_{ij} = 0) = 1 - \pi_i$. The sample proportions $\{p_i = Y_i/n_i\}$ are the ML estimates of $\{\pi_i\}$ for the fixed-effects model

$$\text{logit}(\pi_i) = \alpha + \beta_i, \quad i = 1,\ldots,I,$$

where identifiability requires a constraint such as $\sum \beta_i = 0$ or $\beta_I = 0$. This model is saturated, having I nonredundant parameters for the I binomial observations. For small samples, the sample estimates often display much more variability than the true values, and when $\{\beta_i\}$ are similar it can be helpful to shrink the sample proportions toward the overall mean. One can accomplish this using the random effects model

$$\text{logit}(\pi_i) = \alpha + u_i, \tag{3}$$

where $\{u_i\}$ are assumed to be independent from a $N(0, \sigma^2)$ distribution. After estimating α and σ, one estimates logit(π_i) using $[\hat{\alpha} + \hat{u}_i]$, where $\hat{u}_i$ is the predicted random effect based on the observed data. Section 4.5 outlines the standard method for computing $\hat{u}_i$. This is an example of an *empirical Bayes analysis*, which assumes a prior distribution for unknown parameters and uses the data to estimate parameters of that distribution. This paradigm has been in use for some time—for instance, using normal approximations for distributions of sample proportions (Efron and Morris 1975).

To motivate why the random-effects approach can be highly beneficial, we first use an artificial example. For I coins, let π_i denote the probability of a "head" in a single flip of coin i, and suppose $\{Y_i\}$ are counts of heads based on $\{n_i = 10\}$ flips of each coin. Probably $\{\pi_i\}$ are all close to .50 and the sample data would yield estimates for model (3) close to $\hat{\alpha} = 0$ and $\hat{\sigma} = 0$ (especially if I is large). In fact, if $\hat{\sigma} = 0$ the model fit simplifies to that for the simpler model logit$(\pi_i) = \alpha$, and $\{\hat{\pi}_i = (\sum_h Y_h)/(\sum_h n_h)\}$, the overall sample proportion of heads. This estimate, or estimates that are very close to it (which occur when $\hat{\sigma} > 0$

but is small) tend to be much better than the separate sample proportions $\{p_i = Y_i/n_i\}$. Generally, "borrowing from the whole" provides the advantage of smoothing the sample estimates and effectively basing the resulting estimates on much larger sample sizes than using the data for the separate samples on their own. For instance, in the extreme case that $\sigma = 0$ and $\hat{\sigma} = 0$, the random effects estimate of the common probability of a head uses I times as many observations as the separate sample proportions. Generally, the random-effects estimates provide shrinkage of the separate estimates toward the overall sample proportion. The amount of shrinkage decreases as $\hat{\sigma}$ or n_i grow.

For an illustration based on a more realistic problem, we simulated a sample to mimic a poll taken before the 1996 U.S. presidential election. For a sample of size n_i in state i ($i = 1, \ldots, 51$ with $i = 51$ being the District of Columbia), we generated Y_i as a binomial variate with π_i equal to the actual proportion of votes in state i for Bill Clinton in the 1996 election, conditional on voting for Clinton or Dole. We set n_i proportional to the population size in that state, subject to $\sum n_i = 2000$. The $\{n_i\}$ ranged from 4 to 240. Table 2 shows $\{n_i\}$, $\{\pi_i\}$ and $\{p_i = Y_i/n_i\}$.

The ML fit of the random-effects model (3) (using PROC NLMIXED in SAS) provides $\hat{\alpha} = .164$ and $\hat{\sigma} = .29$. For that model, the predicted random-effects values (also estimated using NLMIXED) yield the corresponding proportion estimates $\{\hat{\pi}_i^{(1)} = \exp(\hat{\alpha} + \hat{u}_i)/[1 + \exp(\hat{\alpha} + \hat{u}_i)]\}$ (also shown in Table 2). Since the sample sizes are mostly small and since $\hat{\sigma}$ is relatively small, the amount of shrinkage for these estimates is considerable. They vary between only .468 (Texas) and .696 (New York), whereas the sample proportions vary between .111 (for Idaho) and 1.0 (DC). Estimates based on fewer observations, such as DC, tend to receive greater shrinkage. Although the random-effects estimates are relatively homogeneous, they do tend to be closer than the sample proportions to the true values. For instance, $\sum |p_i - \pi_i|/51 = .079$ and $\sum |\hat{\pi}_i^{(1)} - \pi_i|/51 = .053$.

To check whether these results are typical, we simulated 10,000 studies with these sample sizes and probabilities. Overall, the mean distance from true probabilities was .060 for the random-effects estimates and .091 for the sample proportions. In 99.6 percent of the studies, the mean distance was smaller for the random-effects estimates.

Although the random-effects estimates tend to be closer than the sample proportions to the true proportions, the amount of shrinkage can be excessive, given other information we know about presidential elections.

TABLE 2

Estimates of Proportion of Vote for Clinton, Conditional on Voting for Clinton or Dole in 1996 U.S. Presidential Election

State	n_i	π_i	p_i	$\hat{\pi}_i^{(1)}$	$\hat{\pi}_i^{(2)}$	State	n_i	π_i	p_i	$\hat{\pi}_i^{(1)}$	$\hat{\pi}_i^{(2)}$
AK	5	0.394	0.200	0.508	0.438	MT	7	0.483	0.429	0.526	0.528
AL	32	0.463	0.500	0.524	0.484	NC	55	0.475	0.455	0.494	0.492
AR	19	0.594	0.526	0.537	0.604	ND	5	0.461	0.600	0.546	0.444
AZ	34	0.512	0.618	0.573	0.531	NE	13	0.395	0.462	0.524	0.408
CA	240	0.572	0.538	0.538	0.557	NH	9	0.567	0.556	0.543	0.527
CO	29	0.492	0.586	0.558	0.553	NJ	60	0.600	0.667	0.611	0.579
CT	25	0.604	0.720	0.602	0.588	NM	13	0.540	0.462	0.524	0.556
DC	4	0.903	1.000	0.576	0.909	NV	12	0.506	0.500	0.533	0.530
DE	5	0.586	0.400	0.527	0.561	NY	137	0.660	0.752	0.696	0.686
FL	108	0.532	0.602	0.583	0.553	OH	84	0.536	0.488	0.507	0.510
GA	56	0.494	0.554	0.548	0.531	OK	23	0.456	0.478	0.520	0.463
HI	9	0.643	0.556	0.543	0.580	OR	24	0.547	0.625	0.569	0.589
IA	22	0.557	0.500	0.528	0.544	PA	90	0.552	0.567	0.558	0.569
ID	9	0.391	0.111	0.472	0.395	RI	7	0.689	0.571	0.545	0.629
IL	89	0.596	0.539	0.540	0.574	SC	28	0.469	0.571	0.552	0.491
IN	44	0.468	0.432	0.488	0.464	SD	6	0.479	0.667	0.555	0.502
KS	19	0.400	0.316	0.477	0.455	TN	40	0.513	0.500	0.522	0.531
KY	29	0.506	0.448	0.506	0.516	TX	144	0.473	0.444	0.468	0.465
LA	33	0.566	0.667	0.592	0.571	UT	15	0.380	0.333	0.490	0.372
MA	46	0.686	0.739	0.637	0.665	VA	51	0.489	0.412	0.473	0.465
MD	38	0.586	0.474	0.511	0.566	VT	4	0.633	0.500	0.538	0.615
ME	9	0.627	0.778	0.578	0.591	WA	42	0.572	0.619	0.578	0.599
MI	73	0.573	0.589	0.570	0.573	WI	39	0.559	0.487	0.517	0.529
MN	35	0.594	0.571	0.554	0.588	WV	14	0.584	0.571	0.548	0.591
MO	41	0.535	0.561	0.550	0.575	WY	4	0.426	0.250	0.518	0.470
MS	21	0.472	0.333	0.477	0.445						

Note: π_i = true, p_i = sample, $\hat{\pi}_i^{(1)}$ = random effects, $\hat{\pi}_i^{(2)}$ = random effects with shrinkage toward 1992 election.

For instance, in 16.1 percent of the simulations $\hat{\sigma}$ was so small that these estimates predicted a Clinton victory in every state. Rather than assuming a common mean for the random effects, one might instead use supplementary information that should improve the predictions. For instance, let q_i denote the true proportion of votes for Clinton in state i in the 1992 election, conditional on voting for Clinton or Bush. This is known information for polls taken in 1996, and one could fit the model

$$\text{logit}(\pi_i) = \text{logit}(q_i) + \alpha + u_i,$$

where $\{q_i\}$ are known and $\{u_i\}$ are independent from a $N(0, \sigma^2)$ distribution. Known terms in the linear predictor, such as $\text{logit}(q_i)$, are referred to as *offsets*. Rearranging the previous equation we obtain

$$\log \frac{\pi_i/(1-\pi_i)}{q_i/(1-q_i)} = \alpha + u_i. \tag{4}$$

Thus, $\alpha + u_i$ represents the log-odds ratio for the ith state of voting for Clinton versus Dole in 1996 relative to voting for Clinton versus Bush in 1992.

Table 2 also shows the resulting estimates $\{\hat{\pi}_i^{(2)}\}$ of $\{\pi_i\}$. Here, $\hat{\sigma} = .19$ and the estimates shrink considerably toward the prior values from 1992, with a slight upward adjustment since $\hat{\alpha} = .205$. For model (4), when $\hat{\sigma} = 0$, $\hat{\pi}_i^{(2)} = q_i \exp(\hat{\alpha})/[1 - q_i + q_i \exp(\hat{\alpha})]$, and when also $\hat{\alpha} = 0$, $\hat{\pi}_i^{(2)} = q_i$. Otherwise when $\hat{\sigma} = 0$, compared to the previous election results, the estimates shift up or down on the logit scale depending on how the overall Democratic vote compares in the current poll to the previous election (i.e., depending on $\hat{\alpha}$).

With model (4), the random effects estimates vary between .372 (for Utah) and .909 (for DC), whereas the true values vary between .380 (for Utah) and .903 (for DC). Now, these random-effect estimates tend to be much closer than the sample proportions to the true values, with, $\sum|p_i - \pi_i|/51 = .079$ and $\sum|\hat{\pi}_i^{(2)} - \pi_i|/51 = .024$. Over 10,000 simulations, the mean distance values were .091 and .027, and the mean distance was smaller for the random-effects estimates in 100 percent of the cases. In 27.5 percent of these cases $\hat{\sigma} = 0$, but in none of them did the random-effects estimates predict a Clinton victory in each state. Figure 1 displays the values of $(\pi_i, \hat{\pi}_i, q_i, \hat{\pi}_i^{(2)})$ for the data in Table 2, with the states ordered by their values of $\{\pi_i\}$.

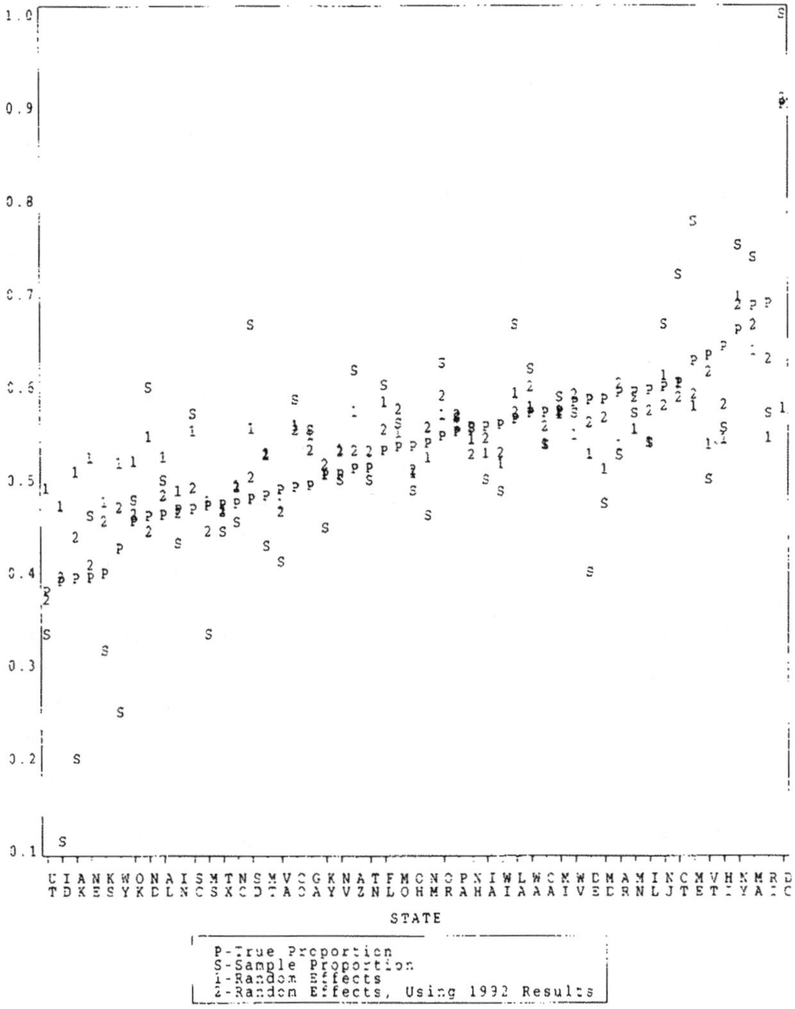

FIGURE 1. Estimates of statewide proportions planning to vote for Clinton in 1996 presidential election (conditional on voting for Clinton or Dole), based on random sample of 2000 voters.

3.2. *Example 2: Modeling Repeated Binary Measurement*

Section 2.1 introduced a random-effects model for repeated categorical measurement with the simple case of binary matched pairs. The model then has the form

$$\text{logit}[P(y_{i1} = 1)] = \alpha + u_i, \qquad \text{logit}[P(y_{i2} = 1)] = \alpha + \beta + u_i,$$

where $\{u_i\}$ are an independent sample from a $N(0, \sigma^2)$ distribution. Let n_{ab} denote the number of observations for which $(y_{i1}, y_{i2}) = (a, b)$, $a = 0,1$, $b = 0,1$. The counts can be summarized in a table such as Table 1. Let $Y_1 = \sum y_{i1}$ and $Y_2 = \sum y_{i2}$. Unconditionally, Y_1 is a binomial random variable with parameter $E\{\exp(\alpha + u)/[1 + \exp(\alpha + u)]\}$, and Y_2 is a binomial random variable with parameter $E\{\exp(\alpha + \beta + u)/[1 + \exp(\alpha + \beta + u)]\}$, where the expectation is taken with respect to u, a $N(0, \sigma^2)$ random variable.

This model implies a nonnegative correlation between the binomial variates Y_1 and Y_2, with greater association resulting from greater heterogeneity (i.e., larger σ). Under this model, Y_1 and Y_2 are independent only if $\sigma = 0$. When the sample data are consistent with this model, in the sense that $\log(n_{00} n_{11} / n_{10} n_{01}) \geq 0$, then the perhaps surprising result (Neuhaus et al. 1994) occurs that $\hat{\beta} = \log(n_{01} / n_{10})$. This is also the estimate with the conditional ML approach, eliminating $\{u_i\}$ by conditioning on their sufficient statistics.

This random-intercept model extends to more than two repeated measurements, with covariates that themselves may or may not vary. We illustrate using Table 3, which contains data from the 1994 General Social Survey. The subjects indicate whether they support legalizing abortion in three situations: (1) if the family has a very low income and cannot afford any more children, (2) when the woman is not married and does not want to marry the father, and (3) if the woman wants to terminate the pregnancy

TABLE 3
Cross Classification of Support for Legalizing Abortion in Three Cases, by Gender

	Sequence of Responses on the Three Items*							
Gender	(1,1,1)†	(1,1,2)	(2,1,1)	(2,1,2)	(1,2,1)	(1,2,2)	(2,2,1)	(2,2,2)
Male	342	26	6	21	11	32	19	356
Female	440	25	14	18	14	47	22	457

Source: Data from *General Social Survey* (1994).

*Respondents were asked about their support for legalizing abortion (1) if the family has a very low income and cannot afford any more children, (2) if the woman is not married and does not want to marry the father, and (3) if the woman wants to terminate the pregnancy for any reason.

†Response 1 is "yes" and 2 is "no."

for any reason. Table 3 also classifies the subjects by gender. Let y_{ij} denote the response for subject i on item j, with a value of 1 representing support. We consider the model

$$\text{logit}[P(y_{ij} = 1)] = \alpha + \beta_j + \gamma x + u_i, \qquad (5)$$

where $x = 1$ for females and 0 for males, $\{u_i\}$ are independent from a $N(0, \sigma^2)$ distribution, and $\{\beta_j\}$ satisfy a constraint such as $\beta_3 = 0$. (Equivalently, one could delete α from the model and then remove the constraint on $\{\beta_j\}$ or allow a nonzero mean for $\{u_i\}$.)

For the ML fit of this model, contrasts of $\{\hat{\beta}_j\}$ provide evidence of greater support for legalized abortion when the family has a low income and cannot afford any more children than in the other two instances ($\hat{\beta}_1 - \hat{\beta}_3 = .83$, $se = .16$, $\hat{\beta}_1 - \hat{\beta}_2 = .54$, $se = .16$) and slight evidence of greater support when the woman is not married and does not want to marry the man than when the woman wants the abortion for any reason ($\hat{\beta}_2 - \hat{\beta}_3 = .29$, $se = .16$). Also, $\hat{\gamma} = .01$ ($se = .49$). The estimates have log-odds ratio interpretations. For each item, for instance, the estimated odds of females supporting legalized abortion equal $\exp(.01) = 1.01$ times the estimated odds for males. For these data, subjects are highly heterogeneous ($\hat{\sigma} = 8.8$, with $se = .54$), resulting in strong associations among the items as reflected by 1595 of the 1850 observations falling in the four cells where subjects made the same response on all three items. We also considered the interaction model having different $\{\beta_j\}$ for men and women, but it did not provide an improved fit (likelihood-ratio statistic = 1.0 with $df = 2$ for testing that the extra parameters equal 0). Essentially, there is no difference between males and females in this study.

3.3. *Example 3: Summarizing Results from Several 2-by-2 Tables*

Many applications refer to comparing two groups on a binary response when data are stratified according to levels of a third variable. The data then take the form of several 2-by-2 contingency tables. The strata are sometimes themselves a sample—for example, schools or medical centers; or they may be levels of a control variable, such as age or severity of the condition being treated, or combinations of levels of several control variables; or, they may be different studies of the same sort evaluated in a meta-analysis. The main concerns for data of this sort relate to investigating the "average" level of association and the degree of variability about that average (i.e., the treatment-by-center interaction); for instance, see DerSimonian and Laird (1986).

When the strata are sampled, a random-effects approach is natural. One then has a structure for extending inferences to the population of strata sampled. Moreover, the random-effects model can provide a simple summary such as an estimated mean and standard deviation of log-odds ratios for the population of centers. It can also provide predicted odds ratios for separate strata that have the benefits of shrinkage, especially when sample sizes in some of the strata are small. Even when the strata are not a sample, the model can be beneficial for these two purposes.

We illustrate using Table 4, which shows the results of admissions decisions for applicants to graduate school in departments of the College of Liberal Arts and Sciences at the University of Florida during the 1997–1998 academic year. Stratifying by the department to which the student applied, the table compares males and females on whether admitted. Overall 983 men applied with 35.9 percent accepted, and 1093 females applied with 34.4 percent accepted.

For a subject of gender j ($j = 1$, males, $j = 2$, females) applying to department i, let π_{ij} denote the probability of being admitted. One possible model is the logit-normal model

$$\text{logit}(\pi_{i1}) = \alpha + \beta/2 + u_i, \qquad \text{logit}(\pi_{i2}) = \alpha - \beta/2 + u_i, \tag{6}$$

assuming that $\{u_i\}$ are independent from a $N(0, \sigma^2)$ distribution. This model assumes that the log-odds ratio β between gender and being admitted is constant over departments. A logit-normal model permitting interaction is

$$\text{logit}(\pi_{i1}) = \alpha + b_i/2 + u_i, \qquad \text{logit}(\pi_{i2}) = \alpha - b_i/2 + u_i, \tag{7}$$

where $\{u_i\}$ are independent from a $N(0, \sigma_u^2)$ distribution, $\{b_i\}$ are independent from a $N(\beta, \sigma_b^2)$ distribution, β is the expected value of study-specific log-odds ratios and σ_b describes the variability in those log-odds ratios. The model parameters are then $(\alpha, \beta, \sigma_u, \sigma_b)$.

For these data, a standard fixed-effects analysis for the lack of interaction model has ML estimate of the gender effect $\hat{\beta} = -.173$ ($se = .112$). The corresponding model (6) in which departments are a random effect also has $\hat{\beta} = -.163$ ($se = .111$). The model (7) permitting interaction but assuming that $\{u_i\}$ are independent of $\{b_i\}$ has $\hat{\beta} = -.18$ ($se = .13$), with $\hat{\sigma}_b = .20$ ($se = .35$). Similar answers result from allowing

TABLE 4
1997–1998 Admissions Decisions to Graduate School at the University of Florida

	Males		Females				Males		Females		
Department	Yes*	No	Yes	No	OR**	Department	Yes*	No	Yes	No	OR**
Anthropology	21	41	32	81	1.30	Linguistics	7	8	21	10	.42
Astronomy	3	8	6	0	0	Mathematics	31	37	25	18	0.60
Chemistry	34	110	12	43	1.11	Philosophy	9	6	3	0	0
Classics	4	0	3	1	∞	Physics	25	53	10	11	.52
Communicative Processes	5	10	52	149	1.43	Political Science	39	49	25	34	1.08
Computer Science	6	12	8	7	.44	Psychology	4	41	2	123	6.00
English	30	112	35	100	.77	Religion	0	2	3	3	0
Geography	11	11	9	1	.11	Romance Languages	6	3	29	13	.90
Geology	15	6	6	3	1.25	Sociology	7	17	16	33	.85
Germanic/Slavic	4	1	17	0	0	Statistics	36	14	23	9	1.01
History	21	19	9	9	1.11	Zoology	10	54	4	62	2.87
Latin American Studies	25	16	26	7	0.42						

*Yes = accept, no = reject; **OR = sample odds ratios.

$\{u_i\}$ and $\{b_i\}$ to be correlated. For all these models the estimated gender effect is not large. For instance, for the interaction model the estimated mean log-odds ratio of $-.176$ corresponds to an odds ratio of .84. The gender effect is not significant. For instance, the likelihood-ratio statistic for testing $H_0: \beta = 0$ is 2.4 ($df = 1$) for the fixed-effects model and 2.0 for the random-effects model allowing interaction. Note that because of the extra source of variability in the interaction models, the standard error of $\hat{\beta}$ is slightly larger than with the other analyses.

As in Example 1, one can obtain smoothed estimates, this time of the department-specific odds ratios. Table 4 shows that the sample odds ratios varied between 0 (for Astronomy, Germanic and Slavic Languages, Philosophy, Religion) and ∞ (Classics); by contrast, the estimates of $\exp(b_i)$ for model (7) vary between .75 (for Astronomy) and .96 (for Zoology). There is not much variability in these predictions, since the estimated variance component for the interaction is so small. Interestingly, Simpson's paradox occurs here, as the marginal sample odds ratio relating gender to whether admitted equals 1.07, whereas the predicted odds ratio for every department is less than 1.0.

Incidentally, in passing we mention that one needs to be careful about implications of the model formula expression and the random-effects structure. For instance, model (7) with uncorrelated $\{b_i\}$ and $\{u_i\}$ is different from the model

$$\text{logit}(\pi_{i1}) = \alpha + b_i + u_i, \qquad \text{logit}(\pi_{i2}) = \alpha + u_i,$$

with uncorrelated $\{b_i\}$ and $\{u_i\}$. Generally, if the interaction model has form $\text{logit}(\pi_{ij}) = \alpha + b_i x_j + u_i$ where x_j is a dummy variable (with, e.g., $x_1 - x_2 = 1$), and if we let $z_j = x_j + c$ for some constant c, then the model is also $\text{logit}(\pi_{ij}) = \alpha + b_i(z_j - c) + u_i = \alpha + b_i z_j + v_i$, where $v_i = u_i - cb_i$. Thus (b_i, v_i) are correlated even if (b_i, u_i) are not.

3.4. *Example 4: Hierarchical Modeling*

Hierarchical data, in which units are grouped at different levels, is common in the social sciences. Models for data in which hierarchical grouping or clustering occurs are often referred to as *multilevel models*. These models fall within the GLMM framework that is the focus of this paper. For example, in a study of factors that affect school performance, the level 1 units might be students, the level 2 units schools, and the level 3 units the county, region, or school district. Clearly, socioeconomic factors that affect school choice will often cause students within the same schools to have correlated responses. Similarly, variation between locations may induce additional correlation at a regional level. Correlations caused by additional sources of variability are accounted for in a multilevel model through the inclusion of random effects at each stage of the hierarchy. The variances of these effects are estimated as part of the model-fitting process, and they measure the amount of variability not explained by fixed effects at each level. For early descriptions of the use of random-effects modeling with binary responses in the context of educational assessment, see Aitkin, Anderson, and Hinde (1981) and Aitkin and Longford (1986). For a recent application of multilevel modeling to social observation of neighborhoods, see Raudenbush and Sampson (1999). Other general references include Bryk and Raudenbush (1992), Goldstein (1995), Plewis (1997), and Muthen (1997).

Goldstein (1995, sec. 7.3) provided an example from a survey of voting behavior in the United Kingdom with a similar multilevel structure. The data in this case were obtained from a series of surveys carried out in Britain following elections held in 1983, 1987, and 1992. Respondents were grouped according to year and by the parliamentary constituency in which they lived at the time. A binary response variable of interest is whether or not an individual voted for the Conservative party as opposed to the Liberal or Labour parties. Some constituencies were sampled in all three years and others in only one or two years, resulting in a multilevel structure with respondent at level 1 and year by constituency combinations at level 2. Let π_{ijk} denote the probability that respondent k in year j from constituency i says that he or she voted for the Conservatives. Then a potential GLMM for this data is

$$\text{logit}(\pi_{ijk}) = \mathbf{x}_{ijk}^{t}\boldsymbol{\beta} + u_{ij}, \tag{8}$$

where $\mathbf{x}_{ijk}^{t}\boldsymbol{\beta}$ models fixed effects such as socioeconomic status and (u_{i1}, u_{i2}, u_{i3}) is a trivariate normal random variable representing the effects of constituency i in the three election years. If we assume that between-constituency variation is the same in each year and that the correlations between pairs of years are all equal, then (8) is equivalent to the model:

$$\eta_{ijk} \equiv \text{logit}(\pi_{ijk}) = \mathbf{x}_{ijk}^{t}\boldsymbol{\beta} + u_{ij} + v_i, \tag{9}$$

where now u_{i1}, u_{i2}, u_{i3} and v_i are independent normal variables, with $u_{ij} \sim N(0, \sigma_u^2)$ and $v_i \sim N(0, \sigma_v^2)$. This model formally has a three-level structure. Level 1 variation between respondents in the same year and constituency (and the same fixed factors) is Bernoulli. This is combined with a normal random effect (u_{ij}) which accounts for year-to-year (level 2) variation in log-odds ratios for respondents in the same constituency. Finally, level 3 variation between respondents in different constituencies is a combination of Bernoulli and two independent normal random effects (u_{ij} and v_i). Contrasting models (8) and (9) illustrates an important point about multilevel modeling. Incorporating an additional level of hierarchy in (9) led to a more parsimonious model requiring only two parameters (σ_u and σ_v) to describe the random-effects distribution compared with six in the two-level model (8).

In the survey of voting behavior data, Goldstein obtained the estimates $\sigma_u^2 = 0.05$ and $\sigma_v^2 = 0.38$. This implies a correlation between the log-odds of a respondent saying they voted Conservative in two different election years of

$$\text{cor}(\eta_{ijk}, \eta_{ij'k}) = \frac{\sigma_u^2}{\sigma_u^2 + \sigma_v^2} = \frac{0.05}{0.05 + 0.38} = 0.12.$$

An interesting feature of the model is that this correlation is the same for two different subjects—i.e., $\text{cor}(\eta_{ijk}, \eta_{ij'k}) = \text{cor}(\eta_{ijk}, \eta_{ij'k'})$. In fact an unattractive property of the model is that equality also holds for the correlation between the corresponding pairs of binary responses:

$$\text{cor}(Y_{ijk}, Y_{ij'k}) = \text{cor}(Y_{ijk}, Y_{ij'k'}).$$

Intuitively, one would expect a higher correlation between responses on the same subject. In principle this "deficiency" could be overcome by adding an additional random effect for each respondent. However, the amount of information for estimating the additional variance component is limited in this example, since there are a maximum of three repeated measurements on each respondent. In addition, Goldstein found little evidence of lack of fit for the simpler model.

3.5. *Example 5: Nonparametric Random-Effects Approach*

The examples discussed so far have assumed a normal distribution for random-effects distributions. An alternative, nonparametric, random-effects approach uses instead a distribution on a finite set of mass points having location that is estimated empirically (Heckman and Singer 1984; Lindsay, Clogg, and Grego 1991; Aitkin 1996, 1999). With latent-class models, one specifies the number of mass points for this mixture distribution. The general approach does not specify the number of mass points, but one treats it as fixed and sequentially increases the sample value until the likelihood is maximized. In fact, maximizing the likelihood usually requires relatively few mass points. Aitkin (1996, 1999) presented examples of the general nonparametric approach. Heckman and Singer (1984) noted that this approach is primarily useful when the mixing distribution is a nuisance parameter rather than of direct interest, since the nonparametric estimate of that distribution may be poor even for large samples.

Follmann and Lambert (1989) provided an interesting example in which the number of mass points was prespecified. They analyzed data on the effect of the dosage of a poison on the death rate of a protozoan of a particular genus, assuming two varieties of that genus. For their model, the probability of death at a particular dosage level x equals $\rho\pi_1(x) + (1-\rho)\pi_2(x)$, where $\text{logit}[\pi_i(x)] = \alpha_i + \beta x$ and the mixing proportion ρ is unknown. The fit of this model was much better than that of a single logistic regression model.

In a similar spirit, Lindsay et al. (1991) studied models of the Rasch form (1) but in which the subject term can assume only an unknown finite number of values. They showed that with k items, the likelihood is maximized when the subject parameter takes at most $(k+1)/2$ values. In related work, Tjur (1982) showed that with a distribution-free approach for the subject term, the fit of the Rasch model satisfies the quasi-symmetry log-linear model; see Conaway (1989), Darroch (1981), Hatzinger (1989), Kelderman (1984), and Agresti (1993, 1995, 1997) for related work and details.

We illustrate the nonparametric approach by fitting model (5) to the attitudes about abortion data in Table 3, now using a finite mixture distribution rather than a normal distribution for the random effect u_i. The likelihood is then maximized with a two-point mixture. The results are very similar to those obtained with the normal mixture model. For instance, with the nonparametric approach $\hat{\beta}_1 - \hat{\beta}_3 = .833$ ($se = .16$) and $\hat{\beta}_2 - \hat{\beta}_3 = .304$ ($se = .16$), compared to $\hat{\beta}_1 - \hat{\beta}_3 = .834$ ($se = .16$) and $\hat{\beta}_2 - \hat{\beta}_3 = .292$ ($se = .16$) with the normal approach.

It follows from the papers cited above that one can also estimate the within-subject comparisons of items $\beta_h - \beta_j$ in model (5) by fitting a quasi-symmetric log-linear model. Let $\mu_g(h_1, h_2, h_3)$ denote the expected frequency for gender g making response h_j to item j, $j = 1, 2, 3$, where $g = 1$ for female and 0 otherwise and where $h_j = 1$ for approval of legalized abortion for item j and 0 otherwise. This model is

$$\log \mu_g(h_1, h_2, h_3) = \beta_1 I(h_1 = 1) + \beta_2 I(h_2 = 1) + \beta_3 I(h_3 = 1) + \tau I(g = 1) + \sum_{k=0}^{3} \lambda_k I(h_1 + h_2 + h_3 = k), \quad (10)$$

where $I(\cdot)$ is the indicator function. Here, λ_k is a parameter referring to all cells in which subjects voiced approval in k of the three items, $k = 0, 1, 2, 3$. Fitting this model with ordinary software for GLMs (such as PROC GENMOD in SAS), we obtain $\hat{\beta}_1 - \hat{\beta}_2 = .521$ ($se = .154$), $\hat{\beta}_1 - \hat{\beta}_3 = .828$ ($se = .160$), $\hat{\beta}_2 - \hat{\beta}_3 = .307$ ($se = .161$), very similar to the normal random effects and nonparametric random-effects estimates. In fact, it follows from Tjur (1982) that these estimates also equal those obtained using conditional ML with model (5), treating the subject terms as fixed. With this approach (and with conditional ML), however, one cannot estimate between-groups effects, such as the gender effect in model (5).

3.6. *Example 6: Matched Pairs with a Bivariate Binary Response*

Examples discussed so far have had univariate random effects or independent random effects. We next show an example in which a multivariate, correlated random-effects structure is natural. We use Table 5, taken from Coleman (1964) and analyzed in several papers by Leo Goodman—e.g., Goodman (1974). A sample of schoolboys were interviewed twice, several months apart, and asked about their self-perceived membership in the "leading crowd" and about whether one must sometimes go against their principles to be part of that leading crowd. Thus there are two variables, which we refer to as membership (M) and attitude (A), measured at each of two interview times for each subject. Table 5 labels the categories for attitude as positive and negative, where positive refers to disagreeing with the statement that students must go against their principles.

For subject i, let π_{ijv} be the probability of response in category 1 for variable v at interview time j. We consider the multivariate logit model

$$\text{logit}(\pi_{ijv}) = \beta_{jv} + u_{iv}, \quad (11)$$

in which (u_{i1}, u_{i2}) describes subject heterogeneity for membership and attitude and $\beta_{2v} - \beta_{1v}$ describes the change in the response distribution for

TABLE 5
Cross Classification Illustrating Matched Pairs with a Bivariate Binary Response

(M, A)* for first interview		(M, A) for second interview				
		(Yes, Positive)	(Yes, Negative)	(No, Positive)	(No, Negative)	Total
Yes	Positive	458	140	110	49	757
		(451.3)	(145.5)	(121.9)	(48.8)	
Yes	Negative	171	182	56	87	496
		(173.5)	(180.5)	(58.2)	(73.4)	
No	Positive	184	75	531	281	1071
		(178.0)	(71.3)	(531.9)	(279.4)	
No	Negative	85	97	338	554	1074
		(85.0)	(107.2)	(333.2)	(558.8)	
Total		898	494	1035	971	3398

Source: From Coleman (1964).
*Membership (M) and attitude (A) toward the "leading crowd"; fitted values for model (11) are in parentheses.

variable v between interview times 2 and 1; that is, there are two nondegenerate random effects, one for attitude and one for membership. We fitted this model assuming that $\{(u_{i1}, u_{i2})\}$ are a random sample from a bivariate normal distribution.

Let M denote the membership variable and A the attitude variable. The ML fit of the bivariate random-effects model yields $\hat{\beta}_{2M} - \hat{\beta}_{1M} = .366$ (std. error = .073) and $\hat{\beta}_{2A} - \hat{\beta}_{1A} = .176$ (std. error = .058). For both variables, the probability of the first response is higher at the second interview; for instance, for each subject the odds of self-perceived membership in the leading crowd at time 2 are estimated to be exp(.366) = 1.44 times the odds at time 1. The values in the estimated covariance matrix (not reported here) suggest that there is more heterogeneity with respect to membership than with respect to attitude, and the estimated correlation between the random effects is 0.33. The model fits well, with likelihood-ratio statistic (deviance) comparing the observed counts to the fitted values equal to $G^2 = 5.5$, based on $df = 8$. The likelihood-ratio test comparing this model to the one that constrains $\beta_{2M} - \beta_{1M} = 0$ and $\beta_{2A} - \beta_{1A} = 0$ has test statistic 35.2 based on $df = 2$. The model constraining the random effects to be uncorrelated also fits poorly ($G^2 = 97.5$, $df = 9$), as does the model with perfectly correlated random effects ($G^2 = 655.5$, $df = 10$).

For this model, Agresti (1997) used a nonparametric approach, whereby a lack of assumption about the distribution of (u_{i1}, u_{i2}) motivates a quasi-symmetric log-linear model. This yields the same estimates as obtained with a conditional ML (CML) approach that eliminates (u_{i1}, u_{i2}) by conditioning on their sufficient statistics. The results reported here are nearly identical to those obtained using that approach (see Agresti 1997, but the attitude labels and the sign of the estimates are incorrectly stated there). There are a few basic differences, however. For instance, the nonparametric/CML approach necessarily provides estimates of $\beta_{2M} - \beta_{1M}$ and $\beta_{2A} - \beta_{1A}$ that are identical to the CML estimates from two separate univariate analyses. In essence, because that approach makes no assumption about the joint distribution of the random effects, the multivariate form of the data does not affect the analysis. This does not happen for the bivariate normal random effects analysis, although the estimates are very close to those obtained with univariate analyses.

The approach described above with correlated normal random effects is a continuous analog to discrete latent-class models proposed by Goodman (1974), based on two associated binary latent variables. Results are similar for the two approaches, although advantages of the random-effects model are that it is more parsimonious and it directly provides estimates $\beta_{2M} - \beta_{1M}$ and $\beta_{2A} - \beta_{1A}$ that compare the margins of the observed classifications. For additional examples of multivariate random effects analyses, see Coull and Agresti (2000).

3.7. *Example 7: Extensions to Ordinal/Nominal Response Data*

Random-effects models for binary data extend to handle multinomial responses, whether measured on ordinal or nominal scales. For instance, let y_{ij} denote the jth response in cluster i, where the possible values for y_{ij} are the response category outcomes $1, 2, \ldots, K$. For ordinal responses, GLMMs have been formulated for the $K - 1$ cumulative logits,

$$\text{logit}[P(y_{ij} \leq k)] = \alpha_k + \mathbf{x}_{ij}^t \boldsymbol{\beta} + \mathbf{z}_{ij}^t \mathbf{u}_i, \quad k = 1, \ldots, K-1, \qquad (12)$$

(e.g., see Ezzet and Whitehead 1991; Hedeker and Gibbons 1994; Tutz and Hennevogl 1996). This model has the simple *proportional odds* form whereby fixed and random effects are the same for all cumulative probabilities, that is for all ways of collapsing the K categories to a binary response.

For nominal response variables, cumulative probabilities are not meaningful. One can then formulate an ordinary binary model by pairing each category with a baseline (e.g., category K) and fit these $K - 1$ models simultaneously while allowing separate effects for each. This necessitates using a vector of random effects, one for each logit. This case has received little attention in the literature.

To illustrate a model of form (12), we analyze data from the 1994 General Social Survey on subjects' opinions on four items (the environment, health, law enforcement, education) relating to whether they believe that government spending on each item should increase, stay the same, or decrease. Subjects are also classified by their gender and their race. (The contingency table has 486 cells and is not shown here.) For subject i, let $G_i = 1$ for females and 0 for males, let $R_{1i} = 1$ for whites and 0 otherwise, $R_{2i} = 1$ for blacks and 0 otherwise. Let y_{ij} denote the response for subject i on spending item j, where outcomes $(1, 2, 3)$ represent (increase, stay the same, decrease). Consider first the random-intercept model

$$\text{logit}[P(y_{ij} \leq k)] = \alpha_k + \beta_j + \beta_g G_i + \beta_{r1} R_{i1} + \beta_{r2} R_{2i} + u_i, \quad k = 1, \ldots, K-1. \qquad (13)$$

Using NLMIXED in SAS with constraint $\beta_4 = 0$, we obtained ML estimates $(-.551, -.603, -.486, 0)$ of the item parameters $\{\beta_j\}$. The first three estimates have absolute values greater than five standard errors, providing strong evidence of greater support for increased government spending on education than on the other items.

However, substantial evidence of interaction exists. For instance, the deviance drops by 33.4 with the addition of a race-by-item interaction term. For that model, Table 6 shows the ML estimates and standard errors. Each race shows relatively more support for spending on education than the other items, with blacks also giving relatively high support for spending on health. To help show how to interpret these estimates, Table 7 shows the linear predictor estimates for males for the logit of the probability of supporting increased spending (category 1 contrasted with the other two). For instance, for white subjects with the environment item, the estimated linear predictor equals $1.065 - .055 - .357 - .170 = .483$, so for a white male at the mean of the random-effects distribution, the estimated probability of supporting increased spending is $e^{.483}/[1 + e^{.483}] = .62$. The

TABLE 6
Parameter Estimates and Standard Errors for Cumulative Logit Model on Government Spending, with Random Subject Intercept, Perm'ting Item-by-Race Interaction

Variable	Estimate	Standard Error
Intercept-1	1.065	.391
Intercept-2	1.919	.051
Gender	.409	.088
Race1-w	−.055	.397
Race2-b	.434	.452
Item1-envir	−.357	.539
Item2-health	−.319	.493
Item3-crime	−.585	.480
Race1*Item1	−.170	.549
Race1*Item2	−.387	.503
Race1*Item3	.197	.491
Race2*Item1	−.452	.606
Race2*Item2	.454	.598
Race2*Item3	−.518	.560

Source: General Social Survey (1994).
Note: Coding 0 for Item 4 (educ.) and race 3 (other).

TABLE 7
Linear Predictor Estimates for Logit Probability of Males Preferring Increased Spending*

	Race		
Item	White	Black	Other
Environment	.48	.69	.71
Health	.30	1.64	.74
Crime	.62	.40	.48
Education	1.01	1.50	1.06

*For model with item-by-race interaction with government spending data (Table 6); this increases by .41 for females and by 1.92 for logit probability of increased or the same spending.

linear predictor values increase by 1.919 for the cumulative probability for the second category—that is, the probability of response in categories "increasing" or "staying the same." For this model, $\hat{\beta}_g = .409$; for females, the (subject-specific) odds of supporting increased spending instead of the same or lower spending, and the odds of supporting increased or the same spending instead of lower spending, are estimated to be $\exp(.409) = 1.51$ times the corresponding odds for males.

Some evidence exists of additional interactions, but the race-by-item interaction provides the strongest departure from the main effects model. For this model, the estimated standard deviation of the random intercept equals 1.0, representing a considerable positive association among repeated responses by each subject.

3.8. *Example 8: Cluster Sampling*

The use of cluster sampling methods has traditionally presented a stumbling block for categorical data methodology. Although numerous methods have been proposed, few are reported in the social science literature or have been adopted by leading software packages. Standard errors based on simple random sampling are too small, and the usual chi-squared test statistics have weighted sums of chi-squared, not chi-squared null distributions. For instance, see Rao and Thomas (1988) for a survey of ways of adjusting standard inferences to take into account complex sampling methods in the analysis and modeling of categorical data.

When the sampling scheme uses a random sample of clusters, with independent observations within each cluster, one can account for the clustering by using random effects for the clusters. To illustrate, we analyze data from Brier (1980), who reported 96 observations taken from 20 neighborhoods (the clusters) on Y = *satisfaction with home* and X = *satisfaction with neighborhood as a whole*. Each variable was measured with the ordinal scale (*unsatisfied, satisfied, very satisfied*). Brier's (1980) analysis adjusted for the clustering by reducing the usual Pearson statistic for testing independence in the 3×3 contingency table relating X and Y from 17.9 to 15.7 ($df = 4$).

Again, let y_{ij} denote the jth response in cluster i, and consider the model

$$\text{logit}[P(y_{ij} \leq k)] = \alpha_k + x_{ij}\beta + u_i, \tag{14}$$

where we use scores (1, 2, 3) for the satisfaction levels of x_{ij}. Assuming a $N(0, \sigma^2)$ distribution for u_i and using NLMIXED in SAS, we obtained $\hat{\beta} = -1.201$, with standard error of .407, and $\hat{\sigma} = .92$ ($se = .37$). By contrast, the analysis treating the 96 observations as a random sample corresponds to this model forcing $\sigma = 0$; it has $\hat{\beta} = -1.226$, with standard error of .370. As in the Brier (1980) analysis, there is a slight reduction in significance from taking the clustering into account. The ratio of Var$(\hat{\beta})$ in the clustered to unclustered analysis is 1.14, as is the ratio of Brier's Pearson statistics in the unclustered to clustered analyses. It is a bit surprising that the cluster-specific $\hat{\beta}$ estimate is not larger (in absolute value) than the unclustered one. A referee has indicated that this may reflect the fact that asymptotics may not apply well with a relatively small number of clusters (20 in this case) or that the cluster factor is confounded with the satisfaction with neighborhood covariate (Neuhaus and Kalbfleisch 1998; Berlin et al. 1999).

3.9. *Example 9: Capture-Recapture Data*

This section has presented a variety of data sets and applications to illustrate the potential use of random-effects modeling with categorical response data in the social sciences. Some alternative forms of such models that have been used in other scientific disciplines also have the potential for social science applications.

An example is random-effects models as employed in capture-recapture problems. These methods have repeated measurement over time, with scale (sampled, not sampled) at each time. Observations are completely missing for the cell corresponding to those subjects not sampled for every list. Such methods have traditionally been used to estimate animal abundance in some habitat. However, they have increasingly been applied to estimate population size in census and public health settings. For instance, Davies, Cormack, and Richardson (1999) estimated population prevalence of injecting drug use and HIV infection in Glasgow, and Darroch et al. (1993) used a three-sample multiple-recapture approach in census population estimation. Another possible application is to estimate the number of files on the World Wide Web relating to some subject by taking samples using several search engines (Fienberg, Johnson, and Junker 1999).

For capture-recapture modeling, Coull and Agresti (1999) recently used a logit model with a random-effects term to represent heterogeneity among subjects in their probability of capture at any given time. This allowance for heterogeneity results in wider prediction intervals for the population size than ordinary methods provide, indicating that intervals based on a possibly unrealistic assumption of homogeneity among subjects may be overly optimistic.

3.10. *Extensions to Discrete Data*

The focus of this paper is on random-effects models for categorical response data. More generally, GLMMs are useful for other types of discrete data as well. For instance, consider Poisson regression modeling of count data. A severe limitation of the Poisson model is that the variance must be identical to the mean; hence, at a fixed mean there is not the potential for the variance to decrease as predictors are added to the model. In particular, count data often show overdispersion, with the variance exceeding the mean.

A flexible way to account for overdispersion with count data is with a mixture model. Traditionally this is done by assuming that, given the mean, the distribution is Poisson, but the mean itself varies according to a gamma distribution. The mixture distribution is then the negative binomial. There are two versions of the negative binomial model, depending on how the gamma is parameterized; one version has variance that is a constant multiple of the mean, and the other has variance that is a quadratic function of the mean (McCullagh and Nelder 1989). ML estimation for the latter case is available with PROC GENMOD in SAS (starting with Version 7).

Alternatively, one can use the GLMM structure (2), typically with the log-link function and a normal random effect. For the log link with random intercept, for instance, the model for the mean μ_{ij} for the jth response in cluster i is

$$\log(\mu_{ij}) = \mathbf{x}_{ij}^t \boldsymbol{\beta} + u_i,$$

where u_i has a $N(0, \sigma^2)$ distribution. This model is an appealing way to account for overdispersion due to important unobserved explanatory variables. The implication about the marginal distribution (averaging out the random effect) is that

$$E(y_{ij}) = E[E(y_{ij}|u_i)] = E[e^{\mathbf{x}_{ij}^t \boldsymbol{\beta} + u_i}] = e^{\mathbf{x}_{ij}^t \boldsymbol{\beta} + \sigma^2/2}$$

since (by its moment-generating function) a $N(0, \sigma^2)$ variate u_i has $E(e^{tu_i}) = e^{t^2\sigma^2/2}$. That is, if this model holds, then the log of the mean unconditionally equals $\mathbf{x}_{ij}^t\boldsymbol{\beta} + \sigma^2/2$, so the cluster-specific effects of the explanatory variables are the same as the marginal effects but the intercept is offset (Zeger et al. 1988). Similarly, the marginal distribution has

$$\begin{aligned}
\text{Var}(y_{ij}) &= E[\text{Var}(y_{ij}|u_i)] + \text{Var}[E(y_{ij}|u_i)] \\
&= E[e^{\mathbf{x}_{ij}^t \boldsymbol{\beta} + u_i}] + e^{2\mathbf{x}_{ij}^t \boldsymbol{\beta}} \text{Var}(e^{u_i}) \\
&= e^{\mathbf{x}_{ij}^t \boldsymbol{\beta} + \sigma^2/2} + e^{2\mathbf{x}_{ij}^t \boldsymbol{\beta}}(e^{2\sigma^2} - e^{\sigma^2}) \\
&= E(y_{ij}) + [E(y_{ij})]^2(e^{\sigma^2} - 1).
\end{aligned}$$

That is, the unconditional variance is a quadratic function of the mean. The ordinary Poisson model results from $\sigma^2 = 0$, and the extent to which the variance exceeds the mean increases as σ^2 increases.

Note that one can obtain the negative binomial model with log link from a GLMM construction by letting $\exp(u_i)$ have a gamma distribution with a mean of 1. The GLMM with normal random effect has the advantage, relative to the negative binomial model, of providing a way of permitting multiple random effects and multilevel models. Land, McCall, and Nagin (1996) discussed a semiparametric version of the GLMM that treats the random effect in a nonparametric manner. This is in the same spirit as the work of Aitkin (1996, 1999) for nonparametric fitting of GLMMs mentioned in Section 3.6.

We illustrate a situation in which it is important to allow for a random effect with count data using a simple data set from the 1990 General Social Survey. We look at one question asked subjects: "Within the past 12 months, how many people have you known personally that were victims of homicide?" We consider this response here for the white and black categories of race. The mean for the 159 blacks who responded was .522 with a variance of 1.150; the mean for the 1149 whites who responded was .092 with a variance of .155. The ratio of the variance to the mean for each race provides evidence of overdispersion for a Poisson model. It is plausible that, for each race, the expected value of the response would vary according to various unmeasured factors such as demographic variables and the location of one's residence.

For the ordinary Poisson model with log link, the estimated difference of 1.733 between the log mean for blacks and the log mean for whites has an estimated standard error of .147. However, it is much more natural to use a model permitting subject heterogeneity. Adding a parameter by using the negative binomial approach with quadratic variance function (using ML fitting in SAS with PROC GENMOD), the log-likelihood increases by 61.1 (deviance decreases by 122.2). The estimated difference is still 1.733 between the log means, since for this case both models provide fitted means equal to the observed ones (and $\log(.522/.092) = 1.733$), but now the estimated standard error increases to .238. The Wald 95 percent confidence interval for the ratio of means for blacks and whites goes from $\exp[1.733 \pm 1.96(.147)] = (4.2, 7.5)$ for the ordinary Poisson model to $\exp[1.733 \pm 1.96(.238)] = (3.5, 9.0)$ for the negative binomial model.

Other examples of applications of models that add random effects to Poisson regression include the analysis of cancer maps in epidemiology (Breslow and Clayton 1993) and modeling variability in bacteria counts (Aitchison and Ho 1989).

4. MODEL FITTING AND PREDICTION

Specification of a parametric GLMM is done in two stages. First, conditional on the random effects $\mathbf{u}$, the data $\mathbf{y}$ are assumed to follow a probability distribution in the exponential family. This is a broad family of probability distributions that includes the normal, binomial, and Poisson. Let $f(\mathbf{y} | \mathbf{u}; \boldsymbol{\beta})$ represent the conditional density (or mass) function of $\mathbf{y}$ given $\mathbf{u}$, where $\boldsymbol{\beta}$ is as in (2). For example, consider the model of Section 2.1. In this case, $\mathbf{y} = (y_{11}, y_{12}, \ldots, y_{I1}, y_{I2})^t$, $\mathbf{u} = (u_1, \ldots, u_I)^t$, $\boldsymbol{\beta} = (\alpha, \beta)^t$, and we have

$$f(\mathbf{y}|\mathbf{u};\alpha,\beta)=\prod_{i=1}^{I}\frac{\exp\{y_{i1}(\alpha+u_i)\}}{(1+\exp\{\alpha+u_i\})}\frac{\exp\{y_{i2}(\alpha+\beta+u_i)\}}{(1+\exp\{\alpha+\beta+u_i\})}.$$

The second part of the specification involves making an assumption about the distribution of the random effects, **u**. Typically, **u** is assumed to be multivariate normal with mean zero and covariance matrix **V**. Often **V** is known up to a vector of *variance components*, $\boldsymbol{\sigma}^2$. Let $f(\mathbf{u};\boldsymbol{\sigma})$ denote the probability density function of **u**. In the model of Section 2.1, the components of **u** are assumed to be independent $N(0,\sigma^2)$, which means that $\boldsymbol{\sigma}$ has only one component and

$$f(\mathbf{u};\sigma)=\prod_{i=1}^{I}\frac{1}{\sqrt{2\pi\sigma^2}}\exp\left\{-\frac{1}{2\sigma^2}u_i^2\right\}.$$

In this section we discuss estimation of $\boldsymbol{\psi}=(\boldsymbol{\beta}^t,\boldsymbol{\sigma}^t)^t$, the vector of unknown parameters in our model, using exact ML estimation as well as two approximate ML techniques: one based on an analytical approximation of the likelihood integrand and the other on Bayes methods with diffuse priors.

4.1. *Exact Maximum Likelihood*

As Searle et al. (1992:232) point out, maximum likelihood is a "well-established and well-respected method of estimation that has a variety of optimality properties." As such, ML estimation is usually the default technique for estimating parameters. In general, the GLMM likelihood function is the marginal mass function of the *observed* data, **y**, viewed as a function of the parameters; that is,

$$L(\boldsymbol{\beta},\boldsymbol{\sigma}|\mathbf{y})=\int f(\mathbf{y}|\mathbf{u};\boldsymbol{\beta})f(\mathbf{u};\boldsymbol{\sigma})\,d\mathbf{u}. \qquad (15)$$

This expression nearly always involves intractable integrals whose dimension depends on the structure of the random effects. For example, the likelihood function for the model of Section 2.1 is given by

$$L(\alpha,\beta,\sigma|\mathbf{y}) = \prod_{i=1}^{I} \int_{-\infty}^{\infty} \frac{\exp\{y_{i1}(\alpha+u_i)\}}{(1+\exp\{\alpha+u_i\})} \frac{\exp\{y_{i2}(\alpha+\beta+u_i)\}}{(1+\exp\{\alpha+\beta+u_i\})} \times \frac{1}{\sqrt{2\pi\sigma^2}} \exp\left\{-\frac{u_i^2}{2\sigma^2}\right\} du_i$$

which has no closed-form solution. When the dimension of the intractable integrals is small, numerical integration can be used to closely approximate the likelihood (Crouch and Spiegelman 1990), as is done in SAS's NLMIXED. However, the error induced by replacing the intractable integral with a finite sum (as is done in Gauss-Hermite quadrature methods) becomes more and more difficult to control as the dimension of the integral increases.

Recently developed Monte Carlo methods for finding the exact maximum-likelihood estimate provide an alternative to numerical integration. These iterative methods can handle high-dimensional integrals better than numerical integration. Unfortunately, they require fairly sophisticated computer programs, and, as of now, there is no general software available. The Monte Carlo-based method that has received the most attention is the Monte Carlo EM (MCEM) algorithm, which is now described.

The EM algorithm (Dempster, Laird, and Rubin 1977) is a popular method of finding ML estimates in normal theory mixed models (Searle et al. 1992, ch. 8). Consider application of the EM algorithm in the GLMM setting with $\mathbf{u}$ assuming the role of *missing data*. The E-step of the EM algorithm requires calculation of

$$E\{\log f(\mathbf{y},\mathbf{u};\boldsymbol{\psi})|\mathbf{y};\boldsymbol{\psi}^{(r)}\}, \qquad (16)$$

where $f(\mathbf{y},\mathbf{u};\boldsymbol{\psi}) = f(\mathbf{y}|\mathbf{u};\boldsymbol{\beta})f(\mathbf{u};\boldsymbol{\sigma})$ is the density of the *complete data* and $\boldsymbol{\psi}^{(r)}$ denotes the value of $\boldsymbol{\psi}$ from the rth iteration of EM. As the notation suggests, the expectation in (16) is with respect to the conditional distribution of $\mathbf{u}$ given $\mathbf{y}$ with parameter value set equal to $\boldsymbol{\psi}^{(r)}$, whose density we write as $f(\mathbf{u}|\mathbf{y};\boldsymbol{\psi}^{(r)})$. Unfortunately, analytical evaluation of (16) is also impossible, because (15) cannot be written in closed form.

The MCEM algorithm, introduced by Wei and Tanner (1990), circumvents this difficulty by replacing the intractable expectation with a Monte Carlo approximation. There are (at least) three different methods of constructing a Monte Carlo estimate of (16) in the GLMM context. The most obvious method is to use independent simulations from $f(\mathbf{u}|\mathbf{y};\boldsymbol{\psi}^{(r)})$.

Booth and Hobert (1999) explained how to obtain such a sample through rejection sampling and also how to form a different estimate using importance sampling. The third method is Markov chain Monte Carlo (MCMC). McCulloch (1994) and Chan and Kuk (1997) showed how to use the Gibbs sampler for some specific binary data models, while McCulloch (1997) gave a general Hastings-Metropolis algorithm that will, in theory, work for any GLMM; see also Liao (1999).

Of course, there is no free lunch. While the use of MCEM circumvents a complicated expectation at each E-step, it requires a method for choosing the Monte Carlo sample size at each MCE-step. Booth and Hobert (1999) and Levine and Casella (1998) discussed methods for choosing an appropriate Monte Carlo sample size at each iteration.

In stating that the methods of this subsection provide "exact" ML estimates, we mean that the approximations converge to the ML estimates as they are applied more finely—for instance, as the number of quadrature points increases in an appropriate manner for numerical integration and as the Monte Carlo sample size increases in the MCEM method. This is in contrast to the approximate methods of the next subsection, which may potentially yield values far from the ML estimates no matter how applied.

4.2. *Penalized Quasi Likelihood*

If one is willing to sacrifice exactness for ease of implementation, there are approximate ML methods that maximize an analytical approximation of the likelihood function instead of the likelihood function itself. The main approaches involve integrating a first-order Taylor series expansion of the likelihood integrand around the approximate posterior modes of the random effects (Goldstein 1991; Schall 1991; Breslow and Clayton 1993; Wolfinger and O'Connell 1993; Longford 1993; Longford 1994; McGilchrist 1994). In particular, Breslow and Clayton's (1993) algorithm, which is motivated using a penalized quasi-likelihood (PQL) argument, is essentially the same as the algorithm proposed by Wolfinger and O'Connell (1993), based on the idea of pseudo-likelihood. This algorithm involves iterative fitting of normal theory linear mixed models and can be implemented using the %GLIMMIX macro in SAS (see Littell et al. 1996). Even though this method is iterative, it involves no numerical integration or Monte Carlo approximation and so is much simpler to program than the exact ML methods. Here is a brief description:

Each iteration contains two steps; the first updates $\boldsymbol{\beta}$ and the second updates $\boldsymbol{\sigma}$. Suppose that $(\boldsymbol{\beta}^{(r)}, \boldsymbol{\sigma}^{(r)})$ are the values after r iterations.

The $\boldsymbol{\beta}$ update can be motivated using Henderson's mixed-model equations (Henderson et al. 1959). To this end, consider the normal theory mixed model—that is, the model in which both $f(\mathbf{y}|\mathbf{u};\boldsymbol{\beta})$ and $f(\mathbf{u};\boldsymbol{\sigma})$ are normal densities. Let $\hat{\boldsymbol{\sigma}}$ be the ML or restricted ML (REML) estimate of $\boldsymbol{\sigma}$. It is well known (Searle et al. 1992, sec. 7.6) that the values of $\boldsymbol{\beta}$ and $\mathbf{u}$ that jointly maximize the function $f(\mathbf{y}|\mathbf{u};\boldsymbol{\beta})f(\mathbf{u};\hat{\boldsymbol{\sigma}})$ are the ML estimate of $\boldsymbol{\beta}$ and the estimated best linear unbiased predictor (EBLUP) of $\mathbf{u}$. This motivates the following update for $\boldsymbol{\beta}$ in the GLMM context. Given $\boldsymbol{\sigma}^{(r)}$, the function $f(\mathbf{y}|\mathbf{u};\boldsymbol{\beta})f(\mathbf{u};\boldsymbol{\sigma}^{(r)})$ is maximized with respect to $\boldsymbol{\beta}$ and $\mathbf{u}$ and $\boldsymbol{\beta}^{(r+1)}$ is assigned the maximizing value of $\boldsymbol{\beta}$. This maximization is not trivial and will almost always require an iterative technique such as Newton-Raphson.

The $\boldsymbol{\sigma}$ update is based on another normal approximation. Given $\boldsymbol{\beta}^{(r)}$ and $\mathbf{u}^{(r)}$, a *working dependent variable*, $\mathbf{z}$, is constructed just as it is in the usual iteratively reweighted least-squares algorithm for fitting generalized linear models (McCullagh and Nelder 1989:40). This working dependent variable is then assumed to follow a normal linear mixed model and ML or REML is used to estimate the variance components (e.g., see Searle et al. 1992, ch. 6). The components of $\boldsymbol{\sigma}^{(r)}$ are then assigned the values of the corresponding ML or REML estimates.

The main advantage of PQL is its relative simplicity, avoiding numerical integration and being computationally feasible for very large data sets and complex multilevel models that may not be feasible with the methods of Section 4.1. However, this iterative scheme does *not* yield the ML estimate of $\boldsymbol{\psi} = (\boldsymbol{\beta}^t, \boldsymbol{\sigma}^t)^t$. Indeed, McCulloch (1997) uses some analytical arguments in conjunction with simulation to show that this method can perform quite poorly relative to ML; see also Booth and Hobert (1999, sec. 7.3) for an analysis of a data set that illustrates the potential for large differences between ML and PQL, and Breslow and Lin (1995) and Lin and Breslow (1996) for "bias-corrected" versions of PQL. Generally, the PQL approach deteriorates as the data depart from normal (e.g., binary) and as the variance components increase. To illustrate, consider the opinion about abortion data of Section 3.2. For the parameterization setting $\beta_3 = 0$, the ML estimates for the random-effects model are $\hat{\beta}_1 = .83$ ($se = .16$), $\hat{\beta}_2 = .29$ ($se = .16$) with $\hat{\sigma} = 8.8$ reflecting a very strong within-subject dependence. By contrast, the PQL estimates (obtained using the %GLIMMIX macro in SAS) are $\hat{\beta}_1 = .87$ ($se = .07$), $\hat{\beta}_2 = .31$ ($se = .07$)

with $\hat{\sigma} = 4.3$. The PQL approximations to the ML estimates are decent for $\{\beta_j\}$, but the standard errors and the estimate of σ are only about half of what they should be. In fact, when true variance components are large, PQL ordinarily tends to produce variance component estimates that have substantial negative bias (Breslow and Lin 1995). The PQL approach provided a good approximation for the ML estimates for the other binary data examples presented here.

Generally speaking, PQL is a good approximation to ML, provided the random-effects variances are relatively small (that is, when the fixed effects dominate the model) or the response is approximately normal. Improvements of such approximations have been proposed for cases in which they may behave poorly (e.g., Breslow and Lin 1995; Lin and Breslow 1996; Goldstein and Rasbash 1996). However, we recommend that analysts attempt to use exact ML, rather than possibly poor approximations such as PQL. We have briefly described the approximate methods above because most current software for GLMMs uses them rather than ML and because of the scope of their computational feasibility. Over time, however, as computational methods continue to be refined, we believe that ML fitting of GLMMs will become more commonplace and the approximate methods will lose their current appeal.

4.3. *A Bayesian Model with a Diffuse Prior*

In a Bayesian version of our model $\boldsymbol{\psi}$ is treated as a random variable with prior density $\pi(\boldsymbol{\psi})$. The posterior density is given by

$$\pi(\mathbf{u}, \boldsymbol{\psi} | \mathbf{y}) = \frac{f(\mathbf{y}, \mathbf{u}; \boldsymbol{\psi})\, \pi(\boldsymbol{\psi})}{c(\mathbf{y})}$$

where

$$c(\mathbf{y}) = \iint f(\mathbf{y}, \mathbf{u}; \boldsymbol{\psi})\, \pi(\boldsymbol{\psi})\, d\mathbf{u}\, d\boldsymbol{\psi},$$

which is typically not available in closed form because of the same intractable integrals that cause trouble in the likelihood function. A flat prior, $\pi(\boldsymbol{\psi}) = 1$, results in a posterior (for $\boldsymbol{\psi}$) that is simply a constant multiple of the likelihood function (15). Therefore, if the resulting posterior is *proper*, MCMC methods that can also be used to study intractable posterior distributions (e.g., the Gibbs sampler) can be used to study the likelihood function. While flat priors typically result in proper posteriors in normal theory mixed models (Hobert and Casella 1996), they lead to improper posteriors for many of the models considered in this paper (Natarajan and McCulloch 1995).

One way to ensure a proper posterior is to use a proper prior. If a "diffuse" but proper prior is used in place of a flat prior, we might hope that the resulting posterior is close to the likelihood function. Furthermore, we can legitimately use MCMC methods to find the posterior mode, which we might hope is a reasonable approximation to the ML estimate. However, the use of a proper diffuse prior need not result in a posterior mode that is close to the ML estimate, especially when the data contain little information about the variance components (Kass and Wasserman 1996). Moreover, the simulation results of Natarajan and McCulloch (1998) showed that using a diffuse prior can lead to Markov chains that converge very slowly. Thus, even if the likelihood and posterior are similar, MCMC techniques may be of no practical use because of slow mixing. In our opinion, this approximate Bayes method is the least attractive of all the approximate methods.

4.4. *Inference for Model Parameters*

After fitting the model, the next step is usually inference about the components of $\boldsymbol{\psi}$. We first consider inference about $\boldsymbol{\beta}$. The asymptotic normality of the ML estimate of $\boldsymbol{\beta}$ can be used to form approximate confidence sets in the usual way (McCullagh and Nelder 1989, app. A). Furthermore, hypotheses involving $\boldsymbol{\beta}$ can be tested using asymptotic likelihood-ratio tests (LRTs); that is, using the fact that minus twice the log of the likelihood-ratio statistic ($-2 \log \lambda$) has an asymptotic χ^2 distribution under the null (McCullagh and Nelder 1989, app. A). If an MCEM program for fitting the model is available, the necessary evaluations of the likelihood and derivatives of the likelihood at the ML estimate can be performed via Monte Carlo with little additional programming; for example, see Booth and Hobert (1999, sec. 6).

Regarding the testing of variance components, it is unfortunate that $-2 \log \lambda$ does not necessarily have an asymptotic χ^2 distribution under the null when the hypothesis involves parameters on the boundary of the parameter space—e.g., when testing that a variance component is equal to zero (Self and Liang 1987). (This difficulty has nothing to do with the categorical nature of the data; indeed, the same problem arises in normal linear mixed models for tests about the variance components (Miller 1977).) While calculation of the true asymptotic distribution can in general be quite difficult, there are several important special cases for which it is known. In particular, suppose that the model contains a single variance component, σ^2, and that we wish to test $H_0 : \sigma^2 = 0$ versus $H_1 : \sigma^2 > 0$. Self and Liang (1987, case 5) show that, in this situation, the asymptotic distribution of $-2 \log \lambda$ under the null is a 50:50 mixture of χ_0^2 and χ_1^2 random variables. (A χ_0^2 is a point mass at 0 and corresponds to $\hat{\sigma} = 0$, for which the maximized likelihoods are identical under H_0 and H_1, and hence their ratio $\lambda = 1$ and $-2 \log \lambda = 0$.) Thus, when $\hat{\sigma} > 0$ and $t = -2 \log \lambda > 0$, the P-value for this large-sample test is $(1/2)P(\chi_1^2 > t)$, half the P-value that applies for χ_1^2 asymptotic tests (such as tests about components of $\boldsymbol{\beta}$).

Recently, Lin (1997) has shown that the score test (McCullagh and Nelder 1989, app. A) is a flexible alternative to the LRT for testing that one or all of the variance components in the model are equal to zero. Again, in the MCEM context, it is straightforward to form Monte Carlo approximations of the likelihood derivatives that comprise the score statistic.

4.5. *Prediction of Random Effects*

In Section 4.1 we discussed a method for forecasting election results by predicting random effects associated with 50 states and the District of Columbia. In that setting the procedure involved estimating/predicting a sum of the form $\alpha + u_i$, where α represented a fixed but unknown nation-wide propensity to vote for Clinton and u_i was a random effect associated with the ith state. More generally, when random effects are used to measure variation among a relatively large number of small areas or domains, it is often of interest to estimate/predict mixed linear combinations of fixed and random effects of the form $\eta = \mathbf{x}^t\boldsymbol{\beta} + \mathbf{z}^t\mathbf{u}$ specific to the domains of interest. For example, in educational surveys, the domains might be schools for which a rating is desired or even individual children whose ability is being predicted.

Except for the presence of the unknown fixed effects parameter $\boldsymbol{\beta}$ and the variance components parameter $\boldsymbol{\sigma}$, the GLMM provides a complete description of the joint distribution of the observable data $\mathbf{y}$ and the unobservable random effect $\mathbf{u}$. After the data have been collected (i.e., observed), all the information about the random effects is contained in the conditional distribution of $\mathbf{u}$ given $\mathbf{y}$. This distribution is implicitly defined by the assumed GLMM via the relationship $f(\mathbf{u}|\mathbf{y}) \propto f(\mathbf{y},\mathbf{u})$. Thus, for example, a point prediction for $\mathbf{u}$ is given by the mean of this conditional distribution, $E(\mathbf{u}|\mathbf{y})$. This predictor is "best" in the sense that its mean squared error is less than that of any other predictor (Searle et al. 1992, sec. 7.2).

Two practical issues that arise with the use of $E(\mathbf{u}|\mathbf{y})$ as a predictor for $\mathbf{u}$ are that the conditional expectation (1) depends on the unknown parameters $\boldsymbol{\beta}$ and $\boldsymbol{\sigma}$ and (2) is usually not available in closed form. The first of these difficulties is overcome in practice by simply plugging in estimates in place of the unknown parameters. In the case of the normal theory linear mixed model, substitution of the ML estimate for $\boldsymbol{\beta}$ results in the best linear unbiased predictor or BLUP while further substitution for $\boldsymbol{\sigma}$, if necessary, results in the so-called "empirical" BLUP (Searle et al. 1992, sec. 9.3). The second complication can be dealt with by numerically calculating the desired expectation, either exactly (using numerical integration or Monte Carlo methods) or approximately. In particular, a minor side benefit of the PQL algorithm used in the SAS macro GLIMMIX is that it automatically produces approximations for the predicted random effects. The predictor $\hat{\mathbf{u}}$ obtained by plugging parameter estimates into the conditional expectation $E(\mathbf{u}|\mathbf{y})$ is often referred to as the *empirical Bayes predictor*; for a detailed discussion of this approach, see Carlin and Louis (1996).

The more data that are available from a particular domain, the more accurately random effects associated with that domain can be predicted. Suppose that $\mathbf{y}_i$ denotes the data collected from the ith domain with associated random effect u_i. The amount of uncertainty about u_i is measured by the conditional variance, $\text{Var}(u_i|\mathbf{y}_i)$, or by the corresponding standard deviation. These *standard errors of prediction* can also be computed or approximated using the conditional distribution implied by the assumed GLMM and by substituting estimates of unknown parameters where necessary. A common criticism of this method is that no adjustment is made for the sampling variability in the parameter estimates. The parameters are effectively treated as though they are known, and hence the amount of uncertainty about the random effects tends to be underestimated. Booth and Hobert (1998) discussed this issue and proposed a method for correcting the "naive" standard errors. However, their adjustments are complicated and difficult to compute. Moreover, unless the total amount of data is very limited (leading to very unreliable parameter estimates), corrections to the naive standard errors are often relatively small and of little practical significance.

5. MARGINALLY SPECIFIED MODELS

Section 2.2 highlighted the conditional (i.e., *subject-specific*) interpretation of the regression parameters in a GLMM. In some instances, however, the marginal (i.e., *population averaged*) effects are of primary interest. For example, consider a survey of opinions of different ethnic groups in which responses on a variety of social issues are measured on a binary scale (yes/no, favor/oppose, etc.). Quantities of primary interest in such a setting would typically include between-group odds ratios among marginal probabilities for the different ethnic groups. In such cases it is more convenient to parameterize the model in such a way that the regression parameters have a direct marginal interpretation.

One popular approach to modeling marginal effects is to use generalized estimating equations (GEE). A brief description of this approach follows. As before let y_{ij} denote the jth response in domain or cluster i and let $\mathbf{x}_{ij}$ denote a vector of associated explanatory variable values, $i = 1, \ldots, I$ and $j = 1, \ldots, n_i$. Now suppose that the marginal mean of the (i, j)th response, $m_{ij} = E(y_{ij})$, is described by the linear model

$$g(m_{ij}) = \mathbf{x}_{ij}^t \boldsymbol{\beta}, \tag{17}$$

where g is a link function. In addition, suppose that the variance of y_{ij} is given by $\mathrm{Var}(y_{ij}) = \phi_{ij} v(m_{ij})$, where $\phi_{ij} = \phi / w_{ij}$. If the assumed variance function corresponds to an exponential family model, this assumed structure for the mean and variance is exactly that of a GLM. However, unlike in a GLM, the GEE method does not require the distribution of the responses to be fully specified. Furthermore, GEE allows for dependence between responses from the same cluster via a *working correlation matrix*. The terminology "working" is used because an adjustment to the standard errors of the regression parameters is usually made using a *sandwich variance* formula to account for misspecification of this part of the correlation structure (Liang and Zeger 1986). For example, for the two-level sampling design considered in this section and in much of the paper, it is often reasonable to assume that responses within the same cluster are equicorrelated. On the other hand, if the responses consist of repeated measurements taken at different times within each cluster then a working correlation matrix incorporating an autocorrelation structure might be more reasonable. For a more detailed description of the GEE approach, see Liang and Zeger (1986), Diggle et al. (1994, ch. 8), and Liang et al. (1992).

A drawback of the GEE approach is that it does not explicitly model random effects and therefore does not allow these effects to be estimated. In addition, likelihood-based inferences are not possible because the joint distribution of the responses is not fully specified. A promising recent proposal by Heagerty (1999) attempts to overcome these deficiencies by defining a marginally specified GLMM. Heagerty notes that the traditional conditionally specified GLMM implicitly determines the relationship between the covariates and the marginal mean through the relation $m_{ij} = E(\mu_{ij})$. For example, we pointed out in Section 2.2 that with binary responses the assumption of a linear relationship between the covariates and the conditional logits implied a nonlinear relationship for the marginal logits. Conversely, if a marginal model for the mean of the form (17) is assumed, then this implicitly determines the form of the fixed portion of η_{ij} in the conditional model. That is, the linear predictor, $\eta_{ij} = \mathbf{x}_{ij}^t \boldsymbol{\beta} + \mathbf{z}_{ij}^t \mathbf{u}_i$, in the conditional GLMM is replaced by $\eta_{ij} = \Delta_{ij} + \mathbf{z}_{ij}^t \mathbf{u}_i$, where Δ_{ij} is a function of $(\boldsymbol{\beta}, \boldsymbol{\sigma})$ implicitly defined by the relation between the marginal and conditional means. Heagerty's idea is to specify the model for the conditional mean or the marginal mean depending upon whether a subject-specific or population-averaged interpretation is more relevant.

6. SOFTWARE

Applications of generalized linear mixed models have undoubtedly been hindered by the lack of adequate software. In recent years perhaps the most popular software has been the GLIMMIX macro provided by SAS. This macro provides estimates based on approximating the likelihood using methods of Breslow and Clayton (1993) and Wolfinger and O'Connell (1993). Having the GLM framework, it can fit models for a variety of response distributions and link functions, assuming normal random effects. Version 7 of SAS has introduced PROC NLMIXED, which can also use an adaptive version of Gauss-Hermite quadrature to approximate the likelihood. This is substantially better when variance components are large or data are far from normal. The availability of this procedure (or its successors) will likely make fitting of models with random effects much more common in the future. However, it has limitations. For instance, quadrature methods are computationally feasible only for integrals of small dimensions, and NLMIXED currently cannot accommodate nested random effects.

Table 8 shows the use of NLMIXED for the shrinkage analyses of Table 2 described in Section 3.1. Although it is easiest to use NLMIXED with standard univariate response distributions such as Poisson and binomial, it is also possible to use it with multinomial models. Table 9 shows its use for the ordinal cumulative logit analyses of the government spending data described in Section 3.7. First, one must define the two linear predictors (one for each cumulative probability) and the relationship between each multinomial probability and the linear predictors. For these data, the response is recoded as a vector, (y_1, y_2, y_3) taking three possible values, (0,0,1), (0,1,0) or (1,0,0), corresponding to the three possible responses, 1, 2, or 3. These response vectors are multinomials

TABLE 8
SAS (PROC NLMIXED) Code for Analyses of Table 2

```
data new;
input x n offset;
sub = _n_;
datalines;
1   5   -0.40898
16  32  -0.29363
10  19  0.26574
21  34  -0.19275
129 240 0.20312
....
8   14  0.17246
1   4   -0.29066
;

proc nlmixed;
 parms alpha = .2 sigma = .04;
 eta = alpha + u + offset;
 p = exp(eta) / (1 + exp(eta));
 model x ~ binomial(n,p);
 random u ~ normal(0,sigma*sigma) subject = sub;
 predict p out = new2;
run;

proc print data=new2;
run;
```

TABLE 9

SAS (PROC NLMIXED) Code for Analyses of Government Spending Data

```
data new;
input subject gender race1 race2 item1 item2 item3 y1 y2 y3 count;
datalines;
/*Subject          Gender   Race1   Race2   Item1   Item2   Item3   Y1   Y2   Y3   Count*/
           1         0        1       0       1       0       0      1    0    0     107
           1         0        1       0       0       1       0      1    0    0     107
           1         0        1       0       0       0       1      1    0    0     107
           1         0        1       0       0       0       0      1    0    0     107
           2         1        0       1       1       0       0      1    0    0      20
           2         1        0       1       0       1       0      0    0    1      20
           2         1        0       1       0       0       1      0    1    0      20
           2         1        0       1       0       0       0      0    0    1      20
           .
           .
           .
;
proc nlmixed data=new;
   bounds i2 > 0;
   eta1 = i1 + gender * beta1 + race1 * beta2 + race2 * beta3
          + item1 * beta4 + item2 * beta5 + item3 * beta6 + u;
   eta2 = i1 + i2 + gender * beta1 + race1 * beta2 + race2 * beta3
          + item1 * beta4 + item2 * beta5 + item3 * beta6 +  u;
   p1 = 1/(1 + exp(-eta1));
   p2 = 1/(1 + exp(-eta2)) - 1/(1 + exp(-eta1));
   p3 = 1 - 1/(1 + exp(-eta2));
   z = (p1**y1)*(p2**y2)*(p3**y3);
   if (z > 1e-8) then ll = log(z);
      else ll=-1e100;
  model y1 ~ general(ll);
  estimate 'thresh2' i1+i2;
  random u ~ normal(0,su * su) subject = subject;
  replicate count;
run;
```

with sample sizes of 1. For outcome probabilities, p_1, p_2, and p_3, the contribution to the multinomial log likelihood is $p_1^{y_1} p_2^{y_2} p_3^{y_3}$. NLMIXED allows the user to code general likelihoods, as we defined it with the statement $z = (p1{*}{*}y1){*}(p2{*}{*}y2){*}(p3{*}{*}y3)$. This likelihood is checked to see if it is numerically too close to zero, then converted to the log likelihood (the statement $ll = log(z)$). The statement $y_1 \sim general(ll)$ tells SAS that *ll* gives the value of the log likelihood. (Since the likelihood is a function of the parameters, it does not matter if y_1, y_2, or y_3 is used for that statement). Finally, an estimate statement is used to obtain an estimate of the second threshold.

A variety of other programs are currently in general circulation. For instance, EGRET (now distributed by Cytel Software, in Cambridge, Massachusetts) can fit certain mixed logit models, approximating the likelihood with Gauss-Hermite quadrature or replacing the normal random-effects distribution by a binomial distribution. Hedeker and Gibbons (1994) supplied a FORTRAN program MIXOR for ML fitting of proportional odds models with random effects. Harvey Goldstein and colleagues at the Institute of Education in London provide a general-purpose program for multilevel modeling called MLn (www.ioe.ac.uk/multilevel/), that can fit the model using an improved version of PQL. One can use a fully Bayesian approach using MCMC with BUGS, available from the MRC Biostatistics Unit at Cambridge (www.mrc-bsu.cam.ac.uk/bugs). Other programs include HLM (Scientific Software International, Chicago), written by A. Bryk, S. Raudenbush, and R. Congdon and which also uses an improved version of PQL, LogXact (from Cytel Software) for the conditional ML approach to eliminating cluster terms, and a GLIM macro for parametric and nonparametric fitting of GLMMs (Aitkin and Francis 1995); see Zhou, Perkins, and Hui (1999) for a description of some software for multilevel models.

The numerical approximations necessary to fit GLMMs require careful use even with software such as NLMIXED in SAS. With quadrature-based software, one should use a sufficient number of quadrature points to obtain simultaneously close approximations to the maximized log-likelihood and to ML estimates of the fixed effects, the standard errors of the fixed effects, the variance components, and the standard errors of the variance components. NLMIXED determines the number of quadrature points adaptively, and the default number selected is often quite low (at least, this is the case for versions 7 and 8 of SAS). Usually this is sufficient for the fixed effects but not the random effects part of the model; obtaining sufficiently precise approximations for the standard errors and for the variance components usually requires considerably more points. In NLMIXED, we recommend checking these estimates while increasing the number of quadrature points (using the **qpoints=** option), to be confident that results have stabilized. We also recommend specifying the variance component in terms of the standard deviation in the model code. This helps in estimating variance components very close to 0, and also the standard deviation is usually preferred over the variance for interpretation.

Using large numbers of quadrature points may require long computing times. This is also true of data with a large number of clusters or several fixed and random effects within a cluster. Accurate starting values help speed convergence. Starting values can be obtained using the faster nonadaptive quadrature—for instance, by specifying *noad* and *noadscale* in the NLMIXED options or using the GLIMMIX macro. Since starting values need not be too accurate, milder convergence bounds can be used to obtain them.

7. CONCLUDING REMARKS

This article has shown a variety of social-science-related applications of generalized linear models for categorical data that contain random effects. Although introductory in nature, the models discussed have had relatively simple random-effects structure. However, there are many situations, especially in multilevel or multivariate settings (Catalano and Ryan 1992; Gueorguieva and Agresti 2000), where more complex models are appropriate. There is also continuing methodological research on random-effects models, such as developing ways of efficiently obtaining ML estimates and ways of checking goodness-of-fit of models.

Although random effects provide a natural way of handling many social science applications, as with any advanced statistical method there is the potential for misuse or inadequate use. For instance, with added complexity of models it can be more difficult to obtain ML estimates, and some algorithms may provide poor approximations for them. There is still much work to be done on the development of model-fitting methodology, as numerical integration is generally infeasible for complex models in which obtaining the likelihood involves high-dimensional integrals. The Bayesian paradigm (e.g., using the software BUGS) is becoming increasingly popular, but again with complex models there is the greater danger of inappropriate choices of priors (e.g., improper priors leading to improper posteriors that are not detected by MCMC methods).

In addition, little work has been done on model checking (e.g., goodness-of-fit tests) and model diagnostics for GLMMs, even in the normal theory case. Also, model comparison of GLMMs can be difficult. As we have seen, in some cases standard methods of comparing likelihoods fail because, under the null hypothesis, certain parameters (e.g., variance components) fall on the boundary of the parameter space, thus violating standard assumptions required to generate the usual asymptotic distributions.

Finally, choice of form of an appropriate model is still an issue. There is a controversy among some statisticians about whether the effects generated in marginal models are more or less relevant than the conditional effects resulting from random-effects models (e.g., Lindsey 1999). Most of the discussion of this has been with relation to biomedical and epidemiological issues, and it is time to consider the practical implications of these matters for social science applications. In particular, it is a challenge for methodologists even to explain to practitioners why marginal and conditional effects differ when one uses a nonlinear link function.

Even with these cautions in mind, we think that the random-effects approach provides a potentially very useful extension of standard generalized linear models for social science applications. We hope that this article contributes toward helping methodologists understand their use.

REFERENCES

Agresti, Alan. 1993. "Distribution-free Fitting of Logit Models with Random Effects of Repeated Categorical Responses." *Statistics in Medicine* 12:1969–87.

———. 1995. "Logit Models and Related Quasi-symmetric Loglinear Models for Comparing Responses to Similar Items in a Survey." *Sociological Methods and Research* 24:68–95.

———. 1997. "A Model for Repeated Measurements of a Multivariate Binary Response." *Journal of the American Statistical Association* 22:315–21.

Agresti, Alan, and Barbara Finlay. 1997. *Statistical Methods for the Social Sciences*, 3rd ed. Upper Saddle River, NJ: Prentice Hall.

Aitchison, John, and C. H. Ho. 1989. "The Multivariate Poisson-log Normal Distribution." *Biometrika* 76:643–53.

Aitkin, Murray. 1996. "A General Maximum Likelihood Analysis of Overdispersion in Generalized Linear Models." *Statistics and Computing* 6:251–62.

———. 1999. "A General Maximum Likelihood Analysis of Variance Components in Generalized Linear Models." *Biometrics* 55:117–28.

Aitkin, Murray, and Brian J. Francis. 1995. "Fitting Overdispersed Generalized Linear Models by Non-parametric Maximum Likelihood." *The GLIM Newsletter* 25:37–45.

Aitkin, Murray, and Nicholas Longford. 1986. "Statistical Modelling in School Effectiveness Studies" (with discussion). *Journal of the Royal Statistical Society*, ser. A, 149:1–43.

Aitkin, Murray, Dorothy Anderson, and John Hinde. 1981. "Statistical Modelling of Data on Teaching Styles" (with discussion). *Journal of the Royal Statistical Society*, ser. A, General 144:419–61.

Akin, John S., David K. Guilkey, and Robin Sickles. 1979. "A Random Coefficient Probit Model with an Application to a Study of Migration." *Journal of Econometrics* 11:233–46.

Albert, James. 1992. "A Bayesian Analysis of a Poisson Random Effects Model for Home Run Hitters." *The American Statistician* 46:246–53.

Anderson, Dorothy A., and Murray Aitkin. 1985. "Variance Component Models with Binary Response: Interviewer Variability." *Journal of the Royal Statistical Society*, ser. B, 47:203–10.

Berlin, Jesse A., Stephen E. Kimmel, Thomas R. Ten Have, and Mary D. Sammel. 1999. "An Empirical Comparison of Several Clustered Data Approaches Under Confounding Due to Cluster Effects in the Analysis of Complications of Coronary Angioplasty." *Biometrics* 55:470–76.

Bock, Darrell R., and Murray Aitkin. 1981. "Marginal Maximum Likelihood Estimation of Item Parameters: Application of an EM Algorithm." *Psychometrika* 46:443–59.

Booth, James G., and James P. Hobert. 1998. "Standard Errors of Prediction in Generalized Linear Mixed Models." *Journal of the American Statistical Association* 93:262–72.

———. 1999. "Maximizing Generalized Linear Mixed Model Likelihoods with an Automated Monte Carlo EM Algorithm." *Journal of the Royal Statistical Society*, ser. B, 61:265–85.

Breslow, Norman E., and David G. Clayton. 1993. "Approximate Inference in Generalized Linear Mixed Models." *Journal of the American Statistical Association* 88:9–25.

Breslow, Norman E., and Xihong Lin. 1995. "Bias Correction in Generalized Linear Mixed Models with a Single Component of Dispersion." *Biometrika* 82:81–91.

Brier, Stephen S. 1980. "Analysis of Contingency Tables Under Cluster Sampling." *Biometrika* 67:591–96.

Bryk, Anthony S., and Stephen W. Raudenbush. 1992. *Hierarchical Linear Models*. Thousand Oaks, CA: Sage.

Carlin, Bradley P., and Thomas A. Louis. 1996. *Bayes and Empirical Bayes Methods for Data Analysis*. London: Chapman and Hall.

Catalano, Paul J., and Louise M. Ryan. 1992. "Bivariate Latent Variable Models for Clustered Discrete and Continuous Outcomes." *Journal of the American Statistical Association* 87:651–58.

Chan, Jennifer S. K., and Anthony Y. C. Kuk. 1997. "Maximum Likelihood Estimation for Probit-linear Mixed Models with Correlated Random Effects." *Biometrics* 53:86–97.

Coleman, James S. 1964. *Introduction to Mathematical Sociology*. London: Free Press of Glencoe.

Conaway, Mark R. 1989. "Analysis of Repeated Categorical Measurements with Conditional Likelihood Methods." *Journal of the American Statistical Association* 84:53–62.

Congdon, Peter. 1996. "General Linear Gravity Models for the Impact of Casualty Unit Closures." *Urban Studies* 33:1707–28.

Coull, Brent A., and Alan Agresti. 1999. "The Use of Mixed Logit Models to Reflect Heterogeneity in Capture-recapture Studies." *Biometrics* 55:294–301.

———. 2000. "Random Effects Modeling of Multiple Binomial Responses Using the Multivariate Binomial Logit-normal Distribution." *Biometrics* 56:73–80.

Crouch, Edmund A. C., and Donna Spiegelman. 1990. "The Evaluation of Integrals of the Form $\int_{-\infty}^{+\infty} f(t)\exp(-t^2)dt$: Application to Logistic-normal Models." *Journal of the American Statistical Association* 85:464–69.

Crowder, Martin J. 1978. "Beta-binomial ANOVA for Proportions." *Applied Statistics* 27:34–37.

Daniels, Michael J., and Constantine Gatsonis. 1997. "Hierarchical Polytomous Regression Models with Applications to Health Services Research." *Statistics in Medicine* 16:2311–26.

———. 1999. "Hierarchical Generalized Linear Models in the Analysis of Variations in Health Care Utilization." *Journal of the American Statistical Association* 94:29–42.

Darroch, John N. 1981. "The Mantel-Haenszel Test and Tests of Marginal Symmetry; Fixed-effects and Mixed Models for a Categorical Response." *International Statistical Review* 49:285–307.

Darroch, John N., Stephen E. Fienberg, Gary F. V. Glonek, and Brian W. Junker. 1993. "A Three-sample Multiple-recapture Approach to Census Population Estimation with Heterogeneous Catchability." *Journal of the American Statistical Association* 88:1137–48.

Davies, A. G., Richard M. Cormack, and A. M. Richardson. 1999. "Estimation of Injecting Drug Users in the City of Edinburgh, Scotland, and Number Infected with Human Immunodeficiency Virus." *International Journal of Epidemiology* 28:117–21.

Dempster, Arthur P., Nan M. Laird, and Donald B. Rubin. 1977. "Maximum Likelihood from Incomplete Data Via the EM Algorithm" (with discussion). *Journal of the Royal Statistical Society*, ser. B, 39:1–38.

DerSimonian, Rebecca, and Nan Laird. 1986. "Meta-analysis in Clinical Trials." *Controlled Clinical Trials* 7:177–88.

Diggle, Peter J., Kung-Yee Liang, and Scott L. Zeger. 1994. *Analysis of Longitudinal Data*. Oxford, England: Clarendon Press.

Efron, Bradley, and Carl N. Morris. 1975. "Data Analysis Using Stein's Estimator and its Generalizations." *Journal of the American Statistical Association* 70:311–19.

Enberg, John, Peter Gottschalk, and Douglas Wolf. 1990. "A Random-effects Logit Model of Work-welfare Transitions." *Journal of Econometrics* 43:63–75.

Ezzet, Farkad, and John Whitehead. 1991. "A Random Effects Model for Ordinal Responses from a Crossover Trial" (with discussion). *Statistics in Medicine* 10:901–906.

Fienberg, Stephen E., Matthew S. Johnson, and Brian W. Junker. 1999. "Classical Multi-level and Bayesian Approaches to Population Size Estimation Using Multiple Lists." *Journal of the Royal Statistical Society*, ser. A, 162:383–406.

Follmann, Dean A., and Diane Lambert. 1989. "Generalizing Logistic Regression by Nonparametric Mixing." *Journal of the American Statistical Association* 84:295–300.

Ghosh, Malay, and J. N. K. Rao. 1994. "Small Area Estimation: An Appraisal." *Statistical Science* 9:55–76.

Gibbons, Robert D., and Donald Hedeker. 1994. "Application of Random-effects Probit Regression Models." *Journal of Consulting and Clinical Psychology* 62:285–96.

Gibbons, Robert D., Donald Hedeker, Sara C. Charles, and Paul Frisch. 1994. "A Random-effects Probit Model for Predicting Medical Malpractice Claims." *Journal of the American Statistical Association* 89:760–67.

Goldstein, Harvey. 1991. "Nonlinear Multilevel Models, with an Application to Discrete Response Data." *Biometrika* 78:45–51.

———. 1995. *Multilevel Statistical Models*, 2nd ed. London: Arnold.

Goldstein, Harvey, and Jon Rasbash. 1996. "Improved Approximations for Multilevel Models with Binary Responses." *Journal of the Royal Statistical Society*, ser. A, General 159:505–13.

Goodman, Leo A. 1974. "Exploratory Latent Structure Analysis Using Both Identifiable and Unidentifiable Models." *Biometrika* 61:215–31.

Gueorguieva, Ralitza V., and Alan Agresti. 2000. "A Correlated Probit Model for Multivariate Repeated Measures of Mixtures of Binary and Continuous Responses." Technical report, University of Florida.

Hatzinger, Reinhold. 1989. "The Rasch Model, Some Extensions and Their Relation to the Class of Generalized Linear Models." Pp. 172–79 in *Statistical Modelling*, edited by A. Decarli, B. J. Francis, R. Gilchrist, and G. V. H. Seeber. New York: Springer-Verlag.

Heagerty, Patrick. 1999. "Marginally Specified Logistic-normal Models for Longitudinal Binary Data." *Biometrics* 55:688–98.

Heckman, James, and Burton Singer. 1984. "A Method for Minimizing the Impact of Distributional Assumptions in Econometric Models for Duration Data." *Econometrica* 52:271–320.

Hedeker, Donald, and Robert D. Gibbons. 1994. "A Random-effects Ordinal Regression Model for Multilevel Analysis." *Biometrics* 50:933–44.

Hedeker, Donald, Robert D. Gibbons, and B. R. Flay. 1994. "Random-effects Regression Models for Clustered Data with an Example from Smoking Prevention Research." *Journal of Consulting and Clinical Psychology* 62:757–65.

Henderson, Charles R., Oscar Kempthorne, Shayle R. Searle, and C. N. VonKrosig. 1959. "Estimation of Environmental and Genetic Trends from Records Subject to Culling." *Biometrics* 15:192–218.

Henretta, John, Martha S. Hill, Wei Li, Beth J. Soldo, and Douglas A. Wolf. 1997. "Selection of Children to Provide Care: The Effect of Earlier Parental Transfers." *Journals of Gerontology*, ser. B, 52:110–19.

Hobert, James P., and George Casella. 1996. "The Effect of Improper Priors on Gibbs Sampling in Hierarchical Linear Mixed Models." *Journal of the American Statistical Association* 91:1461–73.

Jones, K., M. I. Gould, and R. Watt. 1998. "Multiple Contexts as Cross-classified Models: The Labor Vote in the British General Election of 1992." *Geographical Analysis* 30:65–93.

Kass, Robert E., and Larry Wasserman. 1996. "The Selection of Prior Distributions by Formal Rules." *Journal of the American Statistical Association* 91: 1343–70.

Kelderman, Henk. 1984. "Loglinear Rasch Model Tests." *Psychometrika* 49:223–45.

Land, Kenneth C., Patricia L. McCall, and Daniel S. Nagin. 1996. "A Comparison of Poisson, Negative Binomial, and Semiparametric Mixed Poisson Regression Models—with Empirical Applications to Criminal Careers Data." *Sociological Methods and Research* 24:387–442.

Langford, Ian H. 1994. "Using a Generalized Linear Mixed Model to Analyze Dichotomous Choice Contingent Valuation Data." *Land Economics* 70:507–14.

———. 1998. "Improved Estimation of Willingness to Pay in Dichotomous Choice Contingent Valuation Studies." *Land Economics* 74:65–75.

Lawless, Jerald F. 1987. "Negative Binomial and Mixed Poisson Regression." *The Canadian Journal of Statistics* 15:209–25.

Lee, Youngjo, and John A. Nelder. 1996. "Hierarchical Generalized Linear Models" (with discussion). *Journal of the Royal Statistical Society*, ser. B, 58:619–78.

Levine, Richard A., and George Casella. 1998. "Implementations of the Monte Carlo EM Algorithm," Technical report, University of California, Davis.

Liang, Kung-Yee, and Scott L. Zeger. 1986. "Longitudinal Data Analysis Using Generalized Linear Models." *Biometrika* 73:13–22.

Liang, Kung-Yee, Scott L. Zeger, and Bahjat Qaqish. 1992. "Multivariate Regression Analysis for Categorical Data" (with discussion). *Journal of the Royal Statistical Society*, ser. B, 54:3–40.

Liao, Jiangang G. 1999. "Maximum Likelihood Estimation in Generalized Linear Mixed Models," Technical report, University of South Florida.

Lin, Xihong. 1997. "Variance Component Testing in Generalised Linear Models with Random Effects." *Biometrika* 84:309–25.

Lin, Xihong and Norman E. Breslow. 1996. "Bias Correction in Generalised Linear Mixed Models with Multiple Components of Dispersion." *Journal of the American Statistical Association* 91:1007–16.

Lindsay, Bruce, Clifford Clogg, and John Grego. 1991. "Semiparametric Estimation in the Rasch Model and Related Exponential Response Models, Including a Simple Latent Class Model for Item Analysis." *Journal of the American Statistical Association* 86:96–107.

Lindsey, James K. 1999. *Models for Repeated Measurements*, 2nd ed. Oxford, England: Oxford University Press.

Littell, Ramon C., George A. Milliken, Walter W. Stroup, and Russell D. Wolfinger. 1996. *SAS System for Mixed Models*, SAS Institute Inc., Cary, NC.

Longford, Nicholas T. 1993. *Random Coefficient Models*. Oxford, England: Oxford University Press.

———. 1994. "Logistic Regression with Random Coefficients." *Computational Statistics and Data Analysis* 17:1–15.

McArdle, John J., and Fumiaki Hamagami. 1994. "Logit and Multilevel Logit Modeling of College Graduation for 1984–1985 Freshman Student-athletes." *Journal of the American Statistical Association* 89:1107–23.

McCullagh, Peter, and John A. Nelder. 1989. *Generalized Linear Models*, 2nd ed. London: Chapman and Hall.

McCulloch, Charles E. 1994. "Maximum Likelihood Variance Components Estimation for Binary Data." *Journal of the American Statistical Association* 89:330–35.

———. 1997. "Maximum Likelihood Algorithms for Generalized Linear Mixed Models." *Journal of the American Statistical Association* 92:162–70.

McGilchrist, C. A. 1994. "Estimation in Generalized Mixed Models." *Journal of the Royal Statistical Society*, ser. B, 56:61–69.

Miller, John J. 1977. "Asymptotic Properties of Maximum Likelihood Estimates in the Mixed Model of the Analysis of Variance." *The Annals of Statistics* 5:746–62.

Montgomery, Mark R., Toni Richards, and Henry I. Braun. 1986. "Child Health, Breast-feeding and Survival in Malaysia: A Random-effects Logit Approach." *Journal of the American Statistical Association* 81:297–309.

Murphy, Mike, and Duolao Wang. 1998. "Family and Sociodemographic Influences on Patterns of Leaving Home in Postwar Britain." *Demography* 35:293–305.

Murray, David M., Joel M. Moskowitz, and Clyde W. Dent. 1996. "Design and Analysis Issues in Community-based Drug Abuse Prevention." *American Behavioral Scientist* 39:853–67.

Muthen, Bengt. 1997. "Longitudinal and Multilevel Modeling: Latent Variable Modeling of Longitudinal and Multilevel Data." *Sociological Methodology* 27:453–80.

Natarajan, Ranjini, and Charles E. McCulloch. 1995. "A Note on the Existence of the Posterior Distribution for a Class of Mixed Models for Binomial Responses." *Biometrika* 82:638–43.

———. 1998. "Gibbs Sampling with Diffuse Priors: A Valid Approach to Data-driven Inference?" *Journal of Computational and Graphical Statistics* 7:267–77.

Nee, V. 1996. "The Emergence of a Market Society: Changing Mechanisms of Stratification in China." *American Journal of Sociology* 101:908–49.

Neuhaus, John M., and John D. Kalbfleisch. 1998. "Between- and Within-cluster Covariate Effects in the Analysis of Clustered Data." *Biometrics* 54:638–45.

Neuhaus, John M., Walter W. Hauck, and John D. Kalbfleisch. 1992. "The Effects of Mixture Distribution Misspecification when Fitting Mixed-effects Logistic Models." *Biometrika* 79:755–62.

Neuhaus, John M., John D. Kalbfleisch, and Walter W. Hauck. 1991. "A Comparison of Cluster-specific and Population-averaged Approaches for Analyzing Correlated Binary Data." *International Statistical Review* 59:25–35.

———. 1994. "Conditions for Consistent Estimation in Mixed-effects Models for Binary Matched-pairs Data." *Canadian Journal of Statistics* 22:139–48.

Plewis, Ian. 1997. *Statistics in Education*. London: Arnold.

Rao, J. N. K., and D. Roland Thomas. 1988. "The Analysis of Cross-classified Categorical Data from Complex Sample Surveys." *Sociological Methodology* 18: 213–69.

Rasch, Georg. 1961. "On General Laws and the Meaning of Measurement in Psychology." *Proceedings of the 4th Berkeley Symposium on Mathematical Statistics and Probability* 4:321–33.

Raudenbush, Stephen W., Brian Rowan, and Sang Jin Kang. 1991. "A Multilevel, Multivariate Model for Studying School Climate with Estimation via the EM Algorithm and Application to U.S. High-School Data." *Journal of Educational Statistics* 16:295–330.

Raudenbush, Stephen W., and Robert J. Sampson. 1999. "Econometrics: Toward a Science of Assessing Ecological Settings, with Application to the Systematic Social Observation of Neighborhoods." Pp. 1–41 in *Sociological Methodology 1999*, edited by Michael E. Sobel. Cambridge, MA: Blackwell Publishers.

Sampson, Robert J., Stephen W. Raudenbush, and Felton Earls. 1997. "Neighborhoods and Violent Crime: A Multilevel Study of Collective Efficacy." *Science* 277:918–24.

Saunderson, T. R., and Ian H. Langford. 1996. "A Study of the Geographical Distribution of Suicide Rates in England and Wales 1989–92 Using Empirical Bayes Estimates." *Social Science and Medicine* 43:489–502.

Schall, Robert. 1991. "Estimation in Generalized Linear Models with Random Effects." *Biometrika* 78:719–27.

Searle, Shayle R., George Casella, and Charles E. McCulloch. 1992. *Variance Components*. New York: Wiley.

Self, Steven G., and Kung-Yee Liang. 1987. "Asymptotic Properties of Maximum Likelihood Estimators and Likelihood Ratio Tests Under Nonstandard Conditions." *Journal of the American Statistical Association* 82:605–10.

Stiratelli, Robert, Nan Laird, and James H. Ware. 1984. "Random-effects Models for Serial Observations with Binary Response." *Biometrics* 40:961–71.

Tjur, Tue. 1982. "A Connection Between Rasch's Item Analysis Model and a Multiplicative Poisson Model." *Scandinavian Journal of Statistics* 9:23–30.

Tsutakawa, Robert K. 1988. "Mixed Model for Analyzing Geographic Variability in Mortality Rates." *Journal of the American Statistical Association* 83:37–42.

Tutz, Gerhard, and Wolfgang Hennevogl. 1996. "Random Effects in Ordinal Regression Models." *Computational Statistics and Data Analysis* 22:537–57.

Wei, Greg C. G., and Martin A. Tanner. 1990. "A Monte Carlo Implementation of the EM Algorithm and the Poor Man's Data Augmentation Algorithms." *Journal of the American Statistical Association* 85:699–704.

Williams, D. A. 1982. "Extra-binomial Variation in Logistic Linear Models." *Applied Statistics* 31:144–48.

Wolfinger, Russell, and Michael O'Connell. 1993. "Generalized Linear Mixed Models: A Pseudo-likelihood Approach." *Journal of Statistical Computation and Simulation* 48:233–43.

Wong, George Y., and William M. Mason. 1985. "The Hierarchical Logistic Regression Model for Multilevel Analysis." *Journal of the American Statistical Association* 80:513–24.

Zeger, Scott L., Kung-Yee Liang, and Paul S. Albert. 1988. "Models for Longitudinal Data: A Generalized Estimating Equation Approach." *Biometrics* 44:1049–60.

Zhou, Xiao-Hua, Anthony J. Perkins, and Siu L. Hui. 1999. "Comparisons of Software Packages for Generalized Linear Multilevel Models." *American Statistician* 53: 282–90.

3

LOG-MULTIPLICATIVE ASSOCIATION MODELS AS LATENT VARIABLE MODELS FOR NOMINAL AND/OR ORDINAL DATA

*Carolyn J. Anderson**
Jeroen K. Vermunt†

Associations between multiple discrete measures are often due to collapsing over other variables. When the variables collapsed over are unobserved and continuous, log-multiplicative association models, including log-linear models with linear-by-linear interactions for ordinal categorical data and extensions of Goodman's (1979, 1985) RC(M) association model for multiple nominal and/or ordinal categorical variables, can be used to study the relationship between the observed discrete variables and the unobserved continuous ones, and to study the unobserved variables. The derivation and use of log-multiplicative association models as latent variable models for discrete variables are presented in this paper. The models are based on graphical models for discrete and continuous variables where the variables follow a conditional Gaussian distribution. The models have many desirable properties, including having schematic or graphical rep-

This research was supported by grants from the National Science Foundation (#SBR96-17510) and the Bureau of Educational Research at the University of Illinois. We thank Ulf Böckenholt, Rung-Ching Tsai, and Jee-Seon Kim for useful comments and suggestions. Correspondence can be addressed to Carolyn J. Anderson, Educational Psychology, University of Illinois, 1310 South Sixth Street, Champaign, IL 61820 or Jeroen K. Vermunt, Department of Methodology, PO Box 90153, 5000 LE Tilburg, Tilburg University, The Netherlands. E-mail addresses are cja@uiuc.edu and J.K.Vermunt@kub.nl.

*University of Illinois

†Tilburg University, The Netherlands

resentations of the system of observed and unobserved variables, the log-multiplicative models can be read from the graphs, and estimates of the means, variances, and covariances of the latent variables given values on the observed variables are a function of the log-multiplicative model parameters. To illustrate some of the advantageous aspects of these models, two examples are presented. In one example, responses to items from the General Social Survey (Davis and Smith 1996) are modeled, and in the other example, panel data from two groups (Coleman 1964) are analyzed.

1. INTRODUCTION

Associations in multivariate categorical data are often due to collapsing over other variables. For example, consider the following four items from the 1994 General Social Survey (Davis and Smith 1996):

A_1 "Do you approve or disapprove of a married woman earning money in business or industry if she has a husband capable of supporting her?" (approve, disapprove).

A_2 "It is much better for everyone involved if the man is the achiever outside the home and the woman takes care of the home and family." (strongly agree, agree, disagree, strongly disagree).

A_3 "A man's job is to earn money; a woman's job is to look after the home and family." (strongly agree, agree, neither agree nor disagree, disagree, strongly disagree).

A_4 "It is not good if the man stays at home and cares for the children and the woman goes out to work." (strongly agree, agree, neither agree nor disagree, disagree, strongly disagree).

We would expect associations to be present between the responses to these items because all of the items appear to be indicators of a single continuous variable—namely, attitude regarding the proper roles of wives and husbands in terms of employment inside/outside the home.

As a second example, consider the Coleman (1964) panel data that consist of responses made at two time points by boys and girls to two items: their attitude toward (positive, negative) and their self-perception of membership in (yes, no) the leading or popular crowd. These two questions may be indicators of the same (continuous) variable or they may be indicators of different but correlated variables. It is also possible that there may be change over time and/or differences between boys and girls. The underlying latent variable structure has implications for what associations should be present in the observed data and the nature of these associations.

Log-linear models are very effective tools for determining what associations are present in categorical data; however, they are less useful for describing the nature of multiple observed associations. When the associations arise because we have collapsed over unobserved or not directly measurable continuous variables, the description and interpretation of the associations would be greatly facilitated if our models represented the observed associations in terms of the unobserved or latent variables. The models should also allow a researcher to study the underlying structural relationships between the unobserved variables. Ideally, researchers should be able to transform their specific theories and hypotheses about the relationships between the observed and unobserved variables into statistical models, which in turn can be readily fit to observed data. We propose a latent variable model that meets these requirements.

The latent variable models proposed here are based on graphical models for discrete and continuous variables (Lauritzen and Wermuth 1989; Wermuth and Lauritzen 1990; see also Edwards 1995; Lauritzen 1996; Whittaker 1990), and they belong to a family of "location models" for discrete and continuous variables (Olkin and Tate 1960; Afifi and Elashoff 1969; Krzanowski 1980, 1983, 1988). The models presented here differ from previously discussed cases in that the continuous variables are unobserved and we restrict our attention to cases where the discrete (observed) variables are conditionally independent given the continuous (latent) ones. The models implied for the observed data are log-multiplicative association models.

In log-multiplicative association models, which are extensions of log-linear models, dependencies between discrete variables are represented by multiplicative terms. Special cases of these models include many well-known models for categorical data such as linear-by-linear interaction models, ordinal-by-nominal association models, the uniform association model for ordinal categorical variables, the $RC(M)$ association model for two variables, and many generalizations of the $RC(M)$ association model for three or more variables (e.g., Agresti 1984; Becker 1989; Clogg 1982; Clogg and Shihadeh 1994; Goodman 1979, 1985).

A simple case of the models was discussed by Lauritzen and Wermuth (1989; Wermuth and Lauritzen 1990), who provided a latent continuous variable interpretation of Goodman's (1979) RC association model for two items. Whittaker (1989) discusses the case of multiple, uncorrelated latent variables for two and three observed variables. In this paper, we consider more general graphical models for multiple *correlated* latent variables for any number of observed variables. Additionally, we allow the covariance matrix of the latent variables to differ over values of the observed, discrete variables.

The models have many desirable properties, including having schematic or graphical representations. The graphs are useful pictorial representations of theories about phenomena, and the corresponding log-multiplicative models can be read from the graph. In many cases, estimates of the means, variances, and covariances of the latent variables are by-products of the estimation of the parameters of the log-multiplicative model.

The remainder of this paper is structured as follows. In Section 2, we present the basic ideas and approach for cases where each observed (discrete) variable is related to only one latent (continuous) variable. In Section 3, we extend the basic model to cases where the observed variables may be related to multiple latent variables. The models discussed in Sections 2 and 3 are illustrated in Section 4, using data from the 1994 General Social Survey (Davis and Smith 1996) and Coleman's (1964) panel data for the boys. In Section 5, we further generalize the latent variable model by allowing the covariance matrix of the latent variables to differ over levels of the observed discrete variables. In Section 6, we illustrate these heterogeneous covariance models by analyzing Coleman's (1964) data for the girls, and doing a combined analysis of the boys and girls data. In Section 7, we conclude with a discussion of additional possible generalizations and areas for further study. Two appendixes are included. The first describes how log-multiplicative models can be read from graphs representing the latent variable model, and the second describes the maximum-likelihood estimation of the models by the unidimensional Newton method.

2. SINGLE LATENT VARIABLE PER INDICATOR

In this section, we present models where each observed discrete variable is an indicator of only one latent variable. In Section 2.1, we derive the log-multiplicative model for the graphical model where there is one continuous latent variable, and in Section 2.2, we extend the model to cases where there are two or more correlated latent variables. In Section 2.3, we discuss identification constraints for the parameters of single indicator models and their implications.

2.1. *The One Latent Variable Model*

The example of the four items from the General Social Survey is a case where we hypothesize that each item is an indicator of a single, common latent variable; that is, we expect that a single indicator, one latent variable model should fit the data. Such a model is presented in Figure 1, where the discrete variables are represented by the squares and the continuous variable by a circle. The absence of a line connecting two variables indicates that the variables are conditionally independent given all the other variables, while the presence of a line connecting two variables, indicates that the variables are dependent.

In the latent variable models proposed in this paper, the joint distribution of the discrete and continuous variables is assumed to be conditional Gaussian (Lauritzen and Wermuth 1989; see also Edwards 1995; Lauritzen 1996; Whittaker 1990). In a conditional Gaussian distribution, the marginal distribution of the discrete variables is multinomial and the conditional distribution of the continuous variables given the discrete ones is multivariate normal where the mean and covariance matrix may differ over levels of the discrete variables. For now, we assume that the covariance matrix does not differ over levels of the discrete variables; however, this restriction is relaxed in Section 5. In other words, differences between cells of a cross-classification of observations is dealt with by allowing the means of the continuous latent variables to differ between cells. Individual differences within cells are captured by the within-cell variances of continuous variables.

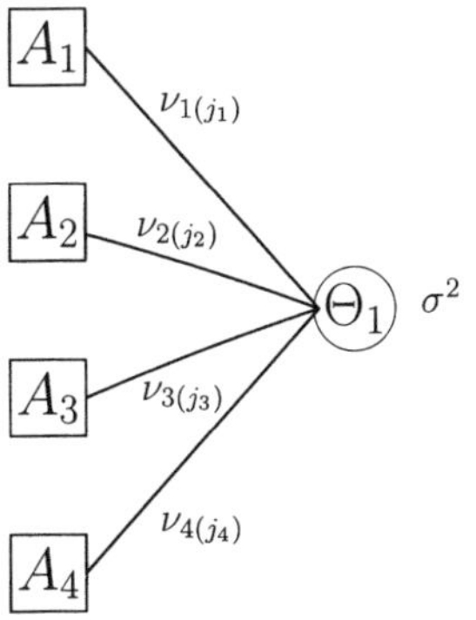

FIGURE 1. Single indicator, one latent variable model for four observed variables.

Let $\mathcal{A} = \{A_1, \ldots, A_I\}$ be a set of I discrete variables, and Θ represent the continuous variable. We denote a realization of the continuous variable by θ and an observation on the discrete variables by $\mathbf{a} = (a_{1(j_1)}, \ldots, a_{I(j_I)})$ (i.e., $\mathbf{a}$ is a cell in the cross-classification of the I discrete variables). The levels of discrete variable A_i are indexed by j_i where $j_i = 1, \ldots, J_i$. The probability that an observation falls into cell $\mathbf{a}$ is denoted by $P(\mathbf{a})$. To obtain the joint distribution of the discrete and continuous variables, we take the product of the marginal distribution of the discrete variables, which is multinomial, and the conditional distribution of the continuous variables, which is a conditional normal distribution; that is,

$$\begin{aligned} f(\mathbf{a}, \theta) &= P(\mathbf{a}) f(\theta | \mathbf{a}) \\ &= P(\mathbf{a}) \frac{1}{\sqrt{2\pi\sigma^2}} \exp\left[-\frac{1}{2} \frac{(\theta - \mu(\mathbf{a}))^2}{\sigma^2}\right] \end{aligned} \tag{1}$$

where $f(\theta|\mathbf{a})$ is a normal distribution with mean $\mu(\mathbf{a})$, which depends on $\mathbf{a}$, and variance σ^2. Equation (1) is the moment form of a (homogeneous) conditional Gaussian distribution.

Since the continuous variable θ is unobserved, we do not have readily available estimates of $\boldsymbol{\mu}(\mathbf{a})$ and σ^2. While the observed cell proportions provide estimates of $P(\mathbf{a})$, we want a model for $P(\mathbf{a})$ that is implied by our specific hypotheses regarding the relationships between the discrete variables and the continuous variable. The model for $P(\mathbf{a})$ will contain interactions between the discrete variables that result from having collapsed over the continuous variable.

Rather than working with the moment form of the conditional Gaussian distribution, it is more useful to work with the canonical form of the distribution. The canonical form of the distribution can be obtained by re-writing equation (1) as

$$\begin{aligned} f(\mathbf{a}, \theta) = \exp\bigg[&\log(P(\mathbf{a})) - \log(\sqrt{2\pi\sigma^2}) - \frac{1}{2}\left(\frac{\mu(\mathbf{a})^2}{\sigma^2}\right) \\ &+ \frac{\mu(\mathbf{a})}{\sigma^2}\theta - \frac{1}{2}\left(\frac{\theta^2}{\sigma^2}\right)\bigg]. \end{aligned} \tag{2}$$

We define

$$h(\mathbf{a}) = \frac{\mu(\mathbf{a})}{\sigma^2}, \tag{3}$$

and

$$g(\mathbf{a}) = \log(P(\mathbf{a})) - \log(\sqrt{2\pi\sigma^2}) - \tfrac{1}{2}\sigma^2 h(\mathbf{a})^2 \ , \tag{4}$$

which are both functions of **a**. Substituting definitions (3) and (4) in equation (2) we obtain

$$f(\mathbf{a}, \theta) = \exp\left[g(\mathbf{a}) + h(\mathbf{a})\theta - \frac{1}{2}\left(\frac{\theta^2}{\sigma^2}\right)\right], \tag{5}$$

which is the canonical form of the conditional Gaussian distribution. In the canonical form, the joint distribution factors into three components: a discrete part $g(\mathbf{a})$, which represents the discrete variables and the dependencies among them after controlling for the continuous variables; a linear part $h(\mathbf{a})\theta$, which represents the dependencies between the discrete variables and the continuous variable; and a quadratic part $-(1/2)\theta^2/\sigma^2$, which represents the continuous variable after controlling for the discrete ones.

The model for the observed data is obtained by rewriting equation (4) in terms of $P(\mathbf{a})$,

$$P(\mathbf{a}) = \sqrt{2\pi\sigma^2} \exp\left[g(\mathbf{a}) + \frac{1}{2}\sigma^2 h(\mathbf{a})^2 \right]. \tag{6}$$

Equation (6) does not include θ, which is unobserved but depends only on observed data. The hypothesis that the discrete variables are conditionally independent given the continuous variable is incorporated into the model through the parameterization we specify for $g(\mathbf{a})$, and the hypothesis that each of the discrete variables is directly related to the latent variable θ is incorporated through the parameterization we specify for $h(\mathbf{a})$.

The function $g(\mathbf{a})$ is set equal to the sum of effect terms as in log-linear models.[1] Since the discrete variables are conditionally independent given the continuous variable, $g(\mathbf{a})$ equals the sum of marginal effect terms for each of the discrete variables; that is,

$$g(\mathbf{a}) = \sum_{i=1}^{I} \lambda_{i(j_i)}, \tag{7}$$

where $\lambda_{i(j_i)}$ is the marginal or main effect term for level j_i of variable A_i. This parameterization of $g(\mathbf{a})$ is used throughout this paper, because in all

[1] If there were no continuous variables, we would have a log-linear model.

of the models considered here, the discrete variables are independent of each other given the continuous variable(s).

From equation (5), we see that $h(\mathbf{a})$ is a coefficient for the strength of the association between the discrete variables and continuous variable. Since each discrete variable is directly related to the continuous variable, we define $h(\mathbf{a})$ as

$$h(\mathbf{a}) = \sum_{i=1}^{I} \nu_{i(j_i)} \tag{8}$$

where $\nu_{i(j_i)}$ is the category score or scale value for level j_i of variable A_i. The category scale values may be estimated from the data or specified *a priori*.

Replacing $g(\mathbf{a})$ and $h(\mathbf{a})$ in equation (6) by the parameterizations given in (7) and (8) yields a log-multiplicative model for the observed data; that is,

$$\begin{aligned}\log(P(\mathbf{a})) &= \lambda + \sum_i \lambda_{i(j_i)} + \frac{1}{2}\sigma^2\left(\sum_{i=1}^{I} \nu_{i(j_i)}\right)^2 \\ &= \lambda + \sum_i \lambda^*_{i(j_i)} + \sigma^2 \sum_i \sum_{k>i} \nu_{i(j_i)}\nu_{k(j_k)} \end{aligned} \tag{9}$$

where λ is a normalizing constant and $\lambda^*_{i(j_i)} = \lambda_{i(j_i)} + (1/2)\sigma^2\nu^2_{i(j_i)}$. Since the term $(1/2)\sigma^2\nu^2_{i(j_i)}$ is only indexed by j_i, it gets "absorbed" into the marginal effect term.

If there are only two discrete variables (i.e., $I = 2$), then equation (9) reduces to the $RC(1)$ association model (Goodman 1979, 1985; see also Clogg and Shihadeh 1994). For our General Social Survey example where $I = 4$ (i.e., Figure 1), we have

$$\begin{aligned} P(\mathbf{a}) = {} & \lambda + \lambda^*_{1(j_1)} + \lambda^*_{2(j_2)} + \lambda^*_{3(j_3)} + \lambda^*_{4(j_4)} \\ & + \sigma^2\nu_{1(j_1)}\nu_{2(j_2)} + \sigma^2\nu_{1(j_1)}\nu_{3(j_3)} + \sigma^2\nu_{1(j_1)}\nu_{4(j_4)} \\ & + \sigma^2\nu_{2(j_2)}\nu_{3(j_3)} + \sigma^2\nu_{2(j_2)}\nu_{4(j_4)} + \sigma^2\nu_{3(j_3)}\nu_{4(j_4)}. \end{aligned} \tag{10}$$

In equation (10) and the more general equation (9), we have multiplicative terms with the same association parameter in each term (i.e., σ^2) and a single set of category scores for each of the variables, which appear in the different multiplicative terms.

Equations (9) and (10) are log-multiplicative association models with bivariate interactions between all pairs of the discrete variables. The best fit that can be attained using equation (9) or (10) is given by the all two-way interaction log-linear model (see Becker 1989). If an all two-way interaction log-linear model fits a data set, then we are justified in considering models such as equation (9) or (10).

2.2. *Multiple Latent Variables*

The one latent variable model is a relatively simple model. In many data sets, the observed variables may be indicators of different latent variables; therefore we generalize the model to the case of multiple latent variables. The derivation given in Section 2.1 is extended to obtain a more general model for the observed data. The one latent variable model is a special case of this more general model. In this section, we will examine two additional special cases, including the most complex single indicator model.

Let $\boldsymbol{\Theta} = \{\Theta_1, \ldots, \Theta_M\}$ be a set of M continuous variables where $M \leq I$ and the $(M \times 1)$ vector $\boldsymbol{\theta} = (\theta_1, \ldots, \theta_M)'$ be a realization of the M latent variables. The moment form of the joint distribution of the I discrete and M latent variables is obtained by multiplying the marginal distribution of the discrete variables, which is multinomial, and the conditional distribution of the continuous variables, which is multivariate normal; that is,

$$
\begin{aligned}
f(\mathbf{a}, \boldsymbol{\theta}) &= P(\mathbf{a}) f(\boldsymbol{\theta}|\mathbf{a}) \\
&= P(\mathbf{a})(2\pi)^{-M/2} |\boldsymbol{\Sigma}|^{-1/2} \\
&\quad \times \exp[-\tfrac{1}{2}(\boldsymbol{\theta} - \boldsymbol{\mu}(\mathbf{a}))' \boldsymbol{\Sigma}^{-1} (\boldsymbol{\theta} - \boldsymbol{\mu}(\mathbf{a}))] \qquad (11)
\end{aligned}
$$

where $f(\boldsymbol{\theta}|\mathbf{a})$ is a multivariate normal distribution with the $(M \times 1)$ mean vector $\boldsymbol{\mu}(\mathbf{a})$, which is a function of $\mathbf{a}$, and the $(M \times M)$ covariance matrix $\boldsymbol{\Sigma}$. The canonical form is obtained from equation (11) by multiplying the terms in the exponent and redefining parameters:

$$
\begin{aligned}
f(\mathbf{a}, \boldsymbol{\theta}) &= P(\mathbf{a})(2\pi)^{-M/2} |\boldsymbol{\Sigma}|^{-1/2} \\
&\quad \times \exp[-\tfrac{1}{2}\boldsymbol{\mu}(\mathbf{a})' \boldsymbol{\Sigma}^{-1} \boldsymbol{\mu}(\mathbf{a}) + \boldsymbol{\mu}(\mathbf{a})' \boldsymbol{\Sigma}^{-1} \boldsymbol{\theta} - \tfrac{1}{2}\boldsymbol{\theta}' \boldsymbol{\Sigma}^{-1} \boldsymbol{\theta}] \\
&= \exp[g(\mathbf{a}) + \mathbf{h}(\mathbf{a})' \boldsymbol{\theta} - \tfrac{1}{2}\boldsymbol{\theta}' \boldsymbol{\Sigma}^{-1} \boldsymbol{\theta}] \qquad (12)
\end{aligned}
$$

where $\mathbf{h}(\mathbf{a})$ is the $(M \times 1)$ vector valued function

$$\mathbf{h}(\mathbf{a}) = \boldsymbol{\Sigma}^{-1}\boldsymbol{\mu}(\mathbf{a}), \tag{13}$$

and

$$g(\mathbf{a}) = \log(P(\mathbf{a})) - \frac{M}{2}\log(2\pi) - \frac{1}{2}\log(|\boldsymbol{\Sigma}|) - \frac{1}{2}\mathbf{h}(\mathbf{a})'\boldsymbol{\Sigma}\mathbf{h}(\mathbf{a}). \tag{14}$$

The model for the observed data is found by rewriting equation (14) in terms of $P(\mathbf{a})$,

$$P(\mathbf{a}) = (2\pi)^{M/2}|\boldsymbol{\Sigma}|^{1/2}\exp[g(\mathbf{a}) + \tfrac{1}{2}\mathbf{h}(\mathbf{a})'\boldsymbol{\Sigma}\mathbf{h}(\mathbf{a})]. \tag{15}$$

In the single indicator multiple latent variable model, to obtain a specific model for the observed data, we must parameterize $g(\mathbf{a})$, $\mathbf{h}(\mathbf{a})$, and $\boldsymbol{\Sigma}$.

An example of a multiple latent variable model that may fit the Coleman panel data is shown in Figure 2. In this model, two items are directly related to one latent variable, the other two items are directly related to a second latent variable, and the two latent variables are correlated. Since the discrete variables (the items) are conditionally independent given the two latent variables, $g(\mathbf{a})$ has the same definition as in the one latent variable model—i.e., equation (4).

The items (discrete variables) have been partitioned into two mutually exclusive sets $\mathcal{A}_1 = \{A_1, \ldots, A_r\}$ and $\mathcal{A}_2 = \{A_{r+1}, \ldots, A_I\}$. For the

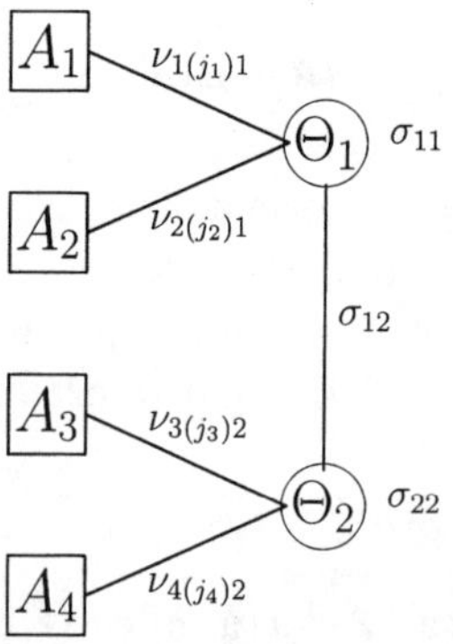

FIGURE 2. Single indicator, two correlated latent variable model for four observed variables.

Coleman data, $r = 2$ and $I = 4$. Since the variables in $\mathcal{A}_1$ are directly related to Θ_1, the first element of the (2×1) vector $\mathbf{h}(\mathbf{a})$ contains coefficients that relate the variables in $\mathcal{A}_1$ and Θ_1. Likewise, the second element of the $\mathbf{h}(\mathbf{a})$ contains coefficients that relate the variables in $\mathcal{A}_2$ and Θ_2. Thus we parameterize $\mathbf{h}(\mathbf{a})$ as

$$\mathbf{h}(\mathbf{a}) = \begin{pmatrix} \sum_{i=1}^{r} \nu_{i(j_i)1} \\ \sum_{i=r+1}^{I} \nu_{i(j_i)2} \end{pmatrix}, \tag{16}$$

where $\nu_{i(j_i)m}$ is the category score or scale value for level j_i of discrete variable A_i for latent variable Θ_m.

Any hypotheses that we have about the relationship between the latent variables are incorporated into the model by the parameterization we specify for $\boldsymbol{\Sigma}$. To complete our model, we define $\boldsymbol{\Sigma}$ as

$$\boldsymbol{\Sigma} = \begin{pmatrix} \sigma_{11} & \sigma_{12} \\ \sigma_{12} & \sigma_{22} \end{pmatrix}. \tag{17}$$

Replacing $g(\mathbf{a})$, $\mathbf{h}(\mathbf{a})$, and $\boldsymbol{\Sigma}$ in equation (15) by their definitions in equations (4), (16), and (17) gives us the model for the observed data,

$$\begin{aligned} \log(P(\mathbf{a})) = \lambda + \sum_{i=1}^{I} \lambda^*_{i(j_i)} + \sigma_{11}\left(\sum_{i=1}^{r-1} \sum_{k=i+1}^{r} \nu_{i(j_i)1}\nu_{k(j_k)1} \right) \\ + \sigma_{22}\left(\sum_{i=r+1}^{I-1} \sum_{k=i+1}^{I} \nu_{i(j_i)2}\nu_{k(j_k)2} \right) \\ + \sigma_{12}\left(\sum_{i=1}^{r} \sum_{k=r+1}^{I} \nu_{i(j_i)1}\nu_{k(j_k)2} \right), \end{aligned} \tag{18}$$

where

$$\lambda^*_{i(j_i)} = \begin{cases} \lambda_{i(j_i)} + (1/2)\sigma_{11}\nu^2_{i(j_i)1} & \text{if } A_i \in \mathcal{A}_1 \\ \lambda_{i(j_i)} + (1/2)\sigma_{22}\nu^2_{i(j_i)2} & \text{if } A_i \in \mathcal{A}_2. \end{cases}$$

For the Coleman data where $I = 4$ and $r = 2$ (i.e., Figure 2), the specific log-multiplicative model based on equation (18) is

$$\begin{aligned}P(\mathbf{a}) = \lambda &+ \lambda^*_{1(j_1)} + \lambda^*_{2(j_2)} + \lambda^*_{3(j_3)} + \lambda^*_{4(j_4)} \\ &+ \sigma_{11}\nu_{1(j_1)1}\nu_{2(j_2)1} + \sigma_{22}\nu_{3(j_3)2}\nu_{4(j_4)2} \\ &+ \sigma_{12}\nu_{1(j_1)1}\nu_{3(j_3)2} + \sigma_{12}\nu_{1(j_1)1}\nu_{4(j_4)2} \\ &+ \sigma_{12}\nu_{2(j_2)1}\nu_{3(j_3)2} + \sigma_{12}\nu_{2(j_2)1}\nu_{4(j_4)2}. \end{aligned} \tag{19}$$

From equation (19), we can see more clearly that the model contains multiplicative terms for all bivariate associations and there is a single set of scale values for each variable. Unlike the one latent variable model, equation (9), where there is a single association parameter for each of the multiplicative terms, in equations (18) and (19) there are three different association parameters for the multiplicative terms: σ_{11}, σ_{22}, and σ_{12}. When the discrete variables within a set are related because they are all indicators of the same latent variable, the association parameter is the variance. When discrete variables from the two different sets are related because the corresponding latent variables are related, the association parameter is the covariance between the latent variables.

In the most complex, single factor per indicator model, each discrete variable is an indicator of (i.e., directly related to) a different latent variable and all the latent variables are correlated. For $I = 4$, the graph of this model is given in Figure 3. With this structure, $M = I$ and

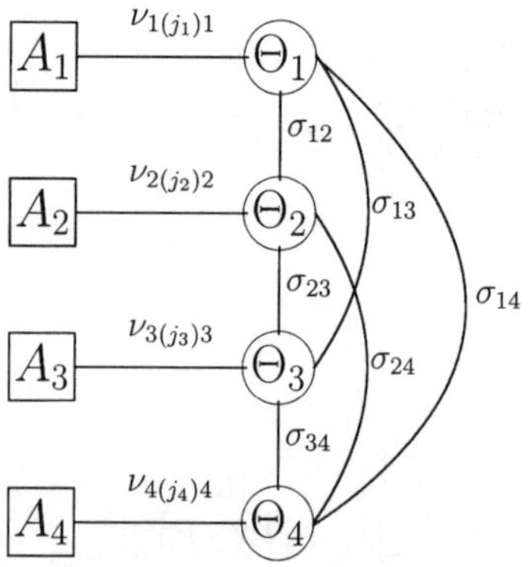

FIGURE 3. The most complex single indicator model for four variables.

$$\mathbf{h}(\mathbf{a}) = \begin{pmatrix} \nu_{1(j_1)1} \\ \vdots \\ \nu_{I(j_I)I} \end{pmatrix}.$$

The definition of $g(\mathbf{a})$ remains the same—i.e., equation (4)—and $\mathbf{\Sigma}$ is now an $(I \times I)$ matrix of variances and covariances between the latent variables. Using these definitions, the model for the observed data is

$$\log(P(\mathbf{a})) = \lambda + \sum_i \lambda^*_{i(j_i)} + \sum_i \sum_{k>i} \sigma_{ik} \nu_{i(j_i)i} \nu_{k(j_k)k} \qquad (20)$$

where $\lambda^*_{i(j_i)} = \lambda_{i(j_i)} + (1/2)\sigma_{ii}\nu^2_{i(j_i)i}$.

Equation (20) is a multivariate generalization of the $RC(1)$ association model, which for three variables is equivalent to models discussed by Clogg (1982; see also Agresti 1984). If category scores are known, then equation (20) is a log-linear model with linear-by-linear interaction terms for each pair of the observed variables (i.e., $\sigma_{ik} x_{i(j_i)i} x_{k(j_k)k}$ where the x's are known scores). If scores for some variables are known but not for others, then equation (20) includes some ordinal-by-nominal interaction terms (e.g., $\sigma_{ik} \nu_{i(j_i)i} x_{k(j_k)k}$).

If no partial association between a pair of discrete variables exists, then the corresponding covariance can be set to zero, which sets the interaction term for the pair of variables equal to zero. But if partial associations between all pairs of variables are present, then it is possible to obtain simpler models by imposing certain restrictions on the model parameters. The models that have fewer latent variables—for example, equations (9) and (18)—can be thought of as special cases of the most complex single indicator model, equation (20), where equality restrictions have been imposed on the association parameters (i.e., covariances) across the multiplicative terms.

All of the single indicator per latent variable models include bivariate interactions between pairs of discrete variables; therefore, a log-linear model that provides a baseline fit (best fit) for the latent variable, log-multiplicative models always exists. Log-linear models are useful in that they indicate whether particular latent variable models may be appropriate. The use of log-linear models in conjunction with the graphical/latent variable, log-multiplicative models is illustrated in the analyses presented in Sections 4 and 6.

When each discrete variable is an indicator of a different latent variable (i.e., equation 20), we can only estimate the covariances between the latent variables. We cannot estimate the variances because they are absorbed into the marginal effect terms (i.e., $\lambda^*_{i(j_i)} = \lambda_{i(j_i)} + (1/2)\sigma_{ii}\nu^2_{i(j_i)i}$). There is no way to tease apart the term $\lambda_{i(j_i)}$ from the terms involving the variances. However, in simpler models such as (9) and (18), we can estimate the variances and the covariances. Given estimates of variances and covariances and using the fact that $\boldsymbol{\mu}(\mathbf{a}) = \boldsymbol{\Sigma}\mathbf{h}(\mathbf{a})$ (see equation 13), we can estimate the conditional means of the latent variables, $\boldsymbol{\mu}(\mathbf{a})$.

2.3. *Identification Constraints*

Identification constraints are required to estimate the parameters of the log-multiplicative models. The choice of constraints sets the scale of the conditional means of the latent variables. Adding conditions beyond those needed for identification correspond to more restrictive latent variable models.

For all log-multiplicative models, location constraints are required for the marginal effect terms, $\lambda^*_{i(j_i)}$, and for the scale values, $\nu_{i(j_i)m}$. These may be setting one value equal to zero (e.g., $\nu_{i(1)m} = 0$), or setting the sum equal to zero (e.g., $\sum_{j_i} \nu_{i(j_i)m} = 0$). We use zero sum constraints in the examples presented in Sections 4 and 6.

One additional constraint is required for each latent variable. While the variance of each latent variable could be set to a constant (e.g., $\sigma_{mm} = 1$ for all m), for reasons that become clear below, it is advantageous to set the scale of the category scores for one discrete variable that is directly related to the latent variable. For example, if A_1 and Θ_m are directly related, then $\sum_{j_1} \nu^2_{1(j_1)m} = 1$. The rule adopted here (assuming $I > 2$) is that a scaling condition is imposed on the scale values of one observed variable per latent variable. For the one common latent variable model, equation (9), the scale values of one variable need to be scaled, and for the two correlated latent variable model in equation (18), the scale values of one variable in $\mathcal{A}_1$ and one variable in $\mathcal{A}_2$ need to be scaled. For model (20), we take this rule to the limit and impose scaling constraints on the scale values for each of the discrete variables.

The category scale values provide two types of information about how the mean of a latent variable differs over levels of an observed variable. This can be seen by expressing the scale values as $\nu_{i(j_i)m} = \omega_{im}\nu^*_{i(j_i)m}$ where $\omega_{im} = (\sum_{j_i} \nu^2_{i(j_i)m})^{1/2}$ and $\sum_{j_i} \nu^{*2}_{i(j_i)m} = 1$. The ω_{im}'s can be interpreted as measures of the overall (relative) strength of the relationship between variable A_i and latent variable Θ_m, and the $\nu^*_{i(j_i)m}$'s represent category specific information about this relationship. For identification purposes, if we impose the scaling condition on the scale values of, for example, A_1 where A_1 is an indicator of Θ_1 (i.e., $\sum_{j_1} \nu^2_{1(j_1)1} = 1$), then for $i \neq 1$, the ω_{i1}'s are free to vary and the variance of Θ_1 is an estimated parameter. Imposing a scaling condition on the scale values of more than one variable per latent variable is a restriction. This restriction can be interpreted as placing equality restrictions on the overall strength of the relationship between the observed variables and the latent variables (i.e., the ω_{im}'s).

We can now show that the case of $I = 3$ is special. The single indicator latent variable model for three observed variables implies the following log-multiplicative model

$$\log(P(\mathbf{a})) = \lambda + \lambda^*_{1(j_1)} + \lambda^*_{2(j_2)} + \lambda^*_{3(j_3)} + \sum_i \sum_{k>i} \sigma^*_{11} \nu_{i(j_i)1} \nu_{k(j_k)1}. \tag{21}$$

Suppose that for identification, the condition $\sum_{j_1} \nu^2_{1(j_1)1} = 1$ is imposed. Since we can represent the scale values for the other two variables as $\nu_{2(j_2)1} = \omega_2 \nu^*_{2(j_2)1}$ and $\nu_{3(j_3)1} = \omega_3 \nu^*_{3(j_3)1}$, model (21) is empirically indistinguishable from model (20), which is seen by setting $\sigma_{12} = \omega_2 \sigma^*_{11}$, $\sigma_{13} = \omega_3 \sigma^*_{11}$, and $\sigma_{23} = \omega_2 \omega_3 \sigma^*_{11}$. This equivalence provides an alternative interpretation for the partial association model for three variables discussed by Clogg (1982; see also Agresti 1984).

3. MULTIPLE LATENT VARIABLES PER INDICATOR

Observed variables may be directly related to more than one latent variable. Adding this complexity to the models does not require the derivation of a more complex model. We use the same general model derived in Section 2.2 (i.e., equation 15), but specify a more complex parameterization for $\mathbf{h}(\mathbf{a})$. Unlike the single indicator models where there is a single set of scale values for each discrete variable, in the multiple indicator models, a discrete variable may have multiple sets of scale values.

The major difficulty in using log-multiplicative models as multiple indicator models is determining the necessary and sufficient constraints needed to uniquely identify the parameters of the log-multiplicative models. For all models, the identification constraints described in Section 2.3 (i.e., location constraints on the marginal effect terms and the scale values and a scaling constraint on the category scores of one observed variable per latent variable) are needed. The additional identification constraints (if any) depend on the complexity of the model.

Since the number of possible multiple indicator models is far too large to consider here, we derive the log-multiplicative models for three of the four models that are used in the examples presented in Sections 4 and 6,[2] and show how to determine the identification constraints for these models. In the first two examples, the latent variables are uncorrelated, and in the third example, the latent variables are correlated.

3.1. *Uncorrelated Latent Variables*

Consider the General Social Survey data where all the items appear to be indicators of one latent variable (i.e., attitude). If the single indicator, one latent variable does not fit, then one possibility is that there is extra pair-specific association that is not accounted for by the common latent variable. To model pair-specific association, we can introduce additional latent variables for pairs of discrete variables. For example, suppose that in addition to being indicators of the latent attitude variable Θ_1, items A_1 and A_2 are directly related to Θ_2 (a pair specific variable), which is uncorrelated with Θ_1. In this case, $\boldsymbol{\Sigma}$ equals a (2×2) diagonal matrix, and $\mathbf{h}(\mathbf{a})$ is parameterized as

$$\mathbf{h}(\mathbf{a}) = \begin{pmatrix} \sum_{i=1}^{4} \nu_{i(j_i)1} \\ \nu_{1(j_1)2} + \nu_{2(j_2)2} \end{pmatrix}.$$

Using this parameterization of $\mathbf{h}(\mathbf{a})$, the parameterization $g(\mathbf{a})$ in equation (7) and a diagonal $\boldsymbol{\Sigma}$ in our general model, equation (15), gives us the log-multiplicative model

$$\log(P(\mathbf{a})) = \lambda + \sum_i \lambda^*_{i(j_i)} + \sigma_{11} \sum_i \sum_{k>i} \nu_{i(j_i)1} \nu_{k(j_k)1} + \sigma_{22} \nu_{1(j_1)2} \nu_{2(j_2)2}. \tag{22}$$

In addition to the identification constraints needed for the common part of the model, the scale values for each discrete variable related to the pair-specific latent variable must have a scaling condition im-

[2] The fourth model, which has a heterogeneous covariance matrix, is discussed in Section 6.2.

posed on them (i.e., $\sum_{j_1} \nu^2_{1(j_1)2} = \sum_{j_2} \nu^2_{2(j_2)2} = 1$). To see this, replace $\nu_{1(j_1)2}$ with $\nu^*_{1(j_1)2} = c\nu_{1(j_1)2}$ where c is a constant. The value of the term $\sigma_{22}\nu_{1(j_1)2}\nu_{2(j_2)2}$ in equation (22) remains the same; that is,

$$\sigma_{22}\nu_{1(j_1)2}\nu_{2(j_2)2} = \sigma^*_{22}\nu^*_{1(j_1)2}\nu^*_{2(j_2)2}$$

where $\sigma^*_{22} = \sigma_{22}/\mathrm{c}^2$ and $\nu^*_{2(j_2)2} = c\nu_{2(j_2)2}$.

Extra association may also be due to multiple uncorrelated latent variables to which each discrete variable is directly related. This would give us

$$\mathbf{h}(\mathbf{a}) = \begin{pmatrix} \sum_i \nu_{i(j_i)1} \\ \vdots \\ \sum_i \nu_{i(j_i)M} \end{pmatrix}. \tag{23}$$

Since the latent variables are uncorrelated, $\mathbf{\Sigma}$ equals a diagonal matrix and the log-multiplicative model is

$$\log(P(\mathbf{a})) = \lambda + \sum_i \lambda^*_{i(j_i)} + \sum_i \sum_{k>i} \sum_m \sigma_{mm}\nu_{i(j_i)m}\nu_{k(j_k)m}. \tag{24}$$

To identify the parameters in equation (24), we need to use only the identification constraints given in Section 2.3 (assuming $I > 2$).

3.2. *Correlated Latent Variables*

Often in the social sciences, latent variables are correlated; therefore, we consider the situation where each of I observed variables is directly related to each of M latent variables ($M > 1$), and the latent variables are correlated. In this case, the parameterization of $\mathbf{h}(\mathbf{a})$ is given in equation (23). Assuming that all of the latent variables are correlated and using equation (15) gives us the log-multiplicative model

$$\log(P(\mathbf{a})) = \lambda + \sum_i \lambda^*_{i(j_i)} + \sum_i \sum_{k>i} \sum_m \sigma_{mm}\nu_{i(j_i)m}\nu_{k(j_k)m}$$

$$+ \sum_i \sum_{k>i} \sum_m \sum_{m'>m} \sigma_{mm'}\nu_{i(j_i)m}\nu_{k(j_k)m'}, \tag{25}$$

where λ is a normalizing constant and $\lambda^*_{i(j_i)} = \lambda_{i(j_i)} + (1/2)\sum_m \times \sum_{m'} \sigma_{mm'} \nu_{i(j_i)m} \nu_{i(j_i)m'}$. Since the sum $(1/2)\sum_m \sum_{m'} \sigma_{mm'} \nu_{i(j_i)m} \nu_{i(j_i)m'}$ is only indexed by j_i, it gets "absorbed" into the marginal effect term. Equation (25) is the most complex multiple indicator model possible, and as shown below, it has more parameters than can be estimated from data.

To show what constraints are needed for equation (25), as well as other multiple indicator models, let $\mathbf{N}_i$ equal the $(J_i \times M)$ matrix whose columns contain the scale values for the categories of variable A_i; that is, $\mathbf{N}_i = (\boldsymbol{\nu}_{i1}, \ldots, \boldsymbol{\nu}_{iM})$ where $\boldsymbol{\nu}_{im}$ equals the $(J_i \times 1)$ vector of scale values $\nu_{i(j_i)m}$. If A_i is conditionally independent of latent variable Θ_m, then all the scale values relating A_i and latent variable Θ_m equal zero and the corresponding column of $\mathbf{N}_i$ contains zeros (i.e., $\boldsymbol{\nu}_{im} = \mathbf{0}$). The interaction term for levels j_i and j_k of variables A_i and A_k equals the (j_i, j_k) element of the matrix product $\mathbf{N}_i \boldsymbol{\Sigma} \mathbf{N}'_k$ where $\boldsymbol{\Sigma}$ is the covariance matrix of the latent variables. For each cell in the cross-classification of the discrete variables, the interaction terms in the model equal the appropriate elements from the matrices in the set

$$\{\mathbf{N}_i \boldsymbol{\Sigma} \mathbf{N}'_k \,|\, i < k\}. \tag{26}$$

Determining the additional constraints needed to identify a model consists of determining whether transformations of the $\mathbf{N}_i$'s and $\boldsymbol{\Sigma}$ exist that have no effect on the value of the elements of the matrix products in (26).

For model (25), none of the columns of the $\mathbf{N}_i$'s equals $\mathbf{0}$. Given any $(M \times M)$ nonsingular matrix T, we can always set $\mathbf{N}^*_i = \mathbf{N}_i \mathbf{T}$ for all i and $\boldsymbol{\Sigma}^* = \mathbf{T}^{-1} \boldsymbol{\Sigma} \mathbf{T}^{-1}$ without changing the values of any of the elements of the matrix products in (26). Given this indeterminacy (and for convenience), we can arbitrarily set all covariances equal to zero and estimate the M variances. This leads us back to the uncorrelated latent variable model in equation (24).

If at least one observed variable is not an indicator of a latent variable, then restrictions exist on the set of possible parameters. For example, consider the case of four variables and two latent variables where A_1 and A_4 are indicators of Θ_1 and Θ_2, respectively, and A_2 and A_3 are indicators of both Θ_1 and Θ_2. The graph for this model is given in Figure 4 and $\mathbf{h}(\mathbf{a})$ is set equal to

$$\mathbf{h}(\mathbf{a}) = \begin{pmatrix} \nu_{1(j_1)1} + \nu_{2(j_2)1} + \nu_{3(j_3)1} \\ \nu_{2(j_2)2} + \nu_{3(j_3)2} + \nu_{4(j_4)2} \end{pmatrix}.$$

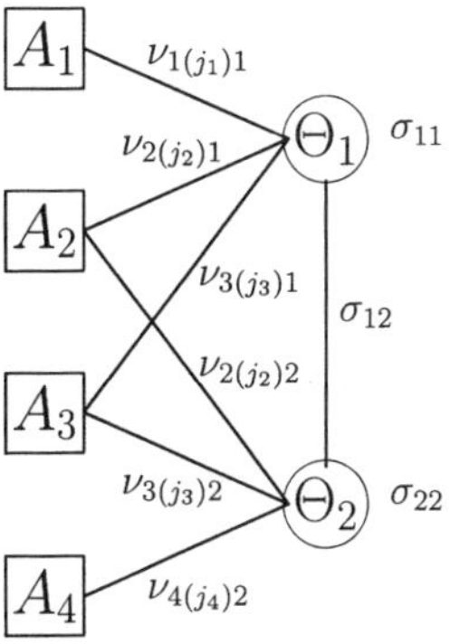

FIGURE 4. Multiple indicator, two correlated latent variable model for four observed variables.

The log-multiplicative model for this case is given in equation (35) in Appendix A. For the log-multiplicative model, the matrices of scale values equal $\mathbf{N}_1 = (\boldsymbol{\nu}_{11}, \mathbf{0})$, $\mathbf{N}_2 = (\boldsymbol{\nu}_{21}, \boldsymbol{\nu}_{22})$, $\mathbf{N}_3 = (\boldsymbol{\nu}_{31}, \boldsymbol{\nu}_{32})$ and $\mathbf{N}_4 = (\mathbf{0}, \boldsymbol{\nu}_{42})$. The covariance σ_{12} cannot be arbitrarily set equal to zero, because $\mathbf{N}_1 \boldsymbol{\Sigma} \mathbf{N}_4' = (\sigma_{12} \boldsymbol{\nu}_{11} \boldsymbol{\nu}_{42}')$. Setting $\sigma_{12} = 0$ implies that there is no (partial) association between A_1 and A_4. After imposing location and scaling conditions, we only need one additional constraint: one variance needs to be set equal to a constant.

When the latent variables are correlated, it can be especially difficult to determine the identification constraints; therefore, we suggest empirically verifying them. Given a set of conditions on the parameters that are believed to be needed for identification, fit the model with fewer conditions. We suggest starting by only imposing those conditions given in Section 2.3, which are known to be required for identification. Successively add conditions on the parameters. If a condition is only needed for identification, then the fit statistics for the model will be exactly the same as the model fit without all of the identification conditions. If a condition on the parameters is a restriction, then the model will not fit the data as well.[3] Once it has been determined that none of the conditions is a restriction, the model with these conditions imposed should be refit several times

[3] In Appendix B, where maximum-likelihood estimation of log-multiplicative models is presented, we discuss a second method for checking whether a condition imposed on the scale values is a restriction.

with random starting values. If the conditions are sufficient for identification, then the parameter estimates will be exactly the same. However, if the conditions imposed are not sufficient, different parameter estimates will likely be obtained, in which case, additional conditions are needed on the parameters to identify a unique solution.

4. EXAMPLES OF SINGLE AND MULTIPLE INDICATOR MODELS

Two example analyses are given here that illustrate the graphical/latent variable models presented in Sections 2 and 3. The models are used here in both an exploratory and a confirmatory fashion.

The log-multiplicative models fit to data in this section and in Section 6 were fit using the unidimensional Newton method described in Appendix A, which was implemented in an experimental version of ℓ_{EM} (Vermunt 1997).

4.1. *General Social Survey Data*

For this example, we analyze the $(2 \times 4 \times 5 \times 5)$ cross-classification of 899 responses from the 1994 General Social Survey (Davis and Smith 1996) to the four items listed in Section 1. Statistics for the models fit to the data are reported in Table 1. Since the data contain many zeros, to assess model goodness-of-fit, we report dissimilarity indices (D) in addition to likelihood ratio statistics (G^2). For model comparisons (most of which are not nested), we use the BIC statistic to take into account goodness-of-fit, sample size, and model complexity.

As baseline models, the independence and all two-way interaction log-linear models were fit to the data. The all two-way model fits the data $(G^2 = 117.93, df = 136, p = .87)$; however, it is complex and estimating the parameters is problematic due to zeros in the observed bivariate margins. While the items appear to measure the same attitude, Model (c), the single indicator one latent variable model (i.e., equation 10), is unsatisfactory. The two uncorrelated latent variable model (Model d) where each item is an indicator of both latent variables (i.e., equation 24), fits the data; however, this model is complex and difficult to interpret.

Given that all the items appear to be indicators of the same attitude, we considered models with one common latent variable and additional

TABLE 1

Statistics for models fit to four items from the 1994 General Social Survey*

	df	G^2	p	D	BIC
Model					
(a) Independence	187	1063.25	<.01	.378	−209
(b) All 2-way interaction log-linear	136	117.93	.87	.089	−807
(c) One latent variable	175	279.50	<.01	.187	−911
(d) Two uncorrelated latent variables	163	170.61	.33	.116	−938
One common latent variable with extra latent variables for					
(e) $A_1A_2, A_1A_3, A_1A_4, A_2A_3, A_2A_4$ & A_3A_4	145	143.60	.52	.100	−843
(f) $A_1A_2, A_1A_3, A_2A_3, A_2A_4$ & A_3A_4	149	144.30	.59	.102	−869
(g) A_1A_2, A_1A_3, A_2A_3 & A_3A_4	155	161.36	.35	.113	−893
(h) A_1A_3, A_2A_3 & A_3A_4	158	164.98	.34	.124	−910
(i) A_2A_3 & A_3A_4	162	168.76	.34	.127	−933
(j) A_3A_4	168	194.41	.08	.138	−948
(k) A_2A_3	169	240.94	<.01	.168	−908
(l) A_2A_4	169	260.16	<.01	.177	−899
(m) A_1A_2	172	271.65	<.01	.183	−898
(n) A_1A_3	171	275.56	<.01	.189	−887
(o) A_1A_4	171	275.61	<.01	.189	−887

*Respondents were asked whether wives and/or husbands should work outside of the home.

uncorrelated latent variables to represent associations between pairs of items not captured by the common variable. Model (e), which has six extra latent variables, fits the data; therefore, we sought simpler models by successively deleting pair-specific latent variables, Models (f)–(j). We also fit the one common latent variable model plus one uncorrelated variable for a pair of items, Models (j)–(o). Since Model (j) has the smallest BIC statistic, fits the data reasonably well,[4] and its interpretation is similar to Models (c) and (i), we report the results from Model (j).

Model (j) has one common latent variable and a second uncorrelated variable that accounts for extra A_3A_4 association. Table 2 contains the estimated association parameters and their standard errors, as well as $\hat{\omega}_{i1}$ computed for each item. The common latent variable is an attitude variable pertaining to the proper roles of wives and husbands in terms of employment inside/outside the home. From the $\hat{\omega}_{i1}$'s, items A_3 and A_2 are most strongly related to the common latent variable, followed by items A_4 and A_1. The conditional mean of the common latent variable is proportional to the sum of the scale values corresponding to a given response pattern (see equation 13). The order of category scores for the common latent variable corresponds to the order of the response options, except for item A_4 where the scale values for "strongly agree" and "agree" are nearly equal but out of order (i.e., $\hat{\nu}_{A_4(1)1} = -.135$ and $\hat{\nu}_{A_4(2)1} = -.145$). The greater the agreement with a statement, the greater the value on the conditional mean of the latent variable.

Relative to the common latent variable, the variable for the extra A_3A_4 association accounts for inconsistent extreme responses "strongly agree" to item A_3 but "strongly disagree" to item A_4, and overly consistent responses for the more moderate responses. These inconsistencies and consistencies may be due in part to the location of the items on the survey and to the wording of item A_4. Item A_4 immediately follows A_3, while A_1 and A_2 are from two different sections of the survey. Item A_4 differs from the other items in that the traditional roles of husbands and wives are reversed and children are explicitly mentioned.

4.2. *Coleman Panel Data*: *The Boys*

The Coleman (1964) panel data, which are reported in Table 3, consist of responses made at two time points by 3398 boys and 3260 girls to two

[4]There are two large standardized residuals; however, these were cells where the observed count equals 1 and the fitted values are between .01 and .02.

TABLE 2

Estimated Parameters (and Standard Errors) from Model (j) in Table 1, Fit to Four Items from the 1994 General Social Survey*

		Response Options				
		Strongly Agree	Agree (approve)†	(neither agree nor disagree)	Disagree (disapprove)†	Strongly Disagree
$\hat{\sigma}_{11} = 11.294$	(4.252)					
$\hat{\omega}_{11} = .077$‡	$\hat{\nu}_{1(j_1)1} =$		.055 (.016)		−.055 (.016)	
$\hat{\omega}_{21} = .587$	$\hat{\nu}_{2(j_2)1} =$	−.306 (.094)	−.211 (.065)		.066 (.030)	.450 (.138)
$\hat{\omega}_{31} = 1.00$	$\hat{\nu}_{3(j_3)1} =$	−.679 (.063)	−.305 (.074)	.083 (.050)	.324 (.024)	.577 (.051)
$\hat{\omega}_{41} = .287$	$\hat{\nu}_{4(j_4)1} =$	−.135 (.048)	−.145 (.034)	.020 (.016)	.064 (.032)	.196 (.049)
$\hat{\sigma}_{22} = 2.642$	(1.094)					
	$\hat{\nu}_{3(j_3)2} =$	.783 (.137)	−.333 (.186)	−.052 (.163)	−.511 (.112)	.113 (.233)
	$\hat{\nu}_{4(j_4)2} =$	.108 (.164)	−.471 (.104)	.097 (.138)	−.467 (.119)	.734 (.122)

*See text for the items.

†The response options for item A_1 were "approve" and "disapprove."

‡$\hat{\omega}_{i1} = (\sum_{j_i} \hat{\nu}^2_{i(j_i)1})^{1/2}$.

TABLE 3
Panel Data Where A_t and B_t Refer to the Attitude and Membership Items at Time Point t*

				Boys			Girls		
$B_1{}^a$	$A_1{}^b$	B_2	A_2	Count	Fitted	Std resid	Count	Fitted	Std resid
2	2	2	2	458	454.83	.15	484	470.58	.62
2	2	2	1	140	151.39	−.93	93	102.49	−.94
2	2	1	2	110	121.46	−1.04	107	103.71	.32
2	2	1	1	49	51.68	−.37	32	29.74	.41
2	1	2	2	171	167.63	.26	112	113.49	−.14
2	1	2	1	182	177.15	.36	110	112.44	−.23
2	1	1	2	56	57.22	−.16	30	32.93	−.51
2	1	1	1	87	77.30	1.10	46	42.96	.46
1	2	2	2	184	171.87	.93	129	146.76	−1.47
1	2	2	1	75	73.13	.22	40	42.09	−.32
1	2	1	2	531	534.85	−.17	768	766.94	.04
1	2	1	1	281	290.89	−.58	321	289.60	1.85
1	1	2	2	85	80.97	.45	74	74.00	.00
1	1	2	1	97	109.38	−1.18	75	60.80	1.82
1	1	1	2	338	322.09	.89	303	320.66	−.99
1	1	1	1	554	556.17	−.09	536	550.80	−.63

Source: Coleman (1964).

*Fitted values and standardized residuals are from Model (f) in Table 6 (i.e., graph in Figure 5 with heterogeneous $\mathbf{\Sigma}$ and $\tau\delta_{1122,G(j)}$).

[a]For items B_1 and B_2, $j = 1$ for "no" and $j = 2$ for "yes."

[b]For items A_1 and A_2, $j = 1$ for "negative" and $j = 2$ for "positive."

items: their attitude toward (positive, negative) and their self-perception of membership in (yes, no) the leading or popular crowd. The data for the boys have been analyzed extensively (e.g., Agresti 1997; Andersen 1988; Goodman 1978; Langeheine 1988; Whittaker 1990), while the data for the girls has not. We analyze the boys in this section, and in Section 6, we model the girls data.

The fit statistics for models estimated for the boys data are reported in the left side of Table 4. We find that the independence log-linear model fails to fit ($G^2 = 1421.68$, $df = 11$, $p < .001$), but the all two-way interaction log-linear model provides a good fit for the boys ($G^2 = 1.21$, $df = 5$, $p = .94$). Given that the all two-way model fits well, we consider log-multiplicative models. The simplest model with one common latent variable (i.e., equation 10) fails to fit ($G^2 = 243.59$, $df = 7$,

TABLE 4
Fit Statistics for Models Estimated Separately to the Boys and Girls Data

	Boys Data			Girls Data					
							with $\tau\delta_{1122}$		
Model	*df*	G^2	*p*	*df*	G^2	*p*	*df*	G^2	*p*
Baseline Models									
(a) Independence	11	1421.68	$<.01$	11	1845.03	$<.01$	10	1725.65	$<.01$
(b) All 2–way loglinear	5	1.21	.94	5	8.39	.14	4	4.44	.34
Latent Variable Models									
(c) 1 latent variable	7	243.59	$<.01$	7	314.32	$<.01$	6	307.59	$<.01$
(d) 2 correlated variables, multiple indicators	5	1.21	.94	5	8.70	.12	4	4.44	.35
(e) 2 correlated variables, single indicator	6	1.21	.98	6	17.13	.01	5	5.22	.39
(f) Model (e) with scaling restrictions	8	5.43	.71	8	23.29	$<.01$	7	9.73	.20
(g) Model (f) with $\sigma_{12} = 0$	9	97.52	$<.01$	9	128.66	$<.01$	8	115.72	$<.01$

$p < .001$). We next estimate a multiple indicator, two correlated latent variable model with the following characteristics: attitude at time one, A_1, is related to one latent variable; membership at time two, B_2, is related to a second latent variable; and the remaining two variables, A_2 and B_1, are allowed to be related to both latent variables (i.e., equation A.1 in Appendix A, and Figure 4 where A_3 and A_4 correspond to B_1 and B_2, respectively). For identification, the category scores for A_1 and B_2 are scaled and $\sigma_{22} = 1$. This model, Model (d) in Table 4, has the same fit and degrees of freedom as the all two-way interaction log-linear model; however, the log-multiplicative model provides us with information regarding the structure underlying the data. The estimated scale values for the boys data from Model (d) are given in Table 5.

The scale values in Table 5 suggest that the two attitude items are indicators of the same latent variable, "attitude," and the two membership items are indicators of a second correlated latent variable, "membership perception," (i.e., Figure 2, where A_3 and A_4 correspond to B_1 and B_2). Model (e), the corresponding single indicator, two correlated latent variable model (i.e., equation 19), fits the data nearly as well as the multiple indicator, two correlated latent variable model ($G^2 = 1.21, df = 6, p = .98$). Also suggested by the estimates in Table 5 is that the strength of the relationship between the observed and latent variables may be equal for all items. Imposing this restriction, Model (f) which is Model (e) with the restriction that $\sum_{j_i} \nu^2_{i(j_i)m} = 1$ for all four items, yields $G^2 = 5.43$, $df = 8$, and $p = .71$. Lastly, to check whether $\sigma_{12} = 0$, we estimate the uncorrelated latent variable version of Model (f); however this model, Model (g), fails to fit ($G^2 = 97.52$, $df = 9$, $p < .001$).

TABLE 5
Estimated Parameters from the Multiple Indicator, Two Correlated Latent Variable Model*

	$\hat{\nu}_{i(j_i)1}$	$\hat{\nu}_{i(j_i)2}$
A_1	±.707	.000
A_2	±.789	±.009
B_1	±.102	±.865
B_2	.000	±.707

Note: $\hat{\sigma}_{11} = .520$, $\hat{\sigma}_{12} = .076$, and $\sigma_{22} = 1.00$.
*Model (d) in Table 4, fit to the boys' data.

Our final model for the boys data, Model (f), is a linear-by-linear interaction model with restrictions across the association parameters. The estimated variances (and standard errors[5]) equal $\hat{\sigma}_{11} = .580(.037)$ for attitude and $\hat{\sigma}_{22} = 1.231(.043)$ for membership, and the covariance equals $\hat{\sigma}_{12} = .123(.013)$. Given the identification constraints and restrictions on the scale values, the category scores for the two levels of each variable equal $-.707$ for $j = 1$ (i.e., "negative" or "no") and .707 for $j = 2$ (i.e., "positive" or "yes").

5. MODELS WITH HETEROGENEOUS COVARIANCE MATRICES

In the models considered so far, $\boldsymbol{\Sigma}$ has been restricted to be constant or homogeneous across levels of the discrete variables. We further generalize the models by allowing $\boldsymbol{\Sigma}$ to differ over cells of the cross-classification of the discrete variables. To make this generalization, we replace $\boldsymbol{\Sigma}$ in the joint distribution by $\boldsymbol{\Sigma}(\mathbf{a})$. Using the canonical form given in equation (12), we obtain

$$f(\mathbf{a}, \boldsymbol{\theta}) = \exp[g(\mathbf{a}) + \mathbf{h}(\mathbf{a})'\boldsymbol{\theta} - \tfrac{1}{2}\boldsymbol{\theta}'\boldsymbol{\Sigma}(\mathbf{a})^{-1}\boldsymbol{\theta}], \tag{27}$$

where

$$\mathbf{h}(\mathbf{a}) = \boldsymbol{\Sigma}(\mathbf{a})^{-1}\boldsymbol{\mu}(\mathbf{a}), \tag{28}$$

and

$$g(\mathbf{a}) = \log(P(\mathbf{a})) - \frac{M}{2}\log(2\pi) - \frac{1}{2}\log(|\boldsymbol{\Sigma}(\mathbf{a})|) - \frac{1}{2}\mathbf{h}(\mathbf{a})'\boldsymbol{\Sigma}(\mathbf{a})\mathbf{h}(\mathbf{a}) \tag{29}$$

(see Lauritzen and Wermuth 1989; Edwards 1995; Lauritzen 1996; Whittaker 1990). The model for observed data is obtained by rewriting equation (29) in terms of $P(\mathbf{a})$,

$$P(\mathbf{a}) = (2\pi)^{M/2}|\boldsymbol{\Sigma}(\mathbf{a})|^{1/2}\exp[g(\mathbf{a}) + \tfrac{1}{2}\mathbf{h}(\mathbf{a})'\boldsymbol{\Sigma}(\mathbf{a})\mathbf{h}(\mathbf{a})]. \tag{30}$$

[5]The estimated standard errors from multidimensional Newton-Raphson and from the jackknife of the unidimensional Newton procedure are equal to within $\pm.0001$.

Much of what is true for the homogeneous models is also true for heterogeneous models. Hypotheses about the relationship between observed variables given the latent variables is incorporated through the parameterization of $g(\mathbf{a})$, hypotheses about the relationship between the observed and latent variables are incorporated into the models through $\mathbf{h}(\mathbf{a})$, and hypotheses about the relationship between the latent variables are incorporated through $\boldsymbol{\Sigma}(\mathbf{a})$. The identification constraints given in Section 2.3 are still required. Whether additional constraints are required depends on how the covariance matrix differs over $\mathbf{a}$. Furthermore, the log-multiplicative models for heterogeneous models can be read from graphs (see Appendix A).

What is different between homogeneous and heterogeneous models is that we must specify how the covariance matrix differs over $\mathbf{a}$. Heterogeneous models may include extra terms relative to homogeneous models due to $|\boldsymbol{\Sigma}(\mathbf{a})|^{1/2}$ in equation (30). For homogeneous models, $|\boldsymbol{\Sigma}(\mathbf{a})|^{1/2} = |\boldsymbol{\Sigma}|^{1/2}$ and it is absorbed into the constant λ. In heterogeneous models, depending on how the covariance matrix differs over cells of the table, $|\boldsymbol{\Sigma}(\mathbf{a})|^{1/2}$ may be absorbed into other terms in the log-multiplicative model or may require the addition of extra parameters. For example, if the covariance matrix differs over the categories of just one observed variable, then $|\boldsymbol{\Sigma}(\mathbf{a})|^{1/2}$ is absorbed into the marginal effect term for that variable. As another example, if the covariance matrix is different for a single cell in the table, then there is one value of $|\boldsymbol{\Sigma}(\mathbf{a})|^{1/2}$ for the single cell and another value of $|\boldsymbol{\Sigma}(\mathbf{a})|^{1/2}$ for the rest of the table. Only one element of $\boldsymbol{\Sigma}(\mathbf{a})$ needs to differ and the single cell will be fit perfectly. In such cases, a parameter needs to be included in the log-multiplicative model such that the cell is fit perfectly (e.g., $\tau\delta_{\mathbf{a}}$ where the indicator $\delta_{\mathbf{a}} = 1$ if $\mathbf{a}$ is the cell with the different covariance matrix, and 0 otherwise).

For graphical/latent variable models with homogeneous and heterogeneous covariance matrices, there is always a log-linear model that provides a baseline (best fit) for a log-multiplicative model.[6] With homogeneous covariance matrices, only bivariate associations are implied for the observed (discrete) variables, and the best fit that could be achieved by a log-multiplicative model is given by some log-linear model with two-

[6]Given enough latent variables, the log-multiplicative model derived from a graphical model will be equivalent to some log-linear model, which implies that a graphical representation of any log-linear model can always be found provided that one is willing to assume the existence of underlying continuous variables.

way interactions. With heterogeneous covariance matrices, three- or higher-way interactions may be present depending on how $\mathbf{\Sigma}(\mathbf{a})$ differs over $\mathbf{a}$.

Since there are many possible ways in which the covariance matrix could differ over levels of the discrete variables, we proceed with an example that requires heterogeneous covariance matrices.

6. THE COLEMAN PANEL DATA REVISITED

In Section 6.1, we analyze the Coleman (1964) data for the girls, and in Section 6.2, we analyze the boys and girls data together with gender as a fifth variable.

6.1. *Girls Data*

For the girls data, we repeat the same analyses performed on the boys data in Section 4.2. It is reasonable to expect that the same structural model should fit both the girls and boys data; however, the simplest latent variable model that fits the girls data is Model (d), the two correlated, multiple indicator model given in Figure 4. Models (e) and (f), the latter of which was the best one for the boys data, fail to fit the girls data;[7] however, the lack-of-fit appears to be due to one cell. The response pattern A_1 = "negative," B_1 = "no," A_2 = "positive," and B_2 = "yes"—i.e., the (1,1,2,2) cell—has a relatively large residual.

For the girls, the covariance matrix for the $(1,1,2,2)$ cell may not equal the one for all the other response patterns. If so, then as discussed in Section 5, we could add a single parameter, τ, to fit the cell perfectly. Refitting all the models adding the term $\tau\delta_{1122}$—where $\delta_{1122} = 1$ for cell $(1,1,2,2)$ and 0 otherwise—greatly improves the fit of Models (d), (e), and (f) for the girls data.[8] Of the models that include the extra term, the best model for the girls data is Model (f).

It would be desirable to compare the boys and girls conditional mean values on the attitude and membership perception (latent) variables;

[7] We could argue that Model (f) is the best, because taking sample size and model complexity into account the most parsimonious model is Model (f). The *BIC* statistics for Models (d), (e), and (f) equal -31.75, -31.41, and -41.42, respectively. Furthermore, Model (f) fits well based on the dissimilarity index for models (d), (e) and (f), which equal .016, .021, and .026, respectively.

[8] BIC statistics for Models (d), (e), and (f) with the τ parameter equal -27.92, -35.23, and -46.89, respectively, and the dissimilarity indices equal .013, .014, and .016, respectively. These statistics again point to Model (f) as the best.

however, to make such comparisons regarding the mean values, gender must be included as an observed variable in the model. An additional reason to include gender in the model is to test whether $\mathbf{\Sigma}_{\text{boys}} = \mathbf{\Sigma}_{\text{girls}}$. The estimates of elements of $\mathbf{\Sigma}$ for the girls are slightly larger than those for the boys. The estimates (and standard errors) for the girls are $\hat{\sigma}_{11,\text{girls}} = .760(.040)$, $\hat{\sigma}_{22,\text{girls}} = 1.586(.052)$, and $\hat{\sigma}_{12,\text{girls}} = .138(.014)$, whereas for the boys, they are $\hat{\sigma}_{11,\text{boys}} = .580(.037)$, $\hat{\sigma}_{22,\text{boys}} = 1.231(.043)$, and $\hat{\sigma}_{12,\text{boys}} = .123(.013)$.

6.2. *Combined Analysis*

Given the results from separately estimating models for the boys and girls, we expect that A_1 and A_2 are related to an unobserved attitude variable, B_1 and B_2 are related to an unobserved membership perception variable, and scale restrictions can be imposed on the scale values for A_1, A_2, B_1, and B_2. We would like to test whether the means of the unobserved variables differ for boys and girls and whether $\mathbf{\Sigma}$ differs. This underlying model is shown in Figure 5.

To derive the most general log-multiplicative model for the figure, we define $g(\mathbf{a})$ as

$$g(\mathbf{a}) = \lambda + \lambda_{A_1(j)} + \lambda_{A_2(j)} + \lambda_{B_1(j)} + \lambda_{B_2(j)} + \lambda_{G(j)}, \tag{31}$$

where λ is a constant, and $\lambda_{A_1(j)}$, $\lambda_{A_2(j)}$, $\lambda_{B_1(j)}$, $\lambda_{B_2(j)}$, and $\lambda_{G(j)}$ are marginal effect terms for the observed variables. For simplicity, we have

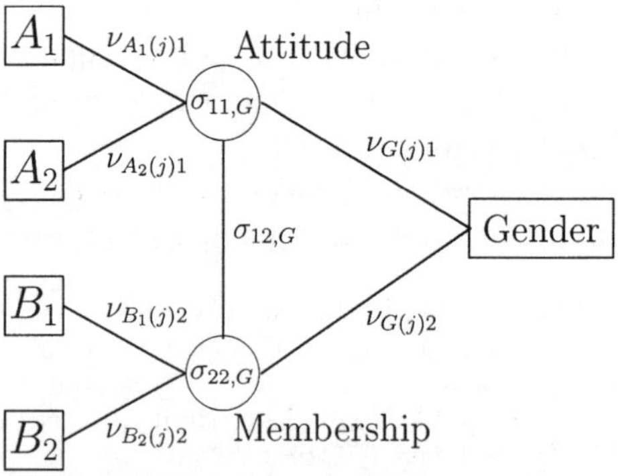

FIGURE 5. Graph corresponding to log-multiplicative Models (c–f) in Table 6 fit to the Coleman panel with gender as the fifth variable.

dropped the subscripts on the j indices. We parameterize $\mathbf{h}(\mathbf{a})$ as

$$\mathbf{h}(\mathbf{a}) = \begin{pmatrix} \nu_{A_1(j)1} + \nu_{A_2(j)1} + \nu_{G(j)1} \\ \nu_{B_1(j)2} + \nu_{B_2(j)2} + \nu_{G(j)2} \end{pmatrix}. \tag{32}$$

The first row in equation (32) equals the sum of the scale values for the unobserved attitude variable and the second row equals the sum of the scale values for the unobserved membership variable. Lastly, we specify a heterogeneous covariance matrix:

$$\mathbf{\Sigma}_{G(j)} = \begin{pmatrix} \sigma_{11G(j)} & \sigma_{12G(j)} \\ \sigma_{12G(j)} & \sigma_{22G(j)} \end{pmatrix}, \tag{33}$$

where this matrix is different for $j = 1$ (boys) and 2 (girls). For the homogeneous models, we set $\mathbf{\Sigma}_{G(j)} = \mathbf{\Sigma}$. Replacing $g(\mathbf{a})$, $\mathbf{h}(\mathbf{a})$, and $\mathbf{\Sigma}(\mathbf{a})$ in equation (30) by their parameterizations in equations (31), (32), and (33), respectively, yields

$$\begin{aligned}
\log(P(\mathbf{a})) = {} & \lambda + \lambda_{A_1(j)} + \lambda_{A_2(j)} + \lambda_{B_1(j)} + \lambda_{B_2(j)} + \lambda^*_{G(j)} \\
& + \tfrac{1}{2}\sigma_{11G(j)}\left[\nu^2_{A_1(j)1} + \nu^2_{A_2(j)1}\right] + \tfrac{1}{2}\sigma_{22G(j)}\left[\nu^2_{B_1(j)2} + \nu^2_{B_2(j)2}\right] \\
& + \sigma_{11G(j)}\left[\nu_{A_1(j)1}\nu_{A_2(j)1} + \nu_{A_1(j)1}\nu_{G(j)1} + \nu_{A_2(j)1}\nu_{G(j)1}\right] \\
& + \sigma_{22G(j)}\left[\nu_{B_1(j)2}\nu_{B_2(j)2} + \nu_{B_1(j)2}\nu_{G(j)2} + \nu_{B_2(j)2}\nu_{G(j)2}\right] \\
& + \sigma_{12G(j)}\left[\nu_{A_1(j)1}\nu_{B_1(j)2} + \nu_{A_1(j)1}\nu_{B_2(j)2} + \nu_{A_2(j)1}\nu_{B_1(j)2}\right. \\
& \qquad + \nu_{A_2(j)1}\nu_{B_2(j)2} + \nu_{A_1(j)1}\nu_{G(j)2} + \nu_{A_2(j)1}\nu_{G(j)2} \\
& \qquad \left. + \nu_{B_1(j)2}\nu_{G(j)1} + \nu_{B_2(j)2}\nu_{G(j)1}\right],
\end{aligned} \tag{34}$$

where $\lambda^*_{G(j)} = \lambda_{G(j)} + \log(|\mathbf{\Sigma}_{G(j)}|^{1/2}) + (1/2)\sum_{m=1}^{2}\sum_{m'=1}^{2}\sigma_{mm'G(j)} \times \nu_{G(j)m}\nu_{G(j)m'}$. While this log-multiplicative model is quite complex, its interpretation is relatively simple and greatly facilitated by Figure 5. The model can be read from its graph using the method outlined in Appendix A.

Based on the previous results, we set $\nu_{A_1(j)1}$, $\nu_{A_2(j)1}$, $\nu_{B_1(j)2}$, and $\nu_{B_2(j)2}$ equal to $\pm.7071$ rather than estimating them. Thus the only scale values estimated are those for gender, $\nu_{G(j)m}$. Other than location constraints on the marginal effects and the scale values for gender, no additional identification constraints are required on the parameters in either the homogeneous or heterogeneous versions of equation (34).

The fit statistics for models with gender as a fifth observed variable are reported in Table 6. While the all two-way interaction log-linear model is the baseline model for the homogeneous version of equation (34), the log-linear model with all three-way interactions that involve gender $(A_1A_2G, A_1B_1G, A_1B_2G, A_2B_1G, A_2B_2G, B_1B_2G)$, is the baseline model for the heterogeneous version of equation (34). Since the all two-way interaction log-linear model, Model (a) in Table 6, fails to fit, the homogeneous latent variable model, Model (c), should also fail. Not only does the homogeneous model fail to fit, but so does the homogeneous model with an extra parameter for the (1,1,2,2) cell for the girls—i.e., $\tau\delta_{1122,G(j)}$ where $\delta_{1122,\text{girls}} = 1$ for the (1,1,2,2) cell for the girls, and 0 otherwise.

Since the log-linear model with the three-way interactions, Model (b), fits the data, we try a heterogeneous model where the covariance matrix differs for boys and girls. The heterogeneous model nearly fits the data ($G^2 = 30.39$, $df = 18$, $p = .03$), and when $\tau\delta_{1122,G(j)}$ is added to the model, the model clearly fits ($G^2 = 19.47$, $df = 17$, $p = .30$). Model (f) is the most parsimonious model that fits the data, so we select it as our final model.

The estimated parameters for Model (f) are given in Table 7. The estimated covariance matrices for the boys and girls are similar to those from the models estimated separately for the boys and girls. Given the scale values and estimated covariance matrices, we compute estimates of the mean values on the latent attitude and membership variables for the cells of the cross-classification of the observed variables using $\boldsymbol{\mu}(\mathbf{a}) = \boldsymbol{\Sigma}(\mathbf{a})\mathbf{h}(\mathbf{a})$ (see equation 28). Since there are only two levels of the variables A_1, A_2, B_1, and B_2 and their scale values are equal, there are only five unique values of the means for the boys and five for the girls. Cells that have the same number of positive responses and yes's have the same mean—for example, the conditional mean for the cell (2,2,2,1) is the same as the mean for (1,2,2,2). The estimated conditional means for attitude and membership perception are plotted in Figure 6 against the numbers 0 through 4, which equal the number of positive responses and yes's. Separate curves are given for boys and girls.

From Figure 6, we see that for response patterns with more negative responses and no's, the boys means are larger than the girls means, while for response patterns with more positive responses and yes's, the girls means are larger than the boys. In both figures, the slopes for the girls are larger than those for the boys. The slopes of the lines for boys and girls differ, because $\hat{\boldsymbol{\Sigma}}_{\text{boys}} \neq \hat{\boldsymbol{\Sigma}}_{\text{girls}}$. If $\hat{\boldsymbol{\Sigma}}_{\text{boys}} = \hat{\boldsymbol{\Sigma}}_{\text{girls}}$, then the lines for boys and girls would be parallel and any difference between them would be due to

TABLE 6
Fit Statistics for Models Fit to Coleman (1964) Panel Data with Gender as a Variable

Model	*df*	G^2	*p*	BIC
Baseline loglinear models				
(a) All 2-way interactions	16	56.31	<.001	−84.31
(b) $(A_1 A_2 G, A_1 B_1 G, A_1 B_2 G, A_2 B_1 G, A_2 B_2 G, B_1 B_2 G)$	10	9.60	.48	−78.44
Latent variable models (equation (34), Figure 5)				
(c) Homogeneous $\mathbf{\Sigma}$	21	63.41	<.001	−121.47
(d) Model (c) with $\tau\delta_{1122,G(j)}$	20	60.90	<.001	−115.17
(e) Heterogeneous $\mathbf{\Sigma}_{G(j)}$	18	30.39	.03	−128.08
(f) Model (e) with $\tau\delta_{1122,G(j)}$	17	19.47	.30	−130.19

TABLE 7
Estimated Parameters from Model (f) in Table 6 Fit to the Panel Data with Gender as a Variable

	Value(s)			Value(s)	
Parameter	$j=1$	$j=2$	Parameter	$j=1$	$j=2$
λ	4.796		$\lambda_{G(j)}$	.276	−.276
$\lambda_{A_1(j)}$	−.134	.134	$\lambda_{B_1(j)}$	.291	−.291
$\lambda_{A_2(j)}$	−.185	.185	$\lambda_{B_2(j)}$	.118	−.118
$\nu_{G(j)1}$	−.125	.125	$\nu_{G(j)2}$	.060	−.060
$\sigma_{11,\text{boys}}$	.578		$\sigma_{11,\text{girls}}$	.757	
$\sigma_{22,\text{boys}}$	1.228		$\sigma_{22,\text{girls}}$	1.583	
$\sigma_{12,\text{boys}}$	.123		$\sigma_{12,\text{girls}}$	.138	
			τ	.462	

Note: Due to restrictions on the scale values for variables A_1, A_2, B_1, and B_2, the scale values $\nu_{A_1(j)1}$, $\nu_{A_2(j)1}$, $\nu_{B_1(j)2}$, and $\nu_{B_2(j)2}$ equal −.707 for $j = 1$ and .707 for $j = 2$.

the scale values for gender. The positive covariance between attitude and membership is reflected by the fact that the higher a child's perception of being a member of the leading crowd, the more positive his or her attitude is toward the leading crowd (and vice versa).

7. DISCUSSION

Log-multiplicative models provide a powerful and flexible approach to studying the relationships between nominal and/or ordinal variables in

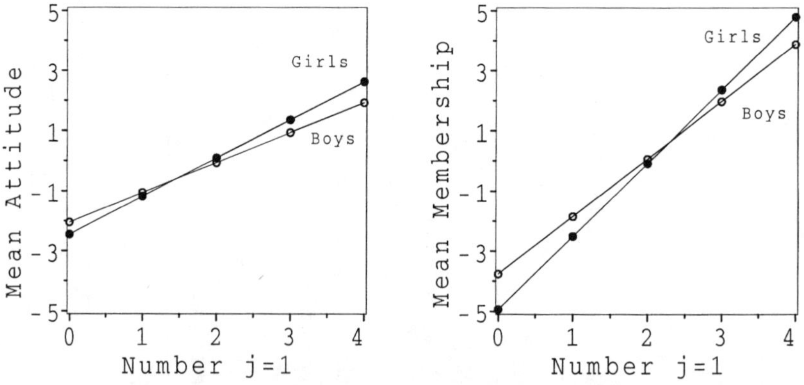

FIGURE 6. Plot of estimated attitude (a) and membership (b) means for boys (circles) and girls (dots) using scale values and estimated covariance matrix from Model (f) in Table 6 fit to the data from Coleman (1964).

terms of unobserved, continuous variables. The approach presented here provides a logical way to incorporate substantive knowledge about a phenomenon into models for studying associations between multiple discrete variables. In the examples presented, we show how to use the models in both an exploratory and confirmatory fashion, how to study group differences in terms of underlying variables, and how to obtain measurements for individuals on the latent variables. Measurement of individuals' values on the latent variables is a byproduct of the estimation of the parameters of log-multiplicative models. Additional possibilities include adding individual level covariates to the models (Anderson and Böckenholt 2000) and imposing inequality restrictions on the category scale values (Ritov and Gilula 1991; Vermunt 1998).

With the conditional Gaussian assumption, the marginal distribution of the continuous variables is a mixture of multivariate normals. This differs from traditional factor analytic and item response theory models where the marginal distribution of latent variables is typically assumed to be multivariate normal. In the traditional models, the conditional distribution within a cell is a mixture of multivariate normals. The models proposed here are alternatives to the more traditional factor analytic models. In some cases, the proposed models may be more appropriate or at least as appropriate as traditional models. Which is better is both a theoretical and an empirical question whose answer depends on the particular phenomenon being studied. A full discussion of the relationships between the latent variable models proposed here and more traditional models is beyond the scope of this paper. Thus, areas for future work include studying the relationship between the log-multiplicative models and traditional factor analytic and item response theory models, and further exploration of the use of log-multiplicative models to estimate individuals' values on latent variables.

APPENDIX A: READING MODELS FROM GRAPHS

Reading log-multiplicative models from graphs is essentially the same for both homogeneous and heterogeneous models. For all models, marginal effect terms are always included for each discrete variable, as well as a constant to ensure that the fitted values sum up to the observed total. In the graphs, the lines connecting the observed and latent variables have been labeled by the corresponding scale values. The interaction terms in the log-multiplicative models equal half the sum of the products of pairs of scale values and the covariance between latent variables from all directed paths between observed variables. There are two types of paths in the graphs: paths from a discrete variable back to itself and paths from one discrete variable to another. Both types of paths may involve either one latent variable or a pair of latent variables.

To illustrate, consider the multiple latent variables per indicator model depicted in Figure 4. The log-multiplicative model for this graph is

$$\begin{aligned}\log(P(\mathbf{a})) = {} & \lambda + \lambda^*_{1(j_1)} + \lambda^*_{2(j_2)} + \lambda^*_{3(j_3)} + \lambda^*_{4(j_4)} \\ & + \sigma_{11}\left[\nu_{1(j_1)1}\nu_{2(j_2)1} + \nu_{1(j_1)1}\nu_{3(j_3)1} + \nu_{2(j_2)1}\nu_{3(j_3)1}\right] \\ & + \sigma_{22}\left[\nu_{2(j_2)2}\nu_{3(j_3)2} + \nu_{2(j_2)2}\nu_{4(j_4)2} + \nu_{3(j_3)2}\nu_{4(j_4)2}\right] \\ & + \sigma_{12}\left[\nu_{1(j_1)1}\nu_{2(j_2)2} + \nu_{1(j_1)1}\nu_{3(j_3)2} + \nu_{1(j_1)1}\nu_{4(j_4)2}\right. \\ & \quad + \nu_{2(j_2)1}\nu_{3(j_3)2} + \nu_{2(j_2)1}\nu_{4(j_4)2} + \nu_{3(j_3)1}\nu_{2(j_2)2} \\ & \quad \left. + \nu_{3(j_3)1}\nu_{4(j_4)2}\right], \end{aligned} \tag{35}$$

where $\lambda^*_{i(j_i)} = \lambda_{i(j_i)} + (1/2)\sum_m \sum_{m'} \sigma_{mm'} \nu_{i(j_i)m} \nu_{i(j_i)m'}$.

With respect to paths from a variable back to itself, when the path goes through a single latent variable, this results in terms such as $(1/2)\sigma_{11}\nu^2_{1(j_1)1}$. This term comes from the directed path $A_1 \rightarrow \Theta_1 \rightarrow A_1$. The covariance of a variable with itself is the variance, so we multiply $(1/2)\nu^2_{1(j_1)1}$ by the variance of Θ_1. Paths from a variable back to itself that involve a pair of latent variables are found only in multiple factors per indicator models. For example, the directed paths $A_2 \rightarrow \Theta_1 \rightarrow \Theta_2 \rightarrow A_2$ and $A_2 \rightarrow \Theta_2 \rightarrow \Theta_1 \rightarrow A_2$ result in the term $(1/2)\sigma_{12}\nu_{2(j_2)1}\nu_{2(j_2)2} + (1/2)\sigma_{12}\nu_{2(j_2)2}\nu_{2(j_2)1} = \sigma_{12}\nu_{2(j_2)1}\nu_{2(j_2)2}$. In homogeneous models, terms that arise from paths from a variable back to itself are absorbed into the marginal effects; however, in heterogeneous models, they are not necessarily absorbed (an example of this is given in Section 6.2).

The second type of path, which connects two different discrete variables, may involve either one latent variable or a pair of correlated latent variables. In the former case, the association parameter is the variance of the latent variable, and in the later, the association parameter is the covariance. For example, the term $\sigma_{11}\nu_{1(j_1)1}\nu_{2(j_2)1}$ results from the directed paths $A_1 \rightarrow \Theta_1 \rightarrow A_2$ and $A_2 \rightarrow \Theta_1 \rightarrow A_1$. The term $\sigma_{12}\nu_{1(j_1)1}\nu_{2(j_2)2}$ results from the directed paths $A_1 \rightarrow \Theta_1 \rightarrow \Theta_2 \rightarrow A_2$ and $A_2 \rightarrow \Theta_2 \rightarrow \Theta_1 \rightarrow A_1$.

As discussed in Section 5, some heterogeneous models may include extra terms due to $|\boldsymbol{\Sigma}(\mathbf{a})|^{1/2}$ in equation (30).

APPENDIX B: MAXIMUM-LIKELIHOOD ESTIMATION

The maximum-likelihood estimation of the parameters of the log-multiplicative models presented in this paper is described here. The starting point is the most general, homogeneous latent variable model, which was given in equation (25). All other (homogeneous) latent variable models can be derived from this model by imposing fixed-value restrictions on some parameters—for instance, by fixing particular sets of category scores to zero, particular variances to one, or particular covariances to zero. The heterogeneous models can be estimated by the same procedure described here. The only difference is that some of the maximum-likelihood equations differ slightly.

Assuming either a multinomial or Poisson sampling scheme, the likelihood equations for the parameters $\lambda^*_{i(j_i)}$, σ_{mm}, $\sigma_{mm'}$, and $\nu_{i(j_i)m}$, which equal zero at the maximum value of the likelihood function, are

$$\frac{\partial \log L}{\partial \lambda^*_{i(j_i)}} = \sum_{\mathbf{a}|j_i} [n(\mathbf{a}) - P(\mathbf{a})],$$

$$\frac{\partial \log L}{\partial \sigma_{mm}} = \sum_{\mathbf{a}} \sum_{i} \sum_{k>i} \nu_{i(j_i)m} \nu_{k(j_k)m} [n(\mathbf{a}) - P(\mathbf{a})],$$

$$\frac{\partial \log L}{\partial \sigma_{mm'}} = \sum_{\mathbf{a}} \sum_{i} \sum_{k\neq i} \nu_{i(j_i)m} \nu_{k(j_k)m'} [n(\mathbf{a}) - P(\mathbf{a})],$$

$$\frac{\partial \log L}{\partial \nu_{i(j_i)m}} = \sum_{\mathbf{a}|j_i} \sum_{k\neq i} \sum_{m'} \sigma_{mm'} \nu_{k(j_k)m'} [n(\mathbf{a}) - P(\mathbf{a})],$$

respectively. Here, $n(\mathbf{a})$ denotes an observed cell entry, $\sum_{\mathbf{a}}$ indicates the summation over all cells, and $\sum_{\mathbf{a}|j_i}$ indicates the summation over the cells in which variable A_i has the value $a_{i(j_i)}$.

A simple algorithm to solve these maximum-likelihood equations is the unidimensional Newton algorithm. This procedure is implemented in an experimental version of the program ℓ_{EM} (Vermunt 1997). We have found that this iterative method, which has also been used by others to obtain ML estimates of log-multiplicative models (for instance, see Goodman 1979; Clogg 1982; Becker 1989), works well for the models discussed in this paper. The method involves updating one parameter at a time fixing the other parameters at their current value. A unidimensional Newton update of a particular parameter, say γ, at the tth iteration cycle is of the form

$$\gamma^{(t)} = \gamma^{(t-1)} - \frac{\partial \log L/\partial\gamma}{\partial^2 \log L/\partial^2\gamma},$$

where the derivatives are evaluated at the current values of all model parameters. The relevant second-order derivatives for the parameters appearing in equation (25) are

$$\frac{\partial^2 \log L}{\partial^2 \lambda^*_{i(j_i)}} = -\sum_{\mathbf{a}|j_i} P(\mathbf{a}),$$

$$\frac{\partial^2 \log L}{\partial^2 \sigma_{mm}} = -\sum_{\mathbf{a}}\sum_{i}\sum_{k>i}[\nu_{i(j_i)m}\nu_{k(j_k)m}]^2 P(\mathbf{a}),$$

$$\frac{\partial^2 \log L}{\partial^2 \sigma_{mm'}} = -\sum_{\mathbf{a}}\sum_{i}\sum_{k\neq i}[\nu_{i(j_i)m}\nu_{k(j_k)m'}]^2 P(\mathbf{a}),$$

$$\frac{\partial^2 \log L}{\partial^2 \nu_{i(j_i)m}} = -\sum_{\mathbf{a}|j_i}\sum_{k\neq i}\sum_{m'}[\sigma_{mm'}\nu_{k(j_k)m'}]^2 P(\mathbf{a}).$$

The location and scaling constraints, which are necessary for identification, can be imposed at each iteration cycle after updating a particular set of λ or ν parameters.

As mentioned in Section 2.3, we sometimes might want to impose a scaling condition on a particular set of the ν parameters that is not necessary for identification. Suppose that the scaling of the mth set of category scores for variable A_i is a model restriction. In such a situation, we have to work with Lagrange terms to obtain the restricted ML solution. The Lagrange likelihood equations for the $\nu_{i(j_i)m}$ parameters, which equal zero at the saddle point of the Lagrange likelihood function, are

$$\frac{\partial \log L}{\partial \nu_{i(j_i)m}} + \beta_{im1} + 2\nu_{i(j_i)m}\beta_{im2}.$$

Here, β_{im1} and β_{im2} are the Lagrange parameters corresponding to the location and scaling restrictions (i.e., $\sum_{j_i} \nu_{i(j_i)m} = 0$ and $\sum_{j_i} \nu^2_{i(j_i)m} = 1$).

Only a slight modification of the unidimensional Newton method is needed with these types of restrictions. Setting the Lagrange likelihood equations for the $\nu_{i(j_i)m}$'s equal to zero, we can compute β_{im1} and β_{im2} by a simple linear regression. This can be seen by rewriting the resulting equations as

$$-\frac{\partial \log L}{\partial \nu_{i(j_i)m}} = \beta_{im1} + 2\nu_{i(j_i)m}\beta_{im2}. \tag{36}$$

The provisional values for β_{im1} and β_{im2} can be obtained by regressing the term on the left-hand side of equation (36) on $2\nu_{i(j_i)m}$. After obtaining new Lagrange terms, the ν's are updated and subsequently centered and rescaled. A nice feature of the Lagrange terms is that they converge to zero if the corresponding location or scaling constraint is necessary for identification. In the models presented in this paper, this is always the case for the location constraints but not always for the scaling conditions.

Since the log-likelihood function of log-multiplicative models is not concave, there may be local maxima. Therefore, models should be estimated multiple times using different sets of random starting values to prevent reporting a local solution.

Contrary to multidimensional Newton methods, the above simple estimation method does not provide standard errors or covariances of the parameter estimates as a by-product. Asymptotic standard errors and covariances of parameter estimates can be obtained by means of jackknifing, which is a method that has been used by a number of authors for this purpose in the context of log-multiplicative models (e.g., Anderson and Böckenholt 2000; Clogg and Shihadeh 1994; Eliason 1995).

REFERENCES

Afifi, Abdelmonem A., and R.M. Elashoff. 1969. "Multivariate Two Sample Tests with Dichotomous and Continuous Variables. I. The Location Model." *Annals of Mathematical Statistics* 40:290–98.

Agresti, Alan. 1984. *Analysis of Ordinal Categorical Data*. New York: Wiley.

———. 1997. "A Model for Repeated Measurements of a Multivariate Binary Response." *Journal of the American Statistical Association* 92:315–21.

Andersen, Erling B. 1988. "Comparison of Latent Structure Models." Pp. 207–29 in *Latent Trait and Latent Class Models*, edited by R. Langeheine and J. Rost. New York: Plenum Press.

Anderson, Carolyn J., and Ulf Böckenholt. In press. "Graphical Regression Models for Polytomous Variables." *Psychometrika*.

Becker, Mark P. 1989. "Models for the Analysis of Association in Multivariate Contingency Tables." *Journal of the American Statistical Association* 84:1014–19.

Clogg, Clifford C. 1982. "Some Models for the Analysis of Association in Multiway Cross-classifications Having Ordered Categories." *Journal of the American Statistical Association* 77:803–15.

Clogg, Clifford C., and Edward Shihadeh. 1994. *Statistical Models for Ordinal Variables*. Thousand Oaks, CA: Sage.

Coleman, James S. 1964. *Introduction to Mathematical Sociology*. Glencoe, IL: Free Press.

Davis, James A., and Tom W. Smith. 1996. *General Social Surveys 1972–1996: Cumulative Codebook*. Chicago, IL: National Opinion Research Center.

Edwards, David. 1995. *Introduction to Graphical Modelling*. New York: Springer-Verlag.

Eliason, Scott R. 1995. "Modeling Manifest and Latent Dimensions of Association in Two-way Cross-classifications." *Sociological Methods and Research* 24:30–67.

Goodman, Leo A. 1978. *Analyzing Qualitative/Categorical Data: Log-linear Models and Latent Structure Analysis*. London: Addison-Wesley.

———. 1979. "Simple Models for the Analysis of Association in Cross-classifications Having Ordered Categories." *Journal of the American Statistical Association* 74:537–52.

———. 1985. "The Analysis of Cross-classified Data Having Ordered and/or Unordered Categories: Association Models, Correlation Models, and Asymmetry Models for Contingency Tables with or without Missing Entries." *Annals of Statistics* 13:10–69.

Krzanowski, Wojtek J. 1980. "Mixtures of Continuous and Categorical Variables in Discriminant Analysis." *Biometrics* 36:493–99.

———. 1983. "Distance Between Populations Using Mixed Continuous and Categorical Variables." *Biometrika* 70:235–43.

———. 1988. *Principles of Multivariate Analysis*. New York: Oxford Press.

Langeheine, Rolf. 1988. "New Developments in Latent Class Theory." Pp. 77–108 in *Latent Trait and Latent Class Models*, edited by Rolf Langeheine and Jürgen Rost. New York: Plenum Press.

Lauritzen, Steffen L. 1996. *Graphical Models*. New York: Oxford University Press.

Lauritzen, Steffen L., and Nancy Wermuth. 1989. "Graphical Models for Associations Between Variables, Some of Which are Qualitative and Some Quantitative." *The Annals of Statistics* 17:31–57.

Olkin, Ingram, and R.F. Tate. 1960. "Multivariate Correlation Models with Mixed Discrete and Continuous Variables." *The Annals of Mathematical Statistics* 32: 448–65.

Ritov, Yaacov, and Zvi Gilula. 1991. "The Order-restricted *RC* Model for Ordered Contingency Tables: Estimation and Testing for Fit." *Annals of Statistics* 19: 2090–101.

Vermunt, Jeroen K. 1997. ℓ_{EM}: A General Program for the Analysis of Categorical Data. The Netherlands: Tilburg University. Internet: http://cwis.kub.nl/~fsw_1/mto/.

———. 1998. "*RC* Association Models with Ordered Row and Column Scores: Estimation and Testing." Presented at the 21st Biennial Conference of the Society for Multivariate Analysis in the Behavioral Sciences, Leuven, Belgium, July 15–17, 1998.

Wermuth, Nancy, and Steffen L. Lauritzen. 1990. "Discussion of Papers by Edwards, Wermuth, and Lauritzen." *Journal of the Royal Statistical Society* ser. B, 52:51–72.

Whittaker, Joe. 1989. "Discussion of Paper by van der Heijden, de Falguerolles, and de Leeuw." *Applied Statistics* 38:278–79.

———. 1990. *Graphical Models in Applied Mathematical Multivariate Statistics*. New York: Wiley.

4

ALGEBRAIC REPRESENTATIONS OF BELIEFS AND ATTITUDES II: MICROBELIEF MODELS FOR DICHOTOMOUS BELIEF DATA

*John Levi Martin**
James A. Wiley†

It may often be the case that the beliefs about which survey researchers query respondents are composed of discrete components, such that holding all of the components is necessary to give a "yes" response. Simple logical relations, which some researchers have proposed may structure belief data, may obtain between these components, and not between the beliefs that are actually measured. This paper demonstrates that an algebraic inversion of a data matrix, first used in test theory by Haertel and Wiley (1993), can be seen as a unique and interpretable decomposition that can recover information regarding the compositional formulas of the measured beliefs as well as the logical relations between the unobserved components. The inversion is illustrated with a set of data from the GSS. Finally, the conditions under which related techniques are then helpful or not helpful for analyzing survey data are discussed.

We would like to thank Ed Haertel, David Wiley, and Ronald Breiger for their comments and critique, two anonymous reviewers, and the editors of *Sociological Methodology* for their comments, which have greatly improved this paper, and great thanks to Phillipa Pattison, who drew our attention to the parallels between this work and work in Boolean matrix theory. Correspondence to John Levi Martin, Rutgers—The State University of New Jersey, Sociology, 54 Joyce Kilmer Avenue, Piscataway, NJ 08854-8045; jlmartin@rci.rutgers.edu.

*Rutgers University
†The Public Health Institute

1. INTRODUCTION

It is commonly understood in survey research that a number of analytically separable components may lie behind respondents' choice of any one response category as opposed to another. These latent variables cannot be directly tapped using the questions at hand (though it is of course possible to design future questions to measure them directly); instead, we must use the aggregate distribution across the manifest variables to generate or confirm plausible models pertaining to these latent variables and their interrelations. Almost invariably, these latent variables have been considered to be *continuous*, despite the generally noncontinuous nature of the manifest variables. Most commonly, these latent variables are seen as *factors*, as in factor analysis (Mulaik 1972; for an example, see Stimson 1975), or as *traits*, as in Item Response Theory (Rasch 1966, Birnbaum 1968; for examples, see Duncan 1984). A multidimensional IRT or factor analysis solution usually involves reducing the complexity of data with M manifest variables to one involving L latent variables, $L<M$. In addition to the parsimony gained, we also have important information as to how respondents are thinking—they can be regarded as weighing (or being moved by) a number of issues or sentiments, and we can even estimate the relative weight each issue or sentiment has when it comes to answering any particular question.

It is perhaps surprising, but there has been much less attention given to representing manifest beliefs in terms of components when those components are thought to be discrete. Yet there is certainly reason to suspect that such discrete components can exist (for one theoretical argument, see Zaller 1992). This paper demonstrates that an algebraic approach wedded to latent-class analysis, first employed in test theory by Haertel and Wiley (1993), can retrieve such components for a set of survey items. Further, it is also possible to retrieve information regarding the internal organization of these components. Since Haertel and Wiley did not present an axiomatic derivation or an algorithm to carry out this procedure, we introduce them here and illustrate them with a set of items from the General Social Survey.

The techniques laid out here may thus be considered one way to approach the problem of retrieving information about the social reasoning producing some matrix of observed data (see D'Andrade 1976 for one of the first such attempts). We demonstrate that this technique is actually closely related to previous attempts to uncover logical relations between beliefs using aggregate data but solves a number of problems—namely, the indeterminacy of solutions, the absence of a justifiable approximation, or the inability to retrieve unobserved components—that made the application of such techniques to survey data unlikely. We also compare this approach to other algebraic techniques and demonstrate that it retrieves different information—and for certain cases, more information—than do these other approaches.

2. DEFINITIONS

In this section and the next, we present a set of algebraic structures that link manifest dichotomous responses to latent discrete components. Our notation is summarized in Appendix A; we denote vectors and matrices in bold font, sets and elements of sets in italics, and scalar variables and indices in roman font. Certain proofs are necessary to demonstrate that it is indeed possible to re-create unobserved components from observed data, and that this re-creation is unique. To facilitate exposition, we relegate theorems, proofs, and most formal definitions to Appendix B. For purposes of convenience, we treat all vectors and matrices as Boolean, and all matrix operations as Boolean (i.e., $1+1=1$). We begin by proposing a reasonable version of the way in which discrete components might aggregate into the beliefs about which we query respondents. We then demonstrate the necessary algebraic consequences of this definition, and finally, how we may make use of these consequences to retrieve information about the discrete components of beliefs from a set of observed data.

Let us begin by considering the case in which each respondent can hold or not hold any or all of a set of K beliefs, $\beta_1, \beta_2 \ldots \beta_K$. In addition, we allow for the existence of logical relations between these beliefs termed "precedence," so that it may be impossible to hold one belief without first holding another (or some set of others). Thus far, we replicate the situation analyzed by Wiley and Martin (1999). But Wiley and Martin (1999), like most formal analysts of qualitative data, assumed that each item measured a distinct belief. Now, however, we consider the situation in which we have not actually asked our respondents questions that tap each of these K beliefs individually. Instead, our actual items combine more than one belief, and hence these beliefs may be considered to be discrete components of the response given to any question.

This does not need to be due to poor questionnaire design (e.g., double-barreled questions)—it is quite plausible that many beliefs may be seen as decomposable into subbeliefs, each of which must be held in order to hold the overarching belief. In some situations, a belief may be functionally unitary, while in others, it is possible to break it down into semi-independent components. Indeed, this is the premise of philosophical analysis in the technical sense (e.g., Kant 1950 [1787]: 48, 152). Hence the basis for the distinction between a measured belief, which we shall call a "macrobelief" (denoted as α) and an unmeasured component, which we shall call a "microbelief" and denote β, is simply that we have not designed an instrument to tap the latter individually. Instead, we tap the joint presence of a set of microbeliefs via the presence of macrobeliefs they compose. In particular, if a set of microbeliefs $\{\beta\}$ are components of any α, each and every one of these microbeliefs must be held in order for the macrobelief to be held. Thus any microbelief is a *necessary* component of any macrobelief of which it is a component; holding all the microbelief components is *sufficient* for one to hold the macrobelief.[1]

For example, the macrobelief "large differences in income are necessary for America's prosperity" might be composed of two microbeliefs: (β_1) "people work hard only when they stand to benefit materially"; and (β_2) "better workers often get higher salaries." Someone who held both of these would agree that "large differences in income are necessary for America's prosperity," but a person who lacked β_1 would believe that there are other motivations that may lead Americans to work hard, and a person who lacked β_2 would believe that since higher income does not go to the meretricious, large income differentials will not provide the needed incentives.

We go on to demonstrate that it is possible to use algebraic techniques to discover meaningful decompositions of macrobeliefs into microbeliefs. Such decompositions, however, only have explanatory utility when we examine a set of macrobeliefs that presents some degree of overlap in components. That is, just as with factor analysis or multidimensional IRT analysis, we wish to examine a set of items that are related but not identical. For example, consider four macrobeliefs ($\alpha_1, \alpha_2, \alpha_3, \alpha_4$) incorporating a total of four microbeliefs ($\beta_1, \beta_2, \beta_3, \beta_4$). We can encapsulate these relations of incorporation in a 4×4 matrix (see Table 1), which shows which microbelief is incorporated in which macrobelief, where a "1" designates incorporation and a "0" lack of incorporation. Thus macrobelief α_1 incorporates microbeliefs β_2 and β_3. We will denote this matrix **D** with elements d_{ij}, where $d_{ij}=1$ iff macrobelief α_j incorporates microbelief β_i.

[1]In this paper, we consider only the case in which the macrobeliefs and microbeliefs can be represented by dichotomies, although we draw attention to representations that allow the microbeliefs to be ordinal.

TABLE 1
Illustrative Microbelief Structure of Macrobeliefs

Microbelief	Macrobelief α_1	α_2	α_3	α_4
β_1	0	1	1	1
β_2	1	1	0	0
β_3	1	0	0	0
β_4	0	0	0	1

This matrix **D** contains a complete summary of the rules for transforming bundles of microbeliefs into a particular pattern of the holding or not holding of macrobeliefs—every possible bundle of microbeliefs, which we shall call a *microbelief state*, implies a consequent set of macrobeliefs, which we shall call a *macrobelief state*. For example, the combination of microbeliefs β_1, β_2, and β_4 transforms, subject to the rules incorporated in **D**, into a macrobelief state in which the first belief is not held, but the others are.

The essence of the technique we introduce can parsimoniously be stated as follows: Given this definition of the mapping from microbelief components to macrobeliefs, as long as the microbeliefs are related to one another in accordance with some rather plausible rules, the set of possible microbelief states forms a particular algebraic structure called a *distributive lattice*; and the set of all macrobelief states forms a different algebraic structure (a potentially nondistributive lattice). Given this, we may not only (1) deduce the possible macrobelief states given the microbelief states but also (2) for a set of macrobelief states, uncover a plausible set of unobserved microbelief components. We go on to illustrate these in order.

3. MAPPINGS BETWEEN MICROBELIEF AND MACROBELIEF STATES

3.1. *From Microbelief to Macrobelief States*

Let us imagine that we have information for each person on whether she holds the ith of K microbeliefs, denoted β_i; we express this through an indicator variable $z_i=1$ if β_i is held, and 0 otherwise, and compose a vector **z** of z_i, $i=1, 2, \ldots K$. Let **Z** denote the matrix whose rows consist of all **z**'s observed in some sample. While there are 2^K possible **z** states for any set of K beliefs, we do not necessarily observe all of these, for there may be logical (or sociological) relations between some of the microbeliefs, such that holding one is impossible if one does not hold some other(s).

In particular, define a transitive, reflexive, and antisymmetric binary relation $\rightarrow$ which we will term "precedence" between microbeliefs as follows: $\beta_i \rightarrow \beta_j$ iff $z_i=0 \Rightarrow$ (read implies) $z_j=0$ for all $\mathbf{z}$.[2] In other words, one cannot hold microbelief β_j without first holding microbelief β_i. The set of microbeliefs $\{\beta\}$ together with the relation $\rightarrow$ forms what is known as a *partially ordered set* (or "poset" for short), which we shall call the microbelief poset (see Appendix B for more detailed and formal definitions). We may denote the set of all possible microbelief states—i.e., subsets of $\{\beta\}$ compatible with the precedence relations in the microbelief poset—as L, and any element of L can be represented in vector form as $\mathbf{z}$. Wiley and Martin (1999) have demonstrated that L is a particular kind of poset, a distributive lattice, in which the transitive, reflexive, and antisymmetric binary relation (here denoted $\leq$) between any $\mathbf{z}_i$ and $\mathbf{z}_j$ consisting of elements z_{ik} and z_{jk} respectively is the Boolean $\leq$: that is, $\mathbf{z}_i \leq \mathbf{z}_j$ iff $z_{ik} \leq z_{jk}\ \forall\ k$. Hence we may term L the "microbelief state lattice."

Any lattice or poset can be represented pictorially as a "Hasse diagram," in which an arrow denotes an unmediated $\leq$ relation; hence an arrow from δ_i to δ_j signifies that δ_j "covers" δ_i (as defined in Appendix B): transitive relations are not explicitly drawn in, but can be assumed. Thus, to continue with the example above, if for our four microbeliefs $\{\beta_1, \ldots \beta_4\}$ we have the following two precedence relations $\beta_2 \rightarrow \beta_3$ and $\beta_1 \rightarrow \beta_4$, we would represent the microbelief poset as shown in Figure 1 (a), and the microbelief state lattice as shown (b) (see Wiley and Martin 1999: 117f).

While for purposes of explication we have assumed that we have information regarding these microbelief states, in general this will not be the case. But each microbelief state maps onto an observed state of M macrobeliefs. (Note that M need not equal K, the number of microbeliefs.) Define an indicator variable $x_i=1$ if the ith macrobelief α_i is held, and $x_i=0$ otherwise. We can term any person's state with regard to the M possible macrobeliefs as a "macrobelief state" and denote it in vector form as

[2] This relation of precedence is identical to the more general definition of "less than," denoted $\leq$, which we use below to describe relations between vectors. However, having the two symbols helps clarify the exposition, by highlighting when we are talking about individual microbeliefs (or macrobeliefs), and when we are talking about states across all microbeliefs (or macrobeliefs).

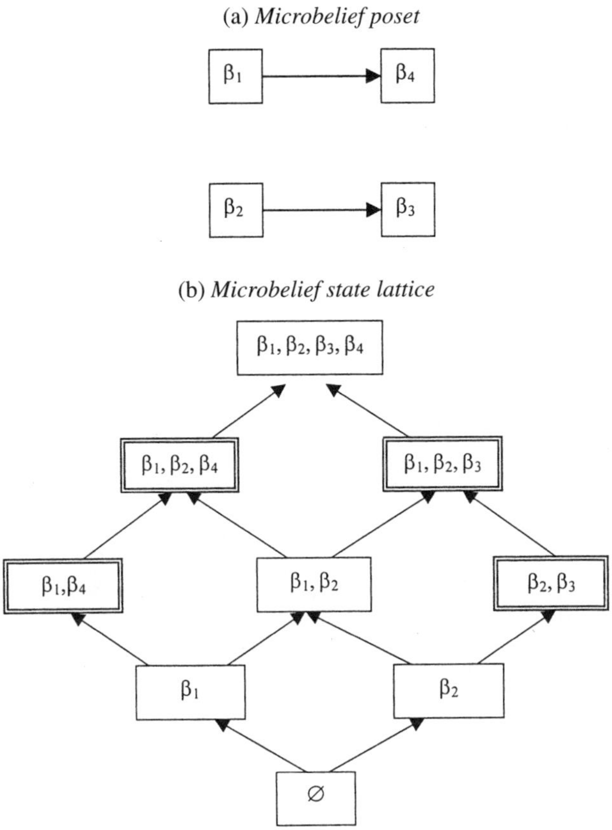

FIGURE 1. Lattice corresponding to microbelief poset.

$\mathbf{x}=[x_1,\ldots x_M]$. (Just as with microbelief states, the macrobelief state refers to the *joint* state of all macrobeliefs.) From every **z** on this lattice, we may construct which macrobeliefs can be observed given the rules incorporated in **D**, according to the simple formula

$$\mathbf{x} = (\mathbf{z}^c\mathbf{D})^c, \tag{1}$$

where the superscript c indicates the complement of the vector (that is, $x_i^c=1$ iff $x_i=0$), and multiplication is Boolean. (In words, for any **z**, only

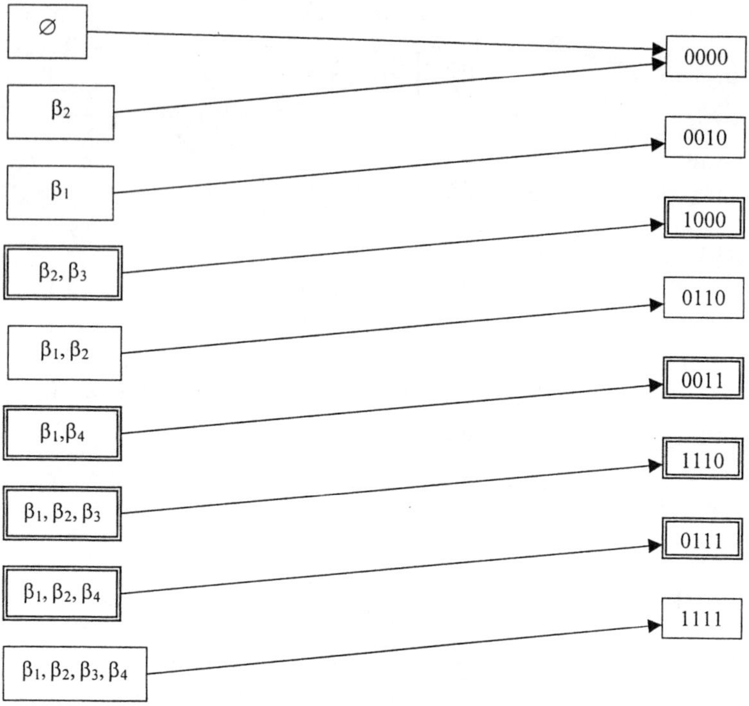

FIGURE 2. Mapping from *L* to *B* via **D**.

those macrobeliefs can be held in which there is no missing microbelief that is required by the mapping rules in **D**.)[3]

Consequently, the matrix **X** whose rows consist of all **x** may also be derived via $\mathbf{X}=(\mathbf{Z}^c\mathbf{D})^c$, though not all **x** in **X** are necessarily unique. **D** thus represents a mapping from **z** (microbelief) states to **x** (macrobelief) states. This mapping for our example, using the **D** matrix in Table 1 and the lattice *L* of Figure 1, is portrayed in Figure 2. In general, the mapping represented by **D** is surjective, since more than one **z**-state can map into a single **x**-state.

This mapping has the following useful implications: (1) The resulting set of macrobelief states (the rows of **X**) forms a lattice which we

[3]We thank Phillipa Pattison for supplying this compact notation, which has greatly simplified exposition and proof.

denote B that is closed under the operation of intersection. Figure 3 takes the states formed by the mapping given in Figure 2 and arranges them in a Hasse diagram; the resulting set is a lattice. (2) As long as no microbeliefs are redundant, such that the omission of one or the fusion of two would produce the same observed structure, and as long as the precedence relations among the microbeliefs satisfy a rather reasonable criterion we term *noninterference* with the mapping **D**, no information about the relations between microbeliefs or about the composition of the macrobeliefs is lost via the mapping, despite the fact that it is not 1-to-1. The principle of noninterference, defined in Appendix B, is simply that the **D** mapping does not call for distinctions between microbeliefs that cannot actually be observed. Thus if macrobelief x_1 requires only microbelief β_1 while macrobelief x_2 requires microbeliefs β_1 and β_2, $\beta_2 \rightarrow \beta_1$ would be an interferent

(a) *Macrobelief state lattice*

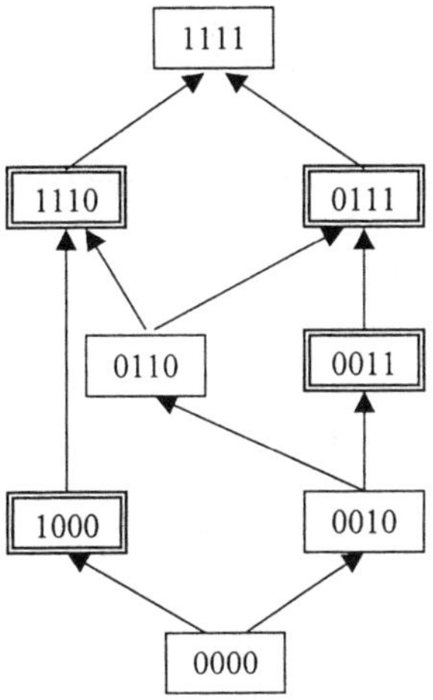

(b) *Inversion applied to this lattice*

MIREs of *B* Complement

$$\mathbf{X}^* = \begin{pmatrix} 1000 \\ 0011 \\ 0111 \\ 1110 \end{pmatrix} \qquad \begin{pmatrix} 0111 \\ 1100 \\ 1000 \\ 0001 \end{pmatrix} = \mathbf{D}$$

FIGURE 3. Macrobelief state lattice.

precedence relation, because we would be unable to distinguish between x_1 and x_2 in the data, though they are in principle distinct.[4]

Our Theorem 2 (Appendix B) proves that B is a lattice (though not necessarily a distributive lattice). We go on to discuss how this allows us to retrieve information about unobserved microbelief components given a lattice of macrobelief states. We note that the techniques we shall lay out below do not require that the observed microbelief states always form a lattice, though they do assume that unobserved states consistent with a lattice structure must have been possible, as we discuss later.

3.2. *A Recovery of Microbeliefs from Observed Macrobeliefs*

Assume that we have a set B of observed macrobelief states $\mathbf{x}$ that is closed under intersection and hence forms a lattice. We may examine the Hasse diagram for B and find all microbelief states that are covered by only one other state—in the example in Figure 3, these are the states that have only one arrow pointing upward. These states, defined as meet-irreducible elements or MIREs in Appendix B, are denoted by double-lined boxes. Let $\{\mathbf{x}^*\}$ be the set of all such MIREs. As Theorem 4 in Appendix B demonstrates, we may re-create the $\mathbf{D}$ matrix quite easily—let $\mathbf{X}^*$ be the matrix whose rows consist of all the elements of $\{\mathbf{x}^*\}$. If we take the complement of $\mathbf{X}^*$, we find that $\mathbf{X}^{*c}=\mathbf{D}$. (The order in which one stacks the MIREs into $\mathbf{X}^*$ is irrelevant, since the rows of $\mathbf{D}$ can be permuted without changing the interpretation.) We call this construction of $\mathbf{D}$ the Haertel-Wiley inversion or HW inversion, since it was introduced by Haertel and D. Wiley (1993). To continue with our example, Figure 3 shows that this inversion does indeed recreate the $\mathbf{D}$ that created this lattice (compare to Table 1). We emphasize that the recovered $\mathbf{D}$ is unique and "minimal," in that it proposes the least number of microbeliefs compatible with the mapping outlined in (1); below, we demonstrate that this also recovers all noninterferent precedence relations between microbeliefs. (These results are proved in Appendix B.)

4. MODEL SELECTION AND FITTING

4.1. *Model Selection*

Up to this point, we have assumed that the observed macrobelief states (or response states) happened to form a lattice. However, in real-world appli-

[4]We note that here we depart from Haertel and Wiley (1993), who did not forbid all interferent precedence relations.

cations, given a set of observations, we may need to add or subtract some response states to produce a lattice structure that is both parsimonious and interpretable. With survey data, which generally has a large number of respondents, this usually involves postulating that some observed response states fall beneath a threshold of importance and can safely be ignored. That is, while for any set of M macrobeliefs about which we have queried respondents, there are 2^M possible belief state vectors, we choose some set $\{\mathbf{x}\}$ of these for our model such that $|\{\mathbf{x}\}|<2^M$. We follow Haertel and Wiley (1993) in proposing that the fact that more than $|\{\mathbf{x}\}|$ response states have been observed is due to response error. (On the importance of the problem of approximation, see Chubb 1986; for different approximation techniques see Duquenne 1996, White 1996.) While each item was designed to tap one macrobelief β_i, it does so imperfectly. The observed response states (henceforward denoted $\{\mathbf{y}\}$) thus differ from the actual macrobelief states $\{\mathbf{x}\}$. We hence need both a way to *generate* a plausible but parsimonious lattice model for any set of data and then a way to *test* that the simplifications entailed by this model are acceptable. We discuss each in turn.

A lattice model may be generated either on *a priori* grounds, or by inspection of the data. An *a priori* specification would be reasonable if one has deliberately written questions to incorporate distinct components or facets expected to be jointly necessary for giving a positive response to any item. One may then on theoretical grounds construct a **D** matrix, which may be used to construct all macrobelief states via equation (1), by letting $\{\mathbf{z}\}$ be all members of the cartesian product $\{0,1\}^K$. (In Appendix B, Corollary 5.1 demonstrates that this maps onto the same *B* as does the smaller microbelief state lattice corresponding to the poset of all noninterferent precedence relations.)

When such *a priori* considerations are not relevant, a testable model may be generated from inspection of the data. Each observed response state $\mathbf{y}$ has a frequency $f(\mathbf{y})$, the number of persons with responses falling into this state. We may rank all observed response states from the most frequent to the least, and begin by selecting a set of the most frequent response states. While such a subset does not necessarily form a lattice, we may create one by adding any states that are formed by all intersections of subsets of this group of states. If this more parsimonious lattice is unable to account for the observed variation (using the latent-class operationalization we describe below), we may continue down the list, and add one or more response states, again, closing our set under intersection. This is somewhat similar to the process whereby factor analysts view a "scree plot" of the decreasing explanatory returns of additional factors during exploratory analysis. In general, one stops at the most parsimonious structure compatible with the data.

4.2. *The Latent-Class Operationalization*

We thus have a model that posits that the underlying response structure is a lattice. But we consider this lattice to be a model for the data, since it is composed of macrobeliefs that we consider to be imperfectly measured by our items. Correspondingly, we assume that the observed response states are probabilistically related to the unobserved macrobelief states according to traditional concepts of latent-class analysis (Lazarsfeld and Henry 1968; Goodman 1974). The latent-class operationalization is identical to that described in Wiley and Martin (1999); here we present a somewhat more condensed description. In essence, we try to account for all the observed data that fall *off* the lattice on the basis of response error from macrobelief states that are *on* the lattice.

Our latent-class model proposes a set of mutually exclusive and exhaustive latent classes, one for each macrobelief state **x** in the lattice *B*. We assume that all responses are conditionally independent, and hence the probability $P[\mathbf{y}|\mathbf{x}]$ of falling into any manifest response state given one's latent macrobelief state is the product of elementary conditional probabilities pertaining to each observed item response. In particular, let $\pi_i = P[y_i = 1 | x_i = 1] = P[y_i = 0 | x_i = 0]$ be the probability that a response to the ith item correctly represents the ith component of the belief state of the respondent. This probability of correct classification is hence a property of the item, is symmetric with regard to the probability of a correct yes and a correct no, and is invariant over macrobelief states. (Other specifications of the elementary misclassification probabilities are possible; for examples, see McCutcheon 1987; Proctor 1970.) Thus $P[\mathbf{y}|\mathbf{x}]$ can be written as

$$P[\mathbf{y}|\mathbf{x}] = \prod_{i=1}^{M} [\pi_i^{x_i y_i + (1-x_i)(1-y_i)}][(1 - \pi_i)^{(x_i - y_i)^2}] \tag{2}$$

The unconditional probability, $P[\mathbf{y}]$, is defined as the sum of products of the form $P[\mathbf{y}|\mathbf{x}]\, P[\mathbf{x}]$ over all **x** in the lattice.

Such a latent-class model, however, can technically fit a set of data by allowing almost all of the observed responses to be due to some form of error. Such a model, whatever the degree of fit, cannot be considered an explanation. Hence we also require that the model's misclassification error (1) be moderate (correct classification probabilities should in general be closer to 1 than to .5); and (2) be theoretically interpretable as response error stemming from misunderstood questions. These are, however, only rather rough and subjective rules of thumb.

We use a version of Clifford Clogg's MLLSA program (Clogg 1977, McCutcheon 1987) to fit the latent-class models, though other similar programs can also be used to fit these models. This routine is integrated with structure building and inverting routines in a program available from the authors.[5] While more complicated models can be fit with other latent-class programs, such as Vermunt's lEM, the models discussed herein can be fitted with extreme ease with this program. We now go on to give an example using an interesting and complex set of data.

5. AN EXAMPLE FROM THE GENERAL SOCIAL SURVEY

For an example of a microstructural analysis of items, we take six of the eight items from a module (EQUAL1 to EQUAL8) on beliefs about economic equality asked in the General Social Survey (Davis and Smith 1988:110ff) in 1984. We eliminated on *a priori* grounds before analysis two items that seemed less connected to the central issues and were also less concrete, one as to whether a person should look out for himself, and another as to whether one is able to live well in America. The sample of persons consists of respondents who gave an *agree* or *disagree* response to all six questions. The item wordings were as follows:

A. "The economy can run only if businessmen make good profits. That benefits everyone in the end."
B. "The government must see to it that everyone has a job and that prices are stable, even if the rights of businessmen have to be restricted."
C. "It is the responsibility of government to meet everyone's needs, even in case of sickness, poverty, unemployment, and old age."
D. "If social welfare benefits such as disability, unemployment compensation, and early retirement pensions are as high as they are now, it only makes people not want to work anymore."

[5]This program, called ELLA, is available from the authors on request. The closure and inversion routines adapted from those originally authored by Edward Haertel are used by his kind permission.

E. "Generally speaking, business profits are distributed fairly in the United States."
F. "If someone has a high social or economic position, that indicates the person has special abilities or great accomplishments."

We collapsed the "strongly agree" and "somewhat agree" categories into "agree" and similarly the "strongly disagree" and "somewhat disagree" categories into "disagree" for illustrative purposes. While in general such dichotomization loses information, we unfortunately do not yet have a rigorous extension to polychotomous data. We coded each item to be 1 if it was in line with laissez-faire economic ideology, and 0 otherwise (thus items B and C are reverse-coded). Of 1473 respondents, 1305 answered all six items in either a positive or negative direction and are included in the analysis. The recoded data are given in Table 2.

We go on to examine a series of substantively meaningful models for the table formed by the cross-classification of these six dichotomies. Model (1) posits that the items are mutually independent. Model (2) posits that the items are interdependent because they all measure one underlying continuous trait using a log-linear Rasch IRT model (Kelderman 1984; Goodman 1990). Model (3) also posits that the items all measure one underlying continuous trait, but allows them to have different discriminating abilities; in return for this increased flexibility, it constrains the latent trait to be normally distributed (the two parameter normal ogive latent-trait model of Bock 1972).[6] Model (4) posits that the items are interdependent because they all measure one underlying *discrete* trait; here we use a Guttman scale model operationalized as a set of latent classes. The same symmetric conditional response structure is used that we discussed above for the lattice models. Model (5) is an unrestricted three-class LCA model, which posits that there are three types of persons in the sample with different marginal propensities to answer any of the six items in a positive direction.[7]

Table 3 presents for each model the likelihood-ratio chi-square, the degrees of freedom, and Raftery's (1985) BIC statistic. BIC, equal to L^2-(df)ln(N), with L^2 the model likelihood-ratio chi-square, df the degrees of freedom of the model, and N the sample size, is a criterion that may be used as a standard for model selection when the models are not

[6] This model was estimated with ℓEM (Vermunt 1997).
[7] We thank a reviewer for drawing our attention to this model's fit to these data.

TABLE 2
GSS Data, Equal Items from 1984

A	B	C	D	E	F	Freq	A	B	C	D	E	F	Freq
0	0	0	0	0	0	51	1	0	0	0	0	0	55
0	0	0	0	0	1	26	1	0	0	0	0	1	52
0	0	0	0	1	0	10	1	0	0	0	1	0	14
0	0	0	0	1	1	6	1	0	0	0	1	1	49
0	0	0	1	0	0	23	1	0	0	1	0	0	27
0	0	0	1	0	1	26	1	0	0	1	0	1	46
0	0	0	1	1	0	3	1	0	0	1	1	0	8
0	0	0	1	1	1	12	1	0	0	1	1	1	52
0	0	1	0	0	0	11	1	0	1	0	0	0	12
0	0	1	0	0	1	6	1	0	1	0	0	1	12
0	0	1	0	1	0	3	1	0	1	0	1	0	3
0	0	1	0	1	1	0	1	0	1	0	1	1	9
0	0	1	1	0	0	8	1	0	1	1	0	0	12
0	0	1	1	0	1	5	1	0	1	1	0	1	14
0	0	1	1	1	0	4	1	0	1	1	1	0	6
0	0	1	1	1	1	4	1	0	1	1	1	1	11
0	1	0	0	0	0	27	1	1	0	0	0	0	45
0	1	0	0	0	1	14	1	1	0	0	0	1	26
0	1	0	0	1	0	3	1	1	0	0	1	0	9
0	1	0	0	1	1	5	1	1	0	0	1	1	30
0	1	0	1	0	0	10	1	1	0	1	0	0	42
0	1	0	1	0	1	4	1	1	0	1	0	1	20
0	1	0	1	1	0	4	1	1	0	1	1	0	11
0	1	0	1	1	1	8	1	1	0	1	1	1	25
0	1	1	0	0	0	40	1	1	1	0	0	0	55
0	1	1	0	0	1	10	1	1	1	0	0	1	29
0	1	1	0	1	0	5	1	1	1	0	1	0	27
0	1	1	0	1	1	3	1	1	1	0	1	1	47
0	1	1	1	0	0	33	1	1	1	1	0	0	54
0	1	1	1	0	1	10	1	1	1	1	0	1	30
0	1	1	1	1	0	9	1	1	1	1	1	0	31
0	1	1	1	1	1	2	1	1	1	1	1	1	57

nested, as is the case for the models of Table 3. The saturated model has a BIC of 0, a model with a BIC below 0 is preferred to the saturated model (even if the chi-square is significant), and the model with the lowest BIC is considered to be the best choice among the models considered. BIC is generally thought to have a tendency to be over-conservative, and may

TABLE 3
List of Models for GSS Data

Model	Likelihood Ratio Chi-sq	Df	BIC
(0) Saturated	0.00	0	0.00
(1) Independence	526.45	57	+117.53
(2) Loglinear Rasch	377.45	51	+11.76
(3) 2 Parameter Normal Ogive	266.38	51	−99.49
(4) Guttman Scale/Latent Class	347.11	51	−18.77
(5) Unrestricted 3 Latent Class	118.08	43	−190.40
(6) Lattice Model	129.14	49	−222.39

give undue preference to more parsimonious models (Raftery 1994; see Weakliem 1999 for an analysis of other shortcomings).

If we use BIC as a criterion for model selection purposes, we find that the model of independence fares quite badly (it is considered worse than the saturated model), while the two parameter normal ogive is preferred to the saturated. (The log-linear Rasch model and the Guttman scale are not very different from the saturated in BIC.) The unrestricted latent-class model and the lattice model do best, with the latter preferred, since it has a somewhat lower BIC. If, however, we test each model on its own merits using classical criteria, we find that all of them are decisively rejected; even the model with the lowest L^2, the unrestricted latent-class model, which fits somewhat better than the lattice model (but uses up additional degrees of freedom), must be rejected at $p<.00001$.

We go on to present the results from this lattice model to illustrate the logic of the decomposition of macrobeliefs into microbeliefs. This lattice model is formed by including the 11 most frequent response states, plus one additional response state that is the intersection of two of these. This model hence includes 12 latent classes, one for each of the macrobelief states. (We choose this lattice, as opposed to one incorporating more states, for ease of exposition, though we note that adding further states allows us to improve the fit of the model somewhat without substantially altering the interpretation.) Above we emphasized that we consider the conditional probabilities of response to be properties of the item, and that misclassification arises because some items are difficult to understand. Consequently, we constrain the misclassification probabilities to be the same for items A, D, and F, which have "if-then" structures, and to be the same for items B and C, which have "even if" structures. Only item E has a simple semantic structure. The retrieved probabilities of correct classification are $\pi_A = \pi_D = \pi_F = .76$; $\pi_B = \pi_C = .85$; and $\pi_E = .87$. It is gratifying not only that the probabilities of correct classification are reasonably high, but also that they seem to be higher for the structurally simpler items.[8]

This lattice is presented in Figure 4; each lattice node represents a macrobelief state **x**, with values for x_1 to x_6, corresponding to the items A through F presented above. Inside each node, we give not only the state **x** but the percentage of the population estimated to be in this macrobelief state (the latent-class probability). The nodes with the double-outline are the MIREs as defined above. This Hasse diagram may be interpreted as the paths by which a person who did not hold any of the pro–laissez faire beliefs might be persuaded to accept all of them.

In Table 4, we present the **D** matrix derived by inverting this lattice in accord with Theorem 4; to facilitate an interpretive analysis of the structure of each macrobelief, we present the matrix with "yes" in cell d_{ij} if $d_{ij} = 1$, blank otherwise. Inspection confirms that the complements of the rows of **D** are the MIREs of Figure 4. In Table 5 we propose a content for each component microbelief, based upon inspection of Table 4. Table 6 then summarizes the construction of each macrobelief. Thus, for example, we argue that the belief that it is not the government's responsibility to ensure full employment and low inflation differs from the last four beliefs in lacking a component of faith in the adequacy of the economic system for distinctly *personal* (as opposed to macroeconomic) outcomes.

Our Theorem 5 demonstrates that we can retrieve all noninterferent precedence relations among the microbeliefs from the **D** matrix. We now illustrate the results of this retrieval for these data. Inspection of **D** demonstrates that there is no case in which a macrobelief incorporates *b*, *c*, *d*, *e*, or *f* without also incorporating *a*. Similarly, while there is a state incorporating microbelief *c* without incorporating *d* (Item E), the reverse is not true. It is therefore *compatible* with our observations that microbelief *a* precedes all the rest, and that microbelief *c* precedes *d*. When we employ Theorem 5 to retrieve the most restrictive partial order of microbeliefs, we come up with the poset shown in Figure 5. While it is not necessary that these precedence relations hold among the microbeliefs, no additional precedence relations are compatible with the inversion.

[8] Further inspection demonstrates that the item with the highest misclassification is D, which contains a negative phrasing, known by cognitive scientists to increase processing complexity (Wason 1959).

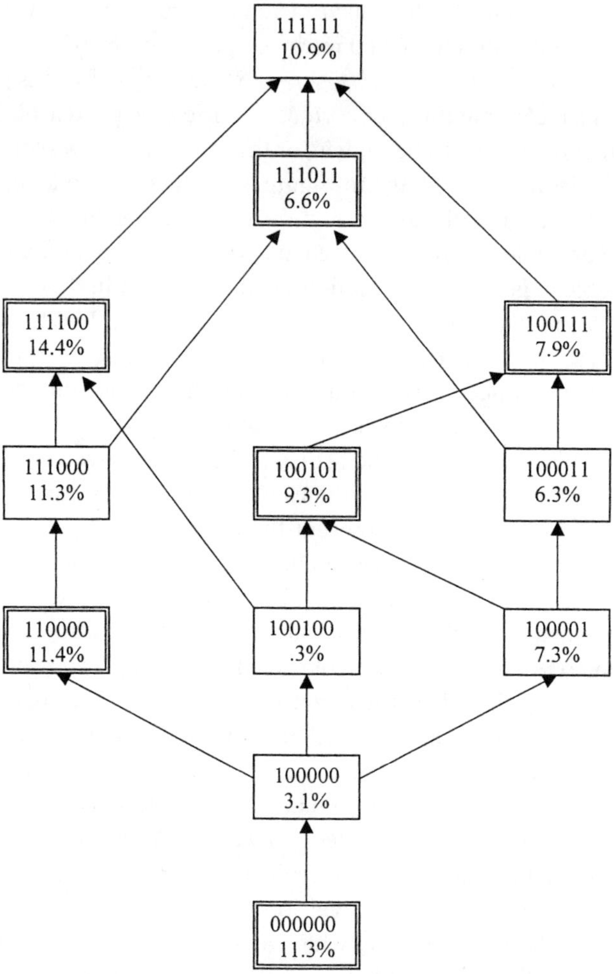

FIGURE 4. Hypothesized belief state lattice for GSS questions on economic inequality.

There is an evident logic to the poset of microbeliefs. The first microbelief, which precedes all others, has to do with general favorability toward business; there is then a split between belief in the adequacy of the system on the *personal* level (b), and the adequacy of the system on the *macroeconomic* level (c). The former (b) precedes more specific beliefs regarding the personal effects of the economic system, one having to do with meritocracy (e) and the other having to do with privation-as-incentive

TABLE 4
D Matrix

Micro-beliefs	Business profits benefit all	The government should NOT manage the economy	Our needs are NOT government's responsibility	Social welfare benefits are a disincentive	Business profits are distributed fairly	Social standing is due to ability
a	yes	yes	yes	yes	yes	yes
b			yes	yes	yes	yes
c		yes	yes		yes	
d		yes	yes			
e					yes	yes
f				yes		

(f), while the latter (c) precedes a more specific belief regarding government regulation of the macroeconomic system (d).

In sum, the approach outlined here allows for the retrieval of information about the latent, discrete components of dichotomous responses. It also gives us information about a possible partial ordering of these latent components. While this technique will not be applicable for all data sets, it may be able to shed considerable light on some otherwise intractable cases. We now wish to discuss the relation of this method to other related algebraic approaches, and demonstrate that this approach connects two different versions of formal analysis, while having certain advantages in the application to survey data.

TABLE 5
Interpretation of Microbeliefs

a: Generally pro-business attitude (or at least not categorically anti-business).
b: The outcomes of the economic system for persons are basically acceptable.
c: The outcomes of the economic system in specifically national economic terms are acceptable.
d: The government has no role to play in regulating the economic system.
e: The existing system is meritocratic.
f: People are moved only by fear of privation.

TABLE 6
Interpretation of Macrobeliefs

Macrobelief	Incorporated Microbeliefs
Business profits benefit all.	Pro-business
No government economic regulation.	Pro-business System is economically acceptable. Government belongs out of economics.
Government shouldn't meet needs.	Pro-business System is economically acceptable. System is personally acceptable. Government belongs out of economics.
Welfare is disincentive.	Pro-business System is personally acceptable. Motivation requires fear.
Profits are distributed fairly.	Pro-business System is economically acceptable. System is personally acceptable. System is meritocratic.
Standing is based on ability.	Pro-business System is personally acceptable. System is meritocratic.

6. RELATION TO OTHER SYSTEMS

6.1. *Partial Order Models*

First of all, we point out that the structures discussed here may be seen as a more general case of the lattices discussed in Wiley and Martin (1999). We began by proposing that the partial ordering discussed by Wiley and Martin held not for observed beliefs but for their unobserved components. However, we may also compare the two approaches in their treatment of the macrobeliefs. In general, the models presented here are more parsimonious than the models introduced by Wiley and Martin (1999), in that they allow us to rule out more macrobelief states than does a model that requires only that the macrobeliefs be partially ordered. These models hence may be more informative than the partial order models.

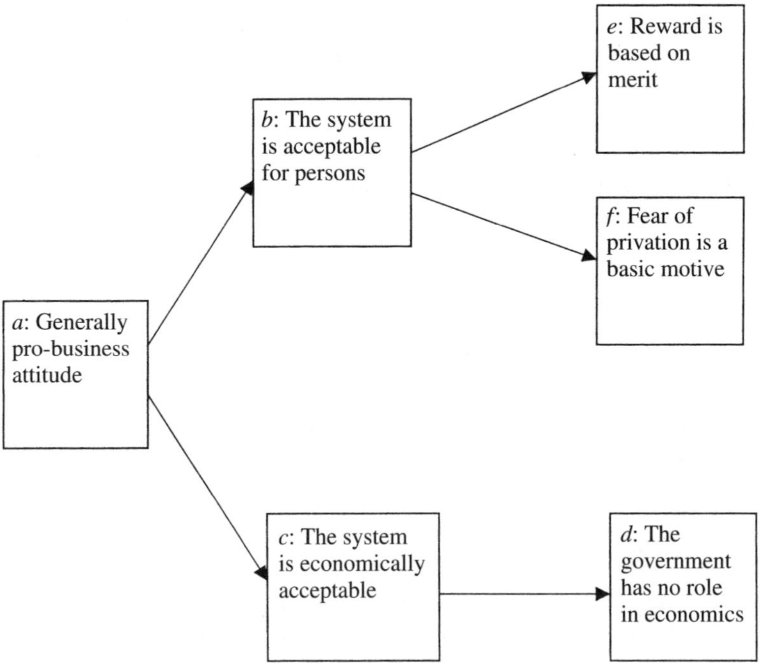

FIGURE 5. Poset of all noninterferent precedence relations.

If, like Wiley and Martin, we define a relation of precedence between macrobeliefs (denoted $\alpha_i \rightarrow \alpha_j$) to mean that it is impossible to hold α_j without first holding α_i, we find that just as we retrieved all possible binary relations of precedence between *microbeliefs* from the **D** matrix, we may also retrieve the binary relations of precedence between *macrobeliefs*, using the simple rule $\alpha_i \rightarrow \alpha_j$ iff there is no microbelief that α_i incorporates but α_j does not. For example, given the data analyzed above, an inspection of the **D** matrix in Table 4 demonstrates that item A precedes all others, item B precedes item C, and item F precedes item E. These precedence relations are observed in the macrobelief state lattice of Figure 4. But the distributive lattice a la Wiley and Martin that would correspond to these precedence relations would be far larger than the lattice presented in Figure 4. Response states that are compatible with these precedence relations, such as [$x_A = x_B = x_D = 1$; $x_C = x_E = x_F = 0$], are ruled out by the lattice in Figure 4. It is only by postulating that the relations of partial ordering hold not for the observed macrobeliefs but for their unobserved microbelief components, that we can parsimoniously account for the observed data.

However, it is still possible for the HW inversion to recover a macrobelief state lattice that is compatible with an underlying partial order of macrobeliefs. If the columns of **D** satisfy a condition we define as "set dependence" in Appendix B, the macrobelief state lattice will *not* be distributive. We can illustrate this condition by inspecting the example of a **D** matrix above (Table 1), in which the microbelief requirements for α_2 are satisfied by the combination (i.e., union) of the requirements for α_1 and α_3, though neither the requirements for α_1 alone nor those for α_3 include all of α_2's requirements. A consequence is that the belief state (1010), which is the union of (1000) and (0010), is inadmissible—i.e., not a member of B—so that B is not closed under union (this is proved in our Lemma 6.2).

If **D** is not set dependent, then B will be closed under union, and hence the special case of a distributive lattice that can be represented by a set of beliefs partially ordered under a precedence relation. Put another way, if a search for a set of response patterns happens to lead to a structure closed under union, this may be taken as strong evidence that each belief has been tapped with a unique item, and hence that there is little utility gained in decomposing macrobeliefs into components (see Theorem 6); it is outside of this special case that the techniques outlined in this paper add information. Further, these techniques are not only more general, they may be seen as "wholly" general, in that they make use of all the algebraic information contained in a Boolean matrix (that is, the row space). Because of this, there are interesting connections to other work which we explore before closing.

6.2. *Biorders*

The algebraic decomposition that produces the representation of microbelief states is formally related to other algebraic techniques that have been used to reduce a data matrix; explicating the connection to these techniques helps demonstrate the fundamental nature of the HW inversion and point toward the unification of a number of approaches. First, we demonstrate that the HW inversion may be seen as producing a special (and especially useful) form of what Doignon and Falmagne (1984) introduced as the reduction of a binary relation to "biorders." While they did not believe that a "straightforward application of the theory to empirical relations was possible,"[9] Doignon and Falmagne proposed a system whereby any binary matrix **X** might be decomposed into a set of simpler binary relations (e.g., such that $\mathbf{X}=\cap\mathbf{R}_i$), each of which establishes an ordinal relation between the row (and, dually, column) elements of the matrix (hence the term *biorder*). Thus Doignon, Ducamp, and Falmagne (1984) demonstrated that any biorder $\mathbf{R}_i$ between a members of some sets $A=\{a\}$ and $M=\{m\}$ can be interpreted as arising only when a has an "amount" of some i^{th} unobserved "resource" that exceeds some threshold for the object m; there are as many resources as there are biorders. The dual ordering arises because "harder" column elements (those that have a higher threshold for resource i) distinguish row elements that are above and below this threshold, and dually, row elements of limited resource distinguish column elements of higher as opposed to lower thresholds.

This emphasis on creating orders is understandable in the psychometric context, given the imperative to rank persons on some dimension(s). However, it leads to certain problems, for given any matrix of observed relations, there may be more than one biorder model that is equally compatible with the data.[10] Such ambiguity, however, is removed if we restrict resources to be dichotomous; this restriction, however, implies the inversion outlined here.[11] The biorder model generated by a set of K ordinal resources, each with T_k distinct levels, corresponds to the HW inversion of a lattice with $\Sigma(T_k - 1)$ components. Instead of searching for some nonunique set of orders, we retrieve a single, unique partial order.

[9] While Falmagne (1989) later suggested a latent-class type approximation for related structures, the works on biorders discussed here did not involve any techniques that would allow them to be fit to noisy data.

[10] The biorder approach begins by constructing a set of rectangular subsets of the $A\times M$ matrix (i.e. $A^*\times M^*$ where $A^*\subseteq A$; $M^*\subseteq M$), such that all cells in this rectangular subset are 0 (or 1). If, say, there is a second subset $A^{**}\times M^{**}$ where $A^{**}\cap A^*=\varnothing$; $M^{**}\subseteq M^*$, these two may be combined into a single biorder, which tells us that members of A^{**} have "less" of some resource than members of A^*, and the members of M^{**} require "more" of this resource than those of M^*.

[11] While Chubb (1986) showed that the search for biorders producing **X** could be restricted to what he termed the "core" of the data set, equivalent to the row-basis or MIREs, he admitted the lack of an approximation procedure, and thus the inability to profitably fit data sets in which all response states had some non-zero frequency. Such a test formulated as a latent model requires that we admit as possibilities all states compatible with the "core" of the data set—that is, the lattice B.

6.3. *Concept and Other Galois Lattices*

Structures termed "concept lattices," which are in certain senses quite similar to biorders, have also been proposed to study the interrelations of concepts (Ganter and Wille 1989). These are based on a data matrix that explicitly links some set of elements to some set of attributes. A reduction to sets of nested rectangles (see Wille 1996: 2) similar to that used by Doignon and Falmagne leads to a Galois lattice, a class of structures that has attracted a great deal of interest in recent years (e.g., Freeman and White 1993; Duquenne 1995, 1996; Mohr and Duquenne 1997). Since a Galois lattice is closed under the intersection of the rows, our *B* lattice is quite similar to a Galois lattice, as we shall show below. Further, as microbelief components clearly may be understood as "attributes" of macrobeliefs, it might be thought that there would be a direct relation between the concept lattices and the lattices we have discussed above. However, this is not so; the concept lattice for some **D** matrix connecting macrobeliefs to microbeliefs would be formed by closure of the rows of **D** under intersection, while the macrobelief state lattice is formed by closure of the complement of the rows of **D** under intersection.

This has two implications: the first is that given the type of interrelations between objects and attributes assumed by a concept lattice, if the attributes are distributed among the population, and the elements arise whenever particular conjunctions of these attributes are present (as would be the case, perhaps, for an analysis of mental disorders that are defined as bundles of separable symptoms), then the population distribution will have the form not of the concept lattice but of the *B* lattice discussed above.[12] The second is that given such a lattice of population states, the concept lattice can be produced from the population distribution even if the attributes are unobserved, by using the HW inversion to retrieve the **D** matrix and then closing the rows of this matrix under intersection.[13]

We mentioned above that the macrobelief state lattice, since it is closed under intersection, is formally similar to a Galois structure. Yet the conventional interpretation of Galois structures from a standard (persons by items) data matrix does not lead to information on discrete components.

[12] This formal relationship is also implied by Pattison (1995: 10, theor. 3).

[13] Note that concept lattices allow for redundancies between objects and attributes that would be lost in an HW inversion.

This is because the Galois lattice deliberately preserves a duality between the two components of a data matrix. Such duality is reasonable in cases in which we expect the mutual definition of one set via another, as in the famous duality of persons and groups (see Breiger 1974), and given actual duality, this can be extremely informative (for a recent example, see Mische 1998). In other cases such a preservation of duality is not theoretically reasonable, and it instead obscures potential further distinctions that could be made among elements of one set, such as may be the case when we use survey data to understand reasoning processes. In this case, a mechanical application of a Galois analysis would retrieve some information about the ordering of the macrobeliefs, and other information about the ordering of the "types" of persons in the sample, which may have no value for us.

However, it is possible to use a Galois type labeling to portray some information regarding the components of the macrobeliefs; the trick is that the Galois analysis retrieves not the microbeliefs but their absence. For example, Figure 6 shows our lattice again, with a Galois-type labeling. Each MIRE may be labeled by the unique microbelief it lacks (Theorem 3, Appendix B); thus node 111100 may be labeled as *e*, indicating that the only difference between it and the one node that covers it is this microbelief *e*. The other element of this lattice is the macrobelief; in the example of Figure 4, we see that all those nodes *not* associated with the absence of a microbelief are associated with the *addition* of a macrobelief (and one node, 110000, is associated with both). This is not necessarily always the case. Instead, as proved in Theorem 7 in Appendix B, the addition of macrobeliefs can be associated with elements that are dual to the MIREs—namely, join-irreducible elements (JIREs); in a Hasse diagram, these are all elements with only one arrow going in to them. (While not all Galois or concept lattices label only JIREs and MIREs, all other labels are redundant, in that they express items that are the intersection of other items; see Wille 1996:5.)

This Galois-type ordering, then, should be read differently from a Galois lattice: both "readings" progress from bottom to top (as opposed to being a bidirectional map). Tracing the possible paths upward from the double-edged boxes, we see the microbelief poset ($a \to b$, $b \to e$, $b \to f$, $a \to c$, $c \to d$ and transitivities). Tracing the possible paths upward connecting the single-edge boxes, we see the precedence relations between macrobeliefs in the macrobelief state lattice; this latter information, however, we consider to be merely a by-product of the microbelief poset and the

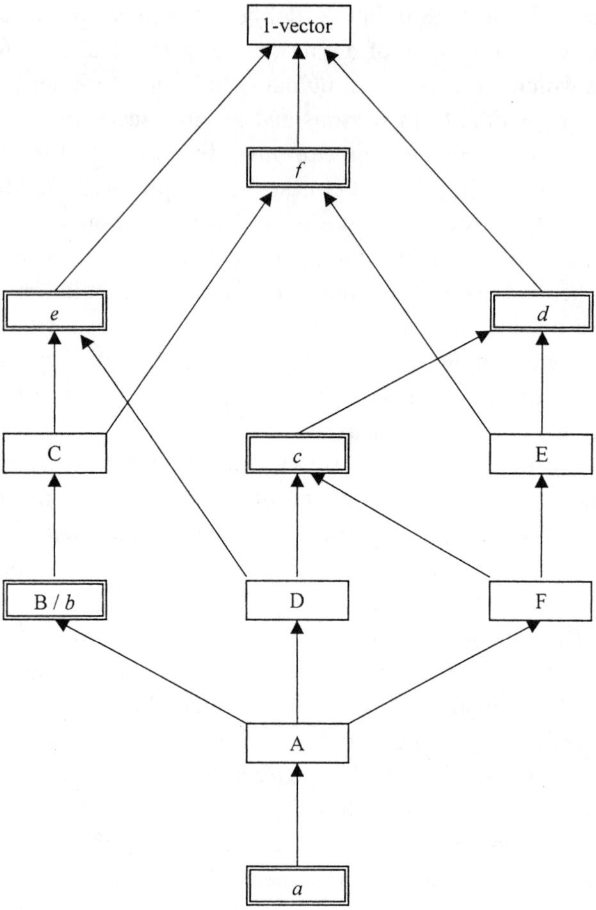

FIGURE 6. Relabeled version of the lattice given above.

rules of composition encompassed in **D**, not recovered by the Galois representation.[14]

[14]This formal identity between the lattices discussed herein and Galois lattices does not mean that given the same data, someone using a Galois-based technique will produce the same structures we do. If the observed data are too complex to be represented, and some form of approximation is required, the final results will depend on the means of approximation. Our latent-class formulation privileges one dimension of this matrix, which is quite reasonable given the form of response. A Galois program such as GLAD (Duquenne 1996) or the HICLAS conjunctive model (Van Mechelen, De Boeck and Rosenberg 1995) may lead to a different structure.

In sum, if aggregate data arise by a process similar to that proposed by formal concept analysis, a Galois type structure arises, but not the concept lattice. Galois analysis of this structure, however, does not retrieve the important information, although a limited retrieval is possible by understanding that the data rows do not represent a (positive) person-phenomenon, but a (negative) component phenomenon.

7. DISCUSSION

There is no reason to believe that discrete responses may not indeed have discrete components; under one reasonable scenario, these discrete components concatenate via an "and" operation—each is necessary but not sufficient for the holding of some belief about which we query respondents. If this is so, then, contrary to our usual assumption regarding discrete beliefs, it is not simply the case that either one believes X or one does not with no "in-between." One may hold some but not all of the components of a belief, and this may be determined by examining what other beliefs a person holds, as well as examining the states of what beliefs can be held (or not held) simultaneously in the sample as a whole. That is in essence the technique outlined here. We have shown that given this scenario, the inversion first discussed by Haertel and Wiley (1993) can retrieve the distribution of these discrete components, and we have illustrated this with a set of data. We have also demonstrated that information about the possible partial ordering of these components can be retrieved from the set of transformation rules that we treat as the **D** matrix. We close by discussing the implications and limitations of this approach.

7.1. *Implications: Coding and Duality*

In most sociological research, our results are not affected by the decision as to whether to code a set of items so that "one" indicates favoring or so that "one" indicates opposing, so long as we are consistent. That is not the case for the structures discussed above. Reverse coding requires that all analyses be dual to those presented here (hence closure should be under union, not intersection, and microbeliefs should concatenate via "or," not "and"). This implies that there can be a difference between holding a belief such as "Generally speaking, business profits are distributed fairly in the United States," and *not* holding the belief "Generally speaking, business profits are *not* distributed fairly in the United States." Such asymmetry may complicate the task of the analyst, but it is quite in keeping with what is known about survey responses, which tend *not* to be symmetric with regard to positive and negative wordings, especially for more abstract items (see Schuman and Presser 1981:296; Hippler and Schwarz 1986; Reiser, Wallace, and Schuessler 1986).

7.2. *Limitations: Simple Logic and Discriminating Power*

We close by pointing to two limitations. First, our ability to recreate thinking patterns is limited by our restriction of the combination of components to "and" relations—all components must be held for the macrobelief to be held. While the duality between union and intersection makes it simple to substitute "or" relations for "and," the techniques outlined here require that we choose only one. But of course, limiting the logic underlying survey responses to only "and" or "or" is unrealistic. Doignon and Falmagne (1985) have made this argument and have considered some systems in which both "and" and "or" operations underlie the construction of complex knowledges. (These lead to Boolean structures somewhat like those explored by Ragin 1987.) Such structures, however, are generally too ambiguous to allow for a unique retrieval of unobserved components.

Second, our ability to identify components is limited by the sampling of the items analyzed. To take our example, if we had eliminated one of our six macrobeliefs from the analysis, we would not have recreated the same **D** matrix, and could not have had exactly the same interpretations. But this does not in any way imply that such interpretations are not robust. Instead, the addition of beliefs to the analysis tends to allow for a greater discrimination between microbeliefs (but involves greater complexity of analysis and requires greater care in specification), and their removal necessarily leads to a loss of discrimination. While different analyses may imply different microstructures, the different analyses may all lead along the same lines, and accentuate the same principles of belief structure. Analogous flexibility is of course also often found in techniques that retrieve continuous components.

In one sense, then, the microbeliefs are merely a heuristic for examining the relations between manifest responses to macrobelief items. But in another sense, they compose a set of strong predictions—predictions that can remove any ambiguity caused by coding issues. If indeed the microbelief composition retrieved via the HW inversion of a lattice is correct, we should be able to write items that tap these component microbeliefs directly; we can also propose *a priori* that we will observe the partial order between these microbeliefs retrieved from the **D** matrix. Thus by writing new questions, we can confirm our analyses of old ones.

APPENDIX A: ABOUT NOTATION AND ORGANIZATION OF TECHNICAL APPENDIX

Symbol	Definition
α_i	The ith macrobelief.
β_i	The ith microbelief.
$\in$	A relation of membership between an element and a set that contains it.
$\subseteq$	A relation between two sets, such that the elements of the first are contained in the second. If $A \subseteq B$ and $\{B \cap \sim A\}$ is not empty (or $A \neq B$), we may say $A \subset B$.
$\rightarrow$	A binary relation between two microbeliefs β_i and β_j.
x_i	The state of the ith macrobelief, where $x_i=1$ if the macrobelief is held and $x_i=0$ otherwise.
z_i	The state of the ith microbelief, where $z_i=1$ if the microbelief is held and $z_i=0$ otherwise.
$\mathbf{x}=[x_1,x_2,\ldots,x_M]$	An arbitrary macrobelief state.
$\mathbf{z}=[z_1, z_1,\ldots, z_K]$	An arbitrary microbelief state.
$\mathbf{I}=[1,1,\ldots,1]$	The unit belief state.
$\varnothing=[0,0,\ldots,0]$	The null belief state.
$\leq$	A binary relation between two members of a partially ordered set.
B	The set of admissible macrobelief states, which is a lattice.
$\cap$	Intersection, binary operation on a pair of belief states.
$\cup$	Union, binary operation on a pair of belief states.
R	M by M matrix constructed by stacking the M meet-irreducible elements of B; equivalently, the row basis of $\mathbf{X}^c$.
$\mathbf{y}=[y_1,y_2,\ldots,y_M]$	An arbitrary manifest response state; $y_i=1$ for a positive response to an item and 0 otherwise.

$\Pr[\mathbf{y}\|\mathbf{x}]$	The conditional probability of a manifest response pattern **y** for a person in macrobelief state **x**; under local independence in a latent-class formulation, this probability is the product of item-specific conditional probabilities.
$\Pr[\mathbf{x}]$	Probability of observing a person in macrobelief state **x** under random sampling from the population of interest.
$\mathbf{D}=[d_{ij}]$	A K (microstates) by M (macrostates) matrix representing the microbelief prerequisite for holding macrobeliefs; $d_{ij}=1$ if $z_i=1$ is required for (a necessary condition of) $x_j=1$ and $d_{ij}=0$ otherwise.
$\mathbf{P}=[p_{ij}]$	A K by K matrix with $p_{ij}=1$ if $\beta_i \to \beta_j$.
L	A distributive lattice of microbelief states corresponding to the poset consisting of $\{\beta\}$ and $\to$ as denoted by **P**.

At some points, it is necessary to distinguish among rows **x** in some matrix **X** using subscripts; in this case, $\mathbf{x}_i$ indicates the ith row of **X**. In other cases, when it does not cause confusion, we may drop this subscript and simply speak of **x**, some row of **X**. In this case, x_i (not bold) indicates the ith element of **x**. When it does not cause confusion, we use matrix notation to indicate a matrix conceived as a set of rows as well as a Boolean matrix. Hence $\mathbf{x}^* \in \mathbf{X}$ signifies $\mathbf{x}^* \in \{\mathbf{x}\}$ where $\{\mathbf{x}\}$ is the set of all rows in **X**; similarly $\mathbf{X} \subseteq \mathbf{Y}$ means $\{\mathbf{x}\} \subseteq \{\mathbf{y}\}$. We use $A \backslash B$ to denote the set-theoretic difference between A and B, that is, $A \cap \sim B$. In some cases, we deal with two elements (say **x** and **y**), one but not necessarily both of which may have some property (say, $\mathbf{x} \leq \mathbf{y}$ or $\mathbf{y} \leq \mathbf{x}$). When the labeling is otherwise indifferent, and hence we can chose to give either element either label, we simply note that "$\mathbf{x} \leq \mathbf{y}$ (or v/v)"; meaning that we are free to adjust the labeling to maintain consistency if things are vice-versa. Sets of indices are generally defined for each purpose, but several set constructions are used regularly and hence are defined as functions, denoted by capital Greek letters.

APPENDIX B: DEFINITIONS, THEOREMS AND PROOFS

We begin with fundamental algebraic definitions that let us describe how unobserved components may create a structure of observed states. A less condensed version of the preliminary discussion of lattice algebras for survey responses is provided in Wiley and Martin (1999); the classic treatment of lattice algebra is Birkhoff (1967 [1940]).

Fundamental Definitions

A "partially ordered set" (or "poset," for short) is a set of elements $\{\delta_1, \delta_2, \delta_3, \ldots\}$ and a binary relation denoted $\leq$, which satisfies the following three conditions:

i. Transitivity: $\delta_1 \leq \delta_2$, $\delta_2 \leq \delta_3$ implies $\delta_1 \leq \delta_3$;
ii. Reflexivity: $\delta_1 \leq \delta_1$;
iii. Antisymmetry: $\delta_1 \leq \delta_2$ and $\delta_2 \leq \delta_1$ implies $\delta_1 = \delta_2$.

Consider a poset A, consisting of elements δ_1, δ_2, δ_3 etc. together with a binary relation $\leq$ as defined above. The "lower bound" of a pair of elements, δ_1 and δ_2, in A is an element δ_3, such that $\delta_3 \leq \delta_1$ and $\delta_3 \leq \delta_2$. Similarly, the "upper bound" of a pair of elements, δ_1 and δ_2, in A is an element δ_3, such that $\delta_1 \leq \delta_3$ and $\delta_2 \leq \delta_3$. The "greatest lower bound" or "meet" of any two elements δ_1 and δ_2 in A, denoted $\delta_1 \wedge \delta_2$, is a unique element δ_3 in A such that $\delta_3 \leq \delta_1$ and $\delta_3 \leq \delta_2$, and there is no δ_4 in A such that $\delta_3 \leq \delta_4 \leq \delta_1$ and $\delta_3 \leq \delta_4 \leq \delta_2$. Similarly, the "least upper bound" or "join" of any two elements, δ_1 and δ_2 in A, denoted $\delta_1 \vee \delta_2$, is a unique element δ_3 in A such that $\delta_1 \leq \delta_3$ and $\delta_2 \leq \delta_3$, and there is no δ_4 in A such that $\delta_1 \leq \delta_4 \leq \delta_3$ and $\delta_2 \leq \delta_4 \leq \delta_3$. A "lattice" is then a poset that is closed under the binary operations of meet and join; that is, for any two elements δ_1 and δ_2 in A, $\delta_1 \vee \delta_2 \in A$, $\delta_1 \wedge \delta_2 \in A$. A lattice is "distributive" if for any three elements δ_1, δ_2, and δ_3 in A, $\delta_1 \wedge (\delta_2 \vee \delta_3) = (\delta_1 \wedge \delta_2) \vee (\delta_1 \wedge \delta_3)$ and $\delta_1 \vee (\delta_2 \wedge \delta_3) = (\delta_1 \vee \delta_2) \wedge (\delta_1 \vee \delta_3)$.

An element δ_1 of some lattice L is "meet-irreducible" if $\delta_1 = \delta_2 \wedge \delta_3$ implies that either $\delta_3 = \delta_1$ or $\delta_2 = \delta_1$, for all δ_2, δ_3 in L. The universal upper-bound I (or the vector $[1,1 \ldots 1]$ in our cases) may be considered trivially meet-irreducible because $I = \delta_1 \wedge \delta_2$ implies $\delta_1 = I$ and $\delta_2 = I$. An element δ_1 of some lattice L is "join-irreducible" if $\delta_1 = \delta_2 \vee \delta_3$ implies that either $\delta_3 = \delta_1$ or $\delta_2 = \delta_1$, for all δ_2, δ_3 in L. The universal lower-bound $\varnothing$ may be considered trivially join-irreducible because $\varnothing = \delta_1 \vee \delta_2$ implies $\delta_1 = \varnothing$ and $\delta_2 = \varnothing$. An element δ_1 in some poset S is said to "cover" some element δ_2 if $\delta_2 \leq \delta_1$ and there is no δ_3 in S such that $\delta_2 \leq \delta_3 \leq \delta_1$.

Definitions: In the text, we defined microbelief vectors $\mathbf{z}\in\{0,1\}^K$, and macrobelief vectors $\mathbf{x}\in\{0,1\}^M$ respectively as $z_i=1$ if the ith microbelief is held, and 0 otherwise, and $x_j=1$ if the jth macrobelief is held, and zero otherwise. The "grade" of such a Boolean vector **x**, denoted $G(\mathbf{x})$, is the sum of x_i over all i. A combination of a set of belief states (whether macrobelief or microbelief) and the relation $\leq$ as defined in the text can be termed a "belief state poset." The "union" of two states, denoted by $\mathbf{v}\cup\mathbf{w}$, is defined as a state **u** where $u_i=1$ if $v_i=1$ or $w_i=1$, and $u_i=0$ otherwise. The "intersection" of two states, denoted $\mathbf{v}\cap\mathbf{w}$, is a belief state **u** such that $u_i=1$ if $v_i=1$ and $w_i=1$ and $u_i=0$ otherwise. Note that scalar union and intersection are equivalent to Boolean addition and multiplication, respectively.

We now proceed to the key theorems underlying the technique, first demonstrating a mapping from a distributive lattice of unobserved microbelief states to a lattice of observed macrobelief states.

Conditions: We assume that no macrobeliefs α_i and α_j are inseparable in the data (i.e., $x_{ki}=x_{kj}$ for all $\mathbf{x}_k\in\mathbf{X}$) and hence redundant; similarly, we assume that no microbeliefs β_i and β_j are inseparable in either their distribution (i.e., $z_{ki}=z_{kj}$ for all $\mathbf{z}_k\in\mathbf{Z}$) or in the mapping (i.e., $d_{ik}=d_{jk}$ for all k), which we call the criteria of separability. The following theorem is stated here without proof, which is trivial.

Theorem 1: For any pair of belief states **w** and **v** in a poset of belief states, (a) $\mathbf{w}\cap\mathbf{v}=\mathbf{w}\wedge\mathbf{v}$ whenever both sides of the equation are contained in the poset. Similarly, (b) $\mathbf{w}\cup\mathbf{v}=\mathbf{w}\vee\mathbf{v}$ whenever both sides of the equation are contained in the poset. Since the distributivity conditions clearly hold for intersection and union of binary vectors, (c) establishing closure under both union and intersection determines a poset of binary vectors to be a distributive lattice.

Corollary 1.1: If **w** and **v** are beliefs states in a lattice L closed under union and intersection, if **w** covers **v**, $G(\mathbf{w}) = G(\mathbf{v})+1$.

Proof: Otherwise, $\exists$ i, j $\mid w_i=w_j=1,\ v_i=v_j=0$. By separability, $\exists\ \mathbf{w}^* \mid w^*_i=0,\ w^*_j=1$ (or v/v). By closure and distributivity, we know $\mathbf{y}=(\mathbf{w}^*\cap\mathbf{w})\cup\mathbf{v}=(\mathbf{w}^*\cup\mathbf{v})\cap(\mathbf{w}\cup\mathbf{v})=(\mathbf{w}^*\cup\mathbf{v})\cap\mathbf{w}$ is in L. But since $\mathbf{v}\leq\mathbf{y}\leq\mathbf{w}$, **w** does not cover **v**, a contradiction.

Definitions: A set of precedence relations (as defined in the text) among a set of K microbeliefs $\{\beta_1, \beta_2 \ldots \beta_K\}$ is said to be "noninterferent" with a mapping into macrobeliefs **D** iff $\exists$ no i, j, m $\mid d_{im}=0,\ d_{jm}=1$, $\beta_i\rightarrow\beta_j$.

Theorem 2: Given a distributive lattice L of microbelief states $\mathbf{z}$, a mapping relation expressed as the Boolean matrix $\mathbf{D}$, the set B of macrobelief states $\mathbf{x}=(\mathbf{z}^c\mathbf{D})^c$ forms a lattice.

Proof: Consider any two elements in B, $\mathbf{x}_1$ and $\mathbf{x}_2$. By the definition of the mapping, $\exists\ \mathbf{z}_1, \mathbf{z}_2 \mid \mathbf{x}_1=(\mathbf{z}_1^c\mathbf{D})^c$ and $\mathbf{x}_2=(\mathbf{z}_2^c\mathbf{D})^c$. Since multiplication is distributive over addition for Boolean vectors $\mathbf{x}_3=\mathbf{x}_1\cap\mathbf{x}_2=(\mathbf{z}_1^c\mathbf{D})^c \cap(\mathbf{z}_2^c\mathbf{D})^c = (\mathbf{z}_1^c\mathbf{D}\cup\mathbf{z}_2^c\mathbf{D})^c = [(\mathbf{z}_1^c\cup\mathbf{z}_2^c)\mathbf{D}]^c = [(\mathbf{z}_1\cap\mathbf{z}_2)^c\mathbf{D}]^c$. But this last is the mapping of $\mathbf{z}_3=\mathbf{z}_1\cap\mathbf{z}_2$ into B, and by Theorem 1(a) $\mathbf{z}_3=\mathbf{z}_1\wedge\mathbf{z}_2$ and hence $\mathbf{z}_3\in L$; hence by the definition of the mapping $\exists\ \mathbf{x}_3= \mathbf{x}_1\cap\mathbf{x}_2=(\mathbf{z}_3^c\mathbf{D})^c \in B$. A theorem of Birkhoff (1967[1940]:7) demonstrates that since B is thus closed under intersection, B is a lattice with (following theorem 1) meet equivalent to intersection. (Note that it is not in general true that B will be closed under union, for it is not the case for Boolean vectors that $\mathbf{a}(\mathbf{b}\cap\mathbf{c})= \mathbf{ab}\cap\mathbf{ac}$.)

Corollary 2.1: If $\mathbf{z}^*$ covers $\mathbf{z}$ in L, and $\mathbf{x}^*=(\mathbf{z}^{*c}\mathbf{D}^c)$; $\mathbf{x}=(\mathbf{z}^c\mathbf{D}^c)$; if $\mathbf{x}$ and $\mathbf{x}^*$ are distinct, $\mathbf{x}^*$covers $\mathbf{x}$ in B.

We now go on to introduce the properties of this mapping that allow us to go the other way, and re-create the matrix $\mathbf{D}$ and the lattice of microbelief states L (as well as the microbelief poset corresponding to this lattice) from any observed lattice of the form of B. We first introduce some notation and a set of lemmas, and then proceed to the central theorems.

Definitions: Given a poset A, consisting of elements δ_1, δ_2, δ_3 etc. together with a binary relation of $\leq$ (or $\rightarrow$), and a subset of A, A^*, δ_i is said to be a "minimal" element of A^* if there is no $\delta_j\in A^* \mid \delta_j \leq$ (or $\rightarrow$) δ_i. Similarly, δ_i is said to be a "maximal" element of A^* if there is no $\delta_j\in A^* \mid \delta_i \leq$ (or $\rightarrow$) δ_j. Note that there may be more than one such minimal or maximal element, but there must be at least one of each by transitivity. For purposes of explication, if $I=\{i\}$ is some set of indices pointing to members of some subset $A^*=\{\delta_i\}$, we may say that "i* is a minimal (maximal) element of I" if δ_{i^*} is a minimal (maximal) element of A^*.

Notation: For any Boolean vector $\mathbf{z}$, let $\Omega^0(\mathbf{z})=\{i|z_i=0\}$ and $\Omega^1(\mathbf{z})=\{i|z_i=1\}$; for any vector $\mathbf{z}$, let $\Psi(\mathbf{z},k)$ be some vector $\mathbf{z}^* \mid z_i^*=1$ if $z_i=1$; $z_k^*=1$, $z_i^*=0$ otherwise. For any macrobelief α_i, let $\Phi(i)=\{j \mid d_{ji}=1\}$ (i.e., all required microbeliefs); for any microbelief β_j let $\Gamma(j)=\{i|d_{ji}=1\}$

(i.e., all requiring macrobeliefs). For any set of macrobelief indices I, $\Phi(I)=\cup\Phi(i)\ \forall i\in I$; for any set of microbelief indices J, $\Gamma(J)=\cup\Gamma(j)\ \forall j\in J$. For two row vectors $\mathbf{z}$ and $\mathbf{z}^*$, let $\Delta(\mathbf{z}^*,\mathbf{z})=\{i \mid z_i^*=1, z_i=0\}$; note that if $\mathbf{z}^*$ covers $\mathbf{z}$ and $G(\mathbf{z}^*)=G(\mathbf{z})+1$, this must have one and only one element. For two column vectors $\mathbf{c}$ and $\mathbf{c}^*$, let $\Delta^T(\mathbf{c}^*,\mathbf{c})=\{i \mid c_i^*=1, c_i=0\}$. This notation is constant over all theorems.

Lemma 3.1: Consider some MIRE $\mathbf{z}$ of L covered by some $\mathbf{z}^*$, with some unique (by corollary 1.1) index $i^*=\Delta(\mathbf{z}^*,\mathbf{z})$. Then either $\mathbf{z}^*=\mathbf{I}$ or $\beta_{i^*}\rightarrow\beta_i\ \forall\ i\in\Omega^0(z^*)$.

Proof: Otherwise take some minimal $k\in\Omega^0(z^*) \mid \beta_{i^*}$ not$\rightarrow \beta_k$; $\mathbf{z}'=\Psi(\mathbf{z},k)$ is in L and covers $\mathbf{z}$ which is not meet-irreducible.

Lemma 3.2: Consider any MIRE in $\mathbf{z}$ in L and $\mathbf{x}=(\mathbf{z}^c\mathbf{D})^c$. The element $\mathbf{z}^*$ covering $\mathbf{z}$ maps into some $\mathbf{x}^*\neq\mathbf{x}$.

Proof: If $\mathbf{z}^*=\mathbf{I}$ (the unit vector), it is obvious (otherwise there is some microbelief which is required by no macrobelief); if $\mathbf{z}^*\neq\mathbf{I}$, let $i^*=\Delta(\mathbf{z}^*,\mathbf{z})$ and $K^*=\Gamma(i^*)\cap\Omega^0(\mathbf{x})$. For any $k\in K^*$, let $G_k=\Phi(k)\cap\Omega^0(\mathbf{z}^*)$, and let $G^*=\cup G_k$; note that each G_k must be non-empty if the addition of β_{i^*} is not to lead to a change in x_k from 0 to 1. By Lemma 3.1 $\beta_{i^*}\rightarrow\beta_i\ \forall\ i\in G^*$. By the definition of noninterference, $\exists$ no $j \mid d_{i^*j}=0, d_{ij}=1$ for any $i\in G^*$, hence the separability condition requires that $\exists\ j^* \mid d_{i^*j^*}=1, d_{ij^*}=0$ for every such i; but since for all $i\in\Omega^0(\mathbf{z}^*)$, $i\notin\Phi(j^*)$, $G_{j^*}=\varnothing$, a contradiction.

Corollary 3.1: Given $\mathbf{z}$, $\mathbf{z}^*$, $\mathbf{x}$, $\mathbf{x}^*$ as defined above, $\exists$ no $\mathbf{x}^{**} \mid \mathbf{x}\leq\mathbf{x}^{**}\leq\mathbf{x}^*$.

Theorem 3: Every microbelief can be associated with one and only one MIRE.

Proof: By corollary 1.1, each MIRE may be associated with the single microbelief added in the microbelief state covering it. To prove uniqueness, imagine two MIREs $\mathbf{z}_1$ and $\mathbf{z}_2$ and associated covering elements $\mathbf{z}_1^*$ and $\mathbf{z}_2^*$ such that $\Delta(\mathbf{z}_1^*,\mathbf{z}_1)=\Delta(\mathbf{z}_2^*,\mathbf{z}_2)=j^*$. If $\mathbf{z}_1^*=\mathbf{z}_2^*=\mathbf{I}$ a contradiction is obvious; otherwise, if $\mathbf{z}_1\neq\mathbf{z}_2$, $P=\Delta(\mathbf{z}_1,\mathbf{z}_2)$ is nonempty (or v/v). Let $Q=\Omega^0(\mathbf{z}_2^*)$; clearly $P\subseteq Q$. If $\mathbf{z}_2$ is a MIRE, this is because

$\beta_{j^*} \rightarrow \beta_i \ \forall \ i \in Q$ (Lemma 3.1) and hence $\forall \ i \in P$. But as $z_{1i}=1$, $z_{1j^*}=0 \ \forall \ i \in P$, this violates the principle of noninterference.

To prove the inversion, we need to show that from any **X**, we can recreate **Z** and **D**. We do this in stages: first we demonstrate that we can recreate **D**, then that we can recreate a subset of **Z**, and then, from this subset, that we can recreate the remainder of **Z**.

Theorem 4: Let $\{\mathbf{x}^*\}$ be the set of all MIREs in B, and $\mathbf{X}^*$ the matrix whose rows consist of all the elements of $\{\mathbf{x}^*\}$. $\mathbf{X}^{*c}=\mathbf{D}$. We begin our proof with some definitions to allow for a parsimonious proof using work of others.

Definitions: (Here we follow Kim 1982: 5–7.) A set of Boolean vectors $\{\mathbf{w}\}$ is called a "subspace" if it is closed under addition (union) and includes the $\varnothing$ vector. The "span" of some matrix **W** (denoted $\langle \mathbf{W} \rangle$) consisting of rows **w** is the intersection of all subspaces containing $\{\mathbf{w}\}$. (In our terminology, the span is simply **W** closed under union.) A set of rows $\{\mathbf{x}\}$ is said to be "independent" if $\exists$ no $\mathbf{x}^* \in \{\mathbf{x}\} | \ \mathbf{x}^* \in \langle \{\mathbf{x}\} \backslash \mathbf{x}^* \rangle$; that is, there are no redundancies such that we can eliminate $\mathbf{x}^*$ and still have the same span of $\{\mathbf{x}\}$. Then the "row basis" of some matrix $\mathbf{W}=\{\mathbf{w}\}$ is a set of rows $\{\mathbf{x}\}$ such that $\langle \{\mathbf{x}\} \rangle = \{\mathbf{w}\}$ and $\{\mathbf{x}\}$ is independent.

Proof of Theorem 4: By the duality of union and intersection, the set of MIREs of some $B=\{\mathbf{x}\}$ closed under intersection is the same as the row basis of $\mathbf{X}^c=\{\mathbf{x}^c\}$, which we shall denote **R**. Any Boolean matrix **W** can be decomposed $\mathbf{W}=\mathbf{UR}$, where **R** is the row basis of **W** and $u_{ik}=1$ iff $\exists$ no $j \mid r_{jk} > w_{ik}$ (Pattison 1995: 8). Hence we may decompose $\mathbf{X}^c$ into $\mathbf{V}^c\mathbf{D}$, where $v_{ik}=1$ iff $\exists \ j \mid d_{kj}=x_{ij}=1$. Note that any row **v** of **V** is a microbelief state vector permissible under the set of noninterferent precedence relations. However, this mapping is bijective, while we know that the mapping from microbelief states to macrobelief states may only be surjective; hence $\mathbf{V} \subseteq \mathbf{Z}$, where **Z** is as defined above. We now go on to show that (i) **Z** can be recreated from the retrieved **D**; that (ii) $\mathbf{X}^c=\mathbf{V}^c\mathbf{D}=\mathbf{Z}^c\mathbf{D}$; and hence we may decompose $\mathbf{X}^c$ into $\mathbf{Z}^c\mathbf{D}$.

Theorem 5: Define a matrix $\mathbf{P}=(\mathbf{D}^c\mathbf{D}^T)^c$, where $\mathbf{D}^T$ indicates the transpose of **D** (i.e., $d^T_{ij}=d_{ji}$). (a) $p_{ij}=1$ iff $\beta_i \rightarrow \beta_j$ is noninterferent with **D**. Hence (b) we can create L from **X**; specifically, let **C** be the matrix of all vectors corresponding to the cartesian product $\{0,1\}^K$; then any row of $(\mathbf{C}^c\mathbf{P})^c$ is a valid microbelief state in L.

Proof: Note that by the definition of **P**, $p_{ij}=1$ iff $\exists$ no k | $d_{jk}=1$; $d_{ik}=0$; the rest then follows directly from definition of interference. Thus we can retrieve all precedence relations among the microbeliefs once we have **D**.

Corollary 5.1: Given a lattice L (expressed in matrix form as **Z**) of all states consistent with all noninterferent precedence relations as contained in **P**, let L^* (and a corresponding $\mathbf{Z}^*$) be some lattice corresponding to a microbelief poset that has a subset of the precedence relations contained in **P** (up to and including the null set); hence $L \subseteq L^*$. (a) If $\mathbf{z}^* \in \{L^* \setminus L\}$; then some $\mathbf{z}=(\mathbf{z}^{*\ c}\mathbf{P})^c$ is in L and $\mathbf{z}^c\mathbf{D}=z^{*c}\mathbf{D}$.

Proof: By theorem 5 $\mathbf{z} \in L$, so we prove only the redundancy of $\mathbf{z}^*$. Let $\mathbf{x}=(\mathbf{z}^c\mathbf{D})^c$ and $\mathbf{x}^*=(\mathbf{z}^{*c}\mathbf{D})^c$, and assume that, to the contrary, $\mathbf{x} \neq \mathbf{x}^*$— i.e., $\mathbf{x} \leq \mathbf{x}^*$, hence $I=\Delta(\mathbf{x}^*,\mathbf{x})$ is nonempty; further, $K=\Delta(\mathbf{z}^*,\mathbf{z}) \cap \Phi(I)$ must be nonempty. But by our definition of $\mathbf{z}^*$, for all $k \in \Delta(\mathbf{z}^*,\mathbf{z})$ $\exists$ j | $z_j^*=0$; $p_{jk}=1$; by definition of **P** $d_{ji}=1$ for any $i \in I$ and hence by definition of mapping $x_i^*=0$ and $\mathbf{x}^*=\mathbf{x}$. This allows us to posit the existence of any $\mathbf{z} \in \{0,1\}^K$, and know that the corresponding **x** is in B whether or not **z** is in L. This also establishes rather directly (b) $\mathbf{X}^c=\mathbf{Z}^c\mathbf{D}=\mathbf{Z}^{*c}\mathbf{D}$.

The final discussion has to do with the relation of these structures to (first) models for partial orders of macrobeliefs, and (second) Galois lattices.

Definitions: Let a column in **D** be denoted by $\mathbf{D}_i$, with the union, intersection, and relation $\leq$ of columns defined analogously to those of rows. A column $\mathbf{D}_k$ is said to be "set dependent" if there exists some set of column indices Q^*, $k \notin Q^*$, such that (a) $\mathbf{D}_k \leq \{\cup \mathbf{D}_i\}$ $\forall$ $i \in Q^*$; (b) $\mathbf{D}_k$ not $\leq \mathbf{D}_i \forall$ $i \in Q^*$. Let F be the set of all such Q^*; define Q as any element of F such that there is no $Q^{**} \in F$ | $Q^{**} \subset Q$. Call Q an "irredundant" set upon which $\mathbf{D}_k$ is dependent. Given a lattice B consisting of macrobelief states **x**, define a "precedence" relation between two macrobeliefs, denoted $\alpha_i \rightarrow \alpha_j$ to be present iff $(x_i=0) \Rightarrow (x_j=0)$ for any **x**.

Theorem 6: If **D** is not set dependent, for any macrobelief α_j, the microbelief requirements of α_j $\Phi(j)=\Phi(I) \cup \beta_{j^*}$, where $I=\{i | \alpha_i \rightarrow \alpha_j\}$ and β_{j^*} is a unique microbelief associated with macrobelief α_j such that $d_{j^*k}=1$ iff $\alpha_j \rightarrow \alpha_k$.

Lemma 6.1: $\alpha_i \rightarrow \alpha_j$ iff $(d_{ki}=1) \Rightarrow (d_{kj}=1)\ \forall$ k.

Proof: (Note in the following, i and j are treated as fixed, while k is generic.) (a) $\alpha_i \rightarrow \alpha_j$ implies $(d_{ki}=1) \Rightarrow (d_{kj}=1)\ \forall$ k. Assume the contrary, that $\alpha_i \rightarrow \alpha_j$ but $\exists\ k^* \mid d_{k^*i}=1,\ d_{k^*j}=0$. Let $Z_{k^*}=\{\mathbf{z} \in L \mid z_{k^*}=0\}$, where L is the microbelief state lattice. There will be some $\mathbf{z}^* \in Z_{k^*} \mid z_k^*=1\ \forall\ k \in \Phi(j)$ unless $\exists\ m \in \Phi(j) \mid \beta_{k^*} \rightarrow \beta_m$. But this violates the condition of noninterference, since $d_{k^*j}=0$, $d_{mj}=1$. Hence $\mathbf{z}^* \in L$. By definition of the mapping, $\mathbf{x}^*=(\mathbf{z}^{*c}\mathbf{D})^c$ will be such that $x_i^*=0$; $x_j^*=1$, violating the precedence relation. (b) $(d_{ki}=1) \Rightarrow (d_{kj}=1)\ \forall$ k implies $\alpha_i \rightarrow \alpha_j$. Assume the contrary, that $(d_{ki}=1) \Rightarrow (d_{kj}=1)\ \forall$ k but $\exists\ \mathbf{x} \mid x_i=0,\ x_j=1$. This $\mathbf{x}$ must map to some $\mathbf{z} \mid z_k=1\ \forall\ k \in \Phi(j)$, while $\exists\ g \in \Phi(i) \mid z_g=0$ (and clearly $g \notin \Phi(j)$). But this is a contradiction of the assumption that $(d_{ki}=1) \Rightarrow (d_{kj}=1)\ \forall$ k, since $(d_{gi}=1)$ but $(d_{gj}=0)$. Lemma 6.1 establishes that $\mathbf{P}'=(\mathbf{D}^T\mathbf{D}^c)^c$ is a matrix where $p_{ij}'=1$ iff $\alpha_i \rightarrow \alpha_j$.

Hence any macrobelief α_j includes all the microbeliefs incorporated in microbeliefs $\{\alpha_i\}$ that precede it. We go on to prove that (1) any macrobelief adds one and only one unique microbelief to the set of microbeliefs required by its immediate predecessor, and that (2) this microbelief is not required by any macrobeliefs that α_j does not precede. But first, we need to prove the following.

Lemma 6.2: D is not set dependent, iff B is closed under union and is hence distributive. (a) If **D** is not set dependent, B is closed under union.

Proof: Let $\mathbf{x}_1$ and $\mathbf{x}_2$ be members of B; let $C_1=\Phi(\Omega^1(\mathbf{x}_1))$; $C_2=\Phi(\Omega^1(\mathbf{x}_2))$; and $C^*=C_1 \cup C_2$. Construct $\mathbf{z}_3$ as follows $z_{3j}=1$ if $j \in C^*$ and 0 otherwise. First, note that $\mathbf{z}_3 \in L$, since it cannot violate any precedence relations, since if $z_{3i}=1$ and $\beta_j \rightarrow \beta_i$, either $j \in C_1$ or $j \in C_2$. Second, note that if we define $\mathbf{x}_3=(\mathbf{z}_3{}^c\mathbf{D})^c$, if $x_{1i}=1$ or $x_{2i}=1$, $\Phi(i) \in C^*$, so $\Phi(i) \in \Omega^1(\mathbf{z}_3)$ and thus $x_{3i}=1$. Finally, note that if $x_{1i}=0$ and $x_{2i}=0$, $x_{3i}=0$ (otherwise $\mathbf{D}_i$ is set dependent on $\Omega^1(\mathbf{x}_1) \cup \Omega^1(\mathbf{x}_2)$, since $\forall\ k \mid d_{ki}=1, k \in C^*$, but $\exists$ no $j \in \Omega^1(\mathbf{x}_1) \cup \Omega^1(\mathbf{x}_2) \mid \mathbf{D}_i \leq \mathbf{D}_j$, since neither x_{1i} nor x_{2i} is 1), and hence $\mathbf{x}_3=\mathbf{x}_1 \cup \mathbf{x}_2$ and B is closed under union.

(b) If **D** is set dependent, B is not closed under union.

Proof: Choose some $\mathbf{D}_i$ that is set dependent on some irredundant set of columns Q as defined above; and for every $k \in \Phi(i)$ define $\mathbf{z}_k^0$ as follows: $z^0_{kj}=1$ unless j=k; and define $\mathbf{x}_k=(\mathbf{z}^{0c}_k\mathbf{D})^c$ and $\mathbf{x}^*=\cup\mathbf{x}_k$ for all $k\in\Phi(i)$. Assume $\mathbf{x}^*\in B$. Clearly $x_{ki}=0$ for all $k\in\Phi(i)$ (since each is missing a microbelief of i) and hence $x^*_i=0$. But for every $j\neq i$ there is some $\mathbf{z}^0_k \mid x_{kj}=1$ (i.e. $z^0_{km}=1\ \forall$ m in $\Phi(j)$). (This is proved as follows: if there is no such $\mathbf{z}^0_k$, it must be because for some m in $\Phi(j)$, $\beta_k\rightarrow\beta_m$ for all $k\in\Phi(i)$. By the principle of noninterference, there can be no $i^* \mid d_{ki^*}=0; d_{mi^*}=1$ for any such k. But then $d_{kj}=1$ for all $k\in\Phi(i)$ and $\mathbf{D}_i\subseteq\mathbf{D}_j$, a contradiction of set-dependence.) Hence $x^*_j=1$ for all $j\neq i$. Choose any $\mathbf{z}^* \mid \mathbf{x}^*=(\mathbf{z}^{*c}\mathbf{D})^c$; by the definition of set dependence, $z^*_k=1\ \forall$ k in $\Phi(i)$. Accordingly, x^*_i must be 1, a contradiction; and so *B* is not closed under union. We now proceed to the proof of Theorem 6.

Proof of Theorem 6: Let $I=\{i\,|\,\alpha_i\rightarrow\alpha_j\}\,|\,\exists$ no $\alpha_k \mid \alpha_i\rightarrow\alpha_k, \alpha_k\rightarrow\alpha_j$. (Note we here treat i and j as fixed.) If **D** is not set-dependent (a) $\Phi(j)\setminus\Phi(I)$ is nonempty and consists of some single j^*.

Proof of (a): By Lemma 6.1 we know this set is nonempty; we prove that it has only one element. Imagine $\{j^*, j^{**}\}\subseteq\Phi(j)\setminus\Phi(I)$. By the separability condition, $\exists$ m $\mid d_{j^*m}=1, d_{j^{**}m}=0$ (or v/v). By definition, $m\notin I$, not α_j, which (Lemma 6.1) means $\exists$ b $\mid d_{bm}=1; d_{bj}=d_{bi}=0\ \forall\ i\in I$. Note that the inversion (Theorems 3 and 4) maps the complement of each row of **D** to a MIRE in *B*; consequently, no row may be the union of two other rows. Since $d_{bi}=d_{j^*i}=d_{j^{**}i}=0\ \ \forall\ \ i\in I;\ \ d_{bj}=0,\ \ d_{j^*j}=d_{j^{**}j}=1;\ \ d_{j^{**}m}=0, d_{j^*m}=d_{bm}=1$; if $\mathbf{d}_{j^*}\neq\mathbf{d}_{j^{**}}\cup\mathbf{d}_b$ $\exists$ h ($h\notin I$) such that one of the following is true (i) $d_{j^*h}=d_{bh}=0, d_{j^{**}h}=1$ (ii) $d_{j^*h}=0, d_{bh}=d_{j^{**}h}=1$ (iii) $d_{j^*h}=d_{j^{**}h}=0, d_{bh}=1$ or (iv) $d_{j^*h}=1, d_{bh}=d_{j^{**}h}=0$. (While there may be more than one b as defined above, this simply translates to more than one h for which the previous statement and the following logic hold true.) Both (i) and (ii) lead to $\mathbf{D}_j$ being set dependent on the columns indexed by $\{I, m, h\}$, a contradiction. (iii) if $\mathbf{D}_m$ is not to be set dependent on $\mathbf{D}_j$ and $\mathbf{D}_h$, $\exists$ c $\mid c\notin\Phi(I), d_{cm}=1, d_{ch}=0$. But then $\mathbf{d}_{j^*}=\mathbf{d}_{j^{**}}\cup\mathbf{d}_c$. (iv) since $h\notin I$ $\exists$ c $\mid d_{ch}=1, d_{ci}=0\ \forall\ i\in I$, but then $\mathbf{d}_{j^*}=\mathbf{d}_{j^{**}}\cup\mathbf{d}_b\cup\mathbf{d}_c$.

(b) β_{j^*} is associated only with α_j and the beliefs it precedes; i.e. $d_{j^*k}=1$ iff $k\in K$ where $K=\{k|\ \alpha_j\rightarrow\alpha_k\}$.

Proof: By Lemma 6.1, we know that $d_{j^*k}=1$ if $k\in K$; hence we need prove only that if $d_{j^*k}=1$, then $k\in K$. Assume the contrary, and hence α_j not $\rightarrow\alpha_k$, which by Lemma 6.1 means that $\exists$ m $\mid d_{mj}=1, d_{mk}=0$. But then

$\mathbf{D}_j \leq \{\mathbf{D}_i \cup \mathbf{D}_k\}$; while $\mathbf{D}_j$ not $\leq \mathbf{D}_i$ and $\mathbf{D}_j$ not $\leq \mathbf{D}_k$. Hence $\mathbf{D}_j$ is set dependent and B is not a distributive lattice.

Theorem 7: While any meet-irreducible element may be uniquely labeled as the absence of a particular microbelief (Theorem 3), any *join-irreducible* element (JIRE) may be labeled as the addition of a particular macrobelief. Hence there are as many join-irreducible elements as there are separable macrobeliefs.

Proof: There are two parts to this proof. (a) Any JIRE may be associated with the addition of only one macrobelief to those contained in the element which it covers; (b) only one such JIRE exists for any macrobelief. (a) Suppose the contrary—namely that for any JIRE $\mathbf{x}$, which covers one element $\mathbf{y}$, $\{j^*, j^{**}\} \subseteq \Delta(\mathbf{x}, \mathbf{y})$. Let $P = \Phi(\Omega^1(\mathbf{y}))$ and let $\mathbf{z}$ be defined $z_i = 1$ iff $i \in P$. Clearly, $\mathbf{y} = (\mathbf{z}^c \mathbf{D})^c$. Define $\mathbf{z}_{j^*}$ and $\mathbf{z}_{j^{**}}$ as follows: $z_{j^*i} = 1$ iff $i \in \Phi(j^*)$ $z_{j^{**}i} = 1$ iff $i \in \Phi(j^{**})$. By definition of noninterference, $\mathbf{z}_{j^*}$, $\mathbf{z}_{j^{**}} \in L$; since L is closed under union, $\mathbf{z}^* = \mathbf{z}_{j^*} \cup \mathbf{z}$ is in L, and maps into some $\mathbf{x}^* \mid x^*_i = 1$ if $y_i = 1$; $x^*_{j*} = 1$; hence $\mathbf{y} \leq \mathbf{x}^*$. Since $\mathbf{x}^* \leq \mathbf{x}$, either $\mathbf{x}^*$ is distinct from $\mathbf{x}$ (which contradicts the assumption that $\mathbf{x}$ cover $\mathbf{y}$), or $\mathbf{x}^* = \mathbf{x}$, i.e., $x_{j^{**}} = 1$, which requires $\Phi(j^{**}) \subseteq \Phi(\Omega^1(\mathbf{y})) \cup \Phi(j^*)$ (i.e., j^{**} is set dependent on $\{\Omega^1(\mathbf{y}), j^*\}$. But the same must be true for j^*—i.e., that $\Phi(j^*) \subseteq \Phi(\Omega^1(\mathbf{y})) \cup \Phi(j^{**})$. But if $A \subseteq B \cup C$ and $B \subseteq A \cup C$, $A = B$; hence $j^* = j^{**}$.

(b) We now demonstrate that there are not two JIREs, $\mathbf{x}$ and $\mathbf{x}'$, covering some $\mathbf{y}$ and $\mathbf{y}'$ respectively, such that $\Delta(\mathbf{x}, \mathbf{y}) = \Delta(\mathbf{x}', \mathbf{y}') = i^*$. Imagine there were, and let $\mathbf{x}^* = \mathbf{x} \cap \mathbf{x}'$. Since B is closed under intersection, $\mathbf{x}^* \in B$; by the definitions of intersection and precedence, $\mathbf{x}^* \leq \mathbf{x}$, $\mathbf{x}'$. But since now $\mathbf{x}^*$ and $\mathbf{y}$ both precede $\mathbf{x}$, and we know there is no $\mathbf{w}$ such that $\mathbf{y} \leq \mathbf{w} \leq \mathbf{x}$, then one of the following is true (i) $\mathbf{x}^* \leq \mathbf{y} \leq \mathbf{x}$, (ii) $\mathbf{x}$ covers both $\mathbf{y}$ and $\mathbf{x}^*$, (iii) $\exists\ \mathbf{w} \mid \mathbf{x}^* \leq \mathbf{w} \leq \mathbf{x}$, $\mathbf{w}$ not $\leq \mathbf{y}$. Either of the last two leads to a contradiction, in that $\mathbf{x}$ is not a JIRE covering $\mathbf{y}$; and (i) is impossible, since $x_{i^*} = x'_{i^*} = 1$, $x^*_{i*} = 1$ and hence $\mathbf{x}^*$ cannot precede $\mathbf{y}$, for $y_{i^*} = 0$.

REFERENCES

Birkhoff, Garrett. 1967 [1940]. *Lattice Theory*, vol. 25, American Mathematical Society Colloquium Publications. Providence: American Mathematical Society.

Birnbaum, Allan. 1968. "Some Latent Trait Models and Their Use in Inferring an Examinee's Ability." Pp. 397–479 in *Statistical Theories of Mental Test Scores*, edited by Frederic M. Lord and Melvin R. Novick. Reading, MA: Addison-Wesley.

Bock, R. Darrell. 1972. "Estimating Item Parameters and Latent Ability When Responses Are Scored in Two or More Nominal Categories." *Psychometrika* 37:29–51.

Breiger, Ronald L., 1974. "The Duality of Persons and Groups." *Social Forces* 53: 181–90.

Chubb, Charles. 1986. "Collapsing Binary Data for Algebraic Multidimensional Representation." *Journal of Mathematical Psychology* 30:161–87.

Clogg, Clifford. 1977. "Unrestricted and Restricted Maximum Likelihood Latent Structure Analysis: A Manual For Users." Working Paper 1977-09. University Park, PA: Population Issues Research Office.

D'Andrade, R. G. 1976. "A Propositional Analysis of U.S. American Beliefs About Illness." Pp. 155–180 in *Meaning in Anthropology*, edited by K. H. Basso and H. A. Selby. Albuquerque: University of New Mexico Press.

Davis, James A., and Tom W. Smith. 1988. *General Social Surveys, 1972–1988*. Chicago: National Opinion Research Center.

Degenne, Alain, and Marie-Odile Lebeauz. 1996. "Boolean Analysis of Questionnaire Data." *Social Networks* 18:231–45.

Doignon, Jean-Paul, André Ducamp, and Jean-Claude Falmagne. 1984. "On Realizable Biorders and the Biorder Dimension of a Relation." *Journal of Mathematical Psychology* 28:73–109.

Doignon, Jean-Paul, and Jean-Claude Falmagne. 1984. "Matching Relations and the Dimensional Structure of Social Choices." *Mathematical Social Sciences* 7: 211–29.

———. 1985. "Spaces for the Assessment of Knowledge." *International Journal of Man-Machine Studies* 23:175–96.

Duncan, Otis D. 1984. "Rasch Measurement in Survey Research: Further Examples and Discussion." Pp. 367–404 in *Surveying Subjective Phenomena* Vol. II, edited by Charles F. Turner and Elizabeth Martin.

Duquenne, Vincent. 1995. "Models of Possessions and Lattice Analysis." *Social Science Information* 34:253–67.

———. 1996. "On Lattice Approximations: Syntactic Aspects." *Social Networks* 18:189–200.

Falmagne, Jean Claude. 1989. "Probabilistic Knowledge Spaces: A Review." Pp. 95–101 in *Applications of Combinatorics and Graph Theory to the Biological and Social Sciences*, edited by Fred Roberts. New York: Springer-Verlag.

Freeman, Linton C., and Douglas R. White. 1993. "Using Galois Lattices to Represent Network Data." Pp. 127–46 in *Sociological Methodology 1993*, edited by Peter V. Marsden. Cambridge, MA: Blackwell Publishers.

Ganter, Bernhard, and Rudolf Wille. 1989. "Conceptual Scaling." Pp. 139–67 in *Applications of Combinatorics and Graph Theory to the Biological and Social Sciences*, edited by Fred Roberts. New York: Springer-Verlag.

Goodman, Leo A. 1974. "The Analysis of Systems of Qualitative Variables When Some of the Variables Are Unobservable. Part I: A Modified Latent Structure Approach." *American Journal of Sociology* 79:1179–2359.

———. 1990. "Total-Score Models and Rasch-Type Models for the Analysis of Multidimensional Contingency Tables, with Specified and/or Unspecified Order for Response Categories." Pp. 249–94 in *Sociological Methodology*, edited by Clifford Clogg. Cambridge, MA: Blackwell Publishers.

Haertel, Edward H., and David E. Wiley. 1993. "Representations of Ability Structures: Implications for Testing." Pp. 359–84 in *Test Theory for a New Generation of Tests,* edited by Norman Frederiksen, Robert Mislevy, and Isaac Bejar. Hillsdale, NJ: Erlbaum.

Hippler, Hans-J., and Norbert Schwarz. 1986. "Not Forbidding Isn't Allowing: The Cognitive Basis of the Forbid-Allow Asymmetry." *Public Opinion Quarterly* 50: 87–96.

Kant, Immanuel. 1950 [1787]. *Critique of Pure Reason*, translated by Norman Kemp Smith. London: Macmillan.

Kelderman, Hendrikus. 1984. "Loglinear Rasch Model Tests." *Psychometrika*: 223–45.

Kim, Ki Hang. 1982. *Boolean Matrix Theory and Applications.* New York: Marcel Dekker, Inc.

Lazarsfeld, Paul F., and Neil W. Henry. 1968. *Latent Structure Analysis.* Boston: Houghton-Mifflin.

McCutcheon, Allan L. 1987. *Latent Class Analysis.* Newbury Park, CA: Sage.

Mische, Ann. 1998. "Projecting Democracy: Contexts and Dynamics of Youth Activism in the Brazilian Impeachment Movement." Ph.D. dissertation, New School for Social Research.

Mohr, John, and Vincent Duquenne. 1997. "The Duality of Culture and Practice: Poverty Relief in New York City, 1888–1917." *Theory and Society* 26:305–56.

Mulaik, S. A. 1972. *The Foundations of Factor Analysis.* New York: McGraw Hill.

Pattison, Phillipa. 1995. "Boolean Decomposition of Binary Matrices." Paper presented at the European Meeting of the Psychometric Society, Leiden, July 4–7.

Proctor, C. H. 1970. "A Probabilistic Formulation and Statistical Analysis of Guttman Scaling." *Psychometrika* 35: 73–78.

Raftery, Adrian. 1985. "A Note on Bayes Factors for Log-Linear Contingency Table Models with Vague Prior Information." *Journal of the Royal Statistical Society*, ser. B, 48:249–50.

———. 1994. "Bayesian Model Selection in Sociology." Working Paper no. 94-12, Center for Studies in Demography and Ecology, University of Washington.

Ragin, Charles C. 1987. *The Comparative Method.* Berkeley: University of California Press.

Rasch, Georg. 1966. "An Individualistic Approach to Item Analysis." Pp. 89–107 in *Readings in Mathematical Social Science*, edited by Paul F. Lazarsfeld and Neil W. Henry. Cambridge, MA: MIT Press.

Reiser, Mark, Michael Wallace, and Karl Schuessler. 1986. "Direction-of-Wording Effects in Dichotomous Social Life Feeling Items." Pp. 1–25 in *Sociological Methodology*, edited by Nancy Brandon Tuma. San Francisco: Jossey-Bass.

Schuman, Howard, and Stanley Presser. 1981. *Questions and Answers in Attitude Surveys.* New York: Academic Press.

Stimson, James A. 1975. "Belief Systems: Constraint, Complexity, and the 1972 Election." *American Journal of Political Science* 19:393–417.

Van Mechelen, Iven, Paul De Boeck, and Seymour Rosenberg. 1995. "The Conjunctive Model of Hierarchical Classes." *Psychometrika* 60:505–21.

Vermunt, Jeroen K. 1993. *Log-linear Models for Event Histories.* Thousand Oaks, CA: Sage.

———. 1997. ℓEM: A General Program for the Analysis of Categorical Data. Tilburg, The Netherlands: Tilburg University.

Wason, P. C. 1959. "The Processing of Positive and Negative Information." *Quarterly Journal of Experimental Psychology* 11:92–107.

Weakliem, David L. 1999. "A Critique of the Bayesian Information Criterion for Model Selection." *Sociological Methods and Research* 27:359–97.

White, Douglas R. 1996. "Statistical Entailments and the Galois Lattice." *Social Networks* 18:201–15.

Wiley, James, and John Levi Martin. 1999. "Algebraic Representations of Beliefs and Attitudes: Partial Order Models." Pp. 113–46 in *Sociological Methodology 1999*, edited by Michael E. Sobel and Mark P. Becker. Cambridge, MA: Blackwell Publishers.

Wille, Rudolf. 1996. "Introduction to Formal Concept Analysis." Preprint #1878, Fachbereich Mathematik, Technische Hochschule Dormstadt.

Zaller, John R. 1992. *The Nature and Origins of Mass Opinion*. Cambridge, England: Cambridge University Press.

5

THREE LIKELIHOOD-BASED METHODS FOR MEAN AND COVARIANCE STRUCTURE ANALYSIS WITH NONNORMAL MISSING DATA

*Ke-Hai Yuan**

Peter M. Bentler†

Survey and longitudinal studies in the social and behavioral sciences generally contain missing data. Mean and covariance structure models play an important role in analyzing such data. Two promising methods for dealing with missing data are a direct maximum-likelihood and a two-stage approach based on the unstructured mean and covariance estimates obtained by the EM-algorithm. Typical assumptions under these two methods are ignorable nonresponse and normality of data. However, data sets in social and behavioral sciences are seldom normal, and experience with these procedures indicates that normal theory based methods for nonnormal data very often lead to incorrect model evaluations. By dropping the normal distribution assumption, we develop more accurate procedures for model inference. Based on the theory of generalized estimating equations, a way to obtain consistent standard errors of the two-stage estimates is given. The asymptotic efficiencies of different estimators are compared under various assumptions. We also propose a minimum chi-square approach and show that the estimator obtained by

This work was supported by National Institute on Drug Abuse Grants DA01070 and DA00017. We gratefully acknowledge the constructive feedback of the editors and two referees.

*University of North Texas

†University of California, Los Angeles

this approach is asymptotically at least as efficient as the two likelihood-based estimators for either normal or nonnormal data. The major contribution of this paper is that for each estimator, we give a test statistic whose asymptotic distribution is chi-square as long as the underlying sampling distribution enjoys finite fourth-order moments. We also give a characterization for each of the two likelihood ratio test statistics when the underlying distribution is nonnormal. Modifications to the likelihood ratio statistics are also given. Our working assumption is that the missing data mechanism is missing completely at random. Examples and Monte Carlo studies indicate that, for commonly encountered nonnormal distributions, the procedures developed in this paper are quite reliable even for samples with missing data that are missing at random.

1. INTRODUCTION

Mean and covariance structure models play an important role in understanding relationships among multivariate observations. With popular software—e.g., LISREL (Jöreskog and Sörbom, 1993) and EQS (Bentler 1995)—these kinds of models are widely used in social and behavioral sciences. Special cases include path analysis, confirmatory factor analysis, errors-in-variables, simultaneous equations, and other latent variable structural equation models (e.g., see Kline 1998; Mueller 1996). With a complete sample, various approaches to estimation and testing in mean and covariance structures have been developed (e.g., Bollen 1989; Browne 1984; Browne and Arminger 1995; Satorra and Bentler 1988, 1994; Yuan and Bentler 1997a, b 1998). However, in the social and behavioral sciences, data collection may involve long questionnaires that are tiring to fill out precisely, and a single study may take several years to complete, so that missing data are almost inevitable. Despite this fact, not many statistically sound approaches to mean and covariance structures with missing data are available, especially, for the typical nonnormal data sets that are found in social and behavioral sciences (Micceri 1989). There is no effective way to evaluate a hypothesized mean and covariance structure $\mu = \mu(\theta_0)$ and $\Sigma = \Sigma(\theta_0)$, generally regarded as the most critical part of modeling hypothetical relations among latent variables.

When data are multivariate normal and the missing data mechanism is ignorable, which includes missing at random (MAR) and missing completely at random (MCAR) (Little and Rubin 1987; Rubin 1987; Schafer 1997), estimation and inference can be accomplished by maximum likelihood (ML) facilitated by the EM-algorithm (Dempster et al. 1977; Little and Rubin 1987; Meng and Pedlow 1992; Schafer 1997). One such approach is a two-stage method (e.g., Brown 1983; Finkbeiner 1979; Rovine 1994). In the first stage of this approach, estimates $\bar{X}_n$ and S_n of μ and Σ are obtained through the EM-algorithm based on a multivariate normality assumption. The second stage is to proceed with the analysis as in the complete data case, treating $\bar{X}_n$ and S_n as the sample mean and sample covariance matrix. In this stage, one obtains an estimate $\tilde{\theta}$ of θ_0 by minimizing the likelihood ratio function based on a normality assumption

$$F_{ML}(\theta) = \mathrm{tr}(S_n\Sigma^{-1}(\theta)) - \log|S_n\Sigma^{-1}(\theta)| + (\bar{X}_n - \mu(\theta))'\Sigma^{-1}(\theta)(\bar{X}_n - \mu(\theta)) - p, \quad (1)$$

where p is the number of variables, and $T_1 = nF_{ML}(\tilde{\theta})$ is a test statistic to evaluate the model structure (e.g., Browne and Arminger 1995). Another approach to obtain an estimate of θ_0 is a direct ML method (e.g., Allison 1987; Arbuckle 1996; Finkbeiner 1979; Jamshidian and Bentler 1999; Lee 1986; Muthén et al. 1987). For the ith observed case X_i with dimension p_i, $E(X_i) = \mu_i$ and $\mathrm{cov}(X_i) = \Sigma_i$, where the latter are a subvector and a submatrix of μ and Σ respectively. With

$$l_i(\theta) = \frac{p_i}{2}\log(2\pi) - \frac{1}{2}\{\log|\Sigma_i(\theta)| + (X_i - \mu_i(\theta))' \times \Sigma_i^{-1}(\theta)(X_i - \mu_i(\theta))\}, \quad (2)$$

the direct maximum-likelihood estimate (MLE) $\hat{\theta}$ can be obtained by maximizing the log-likelihood function

$$l(\theta) = \sum_{i=1}^{n} l_i(\theta).$$

Let vech$(\cdot)$ be an operator that transforms a symmetric matrix into a vector by stacking the columns of the matrix, leaving out the elements above the diagonal. We will use $\sigma = \mathrm{vech}(\Sigma)$ and $\beta = (\sigma', \mu')'$ for convenience. With missing data and a saturated model, the μ_i and Σ_i are functions of β, and the corresponding log-likelihood function is given by

$$l(\beta) = \sum_{i=1}^{n} l_i(\beta). \quad (3)$$

Denote $\hat{\beta}$ the estimator of β_0 obtained by maximizing (3). Based on nesting in the saturated model (μ, Σ), the associated likelihood-ratio statistic T_2 for testing the structure $(\mu(\theta), \Sigma(\theta))$ is (e.g., Arbuckle 1996).

$$T_2 = 2[l(\hat{\beta}) - l(\hat{\theta})].$$

Because no better alternative is available, these two approaches are commonly used in practice even when data are nonnormal. For example, the direct ML approach is implemented in the computer programs LINCS (Schoenberg 1989), AMOS (Arbuckle 1996), Mplus (Muthén and Muthén 1998), and Mx (Neale 1994). Under the assumption of multivariate normality and the null hypothesis, T_2 is asymptotically distributed as $\chi^2_{p+p^*-q}$, where $p^* = p(p+1)/2$ and q is the number of unknown parameters in θ. When data are complete, T_1 equals T_2 and equals the commonly used Wishart likelihood-ratio statistic T_{ML}. For complete data, conditions also exist for T_{ML} to be valid for nonnormal data with some specific models (Amemiya and Anderson 1990; Anderson and Amemiya 1988; Browne 1987; Browne and Shapiro 1988; Mooijaart and Bentler 1991; Satorra and Bentler 1990, 1991; Shapiro 1987; Yuan and Bentler 1999). Unfortunately, there is no effective way of verifying these conditions in practice. When these conditions are not satisfied, normal theory methods generally lead to incorrect model evaluation and misleading substantive conclusion even in the complete data cases (e.g., Hu et al. 1992; Curran et al. 1996; Yuan and Bentler 1998), and it is unlikely that one can avoid the incorrectness with an added missing data problem. Ideally, one would model the data by finding a nonnormal distribution, and inference could proceed with maximum likelihood. Unfortunately, distributions of real data in the social and behavioral sciences tend to be skewed and to have heterogeneous marginal kurtoses. Existing classes of multivariate nonnormal distributions are either too restricted or have unknown distributional forms (e.g., Olkin 1994; Fang et al. 1990; Yuan and Bentler 1999). It is not an exaggeration to say that, in practice, any application of the maximum-likelihood method with multivariate data is at best only an approximation to reality. Normal theory-based methods represent one type of such an approximation.

A breakthrough in mean and covariance structure analysis with nonnormal missing data was made by Arminger and Sobel (1990). Using the pseudo maximum-likelihood (PML) theory developed by Gourieroux et al. (1984), Arminger and Sobel proposed the sandwich-type covariance matrix in describing the distribution of parameter estimates instead of the inverse of the normal theory-based information matrix. Sandwich-type covariance matrices for covariance structure analysis with complete data have been proposed by Dijkstra (1981), Bentler (1983), Shapiro (1983), Browne (1984), Arminger and Schoenberg (1989) and Browne and Arminger (1995). Our experience indicates that standard errors based on the sandwich-type covariance matrix are much more accurate in evaluating parameter significance than those based on normal theory methods. On the other hand, the sandwich-type standard errors behave similarly with those based on normal theory methods when data are multivariate normal (e.g., Yuan and Bentler 1997b). Based on simulation studies with various distribution conditions, Yuan and Bentler recommended the sandwich-type covariance matrix as the default output in structural equation modeling programs.

Almost all the normal theory-based missing data methods assume that the missing data mechanism is MAR. This assumption may not be realistic with practical data (e.g., Allison 1987:77). A more frank attitude should be that some missing variables are MCAR, some are MAR, and some may even be not missing at random (NMAR). Like the normality assumption on distribution, MAR represents only a working assumption for missing data. If data are normal and all the missing variables are either MAR or MCAR, parameter estimates based on maximum likelihood will be consistent (Rubin 1987). However, admitting an incorrect distributional specification, according to Laird (1988) and Rotnitzky and Wypij (1994), the parameter estimates will be inconsistent unless the missing data mechanism is MCAR. With missing data from a distribution having heterogeneous marginal skewness and kurtosis, it is not clear how to specify the likelihood function for obtaining the true MLEs. Normal theory-based maximum likelihood is still a working approach to missing data problems in mean and covariance structures regardless of what the missing data mechanisms are. Actually, whatever the assumption on the missing data mechanism is, once a fitting function as in (1) or (2) is chosen, the MLEs of the model parameters are the same. If there is a bias in a parameter estimate, the bias will not disappear because some untrue assumptions have been accepted. In order to obtain sensible statistical inference, there are two sets of assumptions one can choose: (I) normal data and MAR mechanism; (II) nonnormal data and MCAR mechanism. Besides Arminger and Sobel (1990) and Yuan and Bentler (1996), almost all missing data methods for mean and covariance structure analysis assume normal data. All the likelihood-based methods assume the MAR mechanism. The advantage of picking assumptions (I) is that one can use the likelihood ratio statistic and Fisher information-based standard errors for model inference. Unfortunately, inference based on normal theory can be quite misleading in practice. If assuming (II), one has to develop new statistics and standard errors for model inference.

Arminger and Sobel (1990) developed the sandwich-type covariance matrix for parameter estimates obtained by maximizing (2). With assumptions (II), the present paper has the following four contributions. First, a new and rather natural approach for estimating θ_0 is proposed. The new estimator $\check{\theta}$ is asymptotically at least as efficient as either $\tilde{\theta}$ or $\hat{\theta}$. Second, we will develop a sandwich-type covariance matrix for $\tilde{\theta}$, and study the asymptotic efficiencies of the estimators $\tilde{\theta}$, $\hat{\theta}$, and $\check{\theta}$. Third, we will characterize the asymptotic distributions of T_1 and T_2. Rescaled versions of these test statistics, whose distributions should be better approximated by the proposed chi-square distributions, will be given. Fourth, for each estimator we give a test statistic whose asymptotic distribution is chi-square regardless of the underlying distribution. In addition to the above four contributions, we also study how much bias in parameter estimates occurs when MCAR is not a realistic assumption. Our statistical development of these procedures is based on the approach of the generalized estimating equation developed in Liang and Zeger (1986) (see also Yuan and Jennrich 1998). When applied to mean and covariance structure analysis, the regularity conditions involved are as follows: the population covariance matrix is positive definite, fourth-order moments exist, and the structural model is identified and twice continuously differentiable. These regularity conditions will be assumed throughout our development, without being specified explicitly. A closely related approach is the PML theory set out by Gourieroux et al. (1984) and applied to mean and covariance structure models by Arminger and Schoenberg (1989) and Arminger and Sobel (1990). Parallel developments for covariance structures with complete data are made by Dijkstra (1981), Shapiro (1983), Browne (1984), Arminger and Schoenberg (1989), and Browne and Arminger (1995), and for arbitrary types of structural models by Bentler and Dijkstra (1985).

The rest of this paper will be arranged as follows: The asymptotic distributions of different estimators and their asymptotic efficiencies will be studied in Section 2. Different test statistics for evaluating model structures will be given in Section 3. Since many applications in practice involve only a structured covariance matrix with a nuisance mean vector, we will turn to this special case in Section 4. Illustrations and comparisons among various procedures are presented in Section 5. Simulation studies on parameter bias will be described in Section 6. Some concluding remarks are given at the end of the paper. An outline of relatively complicated proofs will be given in an appendix.

2. ASYMPTOTIC DISTRIBUTION AND EFFICIENCY

In this section, we will study and compare three estimators: (1) the two-stage estimator $\tilde{\theta}$, (2) the direct MLE $\hat{\theta}$, and (3) a minimum chi-square estimator $\check{\theta}$ that will be introduced in this section.

In order to study the asymptotic distribution of $\tilde{\theta}$, we need to know the distribution of $\overline{X}_n$ and S_n. Since the E-step of the EM-algorithm is based on the normality assumption, the parameter estimate $\hat{\beta} = (\text{vech}'(S_n), \overline{X}_n')'$ of $\beta = (\sigma', \mu')'$ actually maximizes the log-likelihood function in (3). Consequently, $\hat{\beta}$ is a stationary point of the generalized estimating equation

$$G(\hat{\beta}) = 0, \tag{4a}$$

where

$$G(\beta) = \frac{1}{n}\sum_{i=1}^{n} \frac{\partial l_i(\beta)}{\partial \beta}. \tag{4b}$$

Let β_0 denote the population counterpart of β. If $E[G(\beta_0)] = 0$, then under some standard regularity conditions, $\hat{\beta}$ is strongly consistent and asymptotically normally distributed (Yuan and Jennrich 1998), and

$$\sqrt{n}(\hat{\beta} - \beta_0) \xrightarrow{\mathcal{L}} N(0, \Omega_{\hat{\beta}}), \tag{5a}$$

where $\Omega_\beta = A_\beta^{-1} B_\beta A_\beta^{-1}$ with

$$A_\beta = -\lim_{n\to\infty} \frac{1}{n}\sum_{i=1}^{n} \frac{\partial^2 l_i(\beta_0)}{\partial \beta_0 \partial \beta_0'}, \qquad B_\beta = \lim_{n\to\infty} \frac{1}{n}\sum_{i=1}^{n} \frac{\partial l_i(\beta_0)}{\partial \beta_0} \frac{\partial l_i(\beta_0)}{\partial \beta_0'}. \tag{5b}$$

Similar results can be obtained using the PML theory (Gourieroux et al. 1984; Arminger and Sobel 1990). The estimating equation (4) is called unbiased if $E[G(\beta_0)] = 0$ (e.g., Godambe and Kale 1991). In such a case, the result in (5) holds regardless of what the underlying distribution of the data is. When the missing data mechanism is MCAR, (4) is unbiased. When data are normal, (4) is also unbiased for MAR data. When $X_i \sim N(\mu_i(\mu), \Sigma_i(\Sigma))$, then $A_\beta = B_\beta$, which corresponds to the normal theory information matrix and $\Omega_\beta = A_\beta^{-1}$ is the minimum asymptotic covariance matrix any estimator can achieve. For a general nonnormal distribution, $\hat{\beta}$ does not enjoy such an optimum property. However, for the unbiased estimating equation (4), regardless of the distribution of the data, consistent estimates of A_β and B_β can be obtained by replacing the unknown parameter β_0 in (5b) by $\hat{\beta}$ and omitting the limit notation; we will denote such an estimator by $\hat{\Omega}_{\hat{\beta}}$. In addition, note that the form of A_β also does not depend on the underlying distribution. Let

$$\kappa_i = \frac{\partial \operatorname{vec}(\Sigma_i)}{\partial \sigma'}, \qquad \text{and} \qquad \tau_i = \frac{\partial \mu_i}{\partial \mu'},$$

which are respectively $p_i^2 \times p^*$ and $p_i \times p$ constant matrices with elements being either 1 or 0, then

$$A_\beta = \begin{pmatrix} \frac{1}{2} \lim_{n\to\infty} \frac{1}{n} \sum_{i=1}^{n} \kappa_i'(\Sigma_i^{-1} \otimes \Sigma_i^{-1})\kappa_i & 0 \\ 0 & \lim_{n\to\infty} \frac{1}{n} \sum_{i=1}^{n} \tau_i' \Sigma_i^{-1} \tau_i \end{pmatrix}.$$

We will denote $H_2 = A_\beta$ for easy comparison of efficiency.

Equation (5) gives a justification for using the normal assumption based EM-algorithm to impute the missing data from a nonnormal distribution. This result is necessary to study the distribution of $\tilde{\theta}$, as well as many other applications in which S_n or $\bar{X}_n$ are used in multivariate analysis.

Now we can study the asymptotic distribution of $\tilde{\theta}$. When $\Sigma_i = \Sigma$, then $\kappa_i = D_p$, which is the duplication matrix as defined in Magnus and Neudecker (1988, p. 49). Let

$$H_1 = \begin{pmatrix} \frac{1}{2} D_p'(\Sigma^{-1} \otimes \Sigma^{-1})D_p & 0 \\ 0 & \Sigma^{-1} \end{pmatrix},$$

then the asymptotic distribution of $\tilde{\theta}$ is given by (e.g., Browne and Arminger 1995)

$$\sqrt{n}(\tilde{\theta} - \theta_0) \xrightarrow{\mathcal{L}} N(0, \Omega_{\tilde{\theta}}), \tag{6a}$$

where

$$\Omega_{\tilde{\theta}} = (\dot{\beta}' H_1 \dot{\beta})^{-1} (\dot{\beta}' H_1 \Omega_{\hat{\beta}} H_1 \dot{\beta}) (\dot{\beta}' H_1 \dot{\beta})^{-1} \tag{6b}$$

with $\dot{\beta} = \partial\beta(\theta_0)/\partial\theta_0'$. A consistent estimate of $\Omega_{\tilde{\theta}}$ can be obtained by replacing Σ by S_n, $\dot{\beta}$ by $\dot{\beta}(\tilde{\theta})$, and $\Omega_{\hat{\beta}}$ by $\hat{\Omega}_{\hat{\beta}}$.Notice that the sandwich-type covariance matrix consists of the normal theory-based covariance matrix $(\dot{\beta}' H_1 \dot{\beta})^{-1}$ on each side, which is due to the normal discrepancy function equation (1). The middle block $(\dot{\beta}' H_1 \Omega_{\hat{\beta}} H_1 \dot{\beta})$ accounts for the missing information and (or) nonnormal data. Actually, for normal data without any missing variables, $\Omega_{\hat{\beta}} = H_1^{-1}$ and $\Omega_{\tilde{\theta}} = (\dot{\beta}' H_1 \dot{\beta})^{-1}$ is just the inverse of the normal theory-based information matrix.

We have obtained the distribution of $\tilde{\theta}$ using the result in (5). Another way of utilizing (5) is to estimate θ_0 by minimizing

$$Q_n(\theta) = (\hat{\beta} - \beta(\theta))' \hat{\Omega}_{\hat{\beta}}^{-1} (\hat{\beta} - \beta(\theta)). \tag{7}$$

This is a minimum chi-square method, as developed in Ferguson (1996, ch. 23), which requires sample size to be large enough, and the number of variables to be not too large, so that $\hat{\Omega}_{\hat{\beta}}$ is invertible. A parallel approach for obtaining parameter estimates with covariance structure analysis for complete data was proposed by Browne (1984). With (5) and the standard regularity conditions, the estimator $\check{\theta}$ is consistent and asymptotically normally distributed with

$$\sqrt{n}(\check{\theta} - \theta_0) \xrightarrow{\mathcal{L}} N(0, \Omega_{\check{\theta}}), \tag{8}$$

where $\Omega_{\check{\theta}} = (\dot{\beta}' \Omega_{\hat{\beta}}^{-1} \dot{\beta})^{-1}$ can be consistently estimated by replacing $\dot{\beta}$ and $\Omega_{\hat{\beta}}$ by $\dot{\beta}(\check{\theta})$ and $\hat{\Omega}_{\hat{\beta}}$ respectively.

Both the estimates $\tilde{\theta}$ and $\check{\theta}$ are two-stage estimates, requiring the initial estimate $\hat{\beta}$. The direct normal theory MLE $\hat{\theta}$ does not need to first obtain $\hat{\beta}$. Using the theory of PML, Arminger and Sobel (1990) gave the asymptotic distribution of $\hat{\theta}$,

$$\sqrt{n}(\hat{\theta} - \theta_0) \xrightarrow{\mathcal{L}} N(0, \Omega_{\hat{\theta}}), \tag{9a}$$

where $\Omega_{\hat{\theta}} = A_\theta^{-1} B_\theta A_\theta^{-1}$ with

$$A_\theta = -\lim_{n\to\infty} \frac{1}{n} \sum_{i=1}^{n} \frac{\partial^2 l_i(\theta_0)}{\partial\theta_0 \partial\theta_0'}, \qquad B_\theta = \lim_{n\to\infty} \frac{1}{n} \sum_{i=1}^{n} \frac{\partial l_i(\theta_0)}{\partial\theta_0} \frac{\partial l_i(\theta_0)}{\partial\theta_0'}. \tag{9b}$$

When data are normal, $A_\theta = B_\theta$, which is the normal theory information matrix associated with the model, and $\Omega_{\hat\theta} = A_\theta^{-1}$ so that $\hat\theta$ is asymptotically fully efficient.

Now we have three methods to estimate θ_0. Even though all the estimators are consistent and asymptotically normally distributed, there exist differences in their efficiencies. When data are normally distributed, we know that $\hat\theta$ is asymptotically fully efficient with $\Omega_{\hat\theta} = A_\theta^{-1}$ and $\Omega_{\tilde\theta} \geq \Omega_{\hat\theta}$ in such a case. Since $\hat\beta$ is also asymptotically efficient when data are normal with $\Omega_{\hat\beta} = A_\beta^{-1}$, we hope this efficiency could be inherited by $\check\theta$. This is actually true. Notice that the $l_i(\theta)$ in equation (2) depends on θ through $\beta = \beta(\theta)$. It follows from a chain rule of differentiation

$$\frac{\partial^2 l_i(\theta)}{\partial\theta\partial\theta'} = \frac{\partial\beta'(\theta)}{\partial\theta}\frac{\partial^2 l_i(\beta)}{\partial\beta\partial\beta'}\frac{\partial\beta(\theta)}{\partial\theta'} \tag{10}$$

that $A_\theta = \dot\beta' H_2 \dot\beta$. It follows from (8) and (9) that $\Omega_{\check\theta} = \Omega_{\hat\theta}$ for normal distributions. When data are not normal, we cannot compare the efficiency of $\hat\theta$ and $\tilde\theta$, but $\check\theta$ is asymptotically at least as efficient as either $\hat\theta$ or $\tilde\theta$. This is shown in the following. Let $Y \sim N(\xi, \Omega_{\hat\beta})$, where ξ is a mean vector of proper dimension, then $\dot\beta'\Omega_{\tilde\beta}^{-1} Y$ regressed on $\dot\beta' H_1 Y$ gives

$$\begin{aligned} E(\dot\beta'\Omega_{\tilde\beta}^{-1} Y | \dot\beta' H_1 Y) = \dot\beta'\Omega_{\tilde\beta}^{-1}\xi + (\dot\beta' H_1 \dot\beta)(\dot\beta' H_1 \Omega_{\hat\beta} H_1 \dot\beta)^{-1} \\ \times \dot\beta' H_1 (Y - \xi). \end{aligned} \tag{11}$$

It follows from (11) that the covariance matrix of the residual $\dot\beta'\Omega_{\tilde\beta}^{-1} Y - E(\dot\beta'\Omega_{\tilde\beta}^{-1} Y | \dot\beta' H_1 Y)$ is given by

$$\dot\beta'\Omega_{\tilde\beta}^{-1}\dot\beta - (\dot\beta' H_1 \dot\beta)(\dot\beta' H_1 \Omega_{\hat\beta} H_1 \dot\beta)^{-1}(\dot\beta' H_1 \dot\beta), \tag{12}$$

which is at least a nonnegative definite matrix. Notice that the first term in (12) is the inverse of $\Omega_{\check\theta}$ and the second term is the inverse of $\Omega_{\tilde\theta}$, it immediately follows that $\Omega_{\check\theta} \leq \Omega_{\tilde\theta}$. Similarly, when sample size is large, $\check\theta$ also has a theoretical advantage over $\hat\theta$ for general nonnormal data. Using (5) and

$$\frac{\partial l_i(\theta)}{\partial\theta'} = \frac{\partial l_i(\beta)}{\partial\beta'}\frac{\partial\beta(\theta)}{\partial\theta'}, \tag{13}$$

we have $B_\theta = \dot\beta' B_\beta \dot\beta = \dot\beta' H_2 \Omega_{\hat\beta} H_2 \dot\beta$ and it follows that

$$\Omega_{\hat\theta} = (\dot\beta' H_2 \dot\beta)^{-1}(\dot\beta' H_2 \Omega_{\hat\beta} H_2 \dot\beta)(\dot\beta' H_2 \dot\beta)^{-1}. \tag{14}$$

Replacing H_1 in (12) by H_2, one obtains the residual covariance matrix of $\dot{\beta}'\Omega_{\bar{\beta}}^{-1} Y$ regressing on $\dot{\beta}' H_2 Y$ as

$$\dot{\beta}'\Omega_{\bar{\beta}}^{-1}\dot{\beta} - (\dot{\beta}' H_2 \dot{\beta})(\dot{\beta}' H_2 \Omega_{\bar{\beta}} H_2 \dot{\beta})^{-1}(\dot{\beta}' H_2 \dot{\beta}), \tag{15}$$

which implies that $\Omega_{\check{\theta}} \leq \Omega_{\hat{\theta}}$. So for both normal and nonnormal data, $\check{\theta}$ is asymptotically at least as efficient as either $\hat{\theta}$ or $\tilde{\theta}$. The inequality in $\Omega_{\check{\theta}} \leq \Omega_{\tilde{\theta}}$ is strict unless data are normal and complete, and the inequality in $\Omega_{\check{\theta}} \leq \Omega_{\hat{\theta}}$ is strict unless data are normal. Notice that the asymptotic efficiency possessed by $\check{\theta}$ may not hold for finite sample sizes, as was demonstrated in Yuan and Bentler (1997b) for complete data. This implies that unless sample size is large or data are extremely nonnormal, $\hat{\theta}$ or $\tilde{\theta}$ may be preferable in practice.

For nonnormal data, the comparison between $\hat{\theta}$ and $\tilde{\theta}$ is not so clear, and their asymptotic efficiencies depend on the underlying sampling distribution. Notice that $H_2 \approx H_1$ if the number of missing cases $n_m \ll n$. From (6b) and (14), it follows that $\Omega_{\tilde{\theta}} \approx \Omega_{\hat{\theta}}$ in such a case. Even though $\hat{\theta}$ is asymptotically more efficient when data are normal, the advantage of using the direct ML method may not be so obvious when the number of missing cases is small compared to the sample size. Also, the direct ML approach may need special programming (Jamshidian and Bentler 1999) while $(\bar{X}_n, S_n)$ can be obtained through the EM-algorithm, which is straightforward. The implication is that the two-stage method may generally be preferred in practice.

3. TEST STATISTICS

In the last section, we have shown the large sample advantage of the minimum chi-square estimator over both the direct ML and the two-stage estimators. The minimum chi-square method also automatically produces a test statistic for evaluating the structural model $\beta = \beta(\theta)$. This is because

$$T_3 = nQ(\check{\theta}) \xrightarrow{\mathcal{L}} \chi_{p+p^*-q}. \tag{16}$$

The statistic T_3 is a generalization of the asymptotically distribution free statistic proposed by Browne (1984) for the complete data case, which has been available in several major statistical software packages (e.g., LISREL, EQS).

Before we construct new test statistics associated with $\tilde{\theta}$ and $\hat{\theta}$, we would like to show that the statistics T_1 and T_2 generally do not asymptotically follow chi-square distributions with nonnormal data. As characterized in the following Lemmas 3.1 and 3.2 whose proofs are given in the appendix to this chapter, these statistics approach some mixtures of chi-square distributions instead. Based on these lemmas, we propose a rescaled version for each of the statistics. The new rescaled statistics are better approximated by the reference chi-square distribution $\chi^2_{p+p^*-q}$.

We will work on the two-stage likelihood ratio test statistic T_1 first. Let

$$V_1 = H_1 - H_1\dot{\beta}(\dot{\beta}'H_1\dot{\beta})^{-1}\dot{\beta}'H_1 \tag{17}$$

and $\lambda_j^{(1)}, j = 1, \cdots, p + p^* - q$ be the nonzero eigenvalues of $\Omega_{\beta}V_1$. The following lemma characterizes the large sample property of T_1.

Lemma 3.1. Under some standard regularity conditions,

$$T_1 \xrightarrow{\mathcal{L}} \sum_{j=1}^{p+p^*-q} \lambda_j^{(1)} \chi^2_{j1},$$

where χ^2_{j1} are independent chi-square random variables each with degree of freedom 1.

So the two-stage likelihood ratio test statistic generally does not approach $\chi^2_{p+p^*-q}$ in distribution. When $\Omega_{\beta}^{-1} = H_1$, $\Omega_{\beta}^{1/2} V_1 \Omega_{\beta}^{1/2}$ is a projection matrix, and all the $\lambda_j^{(1)}$s are equal to 1, $T_1 \xrightarrow{\mathcal{L}} \chi_{p+p^*-q}$. This is the case with complete data sampled from a normal distribution. Since T_1 approaches a distribution of linear combination of chi-squares, and no commonly used distribution is available to describe the behavior of the linear combination of chi-squares, we may rescale T_1 so that it can be better approximated by its proposed distribution. A simple choice is to rescale T_1 to have the asymptotic mean $p + p^* - q$, giving the statistic

$$T_1^* = (p + p^* - q)T_1/\mathrm{tr}(\hat{\Omega}_{\beta}\hat{V}_1), \tag{18}$$

where $\hat{V}_1$ is a consistent estimate of V_1. The statistic T_1^* is parallel to one proposed by Satorra and Bentler (1988, 1994) for the complete data case. Existing empirical experience with nonnormal complete data indicates that the distribution of T_1^* can be approximated by $\chi^2_{p+p^*-q}$ very well (Hu et al. 1992; Curran et al. 1996). More experience needs to be gained to evaluate the performance of this statistic with missing data sets.

In a similar way, the direct likelihood ratio statistic T_2 also has a distribution that approaches a linear combination of chi-square variates. Let

$$V_2 = H_2 - H_2\dot{\beta}(\dot{\beta}'H_2\dot{\beta})^{-1}\dot{\beta}'H_2 \tag{19}$$

and $\lambda_j^{(2)}, j = 1, \cdots, p + p^* - q$ be the nonzero eigenvalues of $\Omega_{\hat{\beta}} V_2$. Then we have the following lemma.

Lemma 3.2. Under regularity conditions stated earlier,

$$T_2 \xrightarrow{\mathcal{L}} \sum_{j=1}^{p+p^*-q} \lambda_j^{(2)} \chi_{j1}^2,$$

where χ_{j1}^2 are independent chi-square random variables each with degree of freedom 1.

Since $\Omega_{\hat{\beta}} = H_2^{-1}$ when data are normal, T_2 will approach $\chi^2_{p+p^*-q}$ in this case. Generally, we may use a rescaled version of this statistic

$$T_2^* = (p + p^* - q)T_2/\mathrm{tr}(\hat{\Omega}_{\hat{\beta}}\hat{V}_2) \tag{20}$$

in applications. As with T_1^*, more experience with T_2^* for different nonnormal data would be useful in guiding the application of such a statistic in data modeling practice.

Since neither T_1 nor T_2 or their rescaled versions asymptotically follow chi-square distributions, we need to have other statistics to better evaluate a structural model associated with the two types of ML-based procedures. This is given in the following lemma and its derivation is given in the appendix to this chapter.

Lemma 3.3. Let $\hat{e}(\theta) = \hat{\beta} - \beta(\theta)$ and

$$T(\theta) = n\hat{e}'(\theta)\{\hat{\Omega}_{\hat{\beta}}^{-1} - \hat{\Omega}_{\hat{\beta}}^{-1}\dot{\beta}(\theta)[\dot{\beta}'(\theta)\hat{\Omega}_{\hat{\beta}}^{-1}\dot{\beta}(\theta)]^{-1}\dot{\beta}'(\theta)\hat{\Omega}_{\hat{\beta}}^{-1}\}\hat{e}(\theta). \tag{21}$$

Then under the regularity conditions stated earlier, the distributions of both $T_4 = T(\tilde{\theta})$ and $T_5 = T(\hat{\theta})$ asymptotically follow $\chi^2_{p+p^*-q}$.

When data are not normal, the improper behavior of likelihood ratio type test statistics is well known. Within the class of elliptical distributions, Muirhead and Waternaux (1980) and Shapiro and Browne (1987) studied rescaled versions of likelihood ratio statistics. When data are not elliptical, the rescaled statistics may not behave properly even when sample size gets larger. However, the statistics T_4 and T_5 always approach

$\chi^2_{p+p^*-q}$ regardless of what the sampling distribution is. Actually, the result in Lemma 3.3 can also be applied to the estimator $\check{\theta}$, which will result in the statistic T_3 defined previously. So statistics T_4 and T_5 can be regarded as a generalization of the minimum chi-square test statistic.

We need to emphasize that the statistics T_3, T_4, and T_5 may not be computable unless $\hat{\Omega}_{\hat{\beta}}$ is invertable. A large sample size is usually needed in order to get a nonsingular $\hat{\Omega}_{\hat{\beta}}$, and even larger sample sizes may be needed for T_3, T_4, and T_5 to behave as nominal chi-squares. With complete data, Yuan and Bentler (1997a, 1998) proposed some asymptotically equivalent versions for these statistics that behave more like the nominal chi-squares for small to medium sample sizes. It would be interesting to see a generalization of these statistics to missing data cases in future studies.

4. STRUCTURAL EQUATION MODELING WITH A NUISANCE MEAN

In many aspects of multivariate analysis—e.g., factor analysis and principal components—the only interest is in covariance matrices, and the population means are best considered to be free nuisance parameters. In such a case, we denote the parameter in the covariance matrix as γ, so the unknown parameter vector now is $\theta' = (\gamma', \mu')'$. In principle, the theory developed in the last two sections also works for this case, but some of the results can be simplified. Our purpose is to give a simplified form of the different test statistics. We will use q to denote the number of unknown parameters in γ.

Since one still needs to estimate μ in the direct ML approach, this approach is the same even though there is no interest in μ. But in the second stage of the two-stage approach, $\tilde{\gamma}$ will be estimated by minimizing the Wishart likelihood function

$$F_{WL}(\gamma) = \mathrm{tr}(S_n\Sigma^{-1}(\gamma)) - \log|S_n\Sigma^{-1}(\gamma)| - p. \tag{22}$$

So the statistic T_1 is now $T_1 = nF_{WL}(\tilde{\gamma})$. Let $\hat{\Omega}_{\hat{\sigma}} = \hat{\Omega}_{\hat{\beta}}^{(11)}$ be the corresponding consistent estimate of the covariance of $\hat{\sigma}$, the statistic T_3 now becomes $T_3 = nQ(\check{\gamma})$, where $\check{\gamma}$ is obtained by minimizing

$$Q(\gamma) = (\hat{\sigma} - \sigma(\gamma))'\hat{\Omega}_{\hat{\sigma}}^{-1}(\hat{\sigma} - \sigma(\gamma)). \tag{23}$$

Similarly, the statistic T_4 and T_5 now become $T_4 = T(\tilde{\gamma})$ and $T_5 = T(\hat{\gamma})$, respectively, where

$$T(\gamma) = n\hat{e}'(\gamma)\{\hat{\Omega}_{\hat{\sigma}}^{-1} - \hat{\Omega}_{\hat{\sigma}}^{-1}\dot{\sigma}(\gamma)[\dot{\sigma}'(\gamma)\hat{\Omega}_{\hat{\sigma}}^{-1}\dot{\sigma}(\gamma)]^{-1}\dot{\sigma}'(\gamma)\Omega_{\hat{\sigma}}^{-1}\}\hat{e}(\gamma)$$

with $\hat{e}(\gamma) = \hat{\sigma} - \sigma(\gamma)$. Each of the statistics T_3, T_4, and T_5 has an asymptotic distribution $\chi^2_{p^*-q}$, regardless of what the underlying distribution of the data is. In order to get the counterparts of T_1^* and T_2^*, let

$$W_1 = \frac{1}{2} D_p'(\Sigma^{-1} \otimes \Sigma^{-1}) D_p, \qquad W_2 = \frac{1}{2n} \sum_{i=1}^{n} \kappa_i'(\Sigma_i^{-1} \otimes \Sigma_i^{-1}) \kappa_i,$$

$$U_1 = W_1 - W_1 \dot{\sigma}(\dot{\sigma}' W_1 \dot{\sigma})^{-1} \dot{\sigma}' W_1, \qquad \text{and}$$

$$U_2 = W_2 - W_2 \dot{\sigma}(\dot{\sigma}' W_2 \dot{\sigma})^{-1} \dot{\sigma}' W_2.$$

Now, both $T_1^* = (p^* - q)T_1/\text{tr}(\hat{\Omega}_{\hat{\sigma}} \hat{U}_1)$ and $T_2^* = (p^* - q)T_2/\text{tr}(\hat{\Omega}_{\hat{\sigma}} \hat{U}_2)$ asymptotically approach mixtures of chi-square distributions, with mean $p^* - q$.

When the sampling distribution is elliptical, all the estimators of γ are asymptotically independent with the estimators of μ. It is known that both T_1^* and T_2^* asymptotically follow $\chi^2_{p^*-q}$ with a complete sample from an elliptical distribution, but we are unable to generalize this property to the missing data case. Notice that the mean vector μ is explicitly estimated in the direct ML approach, and it is implicitly estimated through ML as defined in (4), even when (22) and (23) do not involve mean structures. Although μ is a vector of nuisance parameters, using methods other than ML to obtain its estimate will result in bias in the parameter estimates of γ. More detailed discussion of this aspect was given in Allison (1987).

5. IMPLEMENTATION AND NUMERICAL COMPARISON

We will use a data set from Mardia et al. (1979) to illustrate the steps in implementing the various procedures developed in this paper and to compare the effect of different missing data mechanisms and distribution conditions on these procedures. Mardia et al. (1979, table 1.2.1) give test scores of $n = 88$ students on five subjects. The five subjects are (1) Mechanics, (2) Vectors, (3) Algebra, (4) Analysis, and (5) Statistics. The first two subjects were tested with closed book exams and the last three were tested with open book exams. The original design of this data set is to study if different examination methods measure different abilities of the students. This hypothesis was confirmed by Tanaka et al. (1991) with a two-factor model

$$X = \mu + \Lambda f + e, \qquad \text{and} \qquad \Sigma(\theta) = \Lambda \Phi \Lambda' + \Psi, \tag{24}$$

where

$$\Lambda = \begin{pmatrix} \lambda_{11} & \lambda_{21} & 0 & 0 & 0 \\ 0 & 0 & \lambda_{32} & \lambda_{42} & \lambda_{52} \end{pmatrix}',$$

Φ is a correlation matrix for identification purposes and Ψ is a diagonal matrix. Since the interest is in the factor structure (24), μ is a nuisance parameter. So there are $q = 11$ covariance parameters with $\theta = (\lambda_{11}, \lambda_{21}, \lambda_{32}, \lambda_{42}, \lambda_{52}, \phi_{12}, \psi_{11}, \psi_{22}, \psi_{33}, \psi_{44}, \psi_{55})$. Since $p^* = 15$, the model degrees of freedom are 4. From this complete data set, we created the following missing data samples: (I) The last variable is removed 33 percent, realized by deleting the last variable of the first case in every three cases. So the missing data mechanism in this sample can be regarded as MCAR. (II) To create nonresponses that are missing only at random, we remove the last two variables if the summation of the first three scores is less than 113, which results in 17 (about 20 percent) cases with missing variables. The sample in (II) is a simulation of the situation in which a student may quit the later ones if he or she did not perform well on the first three tests. The advantage here is that we have the parameter estimates for the complete data, which will facilitate the comparison on biases and test statistics of different methods. For all the missing data sets in this section, we use divisor $n - 1$ instead of n when computing the covariance estimates in the M-step of the EM-algorithm, as recommended by Beale and Little (1975).

Considering that none of the current version of the standard software contains the procedures developed here,[1] we would like to outline the necessary steps for implementing these procedures. This will be given next before numerical comparison on these procedures with several missing data sets.

5.1. *Implementation*

For any of the procedures, the MLE S_n of Σ is needed, while $\bar{X}_n$ is also needed if a mean structure is also of interest. They can be obtained by setting the structured model as the saturated model in a program with the direct ML missing data procedure (e.g., LINCS, Mplus, Mx, or AMOS), or one can use the EM-algorithm based on normal assumptions (e.g., Little

[1] We would like to note that EQS 6 (Bentler, in press) will have the new missing data procedures in its future versions.

and Rubin 1987, sec. 8.2). A consistent $\hat{\Omega}_{\hat{\beta}}$ based on (5b) also has to be computed. For the two-stage approach, the S_n and $\overline{X}_n$ can be used as input data in any of the standard programs to get parameter estimates $\tilde{\theta}$ and $T_1 = nF_{ML}(\tilde{\theta})$. For example, for the missing data sample (I) the factor loadings in $\tilde{\theta}$ are given later in Table 2(a) and $T_1 = 2.69$. Standard errors based on the sandwich-type covariance matrix should be evaluated according to (6b). If the rescaled statistic is used for inference, $\hat{V}_1$ based on (17) should be evaluated, which, together with $\hat{\Omega}_{\hat{\beta}}$, will lead to the statistic T_1^* in (18). For example, $T_1^* = 2.04$ for the missing data sample (I). If the asymptotic chi-square statistic T_4 is wanted, one does not need to compute $\hat{V}_1$, instead, $\dot{\beta}(\tilde{\theta})$ should be evaluated and T_4 be obtained according to (21). For the missing data sample (I), $T_4 = 1.74$.

For the direct ML method $\hat{\theta}$ and T_2 are available through standard software (e.g., AMOS, LINCS, Mplus, or Mx). The sandwich-type covariance matrix of $\hat{\theta}$ can be obtained by (9). If the rescaled statistic in (19) is sought, one has to compute $\hat{V}_2$, which together with $\hat{\Omega}_{\hat{\beta}}$ will facilitate the computation of T_2^*. As in the two-stage ML method, one has to compute $\dot{\beta}(\hat{\theta})$ instead of $\hat{V}_2$ if the asymptotic chi-square statistic T_5 is wanted. For the missing data sample (I), $T_2 = 1.96$, $T_2^* = 1.92$, and $T_5 = 1.72$, and the corresponding factor loadings in $\hat{\theta}$ are given in Table 2(a).

The minimum chi-square approach is the easiest one to implement with a programing language such as SAS IML. With $\hat{\beta}$ and $\hat{\Omega}_{\hat{\beta}}$, $\check{\theta}$ is just the generalized least squares estimate with objective function (7). For the missing data sample (I), $T_3 = 1.72$ and the factor loadings corresponding to $\check{\theta}$ are given later in Table 2(a).

5.2. *Comparison*

Previous analysis for the complete data set by Tanaka et al. (1991) indicates that model (24) fits the data very well by either the likelihood method or the minimum chi-square method. Actually, this data set basically follows a multivariate normal distribution with standardized multivariate skewness and kurtosis (Mardia et al. 1979, p. 148) being 3.24 and .057 respectively. Referring these two numbers to distributions χ^2_{35} and $N(0,1)$ respectively, both are far from significant. So we would expect that normal theory methods also work well on missing data samples (I) and (II). Each missing data method was used on each of the two missing data samples. Test statistics corresponding to different methods are given in the upper panel of Table 1. For comparison purpose, the test

TABLE 1
Various Test Statistics with Normal and Nonnormal Data
Under Different Missing Mechanisms

Samples	T_1	T_2	T_1^*	T_2^*	T_3	T_4	T_5
Complete Data	2.07	2.07	2.13	2.13	2.01	1.98	1.98
(I)	2.69	1.96	2.04	1.92	1.72	1.74	1.72
(II)	1.10	.81	.12	.11	.85	.85	.85
Complete Data	42.23	42.23	7.80	7.80	4.14	4.11	4.11
(III)	40.68	35.66	5.64	6.42	3.79	3.82	3.97
(IV)	50.34	37.71	7.34	7.04	2.88	3.04	3.18

statistics for complete data are also included. None of the statistics is statistically significant when referred to χ_4^2, indicating that the proposed model structure cannot be rejected. This suggests that all the statistics give reliable inference when data are approximately normal and the mechanism of nonresponse is ignorable.

In order to further compare the different test statistics, two partially artificial data sets were created. Let r_i, $i = 1, \cdots, n$ be a sample from the population $r = (\chi_3^2 - 3)/\sqrt{6}$, and

$$Y_i = r_i(X_i - E(X)). \tag{25}$$

As $E(r^2) = 1$, and r_i is independent with X_i, the covariance structure of Y_i is

$$\begin{aligned}\text{cov}(Y) &= E(YY') - E(Y)E(Y') = E(r^2)E[(X_i - E(X))(X_i - E(X))'] \\ &= \text{cov}(X)\end{aligned}$$

which is the same as that of the original sample X_i. Applying the transformation (25) to each of the missing data samples (I) and (II) respectively, we obtain two more missing data samples (III) and (IV).[2] Notice that the nonresponses in sample (III) are still completely at random; and the nonresponses in (IV) are still at random. However, since some of the r_i will be

[2] To permit anyone to further study samples (III) and (IV) in this example, we would like to note that the sampling from χ_3^2 was created by $2 \times$ rangam(seed, 1.5) in SAS IML with initial seed = 1234567, where the first 50 random variables were discarded in order to minimize the effects of the arbitrariness of the initial seed.

negative, the nonresponses in sample (IV) will not represent the scores whose first three variables are the lowest. Also, since $E(r^4) = 7$, we can not expect that the sample Y_i in either (III) or (IV) is normally distributed any more. Actually, the standardized Mardia's multivariate kurtosis for the transformed complete sample is 29.60, which is highly significant when referred to $N(0, 1)$. So, theoretically, the normal assumption based methods cannot give reliable inference. Each of the methods was applied to samples (III) and (IV). Results are presented in the lower panel of Table 1. When referring to χ_4^2, both T_1 and T_2 are significant in either sample (III) or (IV), indicating incorrect rejection of a reasonable model. However, as expected, all the other statistics behave very stably and none is significant, yielding the correct conclusion that the proposed model is acceptable. Actually, all the statistics for the two missing data samples behave similarly to their counterparts for the complete data.

Even though we do not know the true population parameters in this example, we know the estimates for the complete sample and also the missing data mechanism for each missing data set. The difference between estimates based on the complete sample and the corresponding population value is because of sampling error. The differences between parameter estimates based on the complete sample and those based on missing data samples are because of loss of efficiency and possible bias due to missing data. Comparing the parameter estimates by different missing data methods with those by complete data will give us valuable information on possible biases. For this, we list only the factor loading estimates in Table 2 to save space, where θ^0 and θ^1 are respectively the MLE and minimum chi-square estimates based on the complete data. Notice that when applying the two-stage and the direct ML methods to the complete data we have $\theta^0 = \tilde{\theta} = \hat{\theta}$, which are generally different from $\theta^1 = \check{\theta}$, because they are obtained from fitting different objective functions. Based on distributions and missing data mechanisms of samples (I) to (IV), we know that theoretically there are no biases for estimates in Table 2 (a) and estimates for sample (III) in Table 2 (b). Discrepancies among different estimates are due to sampling errors or finite sample effects. For easy comparison, the largest discrepancy D^* between parameter estimates for each missing data sample and those for the complete sample are given; an asterisk is used to indicate the specific parameter estimate. Contrasting the D^*s for sample (II) with those for sample (I) in Table 2 (a), we may notice a little bit larger D^* for MAR data than those for MCAR data due to a finite sample effect. This phenomenon will also be observed in the next section. Comparing the

TABLE 2
Estimates of Parameters by Different Methods

(a) Normal Data

	Complete Data		(I)			(II)		
θ	θ^0	θ^1	$\tilde{\theta}$	$\hat{\theta}$	$\check{\theta}$	$\tilde{\theta}$	$\hat{\theta}$	$\check{\theta}$
λ_{11}	12.18	12.53	12.15	12.21	12.43	12.25	12.26	12.31
λ_{21}	10.32	10.25	10.47	10.42	10.34	10.39	10.37	10.32
λ_{32}	9.78	9.71	9.69	9.80	9.74	10.14	10.13	10.01
λ_{42}	11.42	11.47	11.64	11.48	11.40	*13.22	*13.42	*13.88
λ_{52}	12.45	12.64	*11.79	*11.60	*11.38	13.50	13.49	13.90
D^*			−.66	−.85	−1.26	1.80	2.00	2.14

(b) Nonnormal Data

	Complete Data		(III)			(IV)		
θ	θ^0	θ^1	$\tilde{\theta}$	$\hat{\theta}$	$\check{\theta}$	$\tilde{\theta}$	$\hat{\theta}$	$\check{\theta}$
λ_{11}	12.28	13.55	12.58	12.91	13.50	12.79	12.98	14.42
λ_{21}	10.78	9.61	10.64	10.37	10.00	10.47	10.32	9.30
λ_{32}	9.15	8.35	9.52	10.08	8.54	9.90	10.15	9.18
λ_{42}	14.51	12.15	14.61	14.36	12.12	*16.55	*18.09	*13.52
λ_{52}	12.41	12.78	*10.10	*8.74	*10.76	12.53	11.49	13.18
D^*			−2.13	−3.67	−2.02	2.04	3.58	1.37

Note: $\theta^0 = \tilde{\theta} = \hat{\theta}$ is the MLE based on the complete data; $\theta^1 = \check{\theta}$ is the minimum chi-square estimate based on the complete data; D^* is the largest discrepancy between parameter estimates for each missing data sample and those for the complete sample.

D^* for sample (IV) with those for sample (III), one cannot observe greater discrepancies for MAR data than those for MCAR data. From the above comparison we conclude that there is no noticeable bias in MLE based on the wrongly specified distribution for the missing data sample (IV) whose missing data mechanism is MAR.

6. BIAS IN NORMAL THEORY MLE FOR NONNORMAL DATA

Through Monte Carlo, we will continue to study the bias associated with mean and covariance parameters in normal theory-based likelihood estimates when data are not normal. For simplicity and without loss of generality, we choose $p = 2$, $\mu_1 = \mu_2 = 0$, $\sigma_{11} = \sigma_{22} = 1$, and $\sigma_{12} = \sigma_{21} = \rho$

with $\rho = .5$ and .9, respectively. Let x_1 be always observed with sample size N. Only N_1 cases are observed for x_2 according to a missing data mechanism. The biases in parameter estimates of μ and Σ can be obtained by comparing the estimates with the population values. Based on Anderson (1957), there exist analytical solutions for the parameter estimates if a normal distribution assumption is assumed, thus no iteration is necessary for this simple design. Notice that if there is no bias in the parameter estimates $\hat{\beta}$ defined in (4), then there will be no bias in parameter estimates of θ_0. So all possible biases should be reflected in $\hat{\beta}$. Without loss of generality, our interest is in the possible bias in $\hat{\beta}$. Due to a saturated model, parameter estimates for the three estimation methods are identical.

Let e_1 and e_2 be independent standardized random variables, the joint distribution of (x_1, x_2) is generated through

$$x_1 = e_1, \qquad x_2 = \sqrt{1-\rho^2}e_2 + \rho e_1.$$

For different distribution conditions, we choose e_1 as $N(0,1)$ and $e_1 = (\chi_5^2 - 5)/\sqrt{10}$ respectively for symmetric and skewed distributions. Since estimates of μ_1 and σ_{11} are based on complete samples, we would like to create more distributional conditions for x_2 to study the possible biases in estimates of μ_2, σ_{22}, and ρ. For each of the e_1, e_2 is generated respectively from five distributions:

$N(0,1)$;
the standardized t-distribution $t_5/\sqrt{5/3}$;
the standardized uniform distribution $(U(0,1) - 1/2)/\sqrt{1/12}$;
the standardized chi-square distribution $(\chi_3^3 - 3)/\sqrt{6}$;
and the standardized lognormal distribution $(\exp(z) - \exp(1/2))/\sqrt{e(e-1)}$, where $z \sim N(0,1)$.

This design creates a variety of skewnesses and kurtoses in the variable x_2 as given in Table 3. A very severe departure from normality occurs in the case where e_1 follows $N(0,1)$ and e_2 follows lognormal(0,1); the skewness and kurtosis of x_2 are respectively 4.02 and 62.40 with $\rho = .5$. Similarly, when e_1 is χ_5^2 with lognormal e_2, skewness and kurtosis are equally large.

All three missing data mechanisms—MCAR, MAR and NMAR—are included. For comparison purposes, we also include a complete sample for each of the distribution conditions. Since we are interested in possible large sample biases of the MLEs with an incorrect distributional assump-

TABLE 3
Skewness and Kurtosis of x_2

Data e_1 & e_2	$\rho = .5$		$\rho = .9$	
	Skewness	Kurtosis	Skewness	Kurtosis
N(0,1) & N(0,1)	0.00	0.00	0.00	0.00
N(0,1) & t_5	0.00	3.37	0.00	0.22
N(0,1) & U(0,1)	0.00	−0.67	0.00	−0.04
N(0,1) & χ_3^2	1.06	2.25	0.14	0.14
N(0,1) & LN(0,1)	4.02	62.40	0.51	4.00
χ_5^2 & N(0,1)	0.16	0.15	0.92	1.57
χ_5^2 & t_5	0.16	3.52	0.92	1.79
χ_5^2 & U(0,1)	0.16	−0.52	0.92	1.53
χ_5^2 & χ_3^2	1.22	2.40	1.06	1.72
χ_5^2 & LN(0,1)	4.18	62.55	1.43	5.58

tion, we choose $N = 1000$ for the complete data case and $N = 1000$ and 2000 for each of the missing data cases. The MCAR mechanism is created by removing x_2 in every even numbered case. When $x_1 \sim N(0,1)$ the MAR mechanism is realized by removing the corresponding x_2 when $x_1 < 0$; and for x_1 following the standardized χ_5^2, the MAR mechanism is realized by removing x_2 when x_1 is greater than its population median. So for both MCAR and MAR, the missing percentage is about 50 percent. The NMAR mechanism depends on the actual observation of x_2 whose median is not straightforward to obtain. This mechanism was created by removing x_2 if it is less than 0 when $x_1 \sim N(0,1)$ or if it is greater than the median of x_1 when x_1 follows the standardized χ_5^2. For each distribution condition, the average number of observations on x_2 for each of the NMAR samples is reported in Tables 4 and 5.

For each of the designed conditions, 500 replications are used. Since estimates of μ_1 and σ_{11} are just the sample mean and sample variance of x_1, which is completely observed, the asymptotic bias can only be observed on estimates of $\theta = (\mu_2, \sigma_{22}, \rho)'$. Let $\theta^{(i)}$ be the estimate of θ in the ith replication and $\bar{\theta} = \sum_{i=1}^{500} \theta^{(i)}/500$, then typical bias is calculated as $\bar{\theta} - \theta_0$. Since our interest is in contrasting the biases of MLEs from a misspecified distribution for MAR data with MLEs that are known to have zero systematic bias, the biases in Tables 4 and 5 are calculated according to

$$\text{Bias} = (\bar{\theta} - \theta_0)'(\bar{\theta} - \theta_0). \tag{26}$$

TABLE 4
Variance and Bias ($\rho = .5$)

(a) ($N = 1000$)

	Complete		MCAR		MAR		NMAR		
Data e_1 & e_2	Var $\times 10^3$	Bias $\times 10^6$	Var $\times 10^3$	Bias $\times 10^6$	Var $\times 10^3$	Bias $\times 10^6$	N_1	Var $\times 10^3$	Bias $\times 10^6$
N(0,1) & N(0,1)	4.22	1.59	7.34	1.55	17.28	26.16	500	2.36	9.84
N(0,1) & t_5	6.87	4.01	12.35	2.83	21.67	15.41	500	5.77	8.67
N(0,1) & U(0,1)	3.73	3.86	6.51	8.21	16.32	42.85	500	1.69	11.01
N(0,1) & χ_3^2	6.36	5.79	12.17	1.72	19.07	6.42	434	10.49	9.97
N(0,1) & LN(0,1)	83.17	3.76	88.86	101.40	218.79	85.97	414	420.73	9.55
χ_5^2 & N(0,1)	4.78	1.57	7.71	21.07	41.29	75.51	427	2.83	13.01
χ_5^2 & t_5	7.78	2.58	13.68	76.15	46.11	52.00	421	10.76	12.15
χ_5^2 & U(0,1)	4.54	10.41	7.36	11.77	40.62	82.61	435	1.66	13.49
χ_5^2 & χ_3^2	7.18	38.22	12.12	56.38	42.45	110.89	492	1.20	11.09
χ_5^2 & LN(0,1)	70.06	6.47	76.99	436.57	241.07	409.17	507	1.20	9.06

(b) ($N = 2000$)

	MCAR		MAR		NMAR		
Data e_1 & e_2	Var $\times 10^3$	Bias $\times 10^6$	Var $\times 10^3$	Bias $\times 10^6$	N_1	Var $\times 10^3$	Bias $\times 10^6$
N(0,1) & N(0,1)	3.78	15.03	7.49	.90	1000	1.27	9.83
N(0,1) & t_5	6.50	9.47	9.68	4.34	1001	2.99	8.65
N(0,1) & U(0,1)	3.22	2.28	7.34	5.32	999	.87	10.99
N(0,1) & χ_3^2	6.08	4.76	9.14	2.45	868	5.27	9.97
N(0,1) & LN(0,1)	56.92	68.23	87.00	101.23	828	159.10	9.47
χ_5^2 & N(0,1)	3.82	9.87	21.99	69.66	854	1.42	13.02
χ_5^2 & t_5	6.85	17.56	23.07	20.76	842	4.84	12.12
χ_5^2 & U(0,1)	3.70	9.17	22.11	27.34	868	.87	13.49
χ_5^2 & χ_3^2	6.71	10.31	20.94	71.95	985	.63	11.10
χ_5^2 & LN(0,1)	57.51	484.27	88.32	9.00	1015	.60	9.05

Note: $N_1 = N$ for complete data; $N_1 = N/2$ for MCAR data; $N_1 \approx N/2$ for MAR data.

TABLE 5
Variance and Bias ($\rho = .9$)

(a) ($N = 1000$)

Data e_1 & e_2	Complete		MCAR		MAR		NMAR		
	Var $\times 10^3$	Bias $\times 10^6$	Var $\times 10^3$	Bias $\times 10^6$	Var $\times 10^3$	Bias $\times 10^6$	N_1	Var $\times 10^3$	Bias $\times 10^6$
N(0,1) & N(0,1)	4.70	10.26	5.87	7.91	10.18	8.86	500	5.25	3.10
N(0,1) & t_5	4.83	9.16	5.99	7.71	10.38	7.96	500	6.03	2.84
N(0,1) & U(0,1)	4.86	7.64	5.85	5.00	10.46	7.92	500	4.79	3.24
N(0,1) & χ_3^2	4.65	9.46	5.72	3.81	8.83	.92	493	6.50	3.67
N(0,1) & LN(0,1)	9.59	21.75	10.63	54.42	21.83	17.36	488	25.04	2.70
χ_5^2 & N(0,1)	7.76	5.78	8.95	13.23	24.61	8.15	473	5.28	7.33
χ_5^2 & t_5	8.62	2.13	9.80	4.71	24.54	4.56	475	8.30	7.07
χ_5^2 & U(0,1)	8.83	31.16	10.04	28.29	25.06	90.26	470	4.39	7.70
χ_5^2 & χ_3^2	8.53	63.50	9.62	64.47	23.57	44.04	485	5.47	4.03
χ_5^2 & LN(0,1)	11.84	13.27	13.31	81.72	37.32	19.04	495	6.32	2.06

(b) ($N = 2000$)

Data e_1 & e_2	MCAR		MAR		NMAR		
	Var $\times 10^3$	Bias $\times 10^6$	Var $\times 10^3$	Bias $\times 10^6$	N_1	Var $\times 10^3$	Bias $\times 10^6$
N(0,1) & N(0,1)	3.10	9.90	4.62	3.63	999	2.61	3.10
N(0,1) & t_5	3.21	6.47	4.74	3.09	999	3.00	2.84
N(0,1) & U(0,1)	2.93	2.04	4.75	3.20	999	2.31	3.24
N(0,1) & χ_3^2	2.92	.53	4.29	3.31	985	3.08	3.71
N(0,1) & LN(0,1)	6.25	22.00	9.55	4.84	976	11.34	2.66
χ_5^2 & N(0,1)	4.53	2.37	13.31	9.21	945	2.61	7.32
χ_5^2 & t_5	4.01	.53	11.45	.92	950	3.49	7.09
χ_5^2 & U(0,1)	4.78	24.13	12.96	45.28	940	2.09	7.69
χ_5^2 & χ_3^2	4.98	23.63	11.55	6.39	970	2.84	4.00
χ_5^2 & LN(0,1)	7.94	59.11	17.92	2.94	991	3.21	2.04

Note: $N_1 = N$ for complete data; $N_1 = N/2$ for MCAR data; $N_1 \approx N/2$ for MAR data.

It is obvious that any large discrepancy between $\bar{\theta}$ and θ_0 will be reflected in (26). As sampling variation influences the accuracy of an estimate, we also calculated the sample variance of the estimates among the 500 replications according to

$$\text{Var} = \frac{1}{500}\sum_{i=1}^{500}(\theta^{(i)} - \bar{\theta})'(\theta^{(i)} - \bar{\theta}). \tag{27}$$

Table 4 gives the bias and variance corresponding to each condition for $\rho = .5$. Since theoretically there is no asymptotic bias with complete data and MCAR data, the biases reflected by the second and fourth columns of Table 4 (a) and the second column of Table 4 (b) reflect only a finite sample effect. Because of a correct distribution assumption, the corresponding biases for the condition e_1 & e_2 being $N(0,1)$ and the missing data mechanism being MAR in Table 4 also reflect the finite sample effect. We may notice that this effect can be quite large even for complete samples. We will mainly compare biases under MAR and MCAR since both are based on approximately equal sample sizes. From Table 4 (a) we may notice that with the normal sample, the bias under MAR is about 17 times that under MCAR, even though all this is due to a finite sample effect. Similarly, for the normal sample, the variance under MAR is also several times that under MCAR. This indicates that estimates based on MAR data may not be as accurate as estimates based on complete data and MCAR data even though the distributional assumption is correct. A similar proportion of inaccuracy can be observed when the distributional assumption is incorrect. For example, for $N(0,1)$ & t_5 and $N(0,1)$ & $U(0,1)$, biases under MAR are about five times those of MCAR; for conditions $N(0,1)$ & χ_3^2 and χ_5^2 & $N(0,1)$, the biases under MAR are about four times those corresponding to MCAR. For nonnormal data, the largest proportion occurs with χ_5^2 & $U(0,1)$ where the bias corresponding to MAR is about seven times that of MCAR. It is important to note, however, that this is still smaller than that for the normal data. Actually, for conditions $N(0,1)$ & $LN(0,1)$, χ_5^2 & t_5, and χ_5^2 & $LN(0,1)$, the biases under MAR are smaller than those under MCAR, even though these distributions are quite different from normal.

In the last two columns of Table 4 (a) are the variances and biases for data that are NMAR. Regardless of the actual observed sample sizes and the underlying distribution of the data, the bias in the estimates are about 10^4 to 10^5 times of those when data are MCAR or MAR. Even though the maximum-likelihood procedure may perform better than an ad hoc procedure such as listwise deletion (e.g., Schafer 1997, sec. 2.5.2), with an average of about ten times the standard error, the magnitude of biases may render inference on parameters meaningless.

Turning to Table 4 (b), except for a particular phenomenon that for normal data the bias under MAR is much smaller than that under MCAR, which may be due to a finite sample effect, the comparison of biases corresponding to MCAR, MAR, and NMAR is similar to those in Table 4 (a). The results for $\rho = .9$ corresponding to different conditions are given in Table 5, where similar comparisons can be found as with $\rho = .5$ in Table 4. We may also notice from both Tables 4 and 5 with data being MAR and MCAR that larger biases generally go with larger variances. This may indicate that differences between different finite sample estimators may only reflect different efficiencies and not especially biases.

We may conclude from the above comparison that, if there is any large sample bias with normal theory MLE for some commonly encountered nonnormal distributions in practice, the bias is not large enough to worry about. This is rather fortunate since in practice almost any distributional assumption with high dimensional data is likely to be incorrect.

7. DISCUSSION

Since not many multivariate distributions are available to describe the nonnormality of practical data, the normal distribution assumption is commonly used with the analysis of nonnormal missing data in mean and covariance structure analysis. Unfortunately, this generally leads to inaccurate inferences about model structure. We propose several new procedures that do not need any specific distribution assumptions. Statistical development and numerical examples illustrate the merit of procedures that are newly developed over those that are based on a normality assumption. By dropping this assumption, one has to assume the missing data mechanism is MCAR according to Laird (1988) and Rotnitzky and Wypij (1994). We may need to reemphasize that using a normal distribution and a MAR missing data mechanism leads to the same parameter estimates as using an unknown distribution and a MCAR missing data mechanism. Fortunately, our simulation results and examples do not indicate noticeable biases for nonnormal data that are MAR. Taking into consideration the analytical and empirical results, we make the following recommendations: Use the minimum chi-square method for inference when sample size is large; use the direct or the two-stage methods with the rescaled statistics for model inference and sandwich-type covariance matrices for standard errors when sample size is medium. The small sample problem is still open even for complete normal data (e.g., Bentler and Yuan 1999).

When facing a missing data set with nonnormal distributions, we can consider another possible approach: model the data with a multivariate t-distribution, as developed in Little (1988). However, according to Gourieroux et al. (1984), even when data are MCAR, imputation based on such a distribution may not yield consistent estimates of the population covariances unless the data truly follow the multivariate t-distribution. The practical aspect of this inconsistency may not be so serious, as was observed in Lange et al. (1989).

In our development of methods for nonnormal missing data, the focus has been on extending and correcting maximum-likelihood–based methods. Of course, ad hoc methods have been used in data analysis for decades and provide another option in handling incomplete data. These include mean imputation, listwise deletion, pairwise computations, hot deck imputation as well as more recently developed methods such as similar response pattern imputation. In these approaches, a modified data set or a covariance matrix is created that subsequently can be analyzed by any existing standard method designed for complete data. An advantage of these approaches is that they are relatively practical to implement; indeed such methods for dealing with incomplete data can be found in most well-known statistical program packages. Furthermore, nonnormality can be routinely handled when an imputed data matrix is analyzed with a distribution-free method. These methods are all appropriate when the amount of missing data is extremely small. However, there exist several drawbacks of these nonprincipled methods. For example, listwise deletion can render a longitudinal study with few cases left, resulting in grossly inefficient estimates (e.g., Brown 1994). When the missing data mechanism is MAR, existing simulation results indicate that listwise deletion causes parameter estimates to be biased even for normal data (Little and Rubin 1987; Schafer 1997). Similarly, a recent study with a confirmatory factor analysis model by Marsh (1998) indicates that the pairwise computation method leads to substantially biased test statistics, depending on the percent of missing data and its interaction with sample size. On the other hand, the simulation results in the last section imply that there is no noticeable bias even for MLE based on a wrongly specified distribution when the missing data are MAR.

In addition to likelihood-based methods, the multiple imputation technique developed by Rubin (1987) has showed its potential in handling incomplete data problems. In this method each missing value in a data set is replaced by a vector of m simulated values, thus creating m complete data sets that agree with the original incomplete data set on the observed values. Then each of the m imputed data sets is analyzed using a standard complete data routine and the result of the complete data analyses are combined to make inference. Because multiple imputation can remove the difficulty of modeling missing data mechanisms and the computational complications of incomplete data, a variety of multiple imputation techniques have been developed recently (e.g., see Meng 1994; Rubin 1996; Schafer 1997). Extending these techniques to mean and covariance structure analysis would be highly valuable. Due to the typical nonnormality of social science data, however, any such an extension still remains a challenge. For example, when complete data exhibit heterogeneous marginal skewness and kurtosis, it is nearly impossible to find a correct model to generate multiple imputations that conform with the randomness of the missing values. Suppose one uses a model based on the normal distribution to generate the imputed values, then the consequences of replacing the missing values by normal variables on the combined results is not clear (e.g., Rubin 1996; Schafer 1997). As discussed in the introduction, nonnormality is a problem not just with missing data. Even with a complete nonnormal data set, rescaled and generalized least squares type of statistics or recently developed bootstrap techniques (e.g., Bollen and Stine 1993; Yung and Bentler 1996) may have to be used in order to obtain reliable model evaluation.

In spite of our development, additional technical problems for structural equation modeling with missing data remain to be studied in future research. For example, the asymptotic efficiency characterized in Section 3 may not hold for all finite sample sizes. Also, even though the statistics T_3, T_4, and T_5 are asymptotically distribution free, their small sample behavior may not be well described by a chi-square distribution. Furthermore, $\hat{\Omega}_{\hat{\beta}}$ may not be of full rank for smaller sample sizes with a large p. We may have to turn to the statistics T_1^* or T_2^* in such a case, though these are generally not distributed as chi-square even for large sample sizes. More research is necessary for these small sample inference issues to be fully addressed. Another problem is related to the missing data mechanism. Even though the ML-based procedure has little bias when the missing data mechanism is ignorable, MAR is still a strong assumption in practice. It is necessary to develop procedures for dealing with missing data that are NMAR for safer inferences with mean and covariance structure analysis.

Finally, our experience with missing data is limited. The procedures developed in this paper are subject to more empirical verification and modification.

APPENDIX

Proof of Lemma 3.1: Using a Taylor expansion on $F(\tilde{\theta})$, we have

$$F(\tilde{\theta}) = F(\theta_0) + \frac{\partial F(\theta_0)}{\partial \theta_0'}(\tilde{\theta} - \theta_0) + \frac{1}{2}(\tilde{\theta} - \theta_0)' \frac{\partial^2 F(\bar{\theta}_n)}{\partial \bar{\theta}_n \partial \bar{\theta}_n'}(\tilde{\theta} - \theta_0), \tag{A1}$$

where $\bar{\theta}_n$ lies between θ_0 and $\tilde{\theta}$. Using an equation from Muirhead (1982, eq. 15, p. 363),

$$-\log|S_n\Sigma^{-1}| = \mathrm{tr}(I - S_n\Sigma^{-1}) + \frac{1}{2}\mathrm{tr}(I - S_n\Sigma^{-1})^2 + O_p\left(\frac{1}{n^{3/2}}\right).$$

So

$$\begin{aligned} F(\theta_0) &= \frac{1}{2}\mathrm{tr}(I - S_n\Sigma^{-1})^2 + (\bar{X}_n - \mu)'\Sigma^{-1}(\bar{X}_n - \mu) + O_p\left(\frac{1}{n^{3/2}}\right) \\ &= (\hat{\beta} - \beta_0)'H_1(\hat{\beta} - \beta_0) + O_p\left(\frac{1}{n^{3/2}}\right). \end{aligned} \tag{A2}$$

It follows from direct calculations that

$$\sqrt{n}\,\frac{\partial F(\theta_0)}{\partial \theta_0} = -2\dot{\beta}'H_1\sqrt{n}(\hat{\beta} - \beta_0) + o_p(1), \tag{A3}$$

$$\frac{\partial^2 F(\bar{\theta}_n)}{\partial \bar{\theta}_n \partial \bar{\theta}_n'} \xrightarrow{p} 2\dot{\beta}'H_1\dot{\beta}, \tag{A4}$$

and

$$\sqrt{n}(\tilde{\theta} - \theta_0) = (\dot{\beta}'H_1\dot{\beta})^{-1}\dot{\beta}'H_1\sqrt{n}(\hat{\beta} - \beta_0) + o_p(1). \tag{A5}$$

By putting (A2) to (A5) into (A1) we obtain

$$T_1 = \sqrt{n}(\hat{\beta} - \beta_0)'\{H_1 - H_1\dot{\beta}(\dot{\beta}'H_1\dot{\beta})^{-1}\dot{\beta}'H_1\}\sqrt{n}(\hat{\beta} - \beta_0) + o_p(1). \tag{A6}$$

Lemma 3.1 follows from (A6).

Proof of Lemma 3.2: Using Taylor expansions on $l(\hat{\beta})$ and $l(\hat{\theta})$ at β_0 and θ_0 respectively, we obtain

$$l(\hat{\beta}) = l(\beta_0) + \frac{\partial l(\beta_0)}{\partial \beta_0'}(\hat{\beta} - \beta_0) - \frac{n}{2}(\hat{\beta} - \beta_0)'A_\beta(\hat{\beta} - \beta_0) + o_p(1/n) \tag{A7}$$

and

$$l(\hat{\theta}) = l(\theta_0) + \frac{\partial l(\theta_0)}{\partial \theta_0'}(\hat{\theta} - \theta_0) - \frac{n}{2}(\hat{\theta} - \theta_0)'A_\theta(\hat{\theta} - \theta_0) + o_p(1/n), \tag{A8}$$

where we have used (5) and (10), respectively. Similarly, using a Taylor expansion on $\partial l(\hat{\beta})/\partial\hat{\beta} = 0$ and $\partial l(\hat{\theta})/\partial\hat{\theta} = 0$, we have

$$\sqrt{n}(\hat{\beta} - \beta_0) = A_\beta^{-1}\frac{1}{\sqrt{n}}\sum_{i=1}^{n}\frac{\partial l_i(\beta_0)}{\partial \beta_0} + o_p(1) \tag{A9}$$

and

$$\sqrt{n}(\hat{\theta} - \theta_0) = A_\theta^{-1}\frac{1}{\sqrt{n}}\sum_{i=1}^{n}\frac{\partial l_i(\theta_0)}{\partial \theta_0} + o_p(1). \tag{A10}$$

Using (12) on the right-hand side of (A10), it follows from (A9) and (A10) that

$$\begin{aligned}\sqrt{n}(\hat{\theta} - \theta_0) &= A_\theta^{-1}\dot{\beta}'\frac{1}{\sqrt{n}}\sum_{i=1}^{n}\frac{\partial l_i(\beta_0)}{\partial \beta_0} + o_p(1)\\ &= A_\theta^{-1}\dot{\beta}'A_\beta\sqrt{n}(\hat{\beta} - \beta_0) + o_p(1). \end{aligned} \tag{A11}$$

From (A9) to (A11), we also get the following relations

$$\frac{1}{\sqrt{n}}\sum_{i=1}^{n}\frac{\partial l_i(\beta_0)}{\partial \beta_0} = A_\beta\sqrt{n}(\hat{\beta}-\beta_0)+o_p(1); \tag{A12}$$

$$\frac{1}{\sqrt{n}}\sum_{i=1}^{n}\frac{\partial l_i(\theta_0)}{\partial \theta_0} = \dot{\beta}'A_\beta\sqrt{n}(\hat{\beta}-\beta_0)+o_p(1).$$

Since $A_\theta = \dot{\beta}'A_\beta\dot{\beta}$, $l(\beta_0) = l(\theta_0)$ and $T_2 = 2(l(\hat{\beta}) - l(\hat{\theta}))$, it follows from (A7) to (A12) that

$$T_2 = n(\hat{\beta}-\beta_0)'\{A_\beta - A_\beta\dot{\beta}(\dot{\beta}'A_\beta\dot{\beta})^{-1}\dot{\beta}'A_\beta\}(\hat{\beta}-\beta_0)+o_p(1)$$

and the lemma follows by recalling that $H_2 = A_\beta$.

Proof of Lemma 3.3: Since the proofs for T_4 and T_5 are the same, we outline only the proof for T_5. First notice that $\dot{\beta}$ is a $(p+p^*)\times q$ matrix for which $\hat{\dot{\beta}} = \dot{\beta}(\hat{\theta})$ is a consistent estimate. Let $\hat{\dot{\beta}}_c$ be a full column rank $(p+p^*)\times(p+p^*-q)$ matrix whose columns are orthogonal to those of $\hat{\dot{\beta}}$, then $\hat{\dot{\beta}}_c \xrightarrow{P} \dot{\beta}_c$. It follows from (A11) that

$$\begin{aligned}\sqrt{n}(\hat{\beta}-\beta(\hat{\theta})) &= \sqrt{n}\{[\hat{\beta}-\beta_0]-[\beta(\hat{\theta})-\beta(\theta_0)]\}\\ &= \sqrt{n}\{[\hat{\beta}-\beta_0]-\dot{\beta}(\hat{\theta}-\theta_0)\}+o_p(1)\\ &= \{I-\dot{\beta}(\dot{\beta}'A_\beta\dot{\beta})^{-1}\dot{\beta}'A_\beta\}\sqrt{n}(\hat{\beta}-\beta_0)+o_p(1),\end{aligned}$$

and

$$\begin{aligned}T_5 &= n\hat{e}'(\hat{\theta})\hat{\dot{\beta}}_c\{\hat{\dot{\beta}}_c'\hat{\Omega}_{\hat{\beta}}\hat{\dot{\beta}}_c\}^{-1}\hat{\dot{\beta}}_c'\hat{e}'(\hat{\theta})\\ &= \sqrt{n}[\dot{\beta}_c'(\hat{\beta}-\beta_0)]'(\dot{\beta}_c'\Omega_{\hat{\beta}}\dot{\beta}_c)^{-1}\sqrt{n}[\dot{\beta}_c'(\hat{\beta}-\beta_0)]+o_p(1)\\ &\xrightarrow{\mathcal{L}} \chi^2_{p+p^*-q}\end{aligned}$$

The lemma follows from the equality

$$\hat{\dot{\beta}}_c(\hat{\dot{\beta}}_c'\hat{\Omega}_{\hat{\beta}}\hat{\dot{\beta}}_c)^{-1}\hat{\dot{\beta}}_c' = \hat{\Omega}_{\hat{\beta}}^{-1} - \hat{\Omega}_{\hat{\beta}}^{-1}\hat{\dot{\beta}}(\hat{\dot{\beta}}'\hat{\Omega}_{\hat{\beta}}^{-1}\hat{\dot{\beta}})^{-1}\hat{\dot{\beta}}'\hat{\Omega}_{\hat{\beta}}^{-1}$$

which is from lemma 1 of Khatri (1966).

REFERENCES

Allison, Paul D. 1987. "Estimation of Linear Models with Incomplete Data." Pp. 71–103 in *Sociological Methodology 1987*, edited by C.C. Clogg. San Francisco: Jossey-Bass.

Amemiya, Yasuo, and Theodore W. Anderson. 1990. "Asymptotic Chi-Square Tests for a Large Class of Factor Analysis Models." *Annals of Statistics* 18:1453–63.

Anderson, Theodore W. 1957. "Maximum Likelihood Estimates for the Multivariate Normal Distribution When Some Observations are Missing." *Journal of the American Statistical Association* 52:200–203.

Anderson, Theodore W., and Yasuo Amemiya. 1988. "The Asymptotic Normal Distribution of Estimators in Factor Analysis Under General Conditions." *Annals of Statistics* 16:759–71.

Arbuckle, James L. 1996. "Full Information Estimation in the Presence of Incomplete Data." Pp. 243–77 in *Advanced Structural Equation Modeling: Issues and Techniques*, edited by G.A. Marcoulides and R.E. Schumacker. Mahwah, NJ: Lawrence Erlbaum.

Arminger, Gerhard, and Ronald Schoenberg. 1989. "Pseudo Maximum Likelihood Estimation and a Test for Misspecification in Mean and Covariance Structure Models." *Psychometrika*, 54:409–26.

Arminger, Gerhard, and Michael E. Sobel. 1990. "Pseudo-Maximum Likelihood Estimation of Mean and Covariance Structures with Missing Data." *Journal of the American Statistical Association* 85:195–203.

Beale, Evelyn M.L., and Roderick J.A. Little. 1975. "Missing Data in Multivariate Analysis." *Journal of the Royal Statistical Society*, ser. B, 37:129–45.

Bentler, Peter M. 1983. "Some Contributions to Efficient Statistics in Structural Models: Specification and Estimation of Moment Structures." *Psychometrika* 48:493–517.

———. 1995. *EQS Structural Equations Program Manual*. Encino, CA: Multivariate Software.

———. In press. *EQS 6 Structural Equations Program Manual*. Encino, CA: Multivariate Software.

Bentler, Peter M., and Theo K. Dijkstra. 1985. "Efficient Estimation via Linearization in Structural Models." Pp. 9–42 in *Multivariate Analysis VI*, edited by P.R. Krishnaiah. Amsterdam: North-Holland.

Bentler, Peter M., and Ke-Hai Yuan. 1999. "Structural Equation Modeling with Small Samples: Test Statistics." *Multivariate Behavioral Research* 34:181-97.

Bollen, Kenneth A. 1989. *Structural Equations with Latent Variables*. New York: Wiley.

Bollen, Kenneth A. and Robert Stine. 1993. "Bootstrapping Goodness-of-fit Measures in Structural Equation Models." Pp. 111–135 in *Testing Structural Equation Models*, edited by K.A. Bollen and J.S. Long. Newbury Park, CA: Sage.

Brown, C. Hendricks. 1983. "Asymptotic Comparison of Missing Data Procedures for Estimating Factor Loadings." *Psychometrika* 48:269–91.

Brown, Roger L. 1994. "Efficacy of the Indirect Approach for Estimating Structural Equation Models with Missing Data: A Comparison of Five Methods." *Structural Equation Modeling* 1:287–316.

Browne, Michael W. 1984. "Asymptotic Distribution-free Methods for the Analysis of Covariance Structures." *British Journal of Mathematical and Statistical Psychology* 37:62–83.

———. 1987. "Robustness of Statistical Inference in Factor Analysis and Related Models." *Biometrika* 74:375–84.

Browne, Michael W., and Gerhard Arminger. 1995. "Specification and Estimation of Mean and Covariance Structure Models." Pp. 185–249 in *Handbook of Statistical Modeling for the Social and Behavioral Sciences*, edited by G. Arminger, C.C. Clogg, and M.E. Sobel. New York: Plenum.

Browne, Michael W., and Alexander Shapiro. 1988. "Robustness of Normal Theory Methods in the Analysis of Linear Latent Variate Models." *British Journal of Mathematical and Statistical Psychology* 41:193–208.

Curran, Patrick S., Stephen G. West, and John F. Finch. 1996. "The Robustness of Test Statistics to Nonnormality and Specification Error in Confirmatory Factor Analysis." *Psychological Methods* 1:16–29.

Dempster, Arthur P., Nan M. Laird, and Donald B. Rubin. 1977. "Maximum Likelihood Estimation from Incomplete Data via the EM Algorithm" (with discussion). *Journal of the Royal Statistical Society*, ser. B, 39:1–38.

Dijkstra, Theo K. 1981. *Latent Variables in Linear Stochastic Models: Reflections on "Maximum Likelihood" and "Partial Least Squares" Methods*. Ph.D. dissertation, University of Groningen.

Fang, Kai-Tai, Samuel Kotz, and Kaiwang Ng. 1990. *Symmetric Multivariate and Related Distributions*. London: Chapman and Hall.

Ferguson, Thomas S. 1996. *A Course in Large Sample Theory*. London: Chapman and Hall.

Finkbeiner, Carl. 1979. "Estimation for the Multiple Factor Model When Data Are Missing." *Psychometrika* 44:409–20.

Godambe, Vidyadhar P., and Belvant K. Kale. 1991. "Estimating Function: An Overview." Pp. 3–20 in *Estimating Functions*, edited by V.P. Godambe. New York: Oxford University Press.

Gourieroux, Christian, Alain Monfort, and Alain Trognon. 1984. "Pseudo Maximum Likelihood Methods: Theory." *Econometrica* 52:681–700.

Hu, Litze, Peter M. Bentler, and Yutaka Kano. 1992. "Can Test Statistics in Covariance Structure Analysis Be Trusted?" *Psychological Bulletin* 112:351–62.

Jamshidian, Mortaza, and Peter M. Bentler. 1999. "Using Complete Data Routines for ML Estimation of Mean and Covariance Structures with Missing Data." *Journal of Educational and Behavioral Statistics* 23:21–41.

Jöreskog, Karl G., and Dag Sörbom. 1993. *LISREL 8 User's Reference Guide*, Chicago: Scientific Software International.

Khatri, C. G. 1966. "A Note on a MANOVA Model Applied to Problems in Growth Curves." *Annals of the Institute of Statistical Mathematics* 18:75–86.

Kline, Rex B. 1998. *Principles and Practice of Structural Equation Modeling*. New York: Guilford.

Laird, Nan M. 1988. "Missing Data in Longitudinal Studies." *Statistics in Medicine* 7: 305–15.

Lange, Kenneth L., Roderick J.A. Little, and Jeremy M.G. Taylor. 1989. "Robust Statistical Modeling Using the t Distribution." *Journal of the American Statistical Association* 84:881–96.

Lee, Sik-Yum. 1986. "Estimation for Structural Equation Models with Missing Data." *Psychometrika* 51:93–99.

Liang, Kung-Yee, and Scott L. Zeger. 1986. "Longitudinal Data Analysis Using Generalized Linear Models." *Biometrika* 73:13–22.

Little, Roderick J.A. 1988. "Robust Estimation of the Mean and Covariance Matrix from Data with Missing Values." *Applied Statistics* 37:23–38.

Little, Roderick J.A., and Donald E. Rubin. 1987. *Statistical Analysis with Missing Data*. New York: Wiley.

Magnus, Jan R., and Heinz Neudecker. 1988. *Matrix Differential Calculus with Applications in Statistics and Econometrics*. New York: Wiley.

Mardia, Kanti V., John T. Kent, and John M. Bibby. 1979. *Multivariate Analysis*. New York: Academic Press.

Marsh, Herbert W. 1998. "Pairwise Deletion for Missing Data in Structural Equation Models: Nonpositive Definite Matrices, Parameter Estimates, Goodness of Fit, and Adjusted Sample Sizes." *Structural Equation Modeling* 5:22–36.

Meng, Xiao-Li. 1994. "Multiple Imputation Inferences with Uncongenial Sources of Input" (with discussion). *Statistical Science* 9:538–73.

Meng, Xiao-Li, and Steven Pedlow. 1992. "EM: A Bibliographic Review with Missing Articles." Pp. 24–27 in *Statistical Computing Section, Proceedings of the American Statistical Association*.

Micceri, Theodore. 1989. "The Unicorn, the Normal Curve, and Other Improbable Creatures." *Psychological Bulletin* 105:156–66.

Mooijaart, Ab, and Peter M. Bentler. 1991. "Robustness of Normal Theory Statistics in Structural Equation Models." *Statistica Neerlandica* 45:159–71.

Mueller, Ralph O. 1996. *Basic Principles of Structural Equation Modeling*. New York: Springer Verlag.

Muirhead, R. J. 1982. *Aspects of Multivariate Statistical Theory*. New York: Wiley.

Muirhead, Robb J., and Christine M. Waternaux. 1980. "Asymptotic Distributions in Canonical Correlation Analysis and Other Multivariate Procedures for Nonnormal Populations." *Biometrika* 67:31–43.

Muthén, Bengt, David Kaplan, and Michael Hollis. 1987. "On Structural Equation Modeling with Data that Are Not Missing Completely at Random." *Psychometrika* 52:431–62.

Muthén, Linda, and Bengt Muthén. 1998. *Mplus User's Guide*. Los Angeles: Muthén and Muthén.

Neale, Michael C. 1994. "Mx: Statistical Modeling," 2nd ed. Box 710 MCV, Richmond, VA 23298: Department of Psychiatry, Medical College of Virginia.

Olkin, Ingram. 1994. "Multivariate Nonnormal Distributions and Models of Dependency." Pp. 37–53 in *Multivariate Analysis and Its Applications*, edited by T.W. Anderson, K.T. Fang, and I. Olkin. Hayward, CA: IMS.

Rotnitzky, Andrea, and David Wypij. 1994. "A Note on the Bias of Estimators with Missing Data." *Biometrics* 50:1163–70.

Rovine, Michael J. 1994. "Latent Variables Models and Missing Data Analysis." Pp. 181–225 in *Latent Variables Analysis: Applications for Developmental Research*, edited by A. von Eye and C.C. Clogg. Thousand Oaks, CA: Sage.

Rubin, Donald B. 1987. *Multiple Imputation for Nonresponse in Surveys*. New York: Wiley.

———. 1996. "Multiple Imputation after 18 Years." *Journal of the American Statistical Association* 91:473–89.

Satorra, Albert, and Peter M. Bentler. 1988. "Scaling Corrections for Chi-Square Statistics in Covariance Structure Analysis." Pp. 308–13 in *American Statistical Association 1988 Proceedings of Business and Economics Sections*. Alexandria, VA: American Statistical Association.

———. 1990. "Model Conditions for Asymptotic Robustness in the Analysis of Linear Relations." *Computational Statistics and Data Analysis* 10:235–49.

———. 1991. "Goodness-of-fit Test under IV Estimation: Asymptotic Robustness of a NT Test Statistic." Pp. 555–67 in *Applied Stochastic Models and Data Analysis*, edited by R. Gutiérrez and M.J. Valderrama. Singapore: World Scientific.

———. 1994. "Corrections to Test Statistics and Standard Errors in Covariance Structure Analysis." Pp. 399–419 in *Latent Variables Analysis: Applications for Developmental Research*, edited by A. von Eye and C.C. Clogg. Newbury Park, CA: Sage.

Schafer, Joseph L. 1997. *Analysis of Incomplete Multivariate Data*. London: Chapman and Hall.

Schoenberg, Ronald. 1989. *LINCS: Linear Covariance Structure Analysis. User's Guide*. Kent, WA: RJS Software.

Shapiro, Alexander. 1983. "Asymptotic Distribution Theory in the Analysis of Covariance Structures (a Unified Approach)." *South African Statistical Journal* 17:33–81.

———. 1987. "Robustness Properties of the MDF Analysis of Moment Structures." *South African Statistical Journal* 21:39–62.

Shapiro, Alexander, and Michael Browne. 1987. "Analysis of Covariance Structures under Elliptical Distributions." *Journal of the American Statistical Association* 82:1092–97.

Tanaka, Yutaka, Shingo Watadani, and Sung Ho Moon. 1991. "Influence in Covariance Structure Analysis: With an Application to Confirmatory Factor Analysis." *Communication in Statistics-Theory and Method* 20:3805–21.

Yuan, Ke-Hai, and Peter M. Bentler. 1996. "Mean and Covariance Structure Analysis with Missing Data." Pp. 307–26 in *Multidimensional Statistical Analysis and Theory of Random Matrices: Proceedings of Sixth Eugene Lukacs Symposium*, edited by A. Gupta and V. Girko. Utrecht, Netherlands: VSP.

———. 1997a. "Mean and Covariance Structure Analysis: Theoretical and Practical Improvements." *Journal of the American Statistical Association* 92:767–74.

———. 1997b. "Improving Parameter Tests in Covariance Structure Analysis." *Computational Statistics and Data Analysis* 26:177–98.

———. 1998. "Normal Theory Based Test Statistics in Structural Equation Modelling." *British Journal of Mathematical and Statistical Psychology* 51:289–309.

———. 1999. "On Normal Theory and Associated Test Statistics in Covariance Structure Analysis Under Two Classes of Nonnormal Distributions." *Statistica Sinica* 9:831–53.

Yuan, Ke-Hai, and Robert I. Jennrich. 1998. “Asymptotics of Estimating Equations Under Natural Conditions.” *Journal of Multivariate Analysis* 65:245–60.

Yung, Yiu-Fai, and Peter M. Bentler. 1996. “Bootstrapping Techniques in Analysis of Mean and Covariance Structures.” Pp. 195–226 in *Advanced Structural Equation Modeling Techniques*, edited by G.A. Marcoulides & R.E. Schumacker. Mahwah, NJ: Erlbaum.

6

DISCRETE-TIME MULTILEVEL HAZARD ANALYSIS

*Jennifer S. Barber**
*Susan A. Murphy**
*William G. Axinn**
Jerry Maples†

Combining innovations in hazard modeling with those in multilevel modeling, we develop a method to estimate discrete-time multilevel hazard models. We derive the likelihood of and formulate assumptions for a discrete-time multilevel hazard model with time-varying covariates at two levels. We pay special attention to assumptions justifying the estimation method. Next, we demonstrate file construction and estimation of the models using two common software packages, HLM and MLN. We also illustrate the use of both packages by estimating a model of the hazard of contraceptive use in rural Nepal using time-varying covariates at both individual and neighborhood levels.

The first and second authors contributed equally to this paper. This paper benefited substantially from comments and suggestions by the editors and reviewers. This research was supported by National Institute of Child Health and Human Development grant HD32912, by National Science Foundation grants SBR 9811983 and DMS 9802885, by grant P50 DA 10075 from National Institute on Drug Abuse to the Pennsylvania State University's Methodology Center, and by a P30 center grant from NICHD to the University of Michigan's Population Studies Center. Direct correspondence to the first author at the Institute for Social Research, University of Michigan, 426 Thompson St., Ann Arbor, Michigan, 48106-1248 or via e-mail at jebarber@umich.edu.
*University of Michigan
†Pennsylvania State University

1. INTRODUCTION

Over the past two decades, one of the central themes in sociology has been the study of individual life courses: understanding the timing and sequencing of life events such as cohabitation, marriage, labor force entry and exit, and educational attainment (Elder 1977, 1983; Rindfuss, Morgan, and Swicegood 1988; Thornton, Axinn, and Teachman 1995). As a result, sociological models of individual behavior have become increasingly dynamic, even incorporating measures of individual characteristics that change over time. A wide range of advances in the estimation of hazard models with time-varying covariates has fueled this explosion in dynamic modeling (Allison 1984; Petersen 1991; Yamaguchi 1991).

Another central theme in both classic and modern sociology has been the relationship between macro-level social changes and micro-level behavior (Alexander 1988; Coleman 1990; Durkheim [1933] 1984; Smith 1989; Weber 1922). Recent advances in multilevel modeling have dramatically improved efforts to include macro characteristics, sometimes called ecological, neighborhood, or contextual characteristics, in micro-level models of behavior (Bryk and Raudenbush 1992; DiPrete and Forristal 1994; Goldstein 1995; Ringdal 1992). These advances include not only multilevel linear models, but also multilevel generalized linear models such as logistic regression and log-linear regression (see Bryk, Raudenbush, and Congdon 1996; Goldstein 1995; Wong and Mason 1985).

In this paper we combine the dynamic approach to modeling provided by hazard models with multilevel models. We have three goals: (1) to develop a discrete-time multilevel hazard model; (2) to illustrate the use of well known software to estimate models of macrolevel effects on microlevel behavior where there is change over time at both the micro and macro levels of analysis; and (3) to provide details regarding the assumptions that allow the regression coefficients of both the micro- and macro-level covariates to be estimated in a multilevel hazard analysis framework.

Estimation procedures for multilevel models of social behavior must accommodate multilevel data structures. Classical statistical procedures, such as hazard analysis, assume that subjects (or individuals) behave independently, yet it is likely that individuals in the same macro context behave more similarly than individuals from different contexts. As a consequence, statistical procedures that ignore the multilevel data structure underestimate standard errors leading to hypothesis tests with elevated Type 1 error rates (rejecting the null hypothesis in error). Kreft (1994:151) gives a thorough discussion of this issue in the linear regression setting, and Muthén (1997:455–58) gives a similar discussion in the context of linear latent variable models.

The use of a single-level hazard model for multilevel data creates additional complications due to the fact that hazard models are both nonlinear and dynamic. First, if one wants to compare individuals with different characteristics within the same or similar macro contexts, then regression coefficients in the single-level nonlinear model applied to data on individuals grouped within contexts are not the desired regression coefficients (Diggle, Liang, and Zeger 1994). Rather, regression coefficients from the single-level nonlinear model reflect marginal comparisons of individuals from the variety of contexts. In other words, these models do not statistically control for macro contextual characteristics. Thus, if the goal is to compare the contraceptive behavior of educated women to the contraceptive behavior of uneducated women within neighborhoods with similar access to schooling opportunities, then the coefficients from the single-level nonlinear model are inappropriate.

Second, hazard models are dynamic in that the event under study, such as initiation of permanent contraception, unfolds over time. If a single-level hazard model is applied to multilevel data, duration bias results (Trussell and Richards 1985; Vaupel and Yashin 1985; Yamaguchi 1991). Suppose that the event is the initiation of permanent contraception and suppose that the macro context is the neighborhood and neighborhoods are heterogeneous—e.g. some neighborhoods are special in that their characteristics lead to delayed permanent contraceptive use. As time proceeds most of the women who have yet to experience the event will be from the neighborhoods that delay the event time. The estimator of the baseline hazard will not reflect the hazard for any one type of individual; rather it reflects an average hazard, calculated over the variety of macro-level contexts. At later times this average will be primarily over individuals from the special contexts. The unobserved heterogeneity of the contexts results in an underestimation of the baseline hazard. One way to reduce the bias is to include a random intercept in the regression model for the hazard (Vaupel and Yashin 1985).

Suppose that the association of an individual level covariate, such as a woman's educational level, with the event, contraceptive timing, varies across contexts. The unobserved heterogeneity of the contexts then results in a second form of duration bias, a biased regression coefficient. At earlier times the regression coefficient of a woman's education level reflects a comparison of groups of women wherein each group is composed of subjects from the full variety of neighborhoods. But at later times, the regression coefficient for women's education reflects a comparison of groups of women wherein the groups are primarily composed of women from the special neighborhoods. To prevent this bias, we propose a multilevel model including random coefficients. The crux is that multilevel models of social behavior demand not only multilevel data but also multilevel statistical procedures.

A first step in avoiding the above problems is to use statistical procedures that acknowledge the multilevel data structure. However, multilevel *hazard models* are uncommon, particularly models involving both individual and macro-level time-varying covariates. (For examples of multilevel hazard models, see Brewster 1994; Guo 1993; Guo and Rodríguez 1992; Hedeker, Siddiqui, and Hu 1998; Ma and Willms 1999; Massey and Espinosa 1996; Sastry 1996, 1997; Vaupel 1988). Few use a fully dynamic multilevel model with interactions between macro-level and individual level covariates and dynamic time-varying measures at both macro and individual levels in models of individual behavior. One reason has been a dearth of data providing measures of change over time in macro-level characteristics. However, recent advances in data collection methods have led to the development of techniques for collecting a continuous record of change over time in macro-level (e.g., neighborhood) characteristics (Axinn, Barber, and Ghimire 1997). Another reason has been lack of widely available estimation procedures. Widely available software programs developed for multilevel data (e.g., HLM, MLN, Proc Mixed in SAS) have not been explicitly extended to discrete-time hazard analysis with time-varying covariates, and most software programs developed for hazard models (e.g. S-PLUS, STATA) have not been extended to fit multilevel data. The ideal multilevel hazard analysis program would allow both time-varying macro-level and individual level covariates.

2. AN EMPIRICAL EXAMPLE

Our example comes from the Chitwan Valley Family Study. The purpose of the study was to collect detailed information about historical social changes in the neighborhoods in the valley, and to analyze how those social changes relate to individual level behavioral change in the propensity to use contraceptives, to delay marriage, and to limit childbearing. Data were collected from 171 neighborhoods in the Chitwan Valley, located in central Nepal. Every individual in each of the 171 neighborhoods was interviewed. The study collected retrospective histories of change in each neighborhood using the Neighborhood History Calendar method (Axinn et al. 1997), and retrospective histories of each individual's behavior using a life history calendar adapted specifically to the setting (Axinn, Pearce, and Ghimire 1999). Our analysis examines women aged 49 and younger who have had at least one birth.

We will test three hypotheses concerning the timing of permanent contraceptive use, chosen to highlight the model's flexibility for estimating the effects of different types of covariates. The hypotheses are as follows:

H1 (individual level)	Educated women have a higher hazard of using a permanent contraceptive method compared to uneducated women.[1]
H2 (neighborhood level)	Increased access to nearby schooling opportunities is associated with a higher hazard of using a permanent contraceptive method.
H3 (cross level)	The association between education and permanent contraceptive use is stronger in neighborhoods with a school nearby.

With H1, we compare the timing of permanent contraceptive use between women of different levels of education but within the same or similar neighborhoods.[2] With H2, we test whether women who live in neighborhoods with access to schools are more likely to limit their childbearing via contraceptive use. When schooling opportunities are convenient and nearby, a woman is more likely to expect that her children will attend school, which increases the hazard of permanent contraceptive use. H3, our cross-level hypothesis, is a macro-micro interaction: living in a

[1]We focus on *permanent* contraceptive use because the vast majority of contraception in Nepal is used for stopping childbearing rather than spacing births. We consider a woman's own sterilization, her spouse's sterilization, IUD, Norplant, and Depo-provera to be permanent methods in this setting (Axinn and Barber 1999). Because permanent contraception among women who have no children is extremely rare in this setting, we consider women to be at risk of contracepting only after they have given birth to their first child.

[2]Much has been written about the effects of education on contraceptive use, and we refer readers to this vast literature rather than elaborating on this hypothesis here (see Axinn 1993; Axinn and Barber 1999).

neighborhood with a school nearby will strengthen the individual level relationship between a woman's own education and her propensity to use a permanent contraceptive method. Women with formal education may be more likely to limit their family size precisely because they want to send their children to school (Axinn 1993); thus the relationship between a woman's own education and her family-limiting behavior will be stronger if she believes that she will actually have the opportunity to send her children to school.

To construct a model to test these hypotheses, we use the following variables with subscripts denoting the tth calendar year, and the jth woman in the kth neighborhood.

- Y_{tjk} = a dichotomous indicator of whether woman j in neighborhood k initiates permanent contraceptive use during year t. *This is the dependent variable.*
- p_{tjk} = the hazard of initiating permanent contraception by woman j in neighborhood k during year t (given no prior contraceptive use). This is the mean of Y_{tjk} given no prior contraceptive use and all prior covariate measurements.
- Educ_j = a dichotomous indicator of whether woman j attended school (before the birth of her first child). *This is a time-invariant individual level covariate.*
- Chldrn_{tj} = the total number of children woman j has had by year t, minus one.[3] *This is a time-varying individual level covariate.*[4]
- School_{tk} = a dichotomous indicator of whether there is a school within a five-minute walk from neighborhood k during year t. *This is a time-varying group level covariate.*
- Dis_k = distance from the neighborhood to nearest town. Distance in miles to the nearest town was computed using global positioning systems technology. *This is a time-invariant group level covariate.*

[3] Total number of children is coded as the actual number the woman gave birth to minus one because we analyze only women who have given birth to at least one child. If we did not transform the variable in this way, the baseline hazard would be estimated for a woman with zero children, which is outside the valid range in this analysis (Kreft, DeLeeuw, and Aiken 1995).

[4] Our time-varying measures of individual and neighborhood characteristics are measured in the year *prior* to the current year of permanent contraceptive risk. For example, we use the total number of children in the prior year to predict the hazard of permanent contraceptive use in the current year. In other words, all time-varying covariates are lagged by one year.

- The two variables shown below are used to indicate the baseline hazard in the models. They are counter variables where the first person-year for each woman is coded 0, and each subsequent year is incremented accordingly. These two measures form the baseline hazard of permanent contraceptive use.

Time_{tj} = number of years since woman j's first birth.

Time^2_{tj} = number of years since woman j's first birth, squared.[5]

We estimate a multilevel hazard model that allows the effects of education and total number of children to vary by neighborhood. We model the hazard by the logit link; thus the parameters represent additive effects on the log-odds of contraceptive use. The following represents the multilevel model, which we call the conceptual model (CM). Using multilevel terminology, the *individual level model*, or hazard model, for woman j in neighborhood k is

$$\text{Logit}(p_{tjk}) = \beta_{0k} + \beta_{1k}\text{Educ}_j + \beta_{2k}\text{Chldrn}_{tj} + \beta_3\text{Time}_{tj} + \beta_4\text{Time}^2_{tj}. \qquad \text{(CM 1a)}$$

Note that β_0, β_1, and β_2 are indexed by k. This is to allow these effects to vary by neighborhood. We allow β_0 (the intercept in the individual model) to vary by neighborhood so that the overall level of contraceptive use is a function of the neighborhood in which the respondent lives. One way in which the intercept may vary is according to whether a school is nearby. Another way it may vary is by how far from the nearest town the neighborhood lies. We allow β_1 to vary by neighborhood so that the effect of a woman's education on her initiation of permanent contraceptive use may vary by neighborhood because of the different schooling opportunities in each neighborhood. In addition, we allow β_2 to vary by neighborhood because the effect of having a large number of children may differ according to neighborhood.

[5] We also estimated models with dichotomous indicators of each time period. The estimates of the other coefficients in these models did not change. Thus, we chose to parsimoniously represent time in our models with Time and Time^2.

Thus the *neighborhood level model* is

$$\beta_{0k} = \gamma_{00} + \gamma_{01}\text{Dis}_k + \gamma_{02}\text{School}_{tk} + \epsilon_{0k} \qquad \text{(CM 1b)}$$

$$\beta_{1k} = \gamma_{10} + \gamma_{11}\text{School}_{tk} + \epsilon_{1k}$$

$$\beta_{2k} = \gamma_{20} + \epsilon_{2k}$$

$$\beta_3 = \gamma_{30}$$

$$\beta_4 = \gamma_{40}$$

The $\underset{\sim}{\epsilon}$ $(= \epsilon_{0k}, \epsilon_{1k}, \epsilon_{2k})$ are unobserved error terms or random effects that model the correlation between the timing of contraceptive use by women in the same neighborhood; women in the same neighborhood share the same error terms. We assume that $\underset{\sim}{\epsilon}$ is multivariate normal with mean zero and an unknown variance-covariance matrix.

In this model, β_{0k} represents the overall level of contraceptive use in neighborhood k, which varies by the neighborhood's distance to the nearest town and the presence of a school in the neighborhood. β_{1k} represents the effect of women's education for neighborhood k, which varies by the presence of a school in the neighborhood. β_{2k} represents the effects of the woman's total number of children for neighborhood k. Finally, β_3 and β_4 represent the effects of Time since first birth and Time^2 since first birth, respectively.

Note that although this model is expressed at each level, it is actually only one model; to see this, substitute the level 2 equations for the βs in the level 1 equation,

$$\begin{aligned}\text{Logit}(p_{tjk}) = {} & (\gamma_{00} + \gamma_{01}\text{Dis}_k + \gamma_{02}\text{School}_{tk} + \epsilon_{0k}) \\ & + (\gamma_{10} + \gamma_{11}\text{School}_{tk} + \epsilon_{1k})\text{Educ}_j \\ & + (\gamma_{20} + \epsilon_{2k})\text{Chldrn}_{tj} + \gamma_{30}\text{Time}_{tj} \\ & + \gamma_{40}\text{Time}^2_{tj}. \end{aligned} \qquad \text{(CM 1c)}$$

This presentation of the model is likely to be more intuitive to those most familiar with single-level hazard analysis.

Conceptual model CM is used to make the likelihood derivations in the next section concrete. A multilevel model may be of more levels and may include more covariates. Furthermore, the link function need not be the logistic link; other link functions can be used and do not alter the likelihood derivations. For example, the log(-log) function, or the probit function could be used.

3. THE LIKELIHOOD

In this section we demonstrate that conditionally on the $\underset{\sim}{\epsilon}$, the likelihood for a group (a neighborhood in our example) is given by the same formula as in Allison (1982, eqs. 18–20; see also Laird and Olivier 1981). This means that any program for maximum-likelihood estimation in a multilevel regression analysis of a dichotomous dependent variable can be used to estimate the regression coefficients. This is analogous to Allison's (1982:74) result that single-level discrete time hazard models can be estimated using programs for the analysis of dichotomous dependent variables such as Proc Logistic in SAS.

We first formulate the model and the likelihood for one group; so in this section we omit the subscript k. We derive the likelihood in the complete data setting, acting as if the response is not censored. Next, we allow for censoring and include all groups in the likelihood. To highlight our assumptions, we give this derivation for only two levels (individual and group); the derivation for three or more levels is similar. Suppose M is the total number of time periods possible for the entire study. In our example, time (t) is calendar time, a period is one year, and M is 60 years. The jth subject's response is the time to the event, T_j (initiation of contraception in our example). Alternately we denote the jth response by Y_{tj}, $t = 1, \ldots, M$, where Y_{tj} is a time-varying dichotomous random variable with the value 1 if $T_j = t$ and 0 otherwise. Thus $Y_{tj} = 0$ for $t = 1, \ldots, M$ except in the year of the event, when $Y_{tj} = 1$. Or, $Y_{tj} = 0$ for all $t = 1, \ldots, M$ if $T_j > M$ (i.e., the event does not occur within the M periods). The jth subject's at-risk variable, R_{tj}, is 1 if the jth subject is at risk of the event at time t and is 0 otherwise. In our example, a woman is not at risk of contraceptive initiation before the birth of her first child or after age 49. Thus $R_{tj} = 0$ until the period after the jth woman's first childbirth. The year after her first child's birth, $R_{tj} = 1$; it remains 1 until the year after she initiates contraception or until she reaches age 50, whichever occurs first. Sometimes when discussing multiple subjects from the same group simultaneously, we use the subscript i (in addition to the subscript j) to denote the "other" subject.

The collection of error terms in the group level model is denoted by $\underset{\sim}{\epsilon}$ (these are the errors, ϵ_0, ϵ_1, ϵ_2, in our neighborhood level model). The group level covariates at time t are GZ_t. IZ_{tj} denotes the jth subject's individual level covariates at time t. After a subject experiences the event (initiation of contraception), we do not use the individual level covariates. Thus if $t > T_j$, IZ_{tj} is left undefined. All of the time-invariant individual level covariates are contained in IZ_{1j}, and GZ_1 contains all of the time-invariant group level covariates. The variables for a group of size n are summarized in Table 1.

Our primary assumption is a *modeling assumption* for the conditional hazard probability that the jth subject will experience the event at time t. That is, conditional on $T_j \geq t$, on the error terms ($\underset{\sim}{\epsilon}$), on the covariates $\{GZ_s = gz_s, IZ_{sj} = iz_{si}, s \leq t, i = 1, \ldots, n\}$, and on the past responses by the other group members $\{Y_{si}, s < t, i \neq j\}$, the probability that $T_j = t$ (or equivalently $Y_{tj} = 1$), is

$$p_{tj} = p_{tj}(\underset{\sim}{\epsilon}, gz_s, iz_{sj}, s \leq t).$$

That is, the hazard probability (p_{tj}) is assumed to be a function of only the jth subject's past covariates, not the covariates of other subjects. Other subjects' covariates thought to be predictive of the jth subject's event time should be included in the jth subject's covariates. For example, if we believe that other subjects' views on contraceptive use may influence the contraceptive use of the jth subject, then we should include those views in the covariates for the jth subject. Thus in our example we make the modeling assumption that (1) given the woman does not initiate contraceptive use prior to year t; and (2) given her total number of children (Chldrn_{tj}), education level (Educ_j), distance to the nearest town (Dis_k), presence of a nearby school (School_{tk}), and $\underset{\sim}{\epsilon}$, the chance that the jth woman initiates contraceptive use in year t does not depend on other

TABLE 1
Variables for a Group

Responses	$T_j, j = 1, \ldots, n$ OR $Y_{tj}, t = 1, \ldots, M; j = 1, \ldots, n$
At risk indicators	$R_{tj}, t = 1, \ldots, M; j = 1, \ldots, n$
Group level errors	$\underset{\sim}{\epsilon}$
Group level covariates	$GZ_t, t = 1, \ldots, M$
Individual level covariates	$IZ_{tj}, t = 1, \ldots, M; j = 1, \ldots, n$

characteristics of her neighbors. Additionally we assume that the covariates are related to the hazard via the logistic function as given in the conceptual model CM.

The second assumption is *conditional independence*. In the multilevel nonlinear model for binary responses, the residual correlation between responses within a group are modeled by the error terms (e.g., see the conditional likelihoods in Rodriguez and Goldman (1995, eq. 7) or Hedeker and Gibbons (1994, eq. 2)). That is, conditional on the error terms ($\underset{\sim}{\epsilon}$) and the covariates, the responses within the group are modeled as independent. We make a similar conditional independence assumption for the multilevel hazard model. The *conditional independence* assumption is that the responses $(Y_{tj}, j=1,\ldots,n)$ are independent conditional on the error terms ($\underset{\sim}{\epsilon}$), on the covariates $(\{GZ_s, s \leq t\}, \{IZ_{sj}, s \leq t, j=1,\ldots,n\})$, and on the past responses by all group members $\{Y_{sj}, s < t, j=1,\ldots,n\}$. In our example, we are assuming that the jth woman's decision to initiate contraceptive use at time t is independent of her neighbors' contraceptive decisions at time t, given that she has yet to initiate contraceptive use, all other available observations on her neighbors at time t and conditional on the error terms in the neighborhood model. This assumption implies that, at least approximately, all of one woman's influence on her neighbor in terms of contraceptive use is via unmeasured neighborhood level influences (the $\underset{\sim}{\epsilon}$) and via observed shared neighborhood and individual characteristics.

We denote the conditional density of the group level covariates at time t given the error terms, past covariates, and past responses by $g_t(gz_t | \underset{\sim}{\epsilon}, \{gz_s, iz_{sj}, y_{sj}, s < t\}, j = 1,\ldots,n)$ and denote the conditional density of the n group members' individual level covariates at time t given the error terms, past covariates, past responses, and time t group level covariates by $f_t(iz_{tj}, j=1,\ldots,n | \underset{\sim}{\epsilon}, \{gz_s, s \leq t\}, \{iz_{sj}, y_{sj}, s < t\}, j=1,\ldots,n)$. The *modeling assumption* and the *conditional independence* assumption imply that the likelihood for Y_{tj}, GZ_t, IZ_{tj}, $t = 1,\ldots,M; j = 1,\ldots,n$ given $\underset{\sim}{\epsilon}$ is

$$\prod_{t=1}^{M} g_t(gz_t) \prod_{t=1}^{M} f_t(iz_{tj}, j = 1,\ldots,n) \prod_{t=1}^{M} \prod_{j=1}^{n} [(1 - p_{tj})^{(1-y_{tj})} p_{tj}^{y_{tj}}]^{r_{tj}},$$

where we abbreviated p_{tj}, g_t, and f_t by omitting the conditioning sets.

To form the likelihood for the group's observed data, we include the distribution of the error term and integrate out the error term, resulting in the rather complicated formula for the observed likelihood for a group,

$$\int \phi(\underset{\sim}{\epsilon}) \prod_{t=1}^{M} g_t(gz_t) \prod_{t=1}^{M} f_t(iz_{tj}, j = 1, \ldots, n) \prod_{j=1}^{n} \prod_{t=1}^{M} [(1 - p_{tj})^{(1-y_{tj})} p_{tj}^{y_{tj}}]^{r_{tj}} \, d\underset{\sim}{\epsilon}$$

where ϕ is the multivariate normal distribution with mean zero and unknown variance-covariance matrix. Without further assumptions, this likelihood is of little use. This is because the integral is quite complex, due to the fact that the covariate distributions (g_t and f_t) may depend on the error terms ($\underset{\sim}{\epsilon}$). Thus our third assumption is that the covariates are *noninformative* of the error terms. That is, the covariates at time t (GZ_t, IZ_{tj}, $j = 1, \ldots, n$) are independent of the error term ($\underset{\sim}{\epsilon}$) given past responses and covariates (Y_{sj}, GZ_s, IZ_{sj}, $s < t, j = 1, \ldots, n$). This assumption means that both g_t and f_t are not functions of $\underset{\sim}{\epsilon}$ and only p_{tj} remains a function of $\underset{\sim}{\epsilon}$; thus we may rewrite the above likelihood as

$$\prod_{t=1}^{M} g_t(gz_t) \prod_{t=1}^{M} f_t(iz_{tj}, j = 1, \ldots, n) \int \phi(\underset{\sim}{\epsilon}) \prod_{t=1}^{M} \prod_{j=1}^{n} [(1 - p_{tj})^{(1-y_{tj})} p_{tj}^{y_{tj}}]^{r_{tj}} \, d\underset{\sim}{\epsilon}. \tag{2}$$

This is one group's contribution to the likelihood.

The *noninformative covariates* assumption is not innocuous. If we conceptualize the error terms as unmeasured group level covariates, then we are assuming that conditional on past observations, the unmeasured group level covariates are independent of the covariates measured at time t. Thus at first it appears that the covariates should simply be independent of the error terms. However this independence property must hold conditional on the past responses. To illustrate the stringent nature of this assumption, suppose that there is an unmeasured common cause of both the response at time 2 (Y_{2j}) and the individual level covariate at the future time 3 (IZ_{3j}). Denote this unmeasured common cause by U_{1j}. Our model assumes that $\underset{\sim}{\epsilon}$ is a predictor of Y_{2j}. Since Y_{2j} is predicted by both U_{1j} and $\underset{\sim}{\epsilon}$, we may expect that conditional on Y_{2j}, U_{1j} is correlated with $\underset{\sim}{\epsilon}$. Combining this (conditional on Y_{2j}, U_{1j} is correlated with $\underset{\sim}{\epsilon}$) with the fact that U_{1j} is a cause of IZ_{3j} implies that conditionally on Y_{2j}, $\underset{\sim}{\epsilon}$ will be a predictor of IZ_{3j}. Thus, although $\underset{\sim}{\epsilon}$ is marginally independent of the covariate IZ_{3j}, the presence of an unmeasured common cause of both IZ_{3j} and the response (Y_{2j}) will, in general, lead to a violation of the *noninformative covariates* assumption. Of course, if the covariate is exogenous—for example, a randomized treatment—then there are no unmeasured common causes of both the covariate and the response, and the *noninformative covariates* assumption is satisfied. Alternatively, we may believe that we have included all important common predictors of future responses and future covariate values in our collection of past covariates and that all measured covariates are uncorrelated with the error terms. In our extremely simplified model, we are assuming that the distance to the nearest town (Dis) and whether the woman ever went to school (Educ), combined with total number of children (Chldrn) and the presence of a school (School) *in the past*, contain all common predictors of current contraceptive initiation, current number of children (Chldrn), and current presence of a school (School). Furthermore, we are assuming that the total number of children (Chldrn), presence of a school (School), distance to the nearest town (Dis), and whether the woman ever went to school (Educ) are independent of $\underline{\epsilon}$.

Suppose that some members of the group are observed for a shorter, nonrandom period than the entire M intervals. For example, suppose that the jth subject is followed from time 1 until time c_j where c_j is a fixed constant. In this case the data for a group are Y_{sj}, IZ_{sj}, R_{sj}, for $s \leq c_j\ j = 1,\ldots,n$ and GZ_s, for $s \leq M$. The likelihood from (2) is then

$$\prod_{t=1}^{M} g_t(gz_t) \prod_{t=1}^{M} f_t(iz_{tj}, t \leq c_j, j = 1,\ldots,n)$$

$$\times \int \phi(\underline{\epsilon}) \prod_{j=1}^{n} \prod_{t=1}^{c_j} [(1 - p_{tj})^{(1-y_{tj})} p_{tj}^{y_{tj}}]^{r_{tj}} d\underline{\epsilon}, \tag{3}$$

where f_t is the conditional density of the individual level covariates (IZ_{tj}) for which $t \leq c_j$, given the error terms, past covariates, past responses, and time t group level covariates.

Even if the covariate distributions in (3) contain information about the hazard regression coefficients, we can use only the last term in (3) in the estimation of the hazard regression coefficients (Gill 1992). This is because the last term in (3) is a "partial likelihood" as defined by Cox (1975) and Wong (1986). A partial likelihood is the product of conditional densities under the restriction that the conditioning sets are nested. The results of Gill (1992) imply that the last term in (3) is equal to

$$\int \phi(\underset{\sim}{\epsilon}) \prod_{j=1}^{n} \prod_{t=1}^{c_j} [(1 - p_{tj})^{(1-y_{tj})} p_{tj}^{y_{tj}}]^{r_{tj}} \, d\underset{\sim}{\epsilon}$$

$$= \prod_{t=1}^{M} P[Y_{tj} = y_{tj}, t \le c_j, j = 1, \ldots, n \,|\, (GZ_s, IZ_{sj}, s \le \min(t, c_j));$$

$$(Y_{sj}, s < t, s \le c_j), j = 1, \ldots, n].$$

Because the set $\{GZ_s = gz_s, IZ_{sj} = iz_{sj}, s \le \min(u, c_j); Y_{sj} = y_{sj}, s < u, s \le c_j, j = 1, \ldots, n\}$ contains the set $\{GZ_s = gz_s, IZ_{sj} = iz_{sj}, s \le \min(t, c_j); Y_{sj} = y_{sj}, s < t, s \le c_j, j = 1, \ldots, n\}$ for u less than t, this product is a partial likelihood.

We can write the (partial) likelihood for a sample of N groups by adding an additional subscript to denote the kth group and multiplying across groups:

$$\prod_{k=1}^{N} \int \phi(\underset{\sim}{\epsilon}) \prod_{j=1}^{n_k} \prod_{t=1}^{c_{jk}} [(1 - p_{tjk})^{(1-y_{tjk})} p_{tjk}^{y_{tjk}}]^{r_{tjk}} \, d\underset{\sim}{\epsilon}. \quad (4)$$

Wong (1986) showed that estimators found by maximizing a partial likelihood behave like maximum-likelihood estimators. That is, the distribution of the estimators can be approximated by a normal distribution in large samples and the information matrix can be used to form standard errors; therefore we can use maximum-likelihood software for inference on the parameters in the hazard probabilities, p_{tjk}. Note that the products of p_{tjk} in the integral from (4) form the same formulas as given by Allison (1982, eqs. 18–20) and Singer and Willet (1993, eqs. 7–10) for the partial likelihood when there are no unobserved error terms ($\underset{\sim}{\epsilon}$ is a constant).

The above arguments are valid when the c_{jk}'s are fixed constants. However, in most prospective longitudinal studies, subjects may attrit from the study and their response is censored at the time of attrition. In these cases, c_j is the time at which the subject leaves the study; thus $CN_{jk} = c_{jk}$, where the use of "CN" indicates that the censoring time may be chosen by the subject. It is possible and plausible that CN_{jk} will be predictive of future (but unobserved) responses; in this case maximizing (4) to form estimators of the regression coefficients may not result in large-sample-unbiased estimators. Estimators based on (4) will be unbiased under further assumptions. We make a simpler, stronger version of Heitjan and Rubin's (1991) assumption, *coarsening at random*.[6] We assume that

$$P[CN_j = c_{jk}, j = 1, \ldots, n_k | GZ_{sk}, Y_{sjk}, IZ_{sjk}, 1 \leq s \leq M, j = 1, \ldots, n_k]$$

$$= P[CN_{jk} = c_{jk}, j = 1, \ldots, n_k | GZ_{sk}, Y_{sjk}, IZ_{sjk},$$

$$1 \leq s \leq c_{jk}, j = 1, \ldots, n_k]$$

and that the former probability is neither a function of the unknown regression coefficients nor of the unknown variance covariance matrix for $\underset{\sim}{\epsilon}$. In words, we assume that conditional on responses and covariates up to and including time c_{jk}, future values of the responses and covariates are not predictive of the chance that $CN_{jk} = c_{jk}$. When *coarsening at random* holds, Hietjan and Rubin (1991) show that we may treat the observed c_{jk}'s as fixed constants in likelihood inference. Thus under this assumption we may use (4) as our (partial) likelihood.

Because censoring in longitudinal studies is common and may be related to the response, the *coarsening at random* assumption is often difficult to make. However, in our example, the retrospective nature of the data collection implies that this assumption is satisfied. Censoring occurs at the time of the interview and is thus independent not only of the timing of contraception, but also of the covariates. In general, one attempts to measure all common predictors of future censoring and future responses/ covariates and then includes these covariates in the regression model for time t.

Recall that the at-risk indicator (R_{tjk}) is 1 if the jth subject in the kth group is at risk of the event at time t, and is 0 otherwise. Thus when we have censoring, we set R_{tjk} to 0 for $t > CN_{jk}$. We may then rewrite (4) as

$$\prod_{k=1}^{N} \int \phi(\underset{\sim}{\epsilon}) \prod_{j=1}^{n_k} \prod_{t=1}^{M} [(1 - p_{tjk})^{(1-y_{tjk})} p_{tjk}^{y_{tjk}}]^{r_{tjk}} \, d\underset{\sim}{\epsilon}. \tag{5}$$

As Allison notes (1982: 74),

$$\prod_{j=1}^{n_k} \prod_{t=1}^{M} [(1 - p_{tjk})^{(1-y_{tjk})} p_{tjk}^{y_{tjk}}]^{r_{tjk}}$$

[6] See Heitjan and Rubin (1991) or Gill, Van Der Laan, and Robins (1997) for the weaker version of *coarsening at random*.

is the same as the kth group's contribution to the likelihood for the regression analysis of dichotomous dependent variables and thus, when there are no unobserved error terms, discrete-time hazard models can be estimated using programs for the analysis of dichotomous data (for example, Proc Logistic in SAS or logistic in STATA). Similarly, conditional on the unobserved error terms, the above product is the same as the kth group's contribution to the likelihood for a multilevel regression analysis of dichotomous dependent variables. This means that the partial likelihood in (5) is the same as the likelihood we would use in a multilevel regression analysis of a dichotomous dependent variable. Thus under the *modeling, conditional independence*, *noninformative covariates*, and *coarsening at random* assumptions, we may use any program for maximum-likelihood estimation in a multilevel regression analysis of a dichotomous dependent variable. Goldstein (1995), without stating assumptions, notes this when all covariates are time-invariant. The extension described here incorporates time-varying covariates at both the individual and group levels.

4. ESTIMATION WITH COMMON SOFTWARE

We use two software packages, HLM and MLN, to illustrate the estimation of discrete-time multilevel hazard models (Bryk, Raudenbush, and Congdon 1996; Goldstein et al. 1998). These software packages are widely used by sociologists. In order to estimate nonlinear multilevel models, both HLM and MLN use penalized quasi-likelihood to estimate the regression coefficients and variance-covariance matrix of the error terms (Breslow and Clayton 1993). This method is useful when the integral, as in equation (5), cannot be explicitly calculated; these methods approximate the integral and thus the resulting estimation method can be viewed as an approximation to maximum-likelihood estimation for the regression coefficients. When the intraclass correlation is large, the approximation may not perform well;[7] for example, see Rodríguez and Goldman (1995). Better approximations are in progress (Raudenbush and Yang 1998). Additionally MLN provides a second-order approximation, which in simulations appears to work well even when the intraclass correlation is large (Goldstein and Rasbash 1996).

[7] The intraclass correlation represents the correlation between two responses from the same group (Bryk and Raudenbush 1992:18).

Our conceptual model CM in equation (1) must be modified for implementation in both HLM and MLN. Table 2 provides an overview of how CM is implemented differently in HLM and MLN. Nonetheless, both packages can be used to provide appropriate estimates of the γ parameters in a multilevel hazard model that includes time-varying covariates at the group as well as the individual level. We illustrate below how to implement our conceptual model using these software packages. Note also that SAS version 7 includes an experimental procedure, proc NLMIXED, which can be used with multilevel data structures and nonlinear dependent variables. Because proc NLMIXED uses only one input data file, CM in equation (1) must be modified similarly to the MLN modification.

4.1. *Using HLM*

Recall that HLM requires the input of two data sets (or three data sets for a three-level model): an individual and a group level data set. Because we are estimating a discrete-time hazard model, the individual level data set is a person-year data set. The person-year data set has multiple lines for each individual with the number of lines corresponding to the number of years the person is at risk (see Table A.2 in the appendix). The appropriate value for the time-varying individual level covariate in a particular year can be entered on the line corresponding to that year. The group level data set is composed of only one line per group (see Table A.1 in the appendix). In other words, there cannot be multiple observations (at multiple time points) of a particular variable for each neighborhood. Thus, when using HLM, we must include the time-varying group level characteristics (School_{tk} in our example) in the individual (level 1) equation. Thus we can no longer include the time-varying group level characteristic as a predictor of HLM's level 1 intercept in the HLM implementation of CM. However, this HLM implementation is algebraically equivalent to CM, as we demonstrate below.

As before, we substitute the level 2 CM equations for the βs in the level 1 CM equation to express CM in one equation:

$$\begin{aligned}\text{Logit}(p_{tjk}) = {} & (\gamma_{00} + \gamma_{01}\text{Dis}_k + \gamma_{02}\text{School}_{tk} + \epsilon_{0k}) \\ & + (\gamma_{10} + \gamma_{11}\text{School}_{tk} + \epsilon_{1k})\text{Educ}_j + (\gamma_{20} + \epsilon_{2k})\text{Chldrn}_{tj} \\ & + \gamma_{30}\text{Time}_{tj} + \gamma_{40}\text{Time}^2_{tj}.\end{aligned}$$

TABLE 2

Relationship Between Conceptual Model CM, Its Implementation in HLM, and Its Implementation in MLN

Conceptual Model (CM)								
Level 1	β_{0k}	β_{1k}	β_{2k}	β_3	β_4			
Level 2	$\gamma_{00} + \gamma_{01}\text{Dis}_k + \gamma_{02}\text{School}_{tk} + \epsilon_{0k}$	$\gamma_{10} + \gamma_{11}\text{School}_{tk} + \epsilon_{1k}$	$\gamma_{20} + \epsilon_{2k}$	γ_{30}	γ_{40}			
Implementation of CM in HLM								
Level 1	β'_{0k}	β'_{1k}	β_{2k}	β_3	β_4	β'_5	β'_6	
Level 2	$\gamma_{00} + \gamma_{01}\text{Dis}_k + \epsilon_{0k}$	$\gamma_{10} + \epsilon_{1k}$	$\gamma_{20} + \epsilon_{2k}$	γ_{30}	γ_{40}	γ_{02}	γ_{11}	
Implementation of CM in MLN								
Level 1	β''_{0k}	β'_{1k}	β_{2k}	β_3	β_4	β'_5	β'_6	β''_7
Level 2	$\gamma_{00} + \epsilon_{0k}$	$\gamma_{10} + \epsilon_{1k}$	$\gamma_{20} + \epsilon_{2k}$	γ_{30}	γ_{40}	γ_{02}	γ_{11}	γ_{01}

Notes: βs are *not* directly estimated by any software package in implementing CM. Only the γ terms and error variances are estimated.

β_{0k} is the level of contraceptive use in neighborhood k. A predicted value of β_{0k} can be computed for each neighborhood using either HLM or MLN estimates of γ_{00}, γ_{01}, and γ_{02} as shown in the CM level 2 equation ($\beta_{0k} = \gamma_{00} + \gamma_{01}\text{Dis}_k + \gamma_{02}\text{School}_{tk} + \epsilon_{0k}$). β'_{0k} and β''_{0k} are *not* the level of contraceptive use in neighborhood k, according to CM. Rather, β'_{0k} and β''_{0k} represent the groupings of γ terms required by HLM and MLN to estimate CM.

β_{1k} is the effect of women's education in neighborhood k. A predicted value of β_{1k} can be computed for each neighborhood using either HLM or MLN estimates of γ_{10} and γ_{11}, as shown in the CM level 2 equation ($\beta_{1k} = \gamma_{10} + \gamma_{11}\text{School}_{tk} + \epsilon_{1k}$). β'_{1k} is *not* the effect of women's education in neighborhood k according to CM. Rather, β'_{1k} represents the grouping of γ terms required by HLM and MLN to estimate CM.

By rearranging terms and collecting the time-varying presence of a school (School_{tk}) terms in the last line, we get

$$\begin{aligned}\text{Logit}(p_{tjk}) = {} & (\gamma_{00} + \gamma_{01}\text{Dis}_k + \epsilon_{0k}) + (\gamma_{10} + \epsilon_{1k})\text{Educ}_j \\ & + (\gamma_{20} + \epsilon_{2k})\text{Chldrn}_{tj} + \gamma_{30}\text{Time}_{tj} + \gamma_{40}\text{Time}^2_{tj} \\ & + \gamma_{02}\text{School}_{tk} + \gamma_{11}\text{School}_{tk}\text{Educ}_j.\end{aligned}$$

We now rewrite this as an HLM two-level model. We get the HLM *level 1 implementation*:

$$\begin{aligned}\text{Logit}(p_{tjk}) = {} & \beta'_{0k} + \beta'_{1k}\text{Educ}_j + \beta_{2k}\text{Chldrn}_{tj} + \beta_3\text{Time}_{tj} + \beta_4\text{Time}^2_{tj} \\ & + \beta'_5\text{School}_{tk} + \beta'_6\text{School}_{tk}\text{Educ}_{jk}, \qquad \text{(HLM 6a)}\end{aligned}$$

where we have placed primes on the β's that do not coincide with CM, as the following HLM *level 2 implementation* indicates:

$$\begin{aligned}\beta'_{0k} &= \gamma_{00} + \gamma_{01}\text{Dis}_k + \epsilon_{0k} \qquad \text{(HLM 6b)} \\ \beta'_{1k} &= \gamma_{10} + \epsilon_{1k} \\ \beta_{2k} &= \gamma_{20} + \epsilon_{2k} \\ \beta_3 &= \gamma_{30} \\ \beta_4 &= \gamma_{40} \\ \beta'_5 &= \gamma_{02} \\ \beta'_6 &= \gamma_{11}.\end{aligned}$$

Essentially, we are treating the time-varying neighborhood level covariate—distance to the nearest school—as a time-varying individual level covariate. The main difference between this and a real individual level time-varying covariate is that we do not allow β_5 and β_6 to vary by neighborhood. This two-level re-expression of our model can be estimated by the HLM software because the new level 2 equations vary by neighborhood but not over time.

Table 2 explicitly compares CM and its implementation in HLM. Note that if a β term in the HLM equation coincides with the β in CM, we use the same symbol. However, we use a prime symbol ($'$) to indicate that a β does not correspond to CM. For example, because we moved School_{tk} from the level 2 to the level 1 equation, the level 2 equations for β_{0k} and β_{1k}

change. We indicate this by using β'_{0k} and β'_{1k} in the HLM implementation. However, because the level 2 equations for β_{2k}, β_3, and β_4 *do not change*, we continue to use β_{2k}, β_3, and β_4. And, because β'_5 and β'_6 are new terms, we use the prime symbol.

It must be emphasized that the βs and β-primes in equation (6) are used only as a conceptual way to group the γ terms. All implementations produce estimates of the γ terms (and their standard errors) in our conceptual model (CM). HLM forces us to group the γ terms differently because it does not allow time-varying covariates in the level 2 equation. Only the conceptual model corresponds to a grouping of the γ terms that matches the usual understanding of a multilevel model (see description of βs following eq. (1b)). Note that β'_0 *cannot* be interpreted as the average level of contraceptive use in neighborhood k according to our model, CM. β'_0 is used in HLM simply because the software program requires the input of two separate equations: one level 1 equation and a separate level 2 equation for each of the coefficients in the level 1 equation. A predicted level of contraceptive use for each neighborhood can be constructed from the HLM parameters according to the CM level 2 model ($\beta_{0k} = \gamma_{00} + \gamma_{01}\text{Dis}_k + \gamma_{02}\text{School}_{tk}$). Table 2 illustrates the distinct groupings of γ terms within βs that are required when implementing CM in HLM or MLN.

4.2. *Using MLN*

In MLN, *all* of the neighborhood characteristics must be included in the individual level equation. This is because MLN uses only one input data file (see Table A.3 in the appendix). Thus to use MLN we include all individual and neighborhood characteristics in the level 1 equation. Table 2 illustrates the differences between the new model (MLN) and the previous models CM and HLM. In the MLN implementation, distance to the nearest town (Dis_k) is moved from the level 2 equation to the level 1 equation, resulting in a new β parameter, β''_7. This results in a further change to β'_{0k}, indicated by β''_{0k}. This model is still equivalent to CM, and its derivation is similar to the derivation for the HLM implementation, so we do not show it in detail. The resulting *level 1 implementation* in MLN is as follows:

$$\text{Logit}(p_{tjk}) = \beta''_{0k} + \beta'_{1k}\text{Educ}_j + \beta_{2k}\text{Chldrn}_{tj} + \beta_3\text{Time}_{tj} + \beta_4\text{Time}^2_{tj} + \beta'_5\text{School}_{tk} + \beta'_6\text{School}_{tk}\text{Educ}_j + \beta''_7\text{Dis}_k. \quad \text{(MLN 7a)}$$

The MLN *level 2 implementation* is

$$\beta''_{0k} = \gamma_{00} + \epsilon_{0k} \quad \text{(MLN 7b)}$$

$$\beta'_{1k} = \gamma_{10} + \epsilon_{1k}$$

$$\beta_{2k} = \gamma_{20} + \epsilon_{2k}$$

$$\beta_3 = \gamma_{30}$$

$$\beta_4 = \gamma_{40}$$

$$\beta'_5 = \gamma_{02}$$

$$\beta'_6 = \gamma_{11}$$

$$\beta''_7 = \gamma_{01}.$$

Essentially, we have included all of the neighborhood characteristics in the level 1 implementation and use the level 2 implementation only to specify which effects are modeled as random. This model is the statistical equivalent of our more intuitive conceptual model, CM, presented in equation (1) where neighborhood characteristics are included in the level 2 model.

5. RESULTS OF APPLYING THIS TECHNIQUE TO OUR EMPIRICAL EXAMPLE

We now return to our empirical example to demonstrate estimation of the discrete-time multilevel hazard model in HLM and MLN. We relate our results below to the parameters in the conceptual model CM presented in equation (1). Recall that Table 2 illustrates how to reconcile CM with its implementation in both HLM and MLN, illustrated in equations (6) and (7). Descriptive statistics for each of the measures used in analyses are presented in Table 3.

Model 1 in Table 4 includes the cross-level effect term that allows us to test H3. The estimate of the cross-level effect (γ_{11}) is not statistically significant and therefore indicates that the influence of the woman's education level does not vary with the availability of educational opportunities within the neighborhood in which she lives.

Model 2 includes neighborhood characteristics as predictors of the mean hazard of contraceptive use in a particular neighborhood (β_{0k}), but not as predictors of the effect of a woman's education on her propensity to

TABLE 3
Description of Measures Used in Statistical Analyses

	Mean	Standard Deviation	Minimum	Maximum
Neighborhood Level Measures				
($N = 171$)				
Distance to nearest town	8.24	3.93	.02	17.70
School within 5 minute walk[a]	.46		0	1
Individual Level Measures				
($N = 1,395$ women; 17,262 person-years)				
Ever went to school before first birth	.33		0	1
Total number of children[a]	3.17	3.10	1	13
Years since first birth[a]	11.37	8.17	0	34
Years^2 since first birth[a]	196.11	256.26	0	1,156

[a]Descriptive statistics for time-varying measures are computed at the time of first contraceptive use, or if no contraceptive use occurred, at the time of the censoring event (survey interview).

use contraception (β_{1k}). In other words, the cross level effect has been deleted from model 2. The estimates in model 2 correspond to the following conceptual model, which is very similar to CM, except that School_{tk} is not a predictor of β_{1k} in equation (8).

Individual level model

$$\text{Logit}(p_{tjk}) = \beta_{0k} + \beta_{1k}\text{Educ}_j + \beta_{2k}\text{Chldrn}_{tj} + \beta_3\text{Time}_{tj} + \beta_4\text{Time}^2_{tj}. \quad \text{(8a)}$$

Neighborhood level model

$$\beta_{0k} = \gamma_{00} + \gamma_{01}\text{Dis}_k + \gamma_{02}\text{School}_{tk} + \epsilon_{0k} \quad \text{(8b)}$$

$$\beta_{1k} = \gamma_{10} + \epsilon_{1k}$$

$$\beta_{2k} = \gamma_{20} + \epsilon_{2k}$$

$$\beta_3 = \gamma_{30}$$

$$\beta_4 = \gamma_{40}.$$

This model allows us to evaluate H1, which asks whether formal education is associated with a higher hazard of permanent contraceptive use. In this model γ_{10} indicates that formal education *is* associated with a higher hazard of contraceptive use, holding constant other factors in the model. The magnitude of γ_{10} indicates that having attended school is associated with a .58 higher log-odds of permanent contraceptive use. Note that the estimates of the γ terms obtained using HLM and MLN are similar but not exactly the same. This is because HLM and MLN use slightly different methods to approximate the likelihood and because with MLN we used the second-order approximation option.

Model 2 also allows us to evaluate H2, whether nearby schooling opportunities are associated with a higher hazard of permanent contraceptive use. This hypothesis can be evaluated by examining γ_{02}. The coefficient, .29 (.30 in HLM), indicates that having a school within a 5-minute walk is associated with a .29 higher log-odds of permanent contraceptive use. We do not describe the other parameters in the model, but their interpretations are straightforward.

Again, note that the βs are not directly estimated in either statistical package. However, we can compute predicted βs using the estimates of

TABLE 4
Estimates of the Effects of Neighborhood and Individual Level Characteristics on the Hazard of Permanent Contraceptive Use

	Model 1		Model 2		
	HLM	MLN	HLM	MLN	Parameter in CM
Intercept	−4.50***	−4.01***	−4.48***	−4.01***	γ_{00}
	(.18)	(.14)	(.17)	(.15)	
Neighborhood Characteristics					
Distance to nearest town (time-invariant)	−.04**	−.04***	−.04**	−.04***	γ_{01}
	(.01)	(.01)	(.01)	(.01)	
School within 5 minute walk (time-varying)	.36***	.26***	.30***	.29***	γ_{02}
	(.11)	(.09)	(.10)	(.09)	
Individual Characteristics					
Ever went to school before first birth (time-invariant)	.66***	.66***	.58***	.58***	γ_{10}
	(.12)	(.10)	(.09)	(.09)	
Total number of children (time-varying)	.40***	.34***	.40***	.41***	γ_{20}
	(.04)	(.03)	(.04)	(.04)	
Cross-Level Effect					
School within 5 minute walk * Ever went to school	−.19	−.16			γ_{11}
	(.17)	(.16)			

Controls					
Years since first birth	.18***	.18***	.18***	.14***	γ_{30}
	(.03)	(.03)	(.03)	(.03)	
Years^2 since first birth	−.01***	−.01***	−.01***	−.01***	γ_{40}
	(.001)	(.001)	(.001)	(.001)	

Estimated Variances of Random Effects

	Model 1		Model 2	
	HLM	MLN	HLM	MLN
Intercept: Var(ϵ_{0k})	.01	.00	.01	.00
Ever went to school before first birth: Var(ϵ_{1k})	.09	.00	.07	.00
Total number of children: Var(ϵ_{2k})	.02	.02	.01	.02

Note: Standard errors are in parentheses.
$^*p < .05$, $^{**}p < .01$, $^{***}p < .001$, one-tailed tests.

the γ terms provided by either HLM or MLN. For instance, according to our modified conceptual model in equation (8), a predicted value of $\beta_{0k} = \gamma_{00} + \gamma_{01}\text{Dis}_k + \gamma_{02}\text{School}_{tk}$. Thus, according to model 2 in Table 4, for a neighborhood with average distance to the nearest town (8.24) and a school within a 5-minute walk, a predicted value of $\beta_{0k} = -4.48 + -.04(8.24) + .29(1) = -4.5196$.

Finally, note the estimates of the variances of the random effects at the bottom of Table 4. $\text{Var}(\epsilon_{0k})$, which is estimated to be .01 by HLM and .00 by MLN, is the variance in the intercept that is not explained by the neighborhood level variables in the model. For the intercept term, this is quite small. In other words, there is little variation between neighborhoods in the intercept that is not explained by the presence of a school (School) and the distance to the nearest town (Dis). Similarly, $\text{Var}(\epsilon_{1k})$ is the variance in the coefficient for woman's education (Educ) that is not explained by the presence of a school. The estimate of $\text{Var}(\epsilon_{1k})$ computed by HLM in both model 1 and model 2 is quite large relative to the size of the effect; in other words, this indicates substantial variance across neighborhoods in the impact of woman's education on the hazard of contraceptive use net of the presence of a school. Note, however, that the estimate of this variance component computed by MLN is zero. $\text{Var}(\epsilon_{2k})$ is the variance in the estimated effect of total number of children (Chldrn) net of the mean. The estimates produced by both HLM and MLN are substantial relative to the size of the effect of total number of children. This also indicates variability in the effect of total number of children across neighborhoods. Overall, however, note that these variances are not estimated precisely. The different approximations to the likelihood used by HLM and MLN produce different estimates, and the random error inherent in sampling procedures adds to the lack of precision. Thus the variances of the random effects should be interpreted with caution.

6. CONCLUSION

In this paper we described conditions under which any software package using maximum-likelihood estimation for multilevel logistic regression models may be used to perform a multilevel discrete-time hazard analysis with time-varying covariates at both individual and group levels. In particular we have demonstrated the use of HLM and MLN software to estimate this discrete-time multilevel hazard model. Both of these software packages are widely used by sociologists, and either can be used to estimate this type of model. The keys to their use lie in creation of the input data sets and interpretation of the output coefficients. The results generated by these estimation procedures are quite similar, though minor differences result from slight variations in the approximations used in the two packages. Both packages are easily available and a wide range of sociologists will find them useful for estimating discrete-time multilevel hazard models.

In order to use this method we made *modeling, conditional independence*, *noninformative covariates*, and *coarsening at random* assumptions. The last two assumptions imply that we must measure all common predictors of the event time, covariates, and censoring in order to use multilevel hazard analysis. This is rarely successful in sociological studies. Further research is needed on methods for relaxing these assumptions. To test sociological models of macro-micro linkage, it is particularly important to devise methods that provide unbiased estimates of group level effects (neighborhoods, schools, businesses) even when more proximate individual level predictors are omitted. Such methods are required to establish unbiased estimates of the total impact of macro characteristics on micro behavior and outcomes. The research reported here is an initial step toward that goal.

APPENDIX: CONSTRUCTING THE DATA FILES

A.1. *Data File for Use with HLM*

To fit a two-level model with HLM, two data files must be created. The first data file will hold the information on the groups; the second will have the information on the individuals. Note that the current version of HLM (version 4) does not allow missing data when estimating nonlinear models.

In our example, the neighborhood file has one data line per neighborhood, for a total of 171 lines of data. The variables on each line will be the neighborhood ID and the value of the time-invariant neighborhood covariate, distance to the nearest town. Table A.1 shows our neighborhood level data file for use with HLM.

TABLE A.1
Neighborhood Level File for use with HLM

Nbrhd ID (1–30)	Distance to nearest town	Nbrhd ID (31–171)	Distance to nearest town
1	0.04	31	3.66
2	0.02	32	3.54
3	0.03	33	4.35
4	0.07	34	4.77
5	1.24	35	4.37
6	0.82	36	3.64
7	1.69	37	2.82
8	2.15	38	2.99
9	0.22	39	3.16
10	0.41	40	3.39
11	0.20	41	7.52
12	0.40	42	7.85
13	2.71	43	8.19
14	4.58	44	8.48
15	3.38	45	7.84
16	3.24	46	9.23
17	7.07	47	9.22
18	6.31	48	8.29
19	6.00	49	10.28
20	5.68	50	10.63
21	5.25	51	10.67
22	4.67	52	10.76
23	4.89	....	....
24	4.88	166	9.17
25	4.83	167	8.48
26	4.57	168	7.25
27	5.02	169	7.40
28	5.25	170	7.74
29	3.96	171	9.20
30	4.10		

The second data file contains information about the 1,395 women. Because we are conducting a discrete-time hazard analysis, one line of data represents a person-year. For example, if a woman is at risk of permanent contraceptive use for five years (from the year after her first marital birth until contraceptive use or censoring), that woman will be in the data set five times. The first field in the file is the group ID, which in our example is the ID of the neighborhood in which the woman lives. Note that the HLM software requires that all of the individual level observations are grouped together by their respective group level ID. The next columns contain the individual level covariates, both time-invariant and time-varying. The next column contains the time-varying neighborhood level covariate, the presence of a school within a five-minute walk, which we are treating as an individual level covariate for use in HLM. The subsequent column contains the cross-product of the neighborhood level time-varying covariate and individual level variable. In our case, there is one cross-product; the product of the presence of a school and the woman's education. Finally, the last column contains the response variable, contraceptive use. In this data, the response will be 0 if the woman did not use a permanent contraceptive method during that year, and 1 if the woman did use a permanent contraceptive method during that year. Note that most records will have contraceptive use equal to zero. Only the last year for each woman can have a response equal to 1. On the woman's last year she was either censored (did not use a permanent contraceptive method before the end of the study), where contraceptive use is coded 0, or used a permanent contraceptive method, where contraceptive use is coded 1, and is subsequently no longer at risk (and thus subsequent observation-years are not in the data set for this woman). Table A.2 shows the individual level data file for use with HLM.

A.2. Data File for Use with MLN

The data set for use with MLN is simpler because there is only one, rather than two, data files used to estimate the models. Thus time-varying and time-invariant group and individual level covariates are included in the same file. This data set is similar to the individual level file used with HLM; however, it also includes the group level variables. Thus, in this data set, one line again represents one person-year. Note that MLN requires three additional variables, CONS, BCONS, and DENOM, are equal to 1 in all observations (see Goldstein et al. 1998: 97-101). Table A.3 illustrates the MLN data set.

TABLE A.2
Individual Level File for Use with HLM

Neighborhood ID (1–171)	Respondent ID[a]	Respondent Ever Been to School (0,1)	Respondent's Total Number of Children (minus 1)	Years Since First Birth (Time)	Years^2 Since First Birth (Time^2)	School within 5-minute walk (0,1)	School within 5-minute walk * R's Education (0,1)	Contraceptive Use (Dependent Variable) (0,1)
001	1	1	0	0	0	1	1	0
001	1	1	0	1	1	1	1	0
001	1	1	1	2	4	1	1	0
...								
001	5	1	0	0	0	1	1	0
001	5	1	1	1	1	1	1	0
001	5	1	0	2	4	1	1	0
001	5	1	1	3	9	1	1	0
001	5	1	2	4	16	1	1	0
001	5	1	2	5	25	1	1	0
...								
007	205	0	0	0	0	0	0	0
007	205	0	0	1	1	0	0	0
007	205	0	1	2	4	0	0	0
007	205	0	1	3	9	0	0	0
007	205	0	2	4	16	0	0	0
007	205	0	2	5	25	0	0	0
007	205	0	2	6	36	0	0	0
007	205	0	2	7	49	0	0	0
007	205	0	2	8	64	1	0	0
007	205	0	2	9	81	1	0	0
007	205	0	2	10	100	1	0	0
...								
007	212	1	1	0	0	0	0	0
007	212	1	1	1	1	0	0	0
007	212	1	2	2	4	0	0	0
007	212	1	2	3	9	1	1	0
007	212	1	2	4	16	1	1	1
...								

009	263	0	0	0	0	0	0	0
009	263	0	0	1	1	0	0	0
009	263	0	1	2	4	0	0	0
009	263	0	1	3	9	0	0	0
009	263	0	1	4	16	0	0	0
009	263	0	1	5	25	0	0	0
009	263	0	1	6	36	1	0	0
009	263	0	2	7	49	1	0	0
009	263	0	2	8	64	1	0	1
...								
046	1345	0	0	0	0	0	0	0
046	1345	0	1	1	1	0	0	0
046	1345	0	1	2	4	0	0	0
046	1345	0	1	3	9	1	0	0
046	1345	0	1	4	16	1	0	0
046	1345	0	2	5	25	1	0	0
046	1345	0	2	6	36	1	0	0
046	1345	0	3	7	49	1	0	0
046	1345	0	3	8	64	1	0	0
046	1345	0	4	9	81	1	0	0
046	1345	0	4	10	100	1	0	0
046	1345	0	5	11	121	1	0	0
046	1345	0	5	12	144	1	0	0
046	1345	0	5	13	169	1	0	0
046	1345	0	5	14	196	1	0	0
046	1345	0	6	15	225	1	0	0
046	1345	0	6	16	256	1	0	0
046	1345	0	6	17	289	1	0	0
046	1345	0	6	18	324	1	0	0
046	1345	0	6	19	361	1	0	0
046	1345	0	6	20	400	1	0	0
046	1345	0	6	21	441	1	0	0
046	1345	0	6	22	484	1	0	0
046	1345	0	6	23	529	1	0	0
...								

[a]To protect the anonymity of the respondents, ID numbers are artificially constructed for this table.

TABLE A.3
Multilevel Data File for Use with MLN

Neighborhood ID (1–171)	Distance to Nearest Town	Respondent ID[a]	Respondent Ever Been to School (0,1)	Respondent's Total Number of Children (minus 1)	Years Since First Birth (Time)	Years^2 Since First Birth (Time^2)	School within 5-minute walk (0,1)	School within 5-minute walk * R's Education (0,1)	Contraceptive Use (Dependent Variable) (0,1)	CONS	BCONS	DENOM
001	0.04	1	1	0	0	0	1	1	0	1	1	1
001	0.04	1	1	0	1	1	1	1	0	1	1	1
001	0.04	1	1	1	2	4	1	1	0	1	1	1
...												
001	0.04	5	1	0	0	0	1	1	0	1	1	1
001	0.04	5	1	1	1	1	1	1	0	1	1	1
001	0.04	5	1	0	2	4	1	1	0	1	1	1
001	0.04	5	1	1	3	9	1	1	0	1	1	1
001	0.04	5	1	2	4	16	1	1	0	1	1	1
001	0.04	5	1	2	5	25	1	1	0	1	1	1
...												
007	1.69	205	0	0	0	0	0	0	0	1	1	1
007	1.69	205	0	0	1	1	0	0	0	1	1	1
007	1.69	205	0	1	2	4	0	0	0	1	1	1
007	1.69	205	0	1	3	9	0	0	0	1	1	1
007	1.69	205	0	2	4	16	0	0	0	1	1	1
007	1.69	205	0	2	5	25	0	0	0	1	1	1
007	1.69	205	0	2	6	36	0	0	0	1	1	1
007	1.69	205	0	2	7	49	0	0	0	1	1	1
007	1.69	205	0	2	8	64	1	0	0	1	1	1
007	1.69	205	0	2	9	81	1	0	0	1	1	1
007	1.69	205	0	2	10	100	1	0	0	1	1	1
...												

[a]To protect the anonymity of the respondents, ID numbers are artificially constructed for this table.

REFERENCES

Alexander, Jeffrey C. 1988. *Action and Its Environments: Toward a New Synthesis*. New York: Columbia University Press.

Allison, Paul D. 1982. "Discrete-time Methods for the Analysis of Event Histories." Pp. 61–98 in *Sociological Methodology 1982*, edited by Samuel Leinhardt. San Francisco: Jossey-Bass.

———. 1984. *Event History Analysis: Regression for Longitudinal Event Data*. Beverly Hills, CA: Sage.

Axinn, William G. 1993. "The Effects of Children's Schooling on Fertility Limitation." *Population Studies* 47:481–93.

Axinn, William G., and Jennifer S. Barber. 1999. "The Spread of Mass Education and Fertility Limitation." Presented at the annual meeting of the Population Association of America, March 27–29, New York.

Axinn, William G., Jennifer S. Barber, and Dirgha J. Ghimire. 1997. "The Neighborhood History Calendar: A Data Collection Method Designed for Dynamic Multilevel Modeling." Pp. 355–92 in *Sociological Methodology 1997*, edited by Adrian Raftery. Boston: Blackwell Publishers.

Axinn, William G., Lisa D. Pearce, and Dirgha J. Ghimire. 1999. "Innovations in Life History Calendar Applications." *Social Science Research* 28:243–64.

Breslow, N., and D. G. Clayton. 1993. "Approximate Inference in Generalized Linear Mixed Models." *Journal of the American Statistical Association* 88:9–25.

Brewster, Karin L. 1994. "Race Differences in Sexual Activity Among Adolescent Women: The Role of Neighborhood Characteristics." *American Sociological Review* 59:408–24.

Bryk, Anthony S., and Stephen W. Raudenbush. 1992. *Hierarchical Linear Models: Applications and Data Analysis Methods*. Newbury Park, CA: Sage.

Bryk, Anthony, Stephen Raudenbush, and Richard Congdon. 1996. *HLM: Hierarchical Linear and Nonlinear Modeling with the HLM/2l and HLM/3l Programs*. Chicago: Scientific Software International.

Coleman, James S. 1990. *Foundations of Social Theory*. Cambridge, MA: Harvard University Press.

Cox, D. R. 1975. "Partial Likelihood." *Biometrika* 62(2):269–76.

Diggle, Peter J., Kung-Yee Liang, and Scott L. Zeger. 1994. *Analysis of Longitudinal Data*. Oxford, England: Clarendon Press.

DiPrete, Thomas A., and Jerry D. Forristal. 1994. "Multilevel Models: Methods and Substance." *Annual Review of Sociology* 20:331–57.

Durkheim, Emile. 1984 [1933]. *The Division of Labor in Society*. New York: Free Press.

Elder, Glen H., Jr. 1977. "Family History and the Life Course." *Journal of Family History* 2: 279–304.

———. 1983. "The Life Course Perspective." Pp. 54–60 in *The American Family in Social-Historical Perspective, 3rd Edition*, edited by Michael Gordon. New York: St. Martin's Press.

Gill, Richard D. 1992. "Marginal Partial Likelihood." *Scandinavian Journal of Statistics. Theory and Applications* 19:133–37.

Gill, Richard D., M. J. Van Der Laan, and J. M. Robins. 1997. "Coarsening at Random: Characterizations, Conjectures, Counter-Examples." Pp. 255–94 in *The Proceedings of the First Seattle Symposium on Biostatistics: Survival Analysis*, vol. 123 of Springer Lecture Notes in Statistics, edited by D. Y. Lin and T. R. Fleming. New York: Springer-Verlag.

Goldstein, H. 1995. *Multilevel Statistical Models*, 2nd ed. New York: Halsted Press.

Goldstein, H., and J. Rasbash. 1996. "Improved Approximations for Multilevel Models with Binary Responses." *Journal of the Royal Statistical Society*, ser. A, 159: 505–13.

Goldstein, H., J. Rasbash, I. Plewis, D. Draper, W. Browne, M. Yang, G. Woodhouse and M. Healy. 1998. *A User's Guide to MLwiN*. London: Multilevel Models Project.

Guo, Guang. 1993. "Use of Sibling Data to Estimate Family Mortality Effects in Guatemala." *Demography* 30:15–32.

Guo, Guang, and Germán Rodríguez. 1992. "Estimating a Multivariate Proportional Hazards Model for Clustered Data Using the EM Algorithm, with an Application to Child Survival in Guatemala." *Journal of the American Statistical Association* 87: 960–76.

Hedeker, Donald, and Robert D. Gibbons. 1994. "A Random-Effects Ordinal Regression Model for Multilevel Analysis." *Biometrics* 50:993–44.

Hedeker, Donald, Ohidul Siddiqui, and Frank B. Hu. 1998. "Random-effects Regression Analysis of Correlated Grouped-time Survival Data." University of Illinois at Chicago. Unpublished manuscript.

Heitjan, Daniel F., and Donald B. Rubin. 1991. "Ignorability and Coarse Data." *The Annals of Statistics* 19:2244–53.

Kreft, Ita G. G. 1994. "Multilevel Models for Hierarchically Nested Data: Potential Applications in Substance Abuse Prevention Research." Pp. 140–183 in *Advances in Data Analysis for Prevention Intervention Research*, edited by Linda M. Collins and Larry A. Seitz. NIDA Research Monograph No. 142. Washington, D.C.: U.S. Department of Health and Human Services.

Kreft, Ita G. G., Jan DeLeeuw, and Leona S. Aiken. 1995. "The Effect of Different Forms of Centering in Hierarchical Linear Models." *Multivariate Behavioral Research* 30(1):1–21.

Laird, Nan, and Donald Olivier. 1981. "Covariance Analysis of Censored Survival Data Using Log-linear Analysis Techniques." *Journal of the American Statistical Association* 76:231–40.

Ma, Xin, and J. Douglas Willms. 1999. "Dropping Out of Advanced Mathematics: How Much Do Students and Schools Contribute to the Problem?" *Educational Evaluation and Policy Analysis* 21:365–83.

Massey, Douglas S., and Kristin E. Espinosa. 1996. "What's Driving Mexico-U.S. Migration? A Theoretical, Empirical, and Policy Analysis." *American Journal of Sociology* 102:939–99.

Muthén, Bengt. 1997. "Latent Variable Modeling of Longitudinal and Multilevel Data." Pp. 453–80 in *Sociological Methodology 1997*, edited by Adrian E. Raftery. Boston: Blackwell Publishers.

Petersen, Trond. 1991. "The Statistical Analysis of Event Histories." *Sociological Methods and Research* 19:270–323.

Raudenbush, Stephen W., and M. Yang. 1998. "Numerical Integration via High-Order, Multivariate LaPlace Approximation with Application to Multilevel Models." Pp. 11–14 in *Multilevel Modeling Newsletter*, vol. 10(2). London: Multilevel Models Project.

Rindfuss, Ronald R., S. Philip Morgan, and Gray Swicegood. 1988. *First Births in America: Changes in the Timing of Parenthood.* Berkeley: University of California Press.

Ringdal, Kristen. 1992. "Recent Developments in Methods for Multilevel Analysis." *Acta Sociologica* 35:235–43.

Rodríguez, Germán, and Noreen Goldman. 1995. "An Assessment of Estimation Procedures for Multilevel Models with Binary Responses." *Journal of the Royal Statistical Society*, ser. A, 158:73–89.

Sastry, Narayan. 1996. "Community Characteristics, Individual and Household Attributes, and Child Survival in Brazil." *Demography* 33:211–29.

———. 1997. "Family-level Clustering of Childhood Mortality Risk in Northeast Brazil." *Population Studies* 51:245–61.

Singer, J. D., and J. B. Willet. 1993. "It's About Time: Using Discrete-time Survival Analysis to Study Duration and the Timing of Events." *Journal of Education Statistics* 18:155–95.

Smith, Herbert L. 1989. "Integrating Theory and Research on the Institutional Determinants of Fertility." *Demography* 26:171–84.

Thornton, Arland, William G. Axinn, and Jay Teachman. 1995. "The Influence of Educational Experiences on Cohabitation and Marriage in Early Adulthood." *American Sociological Review* 60(5):762–64.

Trussell, James, and Toni Richards. 1985. "Correction for Unmeasured Heterogeneity in Hazard Models Using the Heckman-Singer Procedure." Pp. 242–76 in *Sociological Methodology 1985*, edited by Nancy Brandon Tuma. San Francisco: Jossey-Bass.

Vaupel, James W. 1988. "Inherited Frailty and Longevity." *Demography*, 25:277–87.

Vaupel, James W., and Analtoli I. Yashin. 1985. "Heterogeneity's Ruses: Some Surprising Effects of Selection on Population Dynamics." *American Statistician* 39:176–85.

Weber, Max. 1922. *The Sociology of Religion.* London: Methuer.

Wong, George Y., and William M. Mason. 1985. "The Hierarchical Logistic Regression Model for Multilevel Analysis." *Journal of the American Statistical Association* 80:513–24.

Wong, Wing Hung. 1986. "Theory of Partial Likelihood ." *Annals of Statistics* 14:88–123.

Yamaguchi, Kazuo. 1991. *Event History Analysis.* Newbury Park, CA: Sage.

7

SYSTEMATIC PATTERNS OF ZERO EXPOSURES IN EVENT-HISTORY ANALYSIS

*Jan M. Hoem**

Users of intensity-regression techniques in event-history analysis based on occurrence and exposure matrices frequently encounter zero-valued exposures where there is no observation for selected combinations of factor levels, either because they are logically impossible or because the observational design leaves them out. For example, higher educational levels cannot be attained at very young ages, and observations collected over a given calendar period cannot contain data for older birth cohorts at younger ages or data for younger cohorts at older ages. Unless the exposure matrix is too badly full of zeros, this does not necessarily cause problems for the estimation of regression parameters, but interpretation of results may have to be carried out with extra care. In this paper, we discuss why this is so and show how deft handling of systematic patterns of zero exposures can facilitate analysis.

1. INTRODUCTION

Impossible combinations of regressor values may cause problems in any kind of regression analysis. In analyses that use a person's age and educational attainment as regressors, how do we account for the fact that higher educational levels can only be attained after age 19? Suppose that the age of a woman's youngest child is a determinant of her behavior. How then do

The author thanks Gunnar Andersson for his permission to use the data for Table 2 and Figure 2, Danuta Biterman for enlightening comments on Hoem (1986), and an editor and a referee for *Sociological Methodology* for helpful editorial remarks.

*Max-Planck Institute for Demographic Research

we deal with childless women in an analysis where it is important to compare women with different numbers of children, including no children? (For a childless woman, there is of course no age of a youngest child to include in the analysis.) Suppose our data were collected for a given set of calendar years, and also suppose that we want to include both age attained and year of birth among our regressors. How do we then handle the fact that early birth cohorts have been observed only at higher ages and, conversely, that the data for later birth cohorts cover only younger ages? How do we make sense of your model when there are systematic patterns of regressor-value combinations that are not represented in your data set?

Issues of this nature are encountered in the context of many analyses of individual-level data, and there is no need to grapple with them as if they were new every time. Fortunately, simple solutions exist, and they may deserve more systematic attention than they seem to have received in the current literature, perhaps precisely because they are so simple. We are not certain that a single prescription can be used in all cases, but the purpose of this paper is to present possible devices that will serve well in many connections. Sometimes the data may be split into segments in which such offensive regressor combinations do not appear. Other devices may avoid value combinations that are illogical, impossible, or otherwise not represented in the data by re-coding two or more regressors so as to construct a single, combined covariate where the undesired value combinations do not appear. On rare occasions such evasive action may prove unnecessary provided sufficient care is exercised in the interpretation of the outcome.

These issues are present in all regression analyses, but they may be particularly acute in hazard regression because its estimation methods are especially sensitive. They are typically based on numerical iteration procedures whose convergence may sometimes be jeopardized by unfortunate variable specifications. For these reasons, and because of the applications to be considered here, we focus on general issues and illustrate their solutions by means of a series of concrete examples from the author's own experience in demography.

Hazard (or intensity) regression is a technique used in event-history analysis. It has become a commonplace tool for the study of the types of behavior of individuals that can be represented as transitions between states such as marital statuses, childbearing parities, labor-force activities, progress in educational attainment, spouse selection, sickness risk and health regeneration, and so on. The hazard (or intensity) functions measure the rates at which transitions occur over time. In applications of the kind we will address here, time is a continuous parameter and a transition can occur at any time. Sociologists, demographers, epidemiologists, actuaries, and analysts in several other disciplines often effectively specify a piecewise constant baseline hazard. This means that time is partitioned into a finite number of nonoverlapping intervals and analysis is carried out as if the intensity were constant in each interval. (Note that this does not mean that the analyst works with discrete time.) The baseline hazard is supposed to apply to some baseline group in the study population. Other groups have transition intensities that appear as modifications of the baseline hazard. Such groups may be defined by means of a combination of levels on categorical covariates (regressors). When all covariates are categorical and the baseline hazard is piecewise constant, a matrix of occurrences and one of exposures together constitute a sufficient statistic. All analysis can then be based on this pair of matrices. The occurrence matrix contains counts of transitions in the various subpopulations. The exposure matrix contains corresponding counts of person-months (or other person-time units) during which individuals have been observed to be subject to the risk of the transitions in question. The issue of impossible regressor-value combinations becomes particularly visible in this case, for such combinations correspond to zero-valued entries (also called "empty cells") in the exposure matrix. In this situation, therefore, the discussion of impossible regressor-value combinations becomes a discussion of patterns of zero exposures, which is the topic of the present paper.

The specification of a piecewise-constant baseline intensity and categorical covariates is a modern formulation of procedures that in their simplest version go back to the invention of the life table (Hoem 1993). In principle, this link is well known, but it seems to be forgotten occasionally, perhaps because statistical texts tend to present intensity-regression analysis in notation that emphasizes generality rather than this particular simple and useful connection. To facilitate the presentation of the ideas highlighted here, we therefore provide a correspondence between the formulations normally used by statisticians and those directly geared to the relevant setting. (The literature abounds in general descriptions of these techniques; see for instance Allison 1984; Tuma and Hannan 1984; Andersen et al., 1991; Blossfeld and Rohwer 1995.) Before turning to such generalities, however, we will try to make the issues more concrete by presenting an example.

2. THE ROLE OF EDUCATIONAL ATTAINMENT IN THE FORMATION OF COHABITATIONAL UNIONS

An early study of the formation of cohabitational unions by Swedish women enrolled in education in the 1960s and 1970s failed to detect any effect of educational attainment (Hoem 1986). There were effects of age, birth cohort, and social origin, but it seemed that high-school pupils and college students of the same age, for example, entered consensual unions at the same rates once one controlled for year of birth and social background. When the finding is presented in these terms, it is immediately apparent that there must be a problem with it, for in general a Swedish student cannot be enrolled in college-level studies at ages 17 to 19, the period when most young Swedes are attending high school. The "same-age" assumption is largely spurious for parts of the age range, and the analysis should account for this but did not. In technical terms, a data set that includes educational attainment and covers the age range between, say, 16 to 24 years, will include zero-valued exposures at least for factor-level combinations that involve low age and high attainment, as seen in Table 1.

Analysts face systematic patterns of zero exposures whenever factor-level combinations are substantively impossible (or were left out during data collection). To handle the formalities of our first concrete case of this issue, we note that our data included four explanatory factors—namely, the woman's current age (let us call it Factor A), her birth cohort (Factor B), her class of social origin (Factor C), and her educational level (Factor D). Age was measured in single years (17 through 24), and there were five five-year birth cohorts (1935–1939 through 1955–1959) and three levels of education, which we call "low" (at most ten months of school attendance after September of the year in which the respondent turned 16), "middle" (at least a year of secondary education), and "high" (at least one successful course examination in postsecondary education). The respondents were grouped by social class, essentially into daughters of (1) middle- or high-grade white-collar employees, farmers, and self-employed nonfarmers (group C_1), (2) skilled workers or lower-grade white-collar employees (group C_2), and (3) unskilled workers (C_3). We have added age 16 to the range used in the original investigation (Hoem 1986).

Table 1 is an aggregate over two of the dimensions in a four-dimensional exposure matrix. (There is one dimension for each factor, and we have aggregated over cohort and social class.) The original matrix has zero entries in all cells that correspond to ages 16 to 18 for the

TABLE 1

Months of Exposure to the "Risk" of Union Formation Among Swedish Women Enrolled in Education

	Age								
Educational Level	16	17	18	19	20	21	22	23	24
Low	22,653	9,920	1,769	1,080	433	255	153	89	48
Middle	340	12,778	14,683	10,708	5,914	2,619	1,259	667	336
High	0	0	0	53	2,859	4,141	3,251	1,987	1,153

Source: Derived from data collected in the Swedish Family Survey of 1981.

"high" educational level. Such systematic patterns are frequent in event-history analyses, and we want to address often-asked questions concerning what technical problems (if any) are encountered if one tries to fit intensity models to such data, and what the substantive interpretation is of the model parameters if a fit can be achieved.

In the first approach to the statistical theory involved, note that the empirical analysis resulted in a model where age and cohort operated in combination, class gave a significant but "independent" contribution, and educational level was not needed. Mathematically, the intensity (or hazard) of consensual-union formation had the form $\mu_{ijkm} = a_{ij} c_k$. For each birth cohort j, we faced a very simple proportional-hazards model where a_{ij} is the union-formation intensity at age i for female students (or pupils) in class C_1, which we chose as our baseline group. By definition, respondents in the baseline group have $c_1 = 1$. For $k > 1$, the constant c_k is a multiplicative correction factor representing the super-"risk" of consensual-union formation for daughters from class C_k. The correction factors $\{c_k\}$ had the same values in all cohorts. For daughters of unskilled workers, the factor was estimated at 1.33. For daughters of skilled workers and low-grade white-collar employees, it was 1.38. This means that in each birth cohort the union-formation intensities at each age were well above that of respondents in the baseline group C_1.

At first glance, this model is supposed to hold at all levels m of educational attainment since no parameter depends on m in the above formula for μ_{ijkm}, but this is problematic when certain combinations (i_0, m_0) of (a young) age and ("high") educational attainment are logically impossible. The following solution is almost disappointingly simple. We note that there is an intensity μ_{ijkm} only for meaningful combinations (i, j, k, m). In fact, a formula like $\mu_{ijkm} = a_{ij} c_k$ is incomplete until the range of the subscripts is also specified, and the range is that of those meaningful combinations. *If* the given intensity specification is correct, it can only hold for combinations (i, j, k, m) that do *not* involve the impossible (i_0, m_0).

This looks like a purely semantic way out of a quandary, but it is not the end of the matter in this particular instance. There are substantive reasons to be dissatisfied with an analysis that works with a single intensity specification over the whole age range for this stage of life. In Sweden, "students" at ages 16 (or 17) to 19 are really pupils in upper-secondary school (now the Swedish *gymnasium*) in most cases, and most are regarded as adolescents rather than as young adults. As we pass into the 20–24 age group, things change. At these ages, young people have left the normal *gymnasium*, and they start to regard themselves as adults and to be so regarded by others. Even if some of our respondents took *gymnasium*-level classes at ages 20–24 (and then contributed to the positive exposures for students at the "low" or "middle" levels of education at these ages in Table 1), the institutional setting in which they received that education was different—they participated in *komvux* education (a high-school system directed to adults) rather than the *gymnasieskolan* ("*gymnasium* school") attended by the teenagers. (Our older cohorts attended school forms that were precursors to this system, but the age grading of expectations and behavior persists.) To reflect the largely different life situations of the two age groups, it pays to analyze them separately. When we do so, we discover that educational attainment does have a significant effect on consensual-union formation in both age groups, a feature that was covered up when they were both included in the same analysis.

For the teenagers, a suitable model is $\mu_{ijkm} = a_i b_j d_m$ for $m = 1$ and 2. The age effect $\{a_i\}$ is the same for all cohorts; there is a *separate* cohort effect $\{b_j\}$, and pupils with a low attainment ($m = 1$) had a significant super-risk of union formation of some 46 percent over pupils with a middle-level attainment. (We get $\hat{d}_1 = 1.46$ for the low level when the middle level is our baseline, with $p = .049$.) Moreover, there is no longer any effect of social background (i.e., all c_k equal 1) once we control for the fact that the respondent is enrolled in education and for the level attained (and for birth cohort). In substantive terms, the influence of social class on consensual-union formation behavior is only indirect at these ages; social class works on union formation only via educational behavior.

Similar features also turn up at ages 20 through 24. For this higher age group, it turns out that the best intensity model has the form $\mu_{ijkm} = a_i b_{jm}$. This means that we need to take birth cohort and educational level into account in combination, but the age effect is separate, and we can again leave social background out of account.

The pattern in the estimates of the b_{jm} for ages 20 through 24 is also revealing. (See Figure 1, where we have left out students with a low educational level; they have very small exposures at these ages.) It appears that the more highly educated students were forerunners in the expansion of cohabitational activity that occurred in our first cohorts, who were born between 1935 and 1939 (Cohort 1) and 1940 and 1944 (Cohort 2). For Cohorts 3 and 4 (born in 1945 through 1949 and in 1950 through 1954), students with a middle-level education had caught up. As times turned sour

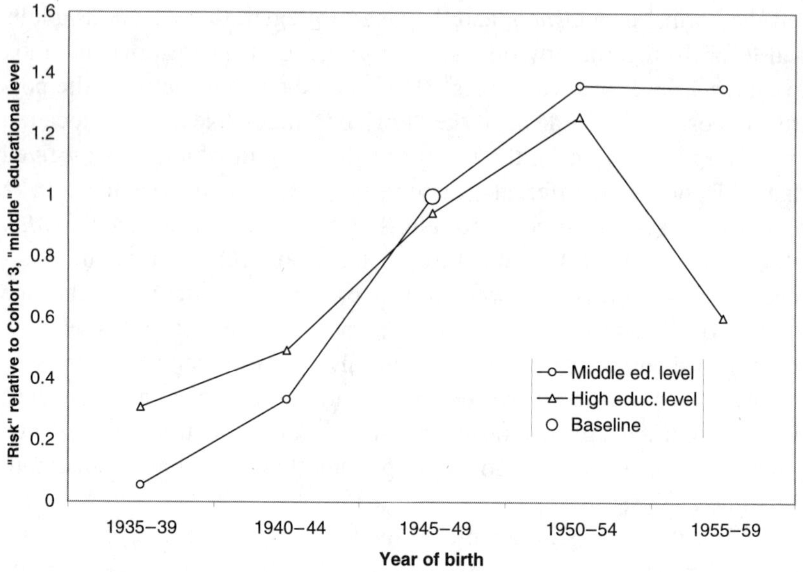

FIGURE 1. Cohort trends in consensual-union formation by Swedish students at ages 20–24, by educational attainment (standardized for age).

for young people in Sweden in the early 1980s, however, the more highly educated in our youngest cohort (born in 1955 through 1959) were the first to read the new signals and to start postponing union formation again.

Once these patterns have been established, a more complete analysis might include more elements. In particular, we may want to try to account for the selection features that help determine who stays enrolled in education. Such analysis goes beyond our current purposes, however. Instead, we turn to a number of questions generated by this simple example. Must we always reorganize our data to make all entries in an exposure matrix positive? (The answer is that we must not.) How can a_{ij} be seen as the union-formation intensity at age i for female students in birth cohort j in the baseline social group *at all levels of educational attainment* when young teenagers cannot have completed the *gymnasium* yet? (The answer is that it cannot.) How can we interpret the intensity μ_{ijkm} for substantively impossible combinations (i, j, k, m)? (The answer is again that we cannot.) Is it at all meaningful to make an analysis across such impossible combinations? (The answer is yes, if we are very careful.) We provide a systematic approach to questions of this nature.

3. MATHEMATICAL REPRESENTATION

A typical general specification of an intensity or hazard function in an analysis of individuals grouped into several permanent strata indexed here by j has the form

$$\mu_{hj}(t) = \mu_{0j}(t)\exp\left\{\sum_q \beta_{jq} x_{hjq}(t)\right\}, \tag{1}$$

where $\mu_{0j}(t)$ is a baseline intensity for stratum j, $x_{hjq}(t)$ is the value at time t of regressor q for individual h in stratum j, and β_{jq} is a regression coefficient that measures the effect of this regressor on the intensity in stratum j. A regressor may be fixed (in which case it does not depend on t) or time-varying (and then it does). When the baseline intensity is piecewise constant and all regressors are sets of binary variables that represent the levels of categorical covariates, the intensity can be given a simpler form. In the original formulation of our four-factor introductory example, this might go as follows.

Suppose that the time axis can be partitioned into intervals I_i and that we can act as if $\mu_{0j}(t) = a_{ij}$ for all t in I_i, for a suitable constant a_{ij} for each (i, j). In our illustration, age corresponds to the time variable t and the factor "birth cohort" acts as a stratum variable. The (single-year) age groups are indexed by i and the cohorts by j. In this example, binary regressors x represent two categorical covariates (social class and educational attainment) whose levels are indexed by k and m, respectively. The first of these is fixed and for individual h in cohort j it has some level k_{hj}. Educational attainment is updated every month and it has some level $m_{hj}(t)$ for this individual at time t. Then the intensity may be presented in the form $\mu_{hj}(t) = a_{i(t),j}\, c_{k_{hj}}\, d_{m_{hj}(t)}$ provided there are no interactions except the one between age and cohort. Here, $i(t)$ is the age interval that includes time t—i.e., exact age t belongs to interval $I_{i(t)}$. When we want to emphasize not individual h but the general format of the intensity, we can write it as $\mu_{ijkm} = a_{ij}\, c_k\, d_m$. This is of course the intensity that applies when $i(t) = i$ and $m_{hj}(t) = m$ for an individual with $k_{hj} = k$. Each *relative risk* c_k and d_m is the antilogarithm of some regression coefficient β_{jq}. It does not depend on j when we do not need an interaction term that involves the birth-cohort factor. To spell this out, suppose that our three social classes are represented by a pair (x_1, x_2) of binaries, and that $(x_1, x_2) = (0,0)$ represents Class C_1, $(x_1, x_2) = (1,0)$

stands for C_2, and $(x_1, x_2) = (0,1)$ for C_3. Let the regression coefficients corresponding to x_1 and x_2 be β_1 and β_2, respectively, with coefficients independent of j. Then $c_2 = \exp(\beta_1)$ and $c_3 = \exp(\beta_2)$, while $c_1 = 1$ as before. In the original model of our introductory example, there was no effect of Factor D, so $d_m = 1$ for all m, corresponding to a set of zero-valued beta coefficients in the exponent of formula (1).

This format allows us to respecify the intensity very easily and to use double-subscript parameters to indicate two-way factor combinations (and multiple-subscript parameters for higher-way combinations). Suppose, for instance, that we need to use the birth cohort and the educational level in a two-way combination but that we need no other interactions. The formula then changes to $\mu_{ijkm} = a_i b_{jm} c_k$. Another possibility is that we may need to combine age and educational level instead; then $\mu_{ijkm} = a_{im} b_j c_k$. Note that we use the same parameter *names*—namely *a*, *b*, *c*, and *d*—as a mnemonic device in all these representations, but that the *interpretation* of the parameters depends on the circumstances. Diacritics can be used if we need to distinguish several parameter representations in the same text. Thus we might write a'_{ij} and a''_{im}, for instance, instead of the symbols a_{ij} and a_{im}. The latter are easily confused, particularly if j and m are given numerical values (What is a_{i2}? Is it a_{ij} for $j = 2$ or is it a_{im} for $m = 2$?) *Statisticians often use a similar device to distinguish parameters from their estimators, and we will mimic this in a minute.*

Suppose now that we want to estimate the parameters a_{im}, b_j, and c_k in the last representation above, based on the occurrences, say D_{ijkm}, and the corresponding exposures R_{ijkm} for the various factor-level combinations. It turns out that the maximum-likelihood estimators $\hat{a}_{im}$, $\hat{b}_j$, and $\hat{c}_k$ are the solutions to the following three sets of equations:

$$\hat{a}_{im} = \frac{D_{i\cdot\cdot m}}{\sum_j \sum_k R_{ijkm} \hat{b}_j \hat{c}_k}, \quad \hat{b}_j = \frac{D_{\cdot j\cdot\cdot}}{\sum_i \sum_k \sum_m R_{ijkm} \hat{a}_{im} \hat{c}_k}, \quad \text{and}$$

$$\hat{c}_k = \frac{D_{\cdot\cdot k\cdot}}{\sum_i \sum_j \sum_m R_{ijkm} \hat{a}_{im} \hat{b}_j}. \tag{2}$$

Here, $D_{i\cdot\cdot m} = \sum_j \sum_k D_{ijkm}$, and the other aggregates are defined similarly. The dot subscript indicates where aggregation has occurred. These equations define the estimators only implicitly. They are solved by some numerical iteration procedure. This is of course less convenient than computing estimates by means of a straightforward formula, but at least the equations above make the handling of zero exposures transparent.

Suppose in fact that for some special combination (i_0, m_0) of levels on Factors A and D, $R_{i_0 jkm_0} = 0$ for all (j, k), as was the case in our initial example, where some combinations of age and educational level were substantively impossible. Then $D_{i_0 jkm_0} = 0$ for all (j, k) as well (you cannot have occurrences where there are no exposures) and the above equation for $\hat{a}_{i_0 m_0}$ in (2) has the form 0/0, so $\hat{a}_{i_0 m_0}$ cannot be found. If we define $\hat{a}_{i_0 m_0}$ to equal 0 in such a case, as is done automatically by some software, this does not however actually cause any problem for the computation of $\hat{a}_{im}$ for the (i, m) that have positive exposures, nor does it cause much trouble for the computation of the $\hat{b}_j$ and the $\hat{c}_k$. As long as a sufficient number of positive R_{ijkm} are located in suitable cells, all that happens is a change to $\sum_{i \neq i_0} \sum_k \sum_{m \neq m_0} R_{ijkm} \hat{a}_{im} \hat{c}_k$ in the denominator of the equation for $\hat{b}_j$ and a similar adjustment in the denominator for $\hat{c}_k$. If the (i_0, m_0) combination is substantively impossible, then there is no meaningful parameter $a_{i_0 m_0}$ in any case, and the lack of a corresponding maximum-likelihood estimator is no defect. (If too many R_{ijkm} are zero in strategic locations, we may run into identifiability problems; see Savage 1973; Harris and Soms 1974.)

The requirement that all parameters should have a meaningful interpretation is the key to the clarification of another issue. Suppose that there is no real need for an interaction between Factors A and D for the (i, m) combinations that *are* substantively possible and meaningful in our illustrative example, which means that for *such* (i, m) we may write $a_{im} = a_i d_m$ for a suitable set of new parameters a_i and d_m. Their maximum-likelihood estimators are computed from relations similar to those in (2) above. In particular,

$$\hat{a}_i = D_{i\ldots} \Big/ \sum_j \sum_k \sum_m R_{ijkm} \hat{b}_j \hat{c}_k \hat{d}_m,$$

and there are corresponding relations for the other parameters. Note that the third sum in the denominator of this expression is really taken only over those values of m that have nonzero exposures, but there is no need to show this explicitly in the formula since elements that have $R_{ijkm} = 0$ automatically drop out of the triple sum. Once the estimators $\{\hat{a}_i\}$ and $\{\hat{d}_m\}$ have been found, the corresponding maximum-likelihood estimator for a_{im} in this case is $a^*_{im} = \hat{a}_i \hat{d}_m$. This quantity can of course be computed for all i and m, but for substantively impossible combinations (i_0, m_0) the resulting quantity $a^*_{i_0 m_0}$ has no sensible interpretation as an estimator of a meaningful parameter.

Before we turn to other examples, let us sum up some operational conclusions from our first illustration. In the analysis of early consensual-union formation, substantive insights into the structure of the educational system and of the age-grading of individuals' transition into adulthood should have caused us to split the data into two segments according to the age of the respondent and to analyze the segments separately. Failing such foresight, the introduction of an interaction between age and educational level could have been used as a diagnostic tool because it would have revealed certain combinations of factor values as nonexistent in the data. Software specifically developed to handle analyses based on occurrence and exposure matrices, such as RocaNova (Martinelle 1993), would produce parameter estimates $\hat{a}_{i_0 m_0} = 0$ for impossible factor-level combinations (i_0, m_0), and so would common computer programs for contingency tables applied for the same purpose. Experimenting with interactions between pairs of factors using such software is a good supplement to incomplete forethought, for it makes any problematic factor-level combinations clearly visible.

We use a representation of the intensity function in terms of distinct levels on a baseline intensity and multiplicative relative risks. This representation is easily but clumsily transformed back to the exponential representation now used conventionally in statistical texts. Suppose our model is $\mu_{ijkm} = a_i b_{jm} c_k$, and let $\mu_0(t) = a_{i(t)}$, $\beta_{jm} = \ln(b_{jm})$, and $\gamma_k = \ln(c_k)$, where $i(t)$ remains the time interval that covers time t. This is the t-dependent level on Factor A. Then the intensity function at time t for an individual h who has level $m_h(t)$ on Factor D at time t, level j_h on Factor B (at all times), and level k_h on Factor C, is

$$\mu_h(t) = \mu_0(t) \exp\left\{ \sum_{j'} \sum_{m'} \beta_{j'm'} \chi[j' = j_h] \chi[m' = m_h(t)] \right.$$
$$\left. + \sum_{k'} \gamma_{k'} \chi[k' = k_h] \right\},$$

where $\chi[S]$ is an indicator of the truth of the statement S. This is a special case of the format in formula (1) for a population with a single, all-encompassing stratum. The respondent's birth cohort is now a covariate, not a stratum indicator, and we drop the stratum index in (1). Our parameters $\beta_{j'm'}$ and $\gamma_{k'}$ then play the role of the general parameters β_q in (the revised version of) formula (1), and our present regressors $y_{hj'm'}(t) = \chi[j' = j_h]\chi[m' = m_h(t)]$ and $z_{hk'}(t) = \chi[k' = k_k]$ (for all t) play the role of the general regressors $x_{hq}(t)$. Maximum-likelihood estimators satisfy relations similar to (2) with the $\beta_{j'm'}$ and $\gamma_{k'}$ substituted for their multiplicative counterparts $b_{j'm'}$ and $c_{k'}$. The maximum-likelihood solutions must again be found by numerical iteration. Most current general software for intensity-regression analysis uses this type of model specification. Unfortunately, it has the disadvantage that it does not offer as easy a way to detect systematic patterns of zero exposures as does the multiplicative formulation we have adhered to here. With exponential representation, such patterns can cause a drift toward minus infinity of the successive approximations to the maximum-likelihood estimates provided by the iteration process, a feature that is uncomfortable for a numerical procedure.

4. REPRESENTATION OF AGE OF YOUNGEST CHILD WHEN CHILDLESS WOMEN ARE INCLUDED

We now turn to a type of application where certain factor-level combinations are so inescapably meaningless that they cry out for special handling. As a first example, consider a study of divorce risks that includes a mother's childbearing parity (i.e., how many children she has borne) and the age of her youngest child among the regressors. These covariates have proved to be important determinants of the divorce risk (Toulemon 1994 and his predecessors), but the inclusion of childless women in the analysis needs special consideration because there is no meaningful age of the youngest child to childless women.

In a recent investigation, Andersson (1997) used a divorce intensity of the form $\mu_{ijk\ell mn} = a_{ijk\ell} c_{mn}$. Here, i indexes the (grouped) duration of marriage (his time variable), j indexes the woman's age group at marriage, k indexes the calendar year (for single calendar years), and ℓ is an indicator of premarital childbearing. The parameters $a_{ijk\ell}$ have their own structure, which need not concern us here. The parameters c_{mn} represent a combination of the woman's childbearing parity m and the age group n of her youngest child (when $m > 0$). The issue is how we can represent the case of $m = 0$.

We could perhaps add a binary indicator of childlessness as a covariate, but childless women would have to be assigned the same arbitrary value (say 1) on the youngest child's age group, and this would produce a great number of zero values in locations in the exposure matrix that represent positive ages of the youngest child for childless women. The following procedure is simpler.

Suppose that for women with children m runs from 1 to some highest parity M and that n runs from 1 to some highest age group N, so there is a total of MN combinations (m, n) with $m > 0$. In Andersson's case (Andersson 1997), $M = 3$ (for parities 1 through 3) and $N = 6$. To include childless women, suppose that we rearrange the pairs (m, n) into a single sequence to produce a combined factor with MN levels. If a particular (m, n) is the vth member of that sequence, let d_v equal c_{mn}. We can then extend the sequence by a single further level—say, level 0, to represent childless women—and perhaps normalize by choosing this as our baseline level (i.e., let $d_0 = 1$). The outcome is direct comparability of the divorce-risk levels of women at all parities and for all ages of the youngest child for women who have children. Empirical results can be presented as in Table 2, or perhaps more lucidly in a diagram like Figure 2. In both cases, $n = 1$ represents women who are pregnant with the child that will give them the parity indicated. (For convenience, the effect is given for pregnant women at parity m when in reality they are pregnant with their mth child.) The main features of the empirical results are (1) that divorce risks for mothers

TABLE 2
Interaction Between Parity and Age of Youngest Child in the Divorce Risk for Swedish Women in First Marriage[a]

	Parity 0	Parity 1	Parity 2	Parity 3
Nonpregnant	1[b]			
Pregnant[c]		0.22	0.10	0.21
Nonpregnant and with a youngest child of age				
< 1 year		0.05	0.05	0.08
1–2 years		0.38	0.24	0.22
3–5 years		0.93	0.44	0.42
6–8 years		0.90	0.49	0.51
9+ years		0.83	0.54	0.64

[a]Analysis includes childless women.

[b]Baseline group.

[c]A pregnant woman at parity 0 is pregnant with her first child and her relative risk is listed under parity 1. Pregnant women at higher parities are listed similarly.

Source: Developed by Andersson (1997) on the basis of register data from Statistics Sweden.

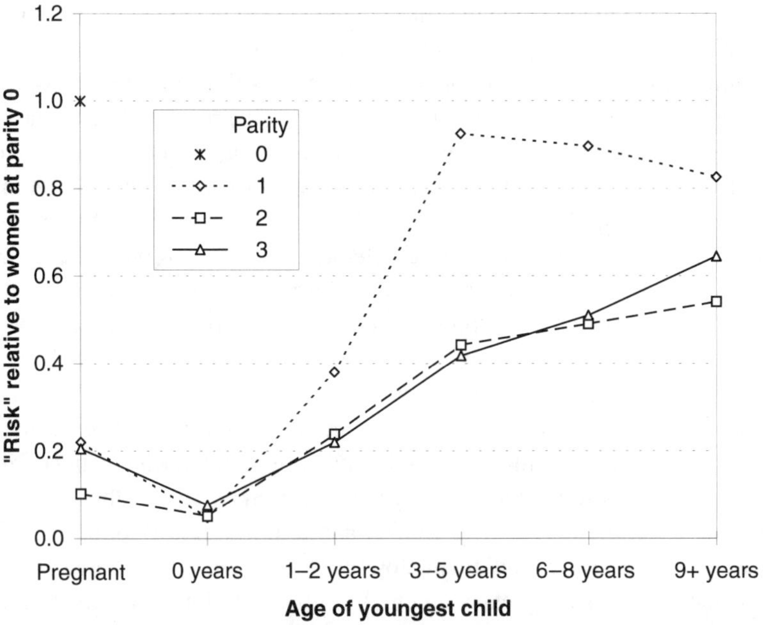

FIGURE 2. Divorce risk for Swedish women in their first marriage, 1971–1994, by parity and age of youngest child. Standardized for current calendar year, age at marriage, duration of marriage, and premarital childbearing. Adapted from Andersson (1997).

are lower than for childless women, but (2) that the risk for mothers of a single child rises to approximately 90 percent of the risk for childless women when the child reaches 3 to 5 years of age. The risks for mothers of two or three children stay lower. In a country with a strong two-child norm like Sweden, remaining a mother of a single child for as long as up to five years may be an indicator that something is wrong with the marriage in many cases. The high divorce risk for single-child mothers at these durations may be largely a selection effect if well-functioning marriages regularly proceed beyond parity 1.

5. REPRESENTATION OF CONDITIONS AT MARRIAGE FORMATION WHEN COHABITANTS ARE INCLUDED

In our previous example, the analysis was confined to married women. The challenge becomes more formidable if we also let the study encompass cohabitants (women in nonmarital unions). It is a standard finding in investigations of disruption risks for marital and nonmarital unions that cohabitants dissolve their unions much more readily than married couples do. Among the married, premarital conception and premarital childbearing increase disruption risks somewhat, as does premarital cohabitation (see Bennett et al. 1988, Hoem and Hoem 1992, and others). (The latter feature may be surprising. It is normally explained as a consequence of selection. Those who marry after preceding cohabitation are thought to have personal values that differ from people who marry directly, and the difference makes the former more divorce-prone.) It is important, therefore, to include the circumstances surrounding marriage formation in the analysis of those who are married. Beside switching attention from formal divorce to union disruption (for marital as well as nonmarital unions) when cohabitants are included, one may want to include pre-cohabitational conception and pre-cohabitational childbearing for cohabitants, but for them there is no meaningful parallel to premarital cohabitation for married individuals. Thus, we encounter a problem analogous to that of defining an age of the youngest child for childless women. A similar solution offers itself, as is illustrated by the following example.

In a study of the patterns of union disruption during the months after the arrival of a woman's first child (Hoem 1997b), we restricted ourselves to the life segments (1) between entry into a first union and the beginning of any second pregnancy in that union, and (2) between entry into a second union while still childless and the beginning of any second pregnancy in that union. Our purpose was to check up on the notion that the arrival of a first child can be a disruptive element in a marital or nonmarital union, a notion that is prevalent in the counseling literature.

The life segments up to any second pregnancy or any disruption in a first union (whichever comes first) are depicted in Figure 3, and an extension of this diagram could capture subsequent life segments through the second union. In the diagram, boxes represent relevant statuses that a woman can be in and arrows represent possible transitions between those statuses. All women start as single, childless, and nonpregnant. Some women marry while still childless and nonpregnant, others become pregnant and then start their first cohabitational union before the arrival of the first child, some marry after some time in a consensual union, and so on. The few women who had a child before their first union could not contribute any information about the substantive issue we addressed and were excluded from the analysis. In the diagram, this

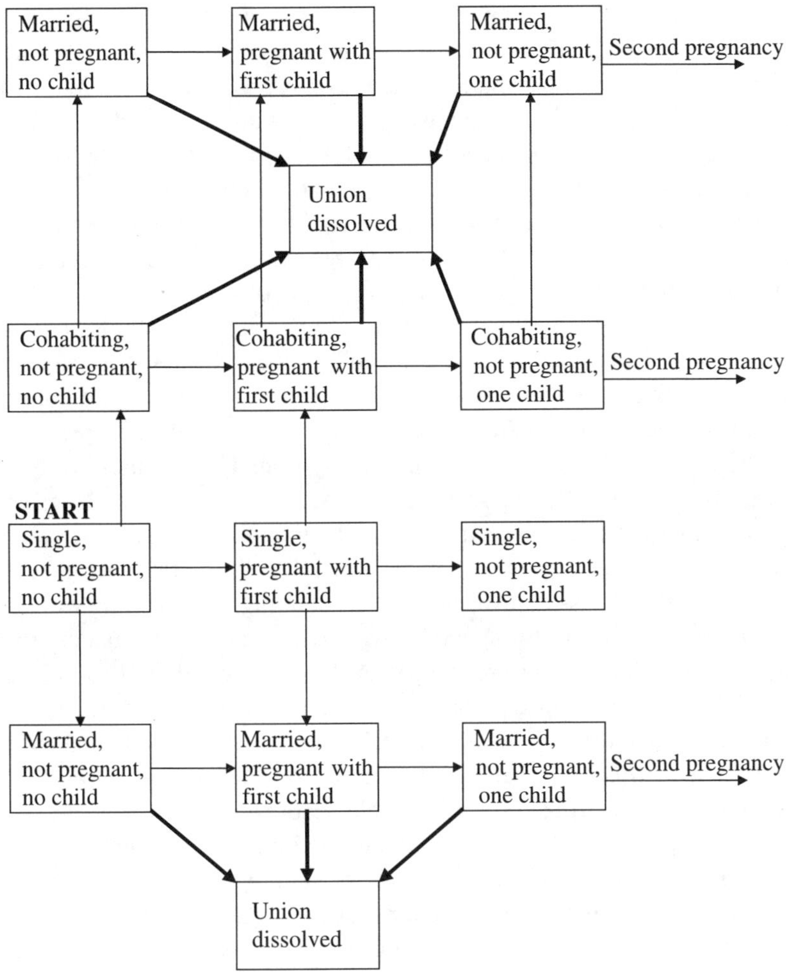

FIGURE 3. Status-and-transition diagram for a study of union disruption risks in first marital and nonmarital unions.

is represented by the absorbing state called "single, not pregnant, one child", out of which there is no arrow.

Our task is to provide an understandable representation of the transition intensities corresponding to the thick arrows in Figure 3 and the corresponding arrows for transitions in the second union (provided it was entered at parity 0). We could have represented many relevant features of behavior by including a number of binary regressors. We could have used one binary variable to distinguish cohabiting from married couples, another to indicate whether marriage had been preceded by cohabitation, a third to flag whether the woman was pregnant with her first child at marriage, and so on. We also needed to take into account whether the woman was pregnant with her first child in any month of observation (as distinct from at marriage formation), whether the couple had a child, and the age of that child. This would have introduced a large number of impossible factor-level combinations and corresponding zero-valued exposures. Couples who were currently cohabiting in any month of observation would have to be assigned the same arbitrary value (0, say) on the indicator that was supposed to pick up premarital cohabitation. Similarly, couples who did not currently have a child would have to be assigned a zero value, for example, for the age of their nonexistent child, and so on. This would have been quite feasible but rather impractical.

A more efficient procedure would be to rearrange those indicators into two multilevel factors, as indicated in Table 3. The first factor, "current civil status," has six levels, one corresponding to cohabiting women, one for previously cohabiting currently married women who had married at parity 0 without being pregnant with their first child, and so on. For simplification we dropped a subdivision of cohabitants according to pregnancy status at entry into the nonmarital union; most were nonpregnant at the time of entry. The other factors used in the analysis are indicated as variables we standardized for in the table heading.

The second factor, "current motherhood status" (for want of a better term), has seven levels, one for childless nonpregnant women, one for women who were pregnant with their first child, and five more levels for women with one child at various young ages. Life histories were censored seven months before the arrival of any second child. This was taken as the time that the woman knew for sure that she was pregnant with her second child.

The first panel of Table 3 has been arranged so as to display the difference in union-dissolution behavior of cohabiting and married couples as well as the effect of the mode of entry into marriage for the latter. Table cells have been left empty when they represent logically impossible combinations or when zero-valued exposures were generated by the observational design, as in the lower-right corner of the first panel.

The second panel contains the main substantive new finding of the study—namely, that the disruption risk rises after the arrival of the first

TABLE 3
Risk of Union Disruption Among Swedish Women, by Current Civil and Motherhood Status[a]

	Current Civil Status		
	Currently cohabiting	Married after cohabitation	Married, no premarital cohabitation
Status at Marriage			
Parity 0	2.99 (74)[b]		
Not pregnant		1[c] (15)	0.86 (5)
Pregnant		1.14 (3)	0.95 (0)
Parity 1		1.34 (3)	[d]
Current Motherhood Status			
Childless		2.51 (65)	
Pregnant		0.65 (7)	
One child at age (in months)			
0–5		1[c] (6)	
6–11		1.53 (6)	
12–17		1.49 (5)	
18–23		2.86 (4)	
24–47		2.53 (7)	

Source: Hoem (1997).

[a]Standardized for duration and order of union, calendar period, and current age; relative risks.

[b]Figures in parentheses represent percentages of the total time of exposure to union disruption. A zero indicates a percentage of less than one half.

[c]Baseline levels are indicated by a relative risk of 1 (without decimals). There is one baseline level on each factor.

[d]The lower-right corner in the first panel is empty because women were excluded from the analysis if they had a child before entry into their current (marital or nonmarital) union. This leaves out women who married at parity 1 if they did not live in a consensual union before marriage.

child and reaches the same level as for childless women when the first child becomes some eighteen months old.

6. SINGLE DEVIATION FROM A MULTIPLICATIVE INTENSITY PATTERN

So far we have mostly indicated how systematic patterns of zero values in the exposure matrix can be avoided. This is done either by (1) a segmentation of the data set or (2) a suitable recombination of the values of two or more underlying factors into a single factor, which is defined in a manner that eliminates levels with no exposures. We will now show that, conversely, the deliberate introduction of a system of zero exposures can be used as a tool to simplify data description.

In some studies of transition intensities, one is able to find a multiplicative form for the combined effect of a pair of factors, except for an occasional factor-level combination. For a case in point, consider our investigation of the impact of educational attainment on divorce risks (Hoem 1997a). Sweden liberalized its divorce law in 1974 and got an immediate rush of divorces in that one year. It mostly affected childless (married) couples, for whom it created a single spike in the divorce risk. Other couples were less involved in 1974 and in subsequent years developments have been much more stable (Andersson 1997). For our purposes, the divorce patterns can be described by an intensity function written as $\mu_{ijk} = a_i b_{jk}$, where j stands for childbearing parity, k for calendar year, and i for a combination of other factors, including educational attainment. The parameters $\{a_i\}$ have their own structure, which depends on the underlying factors, but we will not pay any attention to it here. Our interest right now is directed to the time pattern embedded in the parameters $\{b_{jk}\}$ that represent the combined effects (measured as relative risks) of parity and calendar time. It turns out that to a good approximation b_{jk} can be given a multiplicative representation of the form $b_{jk} = c_j d_k$ for all (j, k) *except* for parity 0 in the calendar year 1974 (i.e., for $j = 0$, $k = 1974$). For this particular (j, k) combination, the divorce risk was almost 50 percent higher than what was projected by the product $c_j d_k$. This single deviation can be handled in the usual intensity-regression framework by an extensive use of zero-valued exposures.

Let us introduce a parameter g given as $g = b_{0,1974}/(c_0 d_{1974})$ to represent the special super-risk of divorce for childless women in 1974, over and above the risk projected by the model for all other combinations of parity and calendar year ($g > 1$). Then $b_{jk} = gc_j d_k$ for $j = 0$ and $k = 1974$, while $b_{jk} = c_j d_k$ for all other combinations of j and k. Let us also introduce a new, binary factor, indexed by m, which equals 1 when $j = 0$ and $k = 1974$, and 0 for all other combinations of j and k. Thus this new factor is a (nonlinear) function of the two factors "parity" and "calendar year." Suppose that the exposure value for cell (i, j, k) is R_{ijk} and define a new, four-index exposure value R_{ijkm} as follows:

$$R_{ijkm} = \begin{cases} R_{ijk} & \text{for } (j,k) \neq (0,1974) \text{ and } m = 0, \\ 0 & \text{for } (j,k) \neq (0,1974) \text{ and } m = 1, \\ 0 & \text{for } (j,k) = (0,1974) \text{ and } m = 0, \text{ and} \\ R_{i,0,1974} & \text{for } (j,k) = (0,1974) \text{ and } m = 1. \end{cases}$$

We define corresponding occurrences D_{ijkm} similarly and introduce $g_0 = 1$, $g_1 = g$, where g was given above. We can then work with a divorce risk formula like $\mu_{ijkm} = a_i c_j d_k g_m$ and estimate it as an ordinary multiplicative intensity whose occurrence and exposure matrices may be unusually full of empty cells, for they consist of our newly defined values D_{ijkm} and R_{ijkm}. This reduces the case of a single deviation from a multiplicative three-factor model to a fully multiplicative four-factor model, which we know how to handle. It should be possible to treat cases with more deviations from a simple pattern in a similar manner.

For numerical computations, it normally pays to switch to a coordinate representation of the matrices if they have many zeros, as in the case above. One would then replace the many-dimensional sparse matrices of occurrences and exposures by a listing that contains records only of the form $(i, j, k, m, D_{ijkm}, R_{ijkm})$ for the (i, j, k, m) where $R_{ijkm} > 0$, and one would feed the latter into the computer program. The fact that some zero-valued exposures are eliminated from the listing of records does not mean that the zero values do not exist, only that they are defined indirectly as the items that are missing from the coordinate representation of the data set.

7. CONCLUDING REMARKS

Systematic patterns of empty cells in occurrence and exposure matrices may be a symptom of substantively impossible factor-level combinations. This is a serious issue in intensity-regression analyses, and it is frequently raised in discussions of their outcomes, but the issue can often be handled without too much difficulty. It is good practice to make sure that the analysis includes interactions between the factors involved. In fact, this can be a diagnostic tool to detect systematic zero-value exposures if pure fore-thought is insufficient. If such analysis can be used to establish a multiplicative model across the *meaningful* factor-level combinations, then all that is needed may be a careful interpretation of parameter estimates to exclude explicitly the impossible cases. A recombination of two or more original factors may produce a new, amalgamated factor that induces the user to avoid the most flagrant misinterpretations. It may also relieve the matrices of a clutter of zero values. It may still be useful to present findings in a pattern that recognizes the original multidimensional factor set-up, as shown earlier in Tables 2 and 3. Our final example also shows that, conversely, it may occasionally be convenient to *introduce* extra zero-valued exposures derived from the original data in order to handle occasional deviations from a multiplicative intensity structure that works across the rest of the factor-value combinations.

REFERENCES

Allison, Paul D. 1984. *Event History Analysis: Regression for Longitudinal Event Data.* Beverly Hills, CA: Sage University Paper No. 46.

Andersen, Per Kragh, Ørnulf Borgan, Richard D. Gill, and Niels Keiding. 1991. *Statistical Models Based on Counting Processes.* Heidelberg, Germany: Springer-Verlag.

Andersson, Gunnar. 1997. "The Impact of Children on Divorce Risks of Swedish Women." *European Journal of Population* 13:109–45.

Bennett, Neil G., Ann K. Blanc, and David E. Bloom. 1988. "Commitment and the Modern Union: Assessing the Link Between Premarital Cohabitation and Subsequent Marital Stability." *American Sociological Review* 53:127–38.

Blossfeld, Hans-Peter, and Götz Rohwer. 1995. *Techniques of Event-History Modeling: New Approaches to Causal Analysis.* Mahwah, NJ: Lawrence Erlbaum.

Harris, Bernard, and Andrew P. Soms. 1974. "Hypothesis Testing and Confidence Intervals for a Multiplicative Poisson Model with Applications to Reliability and Bioassay." Pp. 363–78 in *Reliability and Biometry*, edited by Frank Proschan and R. J. Serfling. Philadelphia: SIAM.

Hoem, Jan M. 1986. "The Impact of Education on Modern Family-Union Initiation." *European Journal of Population* 2:113–33.

———. 1993. "Classical Demographic Methods of Analysis and Modern Event-History Techniques." Liege, Belgium: International Union for the Scientific Study of Population. Presented at the *22nd International Population Conference, Montreal, Canada, 1993*, Vol. 3, pp. 281–91.

———. 1997a. "Educational Gradients in Divorce Risks in Sweden in Recent Decades." *Population Studies* 51:19–27. For a more complete text, see *Stockholm Research Reports in Demography*, no. 84.

———. 1997b. "The Impact of the First Child on Family Stability." *Stockholm Research Reports in Demography*, no. 119.

Hoem, Jan M., and Britta Hoem. 1992. "The Disruption of Marital and Nonmarital Unions in Contemporary Sweden." Pp. 61–93 in *Demographic Applications of Event History Analysis*, edited by James Trussell, Richard Hankinson, and Judith Tilton. Oxford: Clarendon Press.

Martinelle, Sten. 1993. *RocaNova: A Program for Intensity Regression; User's Guide.* Stockholm: Statistics Sweden.

Savage, Jimmy R. 1973. "Incomplete Contingency Tables: Conditions for the Existence of Unique MLE." Pp. 87–99 in *Mathematics and Statistics: Essays in Honor of Harald Bergström*. Gothenburg, Sweden.

Toulemon, Laurent. 1994. "La place des enfants dans l'histoire des couples." *Population* 49:1321–66.

Tuma, Nancy B., and Michael Hannan. 1984. *Social Dynamics, Models, and Methods*. Orlando, FL: Academic Press.

8

THE SELF AS A FUZZY SET OF ROLES, ROLE THEORY AS A FUZZY SYSTEM

*James D. Montgomery**

This paper shows how the socialization process (viewed by role theorists as a "role-person merger") can be represented and analyzed as a fuzzy (dynamical) system. Given a self-concept (a fuzzy set of roles) and social norms (logical implications from roles to actions), an individual infers actions (through approximate reasoning). Given these actions, alters make biased attributions (about the roles in the individual's self-concept) that are gradually internalized by the individual. This feedback loop creates a fuzzy system (a role-space vectorfield) that generates a set of stable long-run selves (role-space attractors). I illustrate this general "endogenous-self" framework with a model based loosely on Tally's Corner; the analysis examines how the individual's long-run self-concept is influenced by a constraint on employment opportunity.

1. INTRODUCTION

Role theorists have viewed socialization as a process by which individuals internalize roles—as a "role-person merger" (Turner 1978). The present paper, inspired by engineering applications of fuzzy logic to control systems, shows how the socialization process may be formalized as a fuzzy (dynamical) system. Addressing intertemporal change in the self-concept, the present "endogenous-self" framework offers a sociological alternative to the endogenous-preference models developed by economists. More gen-

I am grateful to Peter Abell, Tom Fararo, and Matt Rabin for comments on various drafts of this paper.

*London School of Economics

erally, by showing how the key sociological concepts of "self" and "role" and "norm" can be specified using fuzzy sets and relations, how actions and attributions can be derived through fuzzy logic, and how the socialization process may be viewed as a fuzzy system (more specifically, a role-space vectorfield), the paper contributes a new theoretical methodology for representing and analyzing role-theoretic explanations.

The paper is organized as follows. Section 2 describes how the role-person merger may be formalized as a fuzzy system. Section 3 develops the framework and shows how to derive the long-run selves (role-space attractors) generated by the system. To illustrate, I construct a model based loosely on the classic ethnography *Tally's Corner* (Liebow 1967); the analysis examines how the individual's long-run self is influenced by constraints on employment opportunity. Section 4 offers an alternative specification of fuzzy inference and decision-making. Section 5 provides some discussion: I compare the present framework with related perspectives (previous formalizations of role theory, rational choice theory, and social network analysis), discuss fuzzy logic in relation to some alternatives, and indicate some directions for future empirical implementation. Section 6 concludes the paper.

2. THE ROLE-PERSON MERGER AS A FUZZY SYSTEM

Ralph Turner's (1978) conception of the "role-person merger" offers one important role-theoretic view of the socialization process.[1] Reduced to its essence, the role-person merger becomes a simple feedback loop involving a focal individual ("ego"), as illustrated in Figure 1.

Ego's self-concept (or simply "self") is a set of roles; social norms specify the actions that should be taken by roles. Thus, given an initial self, ego may (at least attempt to) choose those actions required by norms. In turn, alters observe ego's actions, attributing her behavior to roles. Following Turner, we might presume that these attributions are systemically biased—that alters tend to *over*attribute roles to ego's self.[2] Finally, to close the feedback loop, we might assume that these (biased) attributions

[1]Future research might consider alternative social-psychological views of the self and self-formation processes, some of which seem equally amenable to formalization using fuzzy sets and fuzzy systems (in particular, see Stryker and Statham 1985).

[2]See Turner's (1978:6) discussion of the "appearance principle." In light of related work in (psychological) social psychology, the appearance principle might be viewed as a manifestation of the "fundamental attribution error" (Ross 1977).

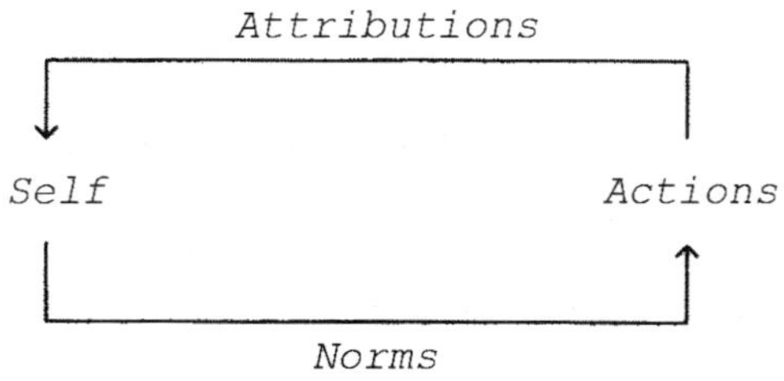

FIGURE 1. The Role-Person Merger

are gradually internalized by ego. In the long run, ego's self contains just those roles that alters attribute to it—ego possesses a "looking-glass" self (Cooley 1983 [1902]).[3]

Building on this preliminary specification of the role-person merger, we might suppose that the self changes through a dialectic process.[4] Having already specified the self as a set of roles, we might further specify norms as logical (material) implications from roles to actions. Each link in the feedback loop would then correspond to a logical syllogism. Ego derives appropriate actions through the syllogism

$$\textit{self, norms} \vdash \textit{actions}$$

which might reflect derivation through *modus ponens* (P and P→Q therefore Q). Alters infer ego's self through the syllogism

$$\textit{actions, norms} \vdash \textit{self}$$

which might reflect derivation through *modus tollens* (−Q and P→Q therefore −P). Alternatively, given alters' tendency to make stronger (logically

[3] My present specification of the role-person merger (formalized in Section 3) is quite stylized. In particular, I assume a representative alter (essentially Mead's [1934] "generalized other") and ignore many details of the attribution process (see Fiske and Taylor 1991). These issues might be addressed in future research once the framework is extended to include ego's personal network (see Section 5).

[4] See Lemmon (1965) for an introduction to formal (classical) logic. Recent sociological application of formal logic has occurred mostly at the metatheoretical level as researchers have checked the logical consistency of various organizational theories (Péli et al. 1994; Masuch and Huang 1996; Hannan 1998); see also Elster (1978) for various sociological applications of formal logic as well as the argument that any proper dialectic argument can and should be specified using formal logic.

more problematic) inferences, their conclusions may stem from abductive reasoning (Q and $P \to Q$ therefore P).[5]

To illustrate, consider an example where ego is a father (i.e., ego's self contains the role f). A social norm requires that a father should provide for his family (an action P). Represented as an implication, this norm becomes $f \to P$. Thus ego derives his obligation through the syllogism

$$f, f \to P \vdash P$$

where the conclusion follows by *modus ponens*. Further suppose that ego is unable to provide for his family (perhaps due to his inability to find a good job). Observing ego's failure to obey the norm, alters might infer that he is not a father. The second syllogism becomes

$$-P, f \to P \vdash -f$$

where the conclusion follows by *modus tollens*. Alternatively, consider a different ego who does provide for his family. Alters observing this action would attribute it to a role in ego's self through the syllogism

$$P, f \to P \vdash f$$

where this conclusion follows by abduction. Note that abductive reasoning yields a strong conclusion that may not be warranted (since ego might have chosen P even if he was not an f).

While a dialectic specification of the role-person merger may be conceptually appealing, sociological applications would seem limited by the inability of classical logic to admit ambiguity. An individual may feel only somewhat attached to a particular role, while norms may prescribe vague actions (compare March [1994, ch. 5] on ambiguity in organizations). Because classical logic presupposes crisp sets (i.e., each element in the universe of discourse has a degree of membership $\mu \in \{0,1\}$), we would be forced to assume that ego's self either does or does not contain f, and that a particular action either does or does not constitute obedience to a norm. In contrast, role theorists might insist that membership is always a

[5] Although Lemmon (1965:17) simply labels it the logical fallacy of "affirming the consequent," abduction does resemble (valid) probabilistic reasoning (through Bayes' Rule) and is permitted (as a tentative derivation) in various nonmonotonic logics (Brewka et al. 1997, ch. 5); see Pearl (1988) on the use of probabilistic techniques within logic.

matter of degree.[6] Thus, my formalization of role theory will make use of fuzzy sets (which generalize crisp sets to allow degree of membership $\mu \in [0,1]$) and fuzzy logic (i.e., approximate reasoning from fuzzy sets).[7]

To illustrate, consider a fuzzy specification of the preceding (crisp) example. Suppose now that ego's self contains the role f only partially, with degree of membership equal to (say) 0.7.[8] More formally, letting S denote the self (now understood as a fuzzy set of roles), and adopting standard fuzzy-set notation, we may write $\mu_S(\mathrm{f}) = 0.7$.[9] (This expression might be read as "the self contains the father role to degree 0.7.") Further, recognizing the ambiguity inherent in norms, the (crisp) action P might be respecified as a fuzzy set. For instance, if we assume that ego provides some level of monetary support $\mathrm{c} \in \mathrm{C} = \{0, 1, \ldots, 9\}$, we might represent "provide for family" as a fuzzy set P characterized by the degrees of membership $\mu_P(\mathrm{c})$. For instance, we might assume

c	0	1	2	3	4	5	6	7	8	9
$\mu_P(\mathrm{c})$	0	0	.1	.25	.4	.6	.75	.9	1	1

Thus monetary payment c = 1 clearly does not constitute "provision for family" since $\mu_P(1) = 0$; payment c = 8 clearly does constitute "provision" since $\mu_P(8) = 1$; payment c = 5 is ambiguous since $\mu_P(5) = 0.6$.

To continue, the norm f→P may be recast as a fuzzy relation N (from roles to actions) with degrees of membership $\mu_N(\mathrm{f,c}) = \mu_P(\mathrm{c})$ for

[6] Compare Turner's (1978) claim that "the person consists of all the roles in an individual's repertoire, with some qualification about how well each is played" (p. 2).

[7] See Zadeh (1965, 1975) for seminal discussions of fuzzy sets and approximate reasoning. Recent texts emphasizing engineering applications include Kosko (1992), Ross (1995), and Tsoukalas and Uhrig (1997); see Kosko (1994) a popular account. Section 5 contains further discussion of (my perspective on) fuzzy logic.

[8] Fuzzy theorists have emphasized that the "vagueness" reflected by degree of membership in a fuzzy set is conceptually distinct from the "randomness" reflected by probability. To illustrate, Kosko (1992:267) draws an irregular oval that might have a high degree of membership (say 0.9) in a fuzzy set of ovals but is not in any probabilistic sense an oval. The distinction between vagueness and randomness seems clear in role-theoretic applications. I am not supposing that ego is a father 70 percent of the time, nor that there is a 70 percent chance that this particular individual is a father. Rather, ego faces a pattern-recognition problem: how should he classify himself within (socially constructed) categories, none of which may fit perfectly? Compare Montgomery (1998:98).

[9] While the standard notation is not explicit, every fuzzy set is defined with respect to some universe of discourse. Here, the fuzzy set S is defined with respect to the set of all social roles R, so that $\mu_S(\mathrm{i}) \in [0,1]$ is defined for every $\mathrm{i} \in \mathrm{R}$.

$c \in C$. Intuitively, ego's obligation to perform action c becomes stronger as $\mu_S(f)$ rises (reflecting ego's stronger identification with the father role) and $\mu_N(f,c)$ rises (reflecting a stronger implication from the father role to action c). Adopting one particular specification of approximate reasoning, we might assume that ego's obligation to choose c is determined by $\min\{\mu_S(f), \mu_N(f,c)\}$. Thus, in place of the (crisp) obligation P drawn from the (crisp) premises f and f→P, a fuzzy specification of ego's problem yields the fuzzy obligations

c	0	1	2	3	4	5	6	7	8	9
$\min\{\mu_S(f), \mu_N(f,c)\}$	0	0	.1	.25	.4	.6	.7	.7	.7	.7

drawn from the fuzzy premises $\mu_S(f)$ and $\mu_N(f,c)$. In the next section, I develop a more complete specification of approximate reasoning, describing how inferences might be made by ego (from self and norms to actions) and alters (from actions and norms to self) in more general settings with multiple roles, actions, and norms.

Given a fuzzy-logic specification of each link in the feedback loop, iteration between ego's choices and alters' attributions creates a fuzzy (dynamical) system.[10] This system may be given a helpful (and hopefully compelling) graphical representation. To begin, note that any fuzzy set may be viewed as a point in a hypercube (Kosko 1992, ch. 7).[11] In particular, the self S may be viewed as a point in "role space" (an n-dimensional unit cube where n is the number of roles in the social system). A mapping between hypercubes is a fuzzy system (Kosko 1992, ch. 8). In the present framework, the feedback loop (which runs from self to actions to self) is a fuzzy system that maps role space into itself, and thus governs change of the self over time. (Adopting dynamical-systems terminology, role space is a manifold; the fuzzy system generates a vectorfield on this manifold.) Given ego's initial self S_0, this fuzzy system determines ego's trajectory

[10] See Fararo (1989, ch. 2) for an introduction to dynamical systems and their application in sociological theory. Vallacher and Nowak (1994) advocate a dynamical systems perspective in social psychology. See Drazin (1992) for a formal introduction to dynamical systems; Abraham and Shaw (1992) provide a helpful graphical introduction.

[11] A fuzzy set associates each element in a universe of discourse with a degree of membership $\mu \in [0,1]$. Thus, if there are n elements in the underlying universe of discourse, the fuzzy set may be viewed as a point in an n-dimensional unit cube.

$\{S_0, S_1, S_2, \ldots\}$ through role space. Of special interest is the set of role-space attractors—the set of stable, long-run selves determined by the norms of the social system.

3. A Model

In this section, I specify and analyze a formal model. The substance of the model is based loosely on *Tally's Corner*, Elliot Liebow's (1967) classic ethnography of streetcorner men. The substantive issues raised by this model (discussed briefly at the end of this section) may be of considerable interest in their own right. However, my primary goal is to show how the role-person merger may be formalized as a fuzzy system and thus illustrate a general theoretical methodology that may enable more precise specification and analysis of many role-theoretic explanations.

3.1. *The Self and Interrole Implications*

Consider a focal male individual ("ego") in a social system with three roles: man (m), father (f), and worker (w). Each of these roles may be contained (perhaps partially) in ego's self-concept (or simply "self"). More formally, the self is a fuzzy set S characterized by degree of membership $\mu_S(\mathrm{i}) \in [0,1]$ for $\mathrm{i} \in \mathrm{R} = \{\mathrm{m}, \mathrm{f}, \mathrm{w}\}$. For purposes of matrix algebra, we may form the corresponding vector of degrees of membership

$$\mathbf{s} = [\mu_S(\mathrm{m})\ \mu_S(\mathrm{f})\ \mu_S(\mathrm{w})].$$

For instance, we might assume (as an initial condition) that

$$\mathbf{s} = [0.7 \quad 0.6 \quad 0.0].$$

That is, ego classifies himself ambiguously as a man ($\mu_S(\mathrm{m}) = 0.7$), somewhat more ambiguously as a father ($\mu_S(\mathrm{f}) = 0.6$), and unambiguously as a nonworker ($\mu_S(\mathrm{w}) = 0.0$).

Roles themselves might be related by logical implication. For instance, we might suppose that men are obligated to be fathers (i.e., $\mathrm{m} \rightarrow \mathrm{f}$).[12] These implications among roles may be represented formally by a fuzzy

[12] Liebow (1967:210) states that the streetcorner man "wants to be publicly, legally married, to support a family and be the head of it, because this is what it is to be a man in our society, whether one lives in a room near the carry-out or in an elegant house in the suburbs."

relation M that characterizes the degree of relation between each ordered pair of roles. For purposes of matrix algebra, these degrees of relation may be collected together in the matrix

$$\mathbf{M} = \begin{bmatrix} \mu_M(\mathrm{m,m}) & \mu_M(\mathrm{m,f}) & \mu_M(\mathrm{m,w}) \\ \mu_M(\mathrm{f,m}) & \mu_M(\mathrm{f,f}) & \mu_M(\mathrm{f,w}) \\ \mu_M(\mathrm{w,m}) & \mu_M(\mathrm{w,f}) & \mu_M(\mathrm{w,w}) \end{bmatrix}.$$

Because each role necessarily implies itself, each of the diagonal elements of **M** are equal to 1 (i.e., $\mu_M(\mathrm{i,i}) = 1$ for all $\mathrm{i} \in \mathrm{R}$). In the current model, I set

$$\mathbf{M} = \begin{bmatrix} 1.0 & 0.3 & 0.2 \\ 0.0 & 1.0 & 0.0 \\ 0.0 & 0.0 & 1.0 \end{bmatrix}$$

so that a man has some obligation to be a father (μ_M (m,f) = 0.3) and a weaker obligation to be a worker (μ_M (m,w) = 0.2) but there are no other implications between roles.[13]

The basic matrix operation in fuzzy logic is max-min composition denoted by the symbol "∘". To define this operation, consider the composition $\mathbf{Z} = \mathbf{X} \circ \mathbf{Y}$ of the matrices $\mathbf{X} = [\mathrm{x_{ij}}]$ and $\mathbf{Y} = [\mathrm{y_{jk}}]$ where $\mathrm{i} \in \mathrm{I}$, $\mathrm{j} \in \mathrm{J}$, and $\mathrm{k} \in \mathrm{K}$. Elements of the **Z** matrix are given by

$$\mathrm{z_{ik}} = \max_{\mathrm{j} \in \mathrm{J}} \{\min\{\mathrm{x_{ij}}, \mathrm{y_{jk}}\}\}, \quad \text{for all } \{\mathrm{i,k}\} \in \mathrm{I} \times \mathrm{K}.$$

Thus composition resembles standard matrix multiplication with multiplication replaced by the min operator and addition replaced by the max operator. To illustrate, consider the composition

$$\mathbf{s} \circ \mathbf{M} = [0.7 \quad 0.6 \quad 0.0] \circ \begin{bmatrix} 1.0 & 0.3 & 0.2 \\ 0.0 & 1.0 & 0.0 \\ 0.0 & 0.0 & 1.0 \end{bmatrix} = [0.7 \quad 0.6 \quad 0.2].$$

[13] Note that roles are nested in this example: **M** is upper triangular. Compare Turner's (1990) distinction between "basic" roles (e.g., man) and "structural status" roles (e.g., father or worker).

Intuitively, this composition yields ego's "effective self," which reflects both direct roles (contained in S) and indirect roles (implied by M).[14]

The preceding matrix algebra may be recast as one-dimensional fuzzy logic. If ego was unambiguously a man ($\mu_S(\mathrm{m}) = 1$) and being a man implied unambiguously being a father ($\mu_M(\mathrm{m,f}) = 1$), then ego would be unambiguously a father ($\mu_{S \circ M}(\mathrm{f}) = 1$). That is, because $\min\{\mu_S(\mathrm{m}), \mu_M(\mathrm{m,f})\} = 1$, we would obtain

$$\mu_{S \circ M}(\mathrm{f}) = \max_{\mathrm{i} \in \mathrm{R}} \{\min\{\mu_S(\mathrm{i}), \mu_M(\mathrm{i,f})\}\} = 1.$$

(Expressed in classical logic, we would simply write the syllogism m, m→f ⊢ f.) But if we now allow both ego's self S and interrole implications M to be fuzzy (i.e., to be held to some degree strictly between 0 and 1), the conclusion itself may be fuzzy. Use of the max-min composition operator implies that the strength of the conclusion derives from the strongest propositional chain leading to that conclusion.[15] In the present example,the conclusion that ego is (ambiguously) a father derives from two different propositional chains:

$$\min\{\mu_S(\mathrm{m}), \mu_M(\mathrm{m,f})\} = \min\{0.7, 0.3\} = 0.3$$

$$\min\{\mu_S(\mathrm{f}), \mu_M(\mathrm{f,f})\} = \min\{0.6, 1.0\} = 0.6$$

where the first chain corresponds to the classical syllogism m, m→f ⊢ f and the second corresponds to f, f→f ⊢ f. Because the second propositional chain is stronger, $\mu_{S \circ M}(\mathrm{f}) = 0.6$.[16]

[14]The composition $\mathbf{s} \circ \mathbf{M}$ captures only the first-order implications between roles. More generally, to include all higher-order implications, one would form the composition $\mathbf{s} \circ \mathbf{M} \circ \mathbf{M} \circ \ldots = \mathbf{s} \circ \mathbf{M}^{\infty}$. In the present (very simple) example, we can ignore this complication because $\mathbf{M} = \mathbf{M}^{\infty}$. Compare the application of matrix composition in social network analysis (Doreian 1974; Hage and Harary 1983, ch. 7).

[15]As a physical analog, Ross (1995:51–52) describes a system of several chains placed together in parallel. The strength of each chain is given by its weakest link (the min operator); the strength of the system is given by the strongest chain (the max operator). Alternatively, adopting a graph-theoretic view of fuzzy logic, the strength of a conclusion corresponds to a network flow (also characterized by max-min composition); see the discussion in Section 5 below.

[16]Classical logic (which admits only binary truth values) would require that the strength of a propositional chain is equal to zero if any link is zero and equal to one if all links are equal to one. Allowing fuzzy truth values, classical logic might be generalized in many ways, so that various forms of composition (such as max-product composition) are sometimes used in fuzzy mathematics; see Ross (1995:210) for a menu of composition operators. Relatedly, social network analysts have offered various measures of network flow; see the discussion in Section 5.

3.2. *Actions and Constraints*

Ego must make choices regarding family support, employment, and time spent with a streetcorner peer group. Each of these three choices corresponds to a universe of discourse over which fuzzy sets of actions may be specified. First, ego makes to his family a monetary payment

$$c \in C = \{0,1,2,\ldots,9\}.$$

As already described in Section 2, we may represent "provide for family" as a fuzzy set of actions P defined over the universe C. Let $\mathbf{p}$ denote the vector of degrees of membership $[\mu_P(0)\ldots\mu_P(9)]$. Retaining the values from the illustration above, I assume

$$\mathbf{p} = [0.0 \quad 0.0 \quad 0.1 \quad 0.25 \quad 0.4 \quad 0.6 \quad 0.75 \quad 0.9 \quad 1.0 \quad 1.0].$$

Second, ego chooses a type of job. While a more realistic model might enumerate all of the relevant occupations in the local economy, I will (for simplicity) adopt a very stylized menu. In particular, ego chooses some type of employment

$$e \in E = \{0,1,2,\ldots,9\},$$

where higher integers denote better (higher-paying) jobs and 0 denotes unemployment. We may represent a "good job" as a fuzzy set G defined over the universe E. In particular, letting $\mathbf{g}$ denote the vector of degrees of membership $[\mu_G(0)\ldots\mu_G(9)]$, I assume

$$\mathbf{g} = [0.0 \quad 0.0 \quad 0.0 \quad 0.0 \quad 0.0 \quad 0.25 \quad 0.50 \quad 0.75 \quad 1.0 \quad 1.0].$$

Finally, ego chooses a level of time spent with a peer group. Again, for simplicity, I specify a highly stylized universe of discourse (instead of the richer universe of streetcorner activities described by Liebow [1967]). In particular, ego chooses some level of time

$$t \in T = \{0,1,2\},$$

where higher integers denote more time and 0 denotes zero time. It will be useful to define two different fuzzy sets over this universe. I specify "a lot of time" with the peer group as the fuzzy set H. In particular, letting $\mathbf{h}$ denote the vector $[\mu_H(0)\ \mu_H(1)\ \mu_H(2)]$, I assume

$$\mathbf{h} = [0.0 \quad 0.4 \quad 1.0].$$

I further specify "little time" with the peer group as a fuzzy set L. In particular, letting $\mathbf{l}$ denote the vector $[\mu_L(0)\ \mu_L(1)\ \mu_L(2)]$, I assume

$$\mathbf{l} = [1.0 \quad 0.1 \quad 0.0].$$[17]

Ego's three choices thus correspond to the (ordered) action triple $\mathrm{a} = \{\mathrm{c,e,t}\}$. That is, given the three-dimensional "action space" $\mathrm{A} = \mathrm{C} \times \mathrm{E} \times \mathrm{T}$, ego must choose some $\mathrm{a} \in \mathrm{A}$. I assume that ego faces the following constraints. First, there is an exogenous ceiling $\mathrm{e}_{\max}$ on employment opportunity. That is, given limited labor-market opportunities (see Liebow 1967, especially ch. 2), ego's choice of employment is restricted to $\mathrm{e} \leq \mathrm{e}_{\max} \leq 9$. Further, assuming that money for family support must derive from employment income, I assume $\mathrm{c} \leq \mathrm{e}$. Finally, recognizing that high levels of time spent with the peer group would preclude employment, I assume that $\mathrm{t} = 2$ implies $\mathrm{e} = 0$.[18] Together, these constraints restrict ego's choice to the (crisp) set of feasible choices $\mathrm{F} \subseteq \mathrm{A}$, where F is characterized by the function

$$\mu_{\mathrm{F}}(\{\mathrm{c,e,t}\}) = \begin{cases} 1 & \text{if } (\mathrm{c} \leq \mathrm{e} \leq \mathrm{e}_{\max} \text{ and } \mathrm{t} < 2) \text{ or } (\mathrm{c} = \mathrm{e} = 0 \text{ and } \mathrm{t} = 2) \\ 0 & \text{otherwise} \end{cases}$$

for all $\{\mathrm{c,e,t}\} \in \mathrm{A}$.[19]

3.3. *Norms and Obligations*

A norm is a mapping from roles to actions. For instance, consider the norm that a father should provide for his family. Applying classical logic, we

[17] We might equate "not a lot of time" with the complement of H—the fuzzy set $\bar{H}$ with the degree-of-membership vector $[1 \quad .6 \quad 0]$. Thus, given my specification of H and L, "little time" is more restrictive (and less fuzzy) than "not a lot of time."

[18] Thus I have implicitly assumed that a moderate level of time spent with the peer group ($\mathrm{t} = 1$) does not interfere with employment (as when ego spends time with the peer group only after the end of his working day).

[19] Bellman and Zadeh (1970) introduce "fuzzy constraints" into decision-making by specifying a degree of constant $\mu(\mathrm{a}) \in [0,1]$ for all $\mathrm{a} \in \mathrm{A}$. Here, constraints are crisp: $\mu_{\mathrm{F}}(\mathrm{a}) \in \{0,1\}$ for all $\mathrm{a} \in \mathrm{A}$.

might represent this norm as f→P, and from the premises f and f→P derive the conclusion P. In fuzzy logic, this inference is embedded in matrix algebra. In particular, representing the first premise as the (crisp) role vector **f** = [0 1 0], the classical syllogism

$$\text{f, f} \rightarrow \text{P} \vdash \text{P}$$

becomes

$$\mathbf{f} \circ \mathbf{N} = \mathbf{p}$$

where **N** is a matrix mapping roles into actions. After the norm has (somehow) been encoded in this matrix, we may infer ego's obligations through approximate reasoning (Zadeh 1975; see also Kosko [1992, ch. 8] and Ross [1995, ch. 7]). That is, given an arbitrary self *S* (that may contain the father role only partially), the composition $\mathbf{s} \circ \mathbf{M} \circ \mathbf{N}$ yields the inferred fuzzy set of actions (that may be a subset of *P*).

To encode a norm in matrix form, we need first to specify an "input" role vector **x** (corresponding to a fuzzy set *X* defined over the universe R) and an "output" action vector **y** (corresponding to a fuzzy set *Y* defined over the universe C or E or T). In the preceding example, the input vector was the crisp role vector **f** = [0 1 0]. More generally, reflecting both the variable strength of norms and the possibility that multiple roles are associated with a particular norm, we might allow input vectors of the form $\mathbf{x} = [\mu_X(\text{m})\ \mu_X(\text{f})\ \mu_X(\text{w})]$ where $\mu_X(\text{i}) \in [0,1]$ reflects the degree to which role i is attached to the norm. Similarly, we might allow the output vector **y** to correspond to a fuzzy (rather than crisp) set of actions. Indeed, in the preceding example, the output vector **p** corresponds to the fuzzy set *P*.

Given an input role vector **x** and output action vector **y**, various schemes have been proposed for encoding the **N** matrix (see Ross [1995, p. 209] for a menu of implication operators). Here, I adopt correlation-minimum encoding (Mamdani 1976; Kosko 1992, ch. 8) so that

$$\mathbf{N} = \mathbf{x}^{\mathrm{T}} \circ \mathbf{y}$$

where the superscript T indicates the transpose of **x** vector. This composition is equivalent to the "fuzzy outer product" of the **x** and **y** vectors; elements of the **N** matrix are given by

$$\text{n}_{\text{ij}} = \mu_N(\text{i,j}) = \min\{\mu_X(\text{i}), \mu_Y(\text{j})\}, \quad \text{for all } \{\text{i,j}\} \in \text{R} \times \text{A}_\text{k} \ ,$$

where N is a fuzzy relation (from roles to actions), and $A_k \in \{C,E,T\}$.[20] Given ego's self S, the interrole implications M, and a norm N, ego infers his (fuzzy set of) obligations through the composition $\mathbf{s} \circ \mathbf{M} \circ \mathbf{N}$.[21]

Suppose that the social system contains four norms: (1) a father should provide for his family (f$\rightarrow$$P$), (2) a worker should hold a good job (w$\rightarrow$$G$), (3) a man should spend a lot of time with his peer group (m$\rightarrow$$H$), and (4) a father should spend little time with his peer group (f$\rightarrow$$L$). To operationalize approximate reasoning, each norm i $\in \{1,2,3,4\}$ is encoded as a matrix $\mathbf{N}_i$. As already described, the first norm may be encoded as $\mathbf{N}_1 = \mathbf{f}^T \circ \mathbf{p}$. Thus,

$$\mathbf{M} \circ \mathbf{N}_1 = \mathbf{M} \circ \mathbf{f}^T \circ \mathbf{p}$$

$$= \begin{bmatrix} 1.0 & 0.3 & 0.2 \\ 0.0 & 1.0 & 0.0 \\ 0.0 & 0.0 & 1.0 \end{bmatrix} \circ \begin{bmatrix} 0 \\ 1 \\ 0 \end{bmatrix}$$

$$\circ [0 \quad 0 \quad .1 \quad .25 \quad .4 \quad .6 \quad .75 \quad .9 \quad 1 \quad 1]$$

$$= \begin{bmatrix} 0.0 & 0.0 & 0.1 & 0.25 & 0.3 & 0.3 & 0.3 & 0.3 & 0.3 & 0.3 \\ 0.0 & 0.0 & 0.1 & 0.25 & 0.4 & 0.6 & 0.75 & 0.9 & 1.0 & 1.0 \\ 0.0 & 0.0 & 0.0 & 0.0 & 0.0 & 0.0 & 0.0 & 0.0 & 0.0 & 0.0 \end{bmatrix}.$$

To formulate the second norm, I assume the crisp input matrix $\mathbf{w} = [0 \quad 0 \quad 1]$ so that $\mathbf{N}_2 = \mathbf{w}^T \circ \mathbf{g}$. Thus

[20] Given correlation-minimum encoding, N is not a proper generalization of the classic material implication X$\rightarrow$Y since it is not the case that $\mu_N(\mathrm{i,j}) = 1$ whenever $\mu_X(\mathrm{i}) = 0$ or $\mu_Y(\mathrm{j}) = 1$. (Compare the binary truth-table for X, Y, and X$\rightarrow$Y.) Rather, N generalizes the classical conjunction $X \wedge Y$. On the other hand, approximate reasoning (with correlation-minimum encoding) does generalize *modus ponens* $(X, X \rightarrow Y \vdash Y)$ in the sense that $\mathbf{x} \circ \mathbf{N} = \mathbf{x} \circ (\mathbf{x}^T \circ \mathbf{y}) = \mathbf{y}$ if $\max_i \{\mu_X(i)\} \geq \max_j \{\mu_Y(j)\}$. Moreover, one can show that $\mathbf{x}' \circ \mathbf{N} \leq \mathbf{y}$ for any $\mathbf{x}'$; see Kosko (1992:310–11) for further discussion. An alternative implication operator will be discussed in Section 4.

[21] Note that max-min composition is associative, so that

$$\mathbf{s} \circ \mathbf{M} \circ \mathbf{N} = (\mathbf{s} \circ \mathbf{M}) \circ \mathbf{N} = \mathbf{s} \circ (\mathbf{M} \circ \mathbf{N}).$$

$$\mathbf{M} \circ \mathbf{N}_2 = \mathbf{M} \circ \mathbf{w}^{\mathrm{T}} \circ \mathbf{g}$$

$$= \begin{bmatrix} 1.0 & 0.3 & 0.2 \\ 0.0 & 1.0 & 0.0 \\ 0.0 & 0.0 & 1.0 \end{bmatrix} \circ \begin{bmatrix} 0 \\ 0 \\ 1 \end{bmatrix}$$

$$\circ [0 \quad 0 \quad 0 \quad 0 \quad 0 \quad .25 \quad .50 \quad .75 \quad 1 \quad 1]$$

$$= \begin{bmatrix} 0.0 & 0.0 & 0.0 & 0.0 & 0.0 & 0.2 & 0.2 & 0.2 & 0.2 & 0.2 \\ 0.0 & 0.0 & 0.0 & 0.0 & 0.0 & 0.0 & 0.0 & 0.0 & 0.0 & 0.0 \\ 0.0 & 0.0 & 0.0 & 0.0 & 0.0 & 0.25 & 0.5 & 0.75 & 1.0 & 1.0 \end{bmatrix}.$$

To formulate the third norm, I assume a crisp input matrix $\mathbf{m} = [1 \quad 0 \quad 0]$ so that $\mathbf{N}_3 = \mathbf{m}^{\mathrm{T}} \circ \mathbf{h}$. Thus

$$\mathbf{M} \circ \mathbf{N}_3 = \mathbf{M} \circ \mathbf{m}^{\mathrm{T}} \circ \mathbf{h}$$

$$= \begin{bmatrix} 1.0 & 0.3 & 0.2 \\ 0.0 & 1.0 & 0.0 \\ 0.0 & 0.0 & 1.0 \end{bmatrix} \circ \begin{bmatrix} 1 \\ 0 \\ 0 \end{bmatrix} \circ [0.0 \quad 0.4 \quad 1.0]$$

$$= \begin{bmatrix} 0.0 & 0.4 & 1.0 \\ 0.0 & 0.0 & 0.0 \\ 0.0 & 0.0 & 0.0 \end{bmatrix}.$$

To reflect an assumption that the fourth norm is less strong than the other norms, I assume a fuzzy input matrix $[0 \quad .6 \quad 0]$. Thus, $\mathbf{N}_4 = [0 \quad .6 \quad 0]^{\mathrm{T}} \circ \mathbf{l}$, and

$$\mathbf{M} \circ \mathbf{N}_4 = \mathbf{M} \circ [0 \quad .6 \quad 0]^{\mathrm{T}} \circ \mathbf{l}$$

$$= \begin{bmatrix} 1.0 & 0.3 & 0.2 \\ 0.0 & 1.0 & 0.0 \\ 0.0 & 0.0 & 1.0 \end{bmatrix} \circ \begin{bmatrix} 0 \\ .6 \\ 0 \end{bmatrix} \circ [1.0 \quad 0.1 \quad 0.0]$$

$$= \begin{bmatrix} 0.3 & 0.1 & 0.0 \\ 0.6 & 0.1 & 0.0 \\ 0.0 & 0.0 & 0.0 \end{bmatrix}.$$

By composing ego's self (the vector **s**) with each of these ($\mathbf{M} \circ \mathbf{N}_i$) matrices, we obtain four vectors representing ego's fuzzy obligations. To illustrate, suppose $S = [.7 \;\; .6 \;\; 0]$ so that

$$\mathbf{s} \circ \mathbf{M} \circ \mathbf{N}_1 = [0.0 \quad 0.0 \quad 0.1 \quad 0.25 \quad 0.4 \quad 0.6 \quad 0.6 \quad 0.6 \quad 0.6 \quad 0.6];$$

$$\mathbf{s} \circ \mathbf{M} \circ \mathbf{N}_2 = [0.0 \quad 0.0 \quad 0.0 \quad 0.0 \quad 0.0 \quad 0.2 \quad 0.2 \quad 0.2 \quad 0.2 \quad 0.2];$$

$$\mathbf{s} \circ \mathbf{M} \circ \mathbf{N}_3 = [0.0 \quad 0.4 \quad 0.7];$$

$$\mathbf{s} \circ \mathbf{M} \circ \mathbf{N}_4 = [0.6 \quad 0.1 \quad 0.0].$$

While my notation does not make this explicit, it is important to recognize that these fuzzy obligations are defined over different dimensions of action space. In particular, the first composition characterizes a fuzzy set defined over the universe C; the second characterizes a fuzzy set defined over E; the third and fourth characterize fuzzy sets defined over T.

3.4. *Deriving Ego's Choices*

I now need to derive ego's action from his fuzzy obligations. Following Kosko's (1992, ch. 8) application of fuzzy logic to control systems, I associate each norm i with a goal $\mathcal{G}_i$, form a decision function $\mathcal{D}$ by summing these goals, and then assume that ego chooses the action $a^* \in F$ that maximizes $\mathcal{D}$.[22] In general, the decision function might be written as

$$\mathcal{D}(a) = \Sigma_i \mathcal{G}_i(a),$$

[22] While this procedure provides one practical method for generating action, its logical foundations are admittedly problematic. Recognizing that each element of each obligation vector represents the strongest propositional chain in a system of parallel chains, there is no obvious logical motivation for simple addition of these elements. Indeed, in fuzzy decision-making (Bellman and Zadeh 1970), the decision function is formed through the intersection (minimum) of goals and constraints: $\mathcal{D} = \mathcal{G} \cap \mathcal{C}$. I return to this issue in Section 4, exploring an alternative inference and decision-making procedure.

where i indexes norms. In the present model, this decision function becomes

$$\mathcal{D}(\{c,e,t\}) = \mu_{S\circ M\circ N_1}(c) + \mu_{S\circ M\circ N_2}(e) + \mu_{S\circ M\circ N_3}(t) + \mu_{S\circ M\circ N_4}(t)$$

defined for all $\{c,e,t\} \in A$. Equivalently, we might write

$$\mathcal{D}(\{c,e,t\}) = (\mathbf{s}\circ\mathbf{M}\circ\mathbf{N}_1)_c + (\mathbf{s}\circ\mathbf{M}\circ\mathbf{N}_2)_e + (\mathbf{s}\circ\mathbf{M}\circ\mathbf{N}_3)_t + (\mathbf{s}\circ\mathbf{M}\circ\mathbf{N}_4)_t$$

where $(\mathbf{s}\circ\mathbf{M}\circ\mathbf{N}_i)_j$ denotes element j of the $\mathbf{s}\circ\mathbf{M}\circ\mathbf{N}_i$ vector. I assume that ego chooses the action

$$a^* = \underset{a \in F}{\operatorname{argmax}}\ \mathcal{D}(a)$$

and that ties—multiple actions yielding the maximum $\mathcal{D}(a)$—might be resolved through randomization.

To illustrate, suppose that ego faces the exogenous constraint $e_{max} = 3$. Given the fuzzy obligation vectors derived above, the decision function is characterized by the stack of matrices:

Time with peer group t = 0

Employment (e)

		0	1	2	3	4	5	6	7	8	9
	0	0.6	0.6	0.6	0.6	·	·	·	·	·	·
	1	·	0.6	0.6	0.6	·	·	·	·	·	·
	2	·	·	0.7	0.7	·	·	·	·	·	·
	3	·	·	·	0.85	·	·	·	·	·	·
Monetary payment (c)	4	·	·	·	·	·	·	·	·	·	·
	5	·	·	·	·	·	·	·	·	·	·
	6	·	·	·	·	·	·	·	·	·	·
	7	·	·	·	·	·	·	·	·	·	·
	8	·	·	·	·	·	·	·	·	·	·
	9	·	·	·	·	·	·	·	·	·	·

Time with peer group t = 1

Employment (e)

Monetary payment (c)	0	1	2	3	4	5	6	7	8	9
0	0.5	0.5	0.5	0.5	·	·	·	·	·	·
1	·	0.5	0.5	0.5	·	·	·	·	·	·
2	·	·	0.6	0.6	·	·	·	·	·	·
3	·	·	·	0.75	·	·	·	·	·	·
4	·	·	·	·	·	·	·	·	·	·
5	·	·	·	·	·	·	·	·	·	·
6	·	·	·	·	·	·	·	·	·	·
7	·	·	·	·	·	·	·	·	·	·
8	·	·	·	·	·	·	·	·	·	·
9	·	·	·	·	·	·	·	·	·	·

Time with peer group t = 2

Employment (e)

Monetary payment (c)	0	1	2	3	4	5	6	7	8	9
0	0.7	·	·	·	·	·	·	·	·	·
1	·	·	·	·	·	·	·	·	·	·
2	·	·	·	·	·	·	·	·	·	·
3	·	·	·	·	·	·	·	·	·	·
4	·	·	·	·	·	·	·	·	·	·
5	·	·	·	·	·	·	·	·	·	·
6	·	·	·	·	·	·	·	·	·	·
7	·	·	·	·	·	·	·	·	·	·
8	·	·	·	·	·	·	·	·	·	·
9	·	·	·	·	·	·	·	·	·	·

In these, "·" denotes infeasible actions. Thus, given $e_{max} = 3$ (and all the other assumptions embedded in the fuzzy obligation vectors), the (unique) optimal action is $a^* = \{3,3,0\}$, which yields $\mathcal{D}(\{3,3,0\}) = 0.85$.

3.5. *Alters' Attributions*

Having specified how ego's self generates action, I now consider the process by which alters make attributions. As discussed above (Section 2), alters tend to overattribute roles to ego's self. In particular, alters might make strong (logically problematic) inferences through abduction. For instance, observing ego in a good job, alters might conclude (through the abductive syllogism $G,\ w \to G \vdash w$) that ego's self contains the worker role. To embed this syllogism in the matrix algebra of approximate reasoning, we might first represent ego's (crisp) action $a^* = \{c^*, e^*, t^*\}$ as three binary action vectors ($\mathbf{c}^*$, $\mathbf{e}^*$, and $\mathbf{t}^*$). Then, for each norm i, we may compose the relevant action vector with the transpose of the $(\mathbf{M} \circ \mathbf{N}_i)$ matrix. In this way, we obtain one fuzzy attribution (a fuzzy set of roles) for each norm.

To illustrate, suppose that ego chooses the action $a^* = \{3,3,0\}$. The choice $c^* = 3$ corresponds to the binary action vector

$$\mathbf{c}^* = [0 \quad 0 \quad 0 \quad 1 \quad 0 \quad 0 \quad 0 \quad 0 \quad 0 \quad 0].$$

Composing this vector with the transpose of $(\mathbf{M} \circ \mathbf{N}_1)$, we obtain

$$\mathbf{c}^* \circ (\mathbf{M}{\circ}\mathbf{N}_1)^{\mathrm{T}} = [0 \quad 0 \quad 0 \quad 1 \quad 0 \quad 0 \quad 0 \quad 0 \quad 0 \quad 0] \circ \begin{bmatrix} 0.0 & 0.0 & 0.0 \\ 0.0 & 0.0 & 0.0 \\ 0.1 & 0.1 & 0.0 \\ 0.25 & 0.25 & 0.0 \\ 0.3 & 0.4 & 0.0 \\ 0.3 & 0.6 & 0.0 \\ 0.3 & 0.75 & 0.0 \\ 0.3 & 0.9 & 0.0 \\ 0.3 & 1.0 & 0.0 \\ 0.3 & 1.0 & 0.0 \end{bmatrix}$$

$$= [0.25 \quad 0.25 \quad 0.0].$$

(Notice that this composition is simply the fourth row of $(\mathbf{M}{\circ}\mathbf{N}_1)^{\mathrm{T}}$.) Similarly, given the other norms (and the relevant action vectors), we obtain

$$\mathbf{e}^* \circ (\mathbf{M}{\circ}\mathbf{N}_2)^{\mathrm{T}} = [0 \quad 0 \quad 0 \quad 1 \quad 0 \quad 0 \quad 0 \quad 0 \quad 0 \quad 0] \circ (\mathbf{M}{\circ}\mathbf{N}_2)^{\mathrm{T}}$$

$$= [0.0 \quad 0.0 \quad 0.0];$$

$$\mathbf{t}^* \circ (\mathbf{M}\circ\mathbf{N}_3)^{\mathrm{T}} = [1 \quad 0 \quad 0] \circ (\mathbf{M}\circ\mathbf{N}_3)^{\mathrm{T}} = [0.0 \quad 0.0 \quad 0.0];$$

$$\mathbf{t}^* \circ (\mathbf{M}\circ\mathbf{N}_4)^{\mathrm{T}} = [1 \quad 0 \quad 0] \circ (\mathbf{M}\circ\mathbf{N}_4)^{\mathrm{T}} = [0.3 \quad 0.6 \quad 0.0].$$

Note that all four vectors characterize fuzzy sets (of roles) defined over the common universe R.

Given these fuzzy attribution vectors, I now construct an overall attribution S' made by alters. Various procedures seem plausible. Here, I assume that alters make the strongest attributions consistent with the fuzzy attribution vectors.[23] Formally,

$$\mu_{S'}(\mathrm{i}) = \max\{(\mathbf{c}^*\circ(\mathbf{M}\circ\mathbf{N}_1)^{\mathrm{T}})_{\mathrm{i}}, (\mathbf{e}^*\circ(\mathbf{M}\circ\mathbf{N}_2)^{\mathrm{T}})_{\mathrm{i}}, (\mathbf{t}^*\circ(\mathbf{M}\circ\mathbf{N}_3)^{\mathrm{T}})_{\mathrm{i}},$$
$$(\mathbf{t}^*\circ(\mathbf{M}\circ\mathbf{N}_4)^{\mathrm{T}})_{\mathrm{i}}\}$$

for $\mathrm{i} \in \mathrm{R}$, where $(\mathbf{z})_{\mathrm{i}}$ denotes element i of the $\mathbf{z}$ vector. Thus, given the fuzzy attribution vectors above, we obtain

$$\mu_{S'}(\mathrm{m}) = \max\{.25, 0, 0, .3\} = .3;$$

$$\mu_{S'}(\mathrm{f}) = \max\{.25, 0, 0, .6\} = .6;$$

$$\mu_{S'}(\mathrm{w}) = \max\{0, 0, 0, 0\} = 0.$$

Thus, on the basis of ego's action $\mathrm{a}^* = \{3, 3, 0\}$, alters attribute to ego the self $S' = \{.3, .6, 0\}$.[24]

3.6. *Dynamics of the Self*

To complete the specification of the model, I need to describe how ego's self is revised over time. Alters' attributions feed back into ego's self through a labeling effect: ego gradually becomes what alters (perhaps wrongly)

[23] Like other aspects of the framework I am developing (in particular, ego's inference procedure and decision function), the modeling choice here is somewhat arbitrary. Arguably, the specification of ego's reasoning process should be rational (presuming that rationality can be well defined in the face of ambiguity over roles and norms). However, having explicitly emphasized the irrationality of alters' attributions, the "correct" attribution procedure should be determined not by criteria of rationality but rather by empirical plausibility. Still, my present procedure may be empirically implausible because it assumes that alters accept the (strongest) evidence in favor of each role attribution, ignoring other evidence that might undermine that attribution.

[24] Note that, in this example, S' is determined solely by ego's choice $\mathrm{t}^* = 0$.

believe him to be. Formally, letting the subscript τ index time periods, I assume

$$\mu_{S_{\tau+1}}(\mathrm{i}) = (1-\gamma)\mu_{S_\tau}(\mathrm{i}) + \gamma\mu_{S'_\tau}(\mathrm{i}), \quad \text{for i} \in \mathrm{R},$$

where γ is an exogenous parameter reflecting both period length and the rate at which ego's self S converges to the self S' attributed by alters to ego. This final equation completes the specification of the feedback loop (fuzzy system) running from self to actions to self: ego's (fuzzy) self S_τ generates a (crisp) set of actions a^*_τ, leading alters to attribute to ego the (fuzzy) self S'_τ, inducing in ego the revised (fuzzy) self $S_{\tau+1}$ that provides a new basis for action.

3.7. *Analysis*

This subsection contains some analysis of the model developed above. I have already described (in Section 2) how ego's self might be viewed as a point in role space (here a three-dimensional unit cube) and the fuzzy system might be viewed as a role-space vectorfield. Thus an analysis of this dynamical system might focus on its short-run dynamics: given ego's initial location in role space (i.e., initial self), what is ego's trajectory through role space (i.e., what is the sequence of selves possessed by ego over time)? Alternatively, analysis might focus on long-run outcomes: given ego's initial location in role space (i.e., initial self), to what role-space attractor does ego's trajectory eventually converge (i.e., what is ego's stable, long-run self)? More generally, does every point in role space lie on a trajectory leading to the same (unique) attractor? Or do there exist multiple attractors (each with its own basin of attraction)? (I.e., does the social system generate more than one stable, long-run self? If so, which initial selves lead to which long-run selves?) My analysis here examines this latter set of (long-run) issues. In particular, I consider how the number and location of role-space attractors are influenced by the parameter $\mathrm{e}_{\max}$, taking (the parameters that determine) social norms as exogenously given.[25]

[25] Readers unfamiliar with dynamical systems concepts might consult Drazin (1992) or Abraham and Shaw (1992). Adopting a dynamical systems perspective, Fararo (1989, ch. 2.8) provides a helpful typology of theorems. The present analysis implicitly entails theorems of type 1–3 (concerning the existence, stability, and comparative statics of social structures) with respect to role-space attractors. Type 4 theorems (concerning change in social structures) would become possible after the microlevel process (developed in the present paper) is nested within a macrolevel process (through which norms themselves evolve).

To build intuition, I first consider the case where $e_{max} = 3$.[26] In this case, there are three role-space attractors. Letting S denote the point $\{\mu_S(m), \mu_S(f), \mu_S(w)\}$ in role space, these attractors are

$$S^0 = \{.3, .6, 0\}, \quad S^1 = \{.4, .25, 0\}, \quad \text{and} \quad S^2 = \{1, 0, 0\}.$$

A steady state in role space is a fixed point $S = S'(a^*(S))$. Thus, we might verify that each of the selves listed above is a steady state by deriving the optimal action a^* implied by each S, deriving the attribution S' implied by this action and then observing that $S' = S$. In this way, one may show

$$S^0 \rightarrow a^*(S^0) = \{3, 3, 0\} \rightarrow S'(a^*(S^0)) = \{.3, .6, 0\} = S^0;$$

$$S^1 \rightarrow a^*(S^1) = \{3, 3, 1\} \rightarrow S'(a^*(S^1)) = \{.4, .25, 0\} = S^1;$$

$$S^2 \rightarrow a^*(S^2) = \{0, 0, 2\} \rightarrow S'(a^*(S^2)) = \{1, 0, 0\} = S^2.$$

Note that the superscript on each attractor corresponds to the level of time (t^*) that ego spends with his peer group. In the steady state S^0, ego classifies himself only weakly as a man ($\mu_S(m) = .3$) but more strongly as a father ($\mu_S(f) = .6$); this attachment to the father role induces him to spend no time with his peer group ($t^* = 0$). In the steady state S^1, ego classifies himself more strongly as a man ($\mu_S(m) = .4$) but more weakly as a father ($\mu_S(f) = .25$). While he continues to support his family to the best of his ability ($c^* = e_{max} = 3$), he spends some time with his peer group ($t^* = 1$). Finally, in the steady state S^2, ego classifies himself even more strongly as a man (indeed, given $\mu_S(m) = 1$, he classifies himself unambiguously as a man) but even more weakly as a father—indeed, given $\mu_S(f) = 0$, he classifies himself unambiguously as a nonfather. Thus he spends all of his time with the peer group ($t^* = 2$) and provides no family support ($c^* = e^* = 0$).

The preceding analysis verifies that the selves S^0, S^1, and S^2 are steady states, but not necessarily attractors (i.e., stable steady states). To demonstrate the stability of these selves, we might plot basins of attraction in role space. In the present model, role space is a three-dimensional cube. However, given $e_{max} < 5$, it is easy to see that $\mu_S(w)$ must equal zero

[26] Perhaps this case resembles most closely the situation of the streetcorner man in *Tally's Corner*. Because only bad jobs are available to him (e_{max} is low), he cannot provide well for his family ($c \leq e_{max}$ implies $\mu_P(c) \leq .25$) and work provides no intrinsic basis for self-esteem ($e \leq e_{max}$ implies $\mu_G(e) = 0$).

in any steady state.[27] Thus, for the case $e_{max} = 3$, we may fix $\mu_S(w) = 0$ and restrict attention to points $\{\mu_S(m), \mu_S(f)\}$ in the two-dimensional unit square. Figure 2 shows the three basins of attraction.[28] Those initial conditions that converge to the attractor S^0 are denoted by "0"; those that converge to S^1 are denoted by "1"; those that converge to S^2 are denoted by "2." The attractors themselves are denoted in boldface while points along the separatrices (between attractors) are denoted by "·".

For comparison, we might briefly consider the case where employment opportunity is increased slightly so that $e_{max} = 4$. In this case, one can show that there are again three attractors:

$$S^0 = \{.3, .6, 0\}, \quad S^1 = \{.4, .4, 0\}, \quad \text{and} \quad S^2 = \{1, 0, 0\}$$

where

$$S^0 \rightarrow a^*(S^0) = \{4, 4, 0\} \rightarrow S'(a^*(S^0)) = \{.3, .6, 0\} = S^0;$$

$$S^1 \rightarrow a^*(S^1) = \{4, 4, 1\} \rightarrow S'(a^*(S^1)) = \{.4, .4, 0\} = S^1;$$

$$S^2 \rightarrow a^*(S^2) = \{0, 0, 2\} \rightarrow S'(a^*(S^2)) = \{1, 0, 0\} = S^2.$$

The basins of attraction are shown in Figure 3. Comparing Figures 2 and 3, note that the increase in e_{max} causes the basin of attraction for S^2 to shrink. Intuitively, increased employment opportunity allows ego to provide more adequately for his family ($\mu_P(4) = .4 > \mu_P(3) = .25$), so that ego derives more value from working and providing for his family (setting $c = e = e_{max}$).

I now offer a more general analysis of the attractors of the system. Given that role space is continuous while action space is discrete (and small), it will be useful to invert the procedure for verifying steady states

[27] Alters will attribute the worker role to ego only if ego holds a good job. But given my specification of the fuzzy set G, $\mu_G(e) = 0$ for $e < 5$. Thus, given $e_{max} < 5$, alters will always make the attribution $\mu_{S'}(w) = 0$, and $\mu_S(w)$ must converge to zero over time.

[28] This figure resulted from a grid search: I derived the trajectory $\{S_0, S_1, \ldots, S_\tau\}$ and observed the limit S_∞ for each initial condition $S_0 \in \{0, .05, \ldots, 1\} \times \{0, .05, \ldots, 1\} \times 0$. This grid search is complicated by the indifference over actions displayed by "weak" selves ($S_0 \in \{0, .05, .1\} \times \{0, .05, .1\} \times 0$). Given this indifference, each of these selves is the origin for *multiple* role-space vectors, generating multiple trajectories through role space. Further analysis reveals that weak (but nonempty) selves are indifferent over the set of actions $a^*(S_0) = \{\{2,2,1\}, \{2,3,1\}, \{3,3,1\}\}$. However, randomization over these actions will inevitably push the self toward the attractor S^1 (see the discussion of the "ratchet effect" in the text below). The empty self ($S_0 = \{0,0,0\}$) is indifferent over all actions. However, if γ is small, the empty self also converges to S^1 regardless of the initial action.

$\mu_S(m)$																					
1.0	2	2	2	2	2	2	2	2	2	2	2	2	2	2	2	2	2	2	2	2	2
	2	2	2	2	2	2	2	2	2	2	2	2	2	2	2	2	2	2	2	2	2
.9	2	2	2	2	2	2	2	2	2	2	2	2	2	2	2	2	2	2	2	2	2
	2	2	2	2	2	2	2	2	2	2	2	2	·	·	·	·	·	·	·	·	·
.8	2	2	2	2	2	2	2	2	2	2	2	·	0	0	0	0	0	0	0	0	0
	·	·	·	·	·	·	·	·	·	·	·	0	0	0	0	0	0	0	0	0	0
.7	1	1	1	1	1	1	1	1	1	1	·	0	0	0	0	0	0	0	0	0	0
	1	1	1	1	1	1	1	1	1	1	·	0	0	0	0	0	0	0	0	0	0
.6	1	1	1	1	1	1	1	1	1	1	·	0	0	0	0	0	0	0	0	0	0
	1	1	1	1	1	1	1	1	1	1	·	0	0	0	0	0	0	0	0	0	0
.5	1	1	1	1	1	1	1	1	1	1	·	0	0	0	0	0	0	0	0	0	0
	1	1	1	1	1	1	1	1	1	1	·	0	0	0	0	0	0	0	0	0	0
.4	1	1	1	1	1	1	1	1	1	1	·	0	0	0	0	0	0	0	0	0	0
	1	1	1	1	1	1	1	1	1	·	0	0	0	0	0	0	0	0	0	0	0
.3	1	1	1	1	1	1	1	1	·	0	0	0	0	0	0	0	0	0	0	0	0
	1	1	1	1	1	1	1	·	0	0	0	0	0	0	0	0	0	0	0	0	0
.2	1	1	1	1	1	1	·	0	0	0	0	0	0	0	0	0	0	0	0	0	0
	1	1	1	1	1	·	0	0	0	0	0	0	0	0	0	0	0	0	0	0	0
.1	1	1	1	1	·	0	0	0	0	0	0	0	0	0	0	0	0	0	0	0	0
	1	1	1	·	0	0	0	0	0	0	0	0	0	0	0	0	0	0	0	0	0
.0	1	1	·	0	0	0	0	0	0	0	0	0	0	0	0	0	0	0	0	0	0
	.0		.1		.2		.3		.4		.5		.6		.7		.8		.9		1.0
																					$\mu_S(f)$

FIGURE 2. Basins of attraction in role space given $e_{max} = 3$.

described above. That is, instead of searching for selves that satisfy the fixed-point equation

$$S = S'(a^*(S)),$$

it will be computationally more efficient to search for actions that satisfy the fixed-point equation

$$a = a^*(S'(a)).$$

Although every action generates a unique attribution $S'(a)$, the self $S'(a)$ may generate indifference over multiple actions. That is, the set of optimal actions $a^*(S'(a))$ may contain more than one member. The self S' might

$\mu_S(m)$																					
1.0	2	2	2	2	2	2	2	2	2	2	2	2	·	·	·	·	·	·	·	·	·
	2	2	2	2	2	2	2	2	2	2	2	·	0	0	0	0	0	0	0	0	0
.9	2	2	2	2	2	2	2	2	·	·	·	0	0	0	0	0	0	0	0	0	0
	2	2	2	2	2	2	2	·	1	1	·	0	0	0	0	0	0	0	0	0	0
.8	·	·	·	·	·	·	·	1	1	1	·	0	0	0	0	0	0	0	0	0	0
	1	1	1	1	1	1	1	1	1	1	·	0	0	0	0	0	0	0	0	0	0
.7	1	1	1	1	1	1	1	1	1	1	·	0	0	0	0	0	0	0	0	0	0
	1	1	1	1	1	1	1	1	1	1	·	0	0	0	0	0	0	0	0	0	0
.6	1	1	1	1	1	1	1	1	1	1	·	0	0	0	0	0	0	0	0	0	0
	1	1	1	1	1	1	1	1	1	1	·	0	0	0	0	0	0	0	0	0	0
.5	1	1	1	1	1	1	1	1	1	1	·	0	0	0	0	0	0	0	0	0	0
	1	1	1	1	1	1	1	1	1	1	·	0	0	0	0	0	0	0	0	0	0
.4	1	1	1	1	1	1	1	1	1	1	·	0	0	0	0	0	0	0	0	0	0
	1	1	1	1	1	1	1	1	1	·	0	0	0	0	0	0	0	0	0	0	0
.3	1	1	1	1	1	1	1	1	·	0	0	0	0	0	0	0	0	0	0	0	0
	1	1	1	1	1	1	1	·	0	0	0	0	0	0	0	0	0	0	0	0	0
.2	1	1	1	1	1	1	·	0	0	0	0	0	0	0	0	0	0	0	0	0	0
	1	1	1	1	1	·	0	0	0	0	0	0	0	0	0	0	0	0	0	0	0
.1	1	1	1	1	·	0	0	0	0	0	0	0	0	0	0	0	0	0	0	0	0
	1	1	1	·	0	0	0	0	0	0	0	0	0	0	0	0	0	0	0	0	0
.0	1	1	·	0	0	0	0	0	0	0	0	0	0	0	0	0	0	0	0	0	0
$\mu_S(f)$	.0		.1		.2		.3		.4		.5		.6		.7		.8		.9		1.0

FIGURE 3. Basins of attraction in role space given $e_{max} = 4$.

persist (at least temporarily) given the existence of a fixed-point action a $\in$ $a^*(S'(a))$. However, long-run stability of this self requires that every action in $a^*(S'(a))$ generate the same attribution S'. (This condition holds trivially when the optimal action is unique so that $a^*(S'(a))$ has only one member.) If this condition does not hold, ego's randomization over these actions would cause his self to vary over time.

To proceed formally, we may construct a square matrix $\mathbf{B} = [b_{ij}]$ with dimensions corresponding to feasible actions. (The label **B** is intended as a mnemonic for "best action.") Each row i of the **B** matrix characterizes the set of optimal actions $a^*(S'(i))$. Thus the elements of the **B** matrix are given by

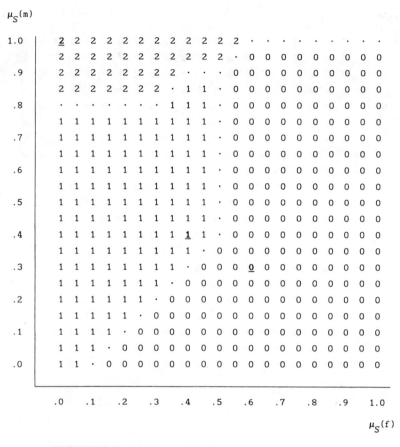

$$b_{ij} = \begin{cases} 1 & \text{if } j \in a^*(S'(i)) \\ 0 & \text{otherwise} \end{cases} \qquad \text{for all } \{i,j\} \in F \times F.$$

To illustrate, Table 1 shows the **B** matrix given $e_{max} = 7$.[29] For instance, the action {4,5,1} induces the set $a^*(S'(\{4,5,1\}))$ with nine members. By construction, fixed points in action space generate $b_{ii} = 1$. Thus, to identify fixed points, we may simply look for the "1"'s along the main diagonal of the **B** matrix (denoted in boldface in Table 1).

Given the **B** matrix, we may derive the set of stable actions (and thus stable selves) by identifying those actions that are the most reachable. To characterize reachability, we first form the matrix

$$\mathbf{R} = \mathbf{I} \circ \mathbf{B} \circ \mathbf{B} \circ \ldots = \mathbf{I} \circ \mathbf{B}^{\infty}$$

where **I** is an identity matrix. The reachability matrix **R** determines a quasiorder over actions; an action is a stable steady state if it is a minimal element of this quasiorder.[30] For instance, given the **B** matrix in Table 1, one can show that the action {7,7,0} is reachable from all other actions but cannot itself reach any other action (since {7,7,0} is the only action in $a^*(S'(\{7,7,0\})$. Thus {7,7,0} is the unique action-space attractor (and $S'(\{7,7,0\}) = \{.3,.9,.75\}$ is the unique role-space attractor) given $e_{max} = 7$.

Repeating this analysis, one may enumerate the fixed points in action space (reported in Table 2) and attractors in role space (reported in Table 3) for all $e_{max} \in \{0,\ldots,9\}$.[31] Table 3 shows that low employment opportunity ($e_{max} \leq 4$) implies three role-space attractors (corresponding to $t^* \in \{0,1,2\}$) while high level of opportunity ($e_{max} \geq 5$) implies a unique role-space attractor (corresponding to the choice $t^* = 0$). On the other hand, Table 2 shows that the number of (unstable) steady states rises with employment opportunity (e_{max}). Intuitively, an ego with high opportunity (say $e_{max} = 7$) but an initially "weak" self-concept (say $S = \{.4,.4,.5\}$)

[29] To reduce the size of this matrix, I have (merely for presentation purposes) omitted the rows and columns of the matrix for actions $a \in \{\{1,1,0\}, \{1,1,1\}, \{1,2,0\},\ldots,\{4,4,1\}, \{4,5,0\}\}$. Because none of these actions is ever optimal, each is associated with a column of "0"'s in the **B** matrix.

[30] Again, compare the application of matrix composition in social network analysis (Hage and Harary 1983, ch. 5); see also Feller (1968, ch. 15) and Kim and Roush (1980, ch. 7.3) on the analysis of Markov chains.

[31] Note that the role-space attractors in the cases $e_{max} = 2$ and $e_{max} = 9$ permit randomization over actions. In both cases, the role-space attractor generates indifference over three actions, but each of these actions leads alters to attribute the same self (the role-space attractor) to ego.

TABLE 1
The B Matrix Given $e_{max} = 7$

Action $a \in F$	Actions in $a^*(S'(a))$																	
{0,0,2}	**1**	1	0	1	0	1	0	1	0	1	0	1	0	1	0	1	0	1
⋮																		
{4,5,1}	0	**1**	0	1	0	1	0	1	0	1	0	1	0	1	0	1	0	1
{4,6,0}	0	0	**0**	0	0	0	0	0	1	0	1	0	1	0	1	0	1	0
{4,6,1}	0	0	0	**1**	0	1	0	0	0	1	0	1	0	1	0	1	0	1
{4,7,0}	0	0	0	0	**0**	0	0	0	0	0	1	0	0	0	1	0	1	0
{4,7,1}	0	0	0	0	0	**1**	0	0	0	0	0	1	0	0	0	1	0	1
{5,5,0}	0	0	0	0	0	0	**1**	0	1	0	1	0	1	0	1	0	1	0
{5,5,1}	0	0	0	0	0	0	1	**0**	1	0	1	0	1	0	1	0	1	0
{5,6,0}	0	0	0	0	0	0	0	0	**1**	0	1	0	1	0	1	0	1	0
{5,6,1}	0	0	0	0	0	0	0	0	1	**0**	1	0	1	0	1	0	1	0
{5,7,0}	0	0	0	0	0	0	0	0	0	0	**1**	0	0	0	1	0	1	0
{5,7,1}	0	0	0	0	0	0	0	0	0	0	1	**0**	0	0	1	0	1	0
{6,6,0}	0	0	0	0	0	0	0	0	0	0	0	0	**1**	0	1	0	1	0
{6,6,1}	0	0	0	0	0	0	0	0	0	0	0	0	1	**0**	1	0	1	0
{6,7,0}	0	0	0	0	0	0	0	0	0	0	0	0	0	0	**1**	0	1	0
{6,7,1}	0	0	0	0	0	0	0	0	0	0	0	0	0	0	1	**0**	1	0
{7,7,0}	0	0	0	0	0	0	0	0	0	0	0	0	0	0	0	0	**1**	0
{7,7,1}	0	0	0	0	0	0	0	0	0	0	0	0	0	0	0	0	1	**0**

Note: I have (for presentation purposes) omitted the rows and columns for actions a ∈ {{1,1,0}, {1,1,1}, {1,2,0},…,{4,4,1}, {4,5,0}}. Elements along the main diagonal are denoted in boldface.

will have no strict preference for choosing a "higher" action (e.g., a = {7,7,1}) over a "lower" action (e.g., a = {4,6,1}).[32] But if ego is given an arbitrarily small "push" to choose the higher action (where this "push" may entail nothing more than randomization by ego over the set of optimal

[32] Given $S = \{.4, .4, .5\}$, ego is indifferent over the seven actions identified in row {4,6,1} of the **B** matrix in Table 1.

TABLE 2
Fixed Points in Action Space

	a	S'(a)	Number of actions in a*(S'(a))		a	S'(a)	Number of actions in a*(S'(a))
$e_{max} = 0$	{0,0,0}	{0.3,0.6,0.0}	1	$e_{max} = 8$	{0,0,2}	{1.0,0.0,0.0}	15
	{0,0,1}	{0.4,0.1,0.0}	1		{4,5,1}	{0.4,0.4,0.25}	14
	{0,0,2}	{1.0,0.0,0.0}	1		{4,6,1}	{0.4,0.4,0.5}	12
$e_{max} = 1$	{0,0,0}	{0.3,0.6,0.0}	3		{4,7,1}	{0.4,0.4,0.75}	9
	{0,0,1}	{0.4,0.1,0.0}	3		{4,8,1}	{0.4,0.4,0.1}	5
	{0,0,2}	{1.0,0.0,0.0}	1		{5,5,0}	{0.3,0.6,0.25}	10
	{0,1,0}	{0.3,0.6,0.0}	3		{5,6,0}	{0.3,0.6,0.5}	9
	{0,1,1}	{0.4,0.1,0.0}	3		{5,7,0}	{0.3,0.6,0.75}	7
	{1,1,0}	{0.3,0.6,0.0}	3		{5,8,0}	{0.3,0.6,1.0}	4
	{1,1,1}	{0.4,0.1,0.0}	3		{6,6,0}	{0.3,0.75,0.5}	6
$e_{max} = 2$	{0,0,2}	{1.0,0.0,0.0}	1		{6,7,0}	{0.3,0.75,0.75}	5
	{2,2,0}	{0.3,0.6,0.0}	1		{6,8,0}	{0.3,0.75,1.0}	3
	{2,2,1}	{0.4,0.1,0.0}	1		{7,7,0}	{0.3,0.9,0.75}	3
$e_{max} = 3$	{0,0,2}	{1.0,0.0,0.0}	1		{7,8,0}	{0.3,0.9,1.0}	2
	{3,3,0}	{0.3,0.6,0.0}	1		{8,8,0}	{0.3,1.0,1.0}	1
	{3,3,1}	{0.4,0.25,0.0}	1	$e_{max} = 9$	{0,0,2}	{1.0,0.0,0.0}	21
$e_{max} = 4$	{0,0,2}	{1.0,0.0,0.0}	1		{4,5,1}	{0.4,0.4,0.25}	20
	{4,4,0}	{0.3,0.6,0.0}	1		{4,6,1}	{0.4,0.4,0.5}	18
	{4,4,1}	{0.4,0.4,0.0}	1		{4,7,1}	{0.4,0.4,0.75}	15
$e_{max} = 5$	{0,0,2}	{1.0,0.0,0.0}	3		{4,8,1}	{0.4,0.4,1.0}	11
	{4,5,1}	{0.4,0.4,0.25}	2		{4,9,1}	{0.4,0.4,1.0}	11
	{5,5,0}	{0.3,0.6,0.25}	1		{5,5,0}	{0.3,0.6,0.25}	15
$e_{max} = 6$	{0,0,2}	{1.0,0.0,0.0}	6		{5,6,0}	{0.3,0.6,0.5}	14
	{4,5,1}	{0.4,0.4,0.25}	5		{5,7,0}	{0.3,0.6,0.75}	12
	{4,6,1}	{0.4,0.4,0.5}	3		{5,8,0}	{0.3,0.6,1.0}	9
	{5,5,0}	{0.3,0.6,0.25}	3		{5,9,0}	{0.3,0.6,1.0}	9
	{5,6,0}	{0.3,0.6,0.5}	2		{6,6,0}	{0.3,0.75,0.5}	10
	{6,6,0}	{0.3,0.75,0.5}	1		{6,7,0}	{0.3,0.75,0.75}	9
$e_{max} = 7$	{0,0,2}	{1.0,0.0,0.0}	10		{6,8,0}	{0.3,0.75,1.0}	7
	{4,5,1}	{0.4,0.4,0.25}	9		{6,9,0}	{0.3,0.75,1.0}	7
	{4,6,1}	{0.4,0.4,0.5}	7		{7,7,0}	{0.3,0.9,0.75}	6
	{4,7,1}	{0.4,0.4,0.75}	4		{7,8,0}	{0.3,0.9,1.0}	5
	{5,5,0}	{0.3,0.6,0.25}	6		{7,9,0}	{0.3,0.9,1.0}	5
	{5,6,0}	{0.3,0.6,0.5}	5		{8,8,0}	{0.3,1.0,1.0}	3
	{5,7,0}	{0.3,0.6,0.75}	3		{8,9,0}	{0.3,1.0,1.0}	3
	{6,6,0}	{0.3,0.75,0.5}	3		{9,9,0}	{0.3,1.0,1.0}	3
	{6,7,0}	{0.3,0.75,0.75}	2				
	{7,7,0}	{0.3,0.9,0.75}	1				

actions), alters would attribute a "stronger" self-concept to ego. And once ego's self-concept is revised upward, he may strictly prefer the higher action to the lower action. Loosely, the attributions of alters create a "ratchet effect" through which ego becomes "locked into" a stronger self-concept.

TABLE 3
Attractors in Role Space

$e_{max} \in \{0,1,2\}$	$S^0 = \{0.3, 0.6, 0.0\}$
	$S^1 = \{0.4, 0.1, 0.0\}$
	$S^2 = \{1.0, 0.0, 0.0\}$
$e_{max} = 3$	$S^0 = \{0.3, 0.6, 0.0\}$
	$S^1 = \{0.4, 0.25, 0.0\}$
	$S^2 = \{1.0, 0.0, 0.0\}$
$e_{max} = 4$	$S^0 = \{0.3, 0.6, 0.0\}$
	$S^1 = \{0.4, 0.4, 0.0\}$
	$S^2 = \{1.0, 0.0, 0.0\}$
$e_{max} = 5$	$S = \{0.3, 0.6, 0.25\}$
$e_{max} = 6$	$S = \{0.3, 0.75, 0.5\}$
$e_{max} = 7$	$S = \{0.3, 0.9, 0.75\}$
$e_{max} \in \{8,9\}$	$S = \{0.3, 1.0, 1.0\}$

To characterize this ratchet effect more formally, we might consider the quasiorder over actions generated by the reachability matrix **R**. Letting "$>$" denote "can reach," one can show that

$$\{4,6,1\} > \{4,7,1\} > \{5,7,1\} > \{5,7,0\} > \{6,7,0\} > \{7,7,0\};$$

$$\{4,6,1\} > \{4,7,1\} > \{6,7,1\} > \{6,7,0\} > \{7,7,0\};$$

$$\{4,6,1\} > \{4,7,1\} > \{7,7,1\} > \{7,7,0\};$$

$$\{4,6,1\} > \{5,6,1\} > \{5,6,0\} > \{5,7,0\} > \{6,7,0\} > \{7,7,0\};$$

$$\{4,6,1\} > \{5,6,1\} > \{6,6,0\} > \{6,7,0\} > \{7,7,0\};$$

$$\{4,6,1\} > \{6,6,1\} > \{6,6,0\} > \{6,7,0\} > \{7,7,0\}.$$

Once ego has developed the self attributed to a "higher" action (i.e., a smaller element of one of these orderings), ego would strictly prefer this action to "lower" actions (i.e., the larger elements of that ordering).

To close the analysis, it may be instructive to consider a particular trajectory through role space. Continuing with the example from above, suppose that ego's initial self is $S_0 = \{.4, .4, .5\}$, and that ego chooses (from among the seven members of $a^*(S_0)$) the action $\{7,7,1\}$. Alters would thus infer $S'(\{7,7,1\}) = \{.4, .9, .75\}$. If we assume $\gamma = .1$, ego's revised self is $S_1 = \{.4, .45, .525\}$. Now $a^*(S_1)$ contains only three members: ego is indifferent over the actions $\{5,7,1\}$, $\{6,7,1\}$, and $\{7,7,1\}$. Suppose that ego again chooses (perhaps through randomization) the action {7,7,1}. Alters again infer $S'(\{7,7,1\}) = \{.4,.9,.75\}$ so that ego's revised self becomes $S_2 = \{.4,.5355,.56775\}$. Now, $a^*(S_2)$ contains three different members: ego is indifferent over the actions {5,7,0}, {6,7,0}, and {7,7,0}. (Intuitively, the increase in ego's attachment to the father role causes him now to prefer actions {c,e,t} with t = 0 over those with t = 1.) Although each of the three actions in $a^*(S_2)$ is associated with a steady state in role space (see Table 2), only the strongest of these selves is an attractor (see Table 3). Thus, while ego's precise trajectory through role space is indeterminate, randomization by ego over the set of optimal actions will (eventually) cause his self to converge to the attractor $S = \{0.3,0.9,0.75\}$.[33]

3.8. *Discussion of the Model*

I have offered the preceding model primarily to illustrate a general theoretical methodology. Still, the model addresses important substantive issues that warrant some discussion. Indeed, the analysis has focused on questions at the heart of the culture-of-poverty debate (Lewis 1966; Patterson 1980). How is ego's self-concept affected by an (exogenous) constraint on labor-market opportunity? Relatedly, (how) does ego respond to changes in opportunity? I hope that my brief discussion here will inspire future research that will extend the present model (and perhaps the theoretical methodology itself) to more fully address these issues.

The role-space vectorfield that governs change in the self is determined (in part) by employment opportunity. Thus, the level of employment opportunity (e_{max}) determines the set of role-space attractors (Table 3). If there exists a unique attractor, ego's self will gradually (but inevitably) converge toward this long-run self; the direction of change depends on ego's initial location in role space. To illustrate, suppose that $e_{max} = 5$. In this case, ego's self will gradually converge toward $S = \{0.3,0.6,0.25\}$. Thus, if ego's initial self was $S_0 = \{1,1,1\}$, he would gradually come to

[33] Given the (extreme) assumption that ego's self conforms immediately to the attributions of alters (i.e., $\gamma = 1$), it would be straightforward to describe ego's stochastic path through role space using the **B** matrix. Dividing each row i of the **B** matrix by the number of elements in $a^*(S'(i))$ (to represent ego's randomization over the set of optimal actions), we obtain a Markov transition matrix. Given ego's initial action $a \in a^*(S_0)$ (represented as a binary vector), iterated multiplication by the transition matrix reveals ego's probabilistic location in action (and thus role) space. Note that this procedure would also identify attractors (and could thus be used as an alternative to the reachability analysis described above).

view himself as less of a man (μ_S(m) falling from 1.0 to 0.3), somewhat less of a father (μ_S(f) falling from 1.0 to 0.6), and less of a worker (μ_S(w) falling from 1.0 to 0.25). Comparing role-space attractors as e_{max} rises (see Table 3), higher levels of opportunity enable ego to maintain a stronger self-conception as a father and worker. In this way, the model captures Liebow's (1967) observation that individuals who face limited opportunity are less able to retain those roles.[34]

Liebow's (1967) streetcorner men face relatively low levels of opportunity (corresponding to $e_{max} \leq 4$). Given the parameters of the model, low opportunity implies multiple role-space attractors (Table 3; Figures 2 and 3).[35] The existence of multiple attractors might help explain why different types of individuals—different stable self-concepts—persist in impoverished neighborhoods even when all individuals face the same constraints. While Liebow (1967) focused narrowly on one type, other ethnographers have distinguished "mainstreamers" from "streetcorner men" (Hannerz 1969) or contrasted "regulars" with "wineheads" and "hoodlums" (Anderson 1978). Fixing $e_{max} = 3$, mainstreamers might correspond to the attractors $S^0 = \{0.3, 0.6, 0.0\}$ or $S^1 = \{0.4, 0.1, 0\}$ (which induce the actions $a^*(S^0) = \{3,3,0\}$ and $a^*(S^1) = \{3,3,1\}$); streetcorner men would correspond to the attractor $S^2 = \{1,0,0\}$ (which induces the action $a^* = \{0,0,2\}$). Given multiple attractors, ego's long-run self depends crucially on his initial self.[36] Figure 2 shows that individuals with strong initial attachment to the man role (μ_S(m) close to 1) become streetcorner men (S^2), while those with lower initial attachment to this role become mainstreamers (S^0 or S^1 depending on their initial attachment to the father role, μ_S(f)).

[34] Compare Liebow (1967:86): "The more demonstrative and accepting he is of his children, the greater is [the streetcorner man's] public and private commitment to the duties and responsibilities of fatherhood; and the greater his commitment, the greater and sharper his failure as the provider and head of the family. To soften his failure, and to lessen the damage to his public and self-esteem, he pushes the children away from him, saying, in effect, 'I'm not even trying to be your father so now I can't be blamed for failing to accomplish what I'm not trying to do.'"

[35] Given alternative parameter values, one can generate multiple equilibria for every value of e_{max}. In particular, one can select parameters so that $S = \{1,0,0\}$ (which induces the action $a^* = \{0,0,2\}$) always remains a role-space attractor regardless of ego's labor-market opportunities (i.e., for all $e_{max} \in \{0, \ldots, 9\}$).

[36] Presumably, ego's initial self is determined by early socialization, which is not addressed in the present model. A more complete model would attempt to explain the trajectory of ego's self over his entire life-cycle, with the initial condition his (presumably empty) self-concept at birth.

Although change in ego's labor-market opportunity does not immediately affect his location in role space, it does alter the role-space vector-field (and thus the set of role-space attractors). To illustrate, suppose that opportunity is low (say $e_{max} = 3$) and that ego's self has converged to the (streetcorner man) self $S^2 = \{1,0,0\}$ (which induces the action $a^* = \{0,0,2\}$). If opportunity increases (to say $e_{max} = 5$), this self is no longer an attractor. Ego will "take advantage" of increased opportunity by choosing higher levels of family support and employment (and a lower level of time with the peer group); alters will attribute to ego's self less of the man role, more of the father role, and more of the worker role; ego's self will gradually converge to the unique attractor $S = \{0.3, 0.6, 0.25\}$ (which induces the action $a^* = \{5,5,0\}$).[37] Thus the question about ego's response to opportunity becomes a question about change in the set of role-space attractors.[38] Note that a smaller increase in opportunity (from $e_{max} = 3$ to $e_{max} = 4$) would have had no effect on ego's self (or actions) since $S = \{1,0,0\}$ remains an attractor in both cases.

Finally, assuming that the government wished to change ego's behavior, note that the appropriate public-policy interventions would seem to depend crucially on the number of role-space attractors for each opportunity level, and how the set of attractors changes as opportunity rises. Suppose that, for each level of opportunity, there exists a unique role-space attractor. Further suppose that, as opportunity rises, this attractor is associated with higher levels of family support and employment. (For concreteness, consider the role-space attractors for $e_{max} \geq 5$ listed in Table 3.) Under these conditions, permanent change in ego's self and behavior would seem to require structural changes in the labor market: ego will change if and only if he is faced with a different level of opportunity.

[37] It is important to recognize the ego only gradually loses the identity of (and no longer behaves as) a streetcorner man. Given $e_{max} = 5$, the self $\{1,0,0\}$ is indifferent over the three actions $\{0,0,2\}$, $\{4,5,1\}$, and $\{5,5,1\}$. Once ego has chosen either $\{4,5,1\}$ or $\{5,5,1\}$, his new self (which has partially internalized the attributions of alters) will strictly prefer these actions to $\{0,0,2\}$. Eventually, as ego's self continues to change (so that he views himself as less of a man and more of a father), he will begin to prefer action $\{5,5,0\}$ to $\{5,5,1\}$.

[38] I might add two caveats. First, ego's transition to a new self may occur only slowly through the ratchet effect described above (see preceding note). Second, my present discussion presumes that ego does not foresee (nor respond to) future changes in opportunity; I have thus ignored the possibility of anticipatory socialization. In Section 5, I briefly discuss how the present framework might be extended to allow (ego's) foresight.

Now suppose that, for some fixed level of opportunity, there exist multiple role-space attractors. (Consider the set of role-space attractors for some particular $e_{max} \leq 4$ in Table 3.) Even without changing ego's level of opportunity, policy interventions that (even temporarily) change ego's self might have permanent effects on ego's self and behavior (by pushing ego's self into a different role-space basin of attraction). Such interventions might operate directly on ego's self-concept, less directly on alters' attributions (that are gradually internalized into ego's self), or even less directly on ego's actions (that generate attributions); interventions might attempt to influence either ego's initial self (through his early socialization) or his current self.[39]

4. AN ALTERNATIVE SPECIFICATION OF FUZZY INFERENCE AND DECISION-MAKING

The fuzzy inference and decision-making procedure specified in the preceding section offers one possible method for deriving ego's action a^* from his self-concept and social norms. However, viewing fuzzy logic as a flexible framework for building descriptive models of reasoning and choice (rather than a prescriptive theory), we might consider alternative specifications of this procedure (which might ultimately be compared and tested against each other). Loosely, the previous procedure identified those actions that ego *should* take. Here, the procedure will identify those actions that ego should *not* take.

To be more precise, the preceding section demonstrated how the classical syllogism

$$f, f \rightarrow P \vdash P$$

could be embedded in the matrix algebra of approximate reasoning as

$$\mathbf{f} \circ \mathbf{N}_1 = \mathbf{p}$$

[39] I have already noted that the present model can generate either a unique role-space attractor or multiple attractors depending on the precise specification of interrole implications and social norms. Thus my point here is not to adjudicate the culture-of-poverty debate (nor offer any particular policy recommendation), but merely to suggest how the present framework (by allowing precise specification and careful analysis of the arguments made by each side) might transform that highly polemical debate into more tractable questions about social norms, the process governing change in the self-concept, and the resulting role-space attractors.

where $\mathbf{p}$ is a vector with elements $[\mu_P(c)]$. Thus the composition $\mathbf{f} \circ \mathbf{N}_1$ yields a vector that corresponds to the fuzzy set P. To motivate an alternative specification of approximate reasoning, we might now begin with the syllogism

$$f, -(f \rightarrow P) \vdash -P.$$

Embedded in the matrix algebra of fuzzy logic, this syllogism becomes

$$\mathbf{f} \circ \bar{\mathbf{N}}_1 = \bar{\mathbf{p}}$$

where $\bar{\mathbf{p}}$ is a vector with elements $[1 - \mu_P(c)]$. In this way, the composition $\mathbf{f} \circ \bar{\mathbf{N}}_1$ yields a vector that corresponds to the *complement* of the fuzzy set P.[40] Thus, in the approximate-reasoning procedure specified below, matrix composition identifies those actions that are logically inconsistent with ego's self-concept.

In place of the correlation-minimum implication operator adopted previously, I now obtain the fuzzy relation N using the implication operator

$$\mu_N(i,j) = \max\{1 - \mu_X(i), \mu_Y(j)\} \quad \text{for all } \{i,j\} \in R \times A_k,$$

where $A_k \in \{C,E,T\}$.[41] The complement of N is given by the fuzzy relation $\bar{N}$, where

$$\mu_{\bar{N}}(i,j) = 1 - \mu_N(i,j) = 1 - \max\{1 - \mu_X(i), \mu_Y(j)\}$$
$$= \min\{\mu_X(i), 1 - \mu_Y(j)\} = \min\{\mu_X(i), \mu_{\bar{Y}}(j)\}$$

for all $\{i,j\} \in R \times A_k$. Thus the corresponding matrix $\bar{\mathbf{N}}$ is equal to the fuzzy outer product of the input role vector $\mathbf{x} = [\mu_X(i)]$ and output action vector $\bar{\mathbf{y}} = [1 - \mu_Y(j)]$. That is,

$$\bar{\mathbf{N}} = \mathbf{x}^T \circ \bar{\mathbf{y}}.$$

[40] In general, given a fuzzy set X characterized by degrees of membership $\mu_X(i)$ for $i \in I$, the complement of X (denoted $\bar{X}$) is characterized by degrees of membership $\mu_{\bar{X}}(i) = 1 - \mu_X(i)$ for $i \in I$; see Ross (1995:27).

[41] Note that this implication operator (μ_N) is never smaller than the Zadeh operator (μ_N^Z) nor larger than the Lukasiewicz operator (μ_N^L):

$$\mu_N^Z(i,j) \equiv \max\{1 - \mu_X(i), \min\{\mu_X(i), \mu_Y(j)\}\}$$
$$\leq \mu_N(i,j) \leq \mu_N^L(i,j) \equiv \min\{1, 1 - \mu_X(i) + \mu_Y(j)\}.$$

In contrast to the correlation-minimum operator, each of these three operators does properly generalize classical (material) implication, yielding $\mu_N(i,j) = 1$ whenever $\mu_X(i) = 0$ or $\mu_Y(j) = 1$.

To illustrate, note that

$$\bar{\mathbf{N}}_1 = \mathbf{f}^{\mathrm{T}} \circ \bar{\mathbf{p}} = \begin{bmatrix} 0 \\ 1 \\ 0 \end{bmatrix} \circ [1 \quad 1 \quad .9 \quad .75 \quad .6 \quad .4 \quad .25 \quad .1 \quad 0 \quad 0]$$

$$= \begin{bmatrix} 0.0 & 0.0 & 0.0 & 0.0 & 0.0 & 0.0 & 0.0 & 0.0 & 0.0 & 0.0 \\ 1.0 & 1.0 & 0.9 & 0.75 & 0.6 & 0.4 & 0.25 & 0.1 & 0.0 & 0.0 \\ 0.0 & 0.0 & 0.0 & 0.0 & 0.0 & 0.0 & 0.0 & 0.0 & 0.0 & 0.0 \end{bmatrix}.$$

Comparing this matrix to

$$\mathbf{N}_1 = \begin{bmatrix} 1.0 & 1.0 & 1.0 & 1.0 & 1.0 & 1.0 & 1.0 & 1.0 & 1.0 & 1.0 \\ 0.0 & 0.0 & 0.1 & 0.25 & 0.4 & 0.6 & 0.75 & 0.9 & 1.0 & 1.0 \\ 1.0 & 1.0 & 1.0 & 1.0 & 1.0 & 1.0 & 1.0 & 1.0 & 1.0 & 1.0 \end{bmatrix},$$

note that $\bar{\mathbf{N}}_1$ reflects the degree of logical inconsistency (between each role-action pair {i,j}) while $\mathbf{N}_1$ reflects logical possibility.

For each norm i specified in the model above, we may now compute the matrix $\bar{\mathbf{N}}_i$. Composing the **M** matrix with each $\bar{\mathbf{N}}_i$ matrix, we obtain four matrices that reflect the logical contractions (both direct and indirect) between roles and actions. In particular,

$$\mathbf{M} \circ \bar{\mathbf{N}}_1 = \mathbf{M} \circ \mathbf{f}^{\mathrm{T}} \circ \bar{\mathbf{p}}$$

$$= \begin{bmatrix} 1.0 & 0.3 & 0.2 \\ 0.0 & 1.0 & 0.0 \\ 0.0 & 0.0 & 1.0 \end{bmatrix} \circ \begin{bmatrix} 0 \\ 1 \\ 0 \end{bmatrix}$$

$$\circ [1 \quad 1 \quad .9 \quad .75 \quad .6 \quad .4 \quad .25 \quad .1 \quad 0 \quad 0]$$

$$= \begin{bmatrix} 0.3 & 0.3 & 0.3 & 0.3 & 0.3 & 0.3 & 0.25 & 0.1 & 0.0 & 0.0 \\ 1.0 & 1.0 & 0.9 & 0.75 & 0.6 & 0.4 & 0.25 & 0.1 & 0.0 & 0.0 \\ 0.0 & 0.0 & 0.0 & 0.0 & 0.0 & 0.0 & 0.0 & 0.0 & 0.0 & 0.0 \end{bmatrix};$$

$$\mathbf{M} \circ \bar{\mathbf{N}}_2 = \mathbf{M} \circ \mathbf{w}^{\mathrm{T}} \circ \bar{\mathbf{g}}$$

$$= \begin{bmatrix} 1.0 & 0.3 & 0.2 \\ 0.0 & 1.0 & 0.0 \\ 0.0 & 0.0 & 1.0 \end{bmatrix} \circ \begin{bmatrix} 0 \\ 0 \\ 1 \end{bmatrix}$$

$$\circ [1 \quad 1 \quad 1 \quad 1 \quad 1 \quad .75 \quad .50 \quad .25 \quad 0 \quad 0]$$

$$= \begin{bmatrix} 0.2 & 0.2 & 0.2 & 0.2 & 0.2 & 0.2 & 0.2 & 0.2 & 0.0 & 0.0 \\ 0.0 & 0.0 & 0.0 & 0.0 & 0.0 & 0.0 & 0.0 & 0.0 & 0.0 & 0.0 \\ 1.0 & 1.0 & 1.0 & 1.0 & 1.0 & 0.75 & 0.5 & 0.25 & 0.0 & 0.0 \end{bmatrix};$$

$$\mathbf{M} \circ \bar{\mathbf{N}}_3 = \mathbf{M} \circ \mathbf{m}^{\mathrm{T}} \circ \bar{\mathbf{h}}$$

$$= \begin{bmatrix} 1.0 & 0.3 & 0.2 \\ 0.0 & 1.0 & 0.0 \\ 0.0 & 0.0 & 1.0 \end{bmatrix} \circ \begin{bmatrix} 1 \\ 0 \\ 0 \end{bmatrix} \circ [1.0 \quad 0.6 \quad 0.0]$$

$$= \begin{bmatrix} 1.0 & 0.6 & 0.0 \\ 0.0 & 0.0 & 0.0 \\ 0.0 & 0.0 & 0.0 \end{bmatrix};$$

$$\mathbf{M} \circ \bar{\mathbf{N}}_4 = \mathbf{M} \circ [0 \quad .6 \quad 0]^{\mathrm{T}} \circ \bar{\mathbf{l}}$$

$$= \begin{bmatrix} 1.0 & 0.3 & 0.2 \\ 0.0 & 1.0 & 0.0 \\ 0.0 & 0.0 & 1.0 \end{bmatrix} \circ \begin{bmatrix} 0 \\ .6 \\ 0 \end{bmatrix} \circ [0.0 \quad 0.9 \quad 1.0]$$

$$= \begin{bmatrix} 0.0 & 0.3 & 0.3 \\ 0.0 & 0.6 & 0.6 \\ 0.0 & 0.0 & 0.0 \end{bmatrix}.$$

Finally, by composing the vector **s** with each of these matrices, we obtain the degrees of logical contradiction between ego's self and actions. To illustrate, suppose $\mathbf{s} = [.7 \quad .6 \quad 0]$ so that

$$\mathbf{s} \circ \mathbf{M} \circ \bar{\mathbf{N}}_1 = [0.6 \quad 0.6 \quad 0.6 \quad 0.6 \quad 0.6 \quad 0.4 \quad 0.25 \quad 0.1 \quad 0.0 \quad 0.0];$$

$$\mathbf{s} \circ \mathbf{M} \circ \bar{\mathbf{N}}_2 = [0.2 \quad 0.2 \quad 0.2 \quad 0.2 \quad 0.2 \quad 0.2 \quad 0.2 \quad 0.2 \quad 0.0 \quad 0.0];$$

$$\mathbf{s} \circ \mathbf{M} \circ \bar{\mathbf{N}}_3 = [0.7 \quad 0.6 \quad 0.0];$$

$$\mathbf{s} \circ \mathbf{M} \circ \bar{\mathbf{N}}_4 = [0.0 \quad 0.6 \quad 0.6].$$

Following the previous (Section 3) specification, I now need to derive ego's actions from the preceding vectors. In their specification of fuzzy decision-making, Bellman and Zadeh (1970; see also Bojadziev and Bojadziev 1995, ch. 10) view a decision ($\mathcal{D}$) as a "confluence" of goals ($\mathcal{G}_1,\ldots,\mathcal{G}_m$) and constraints ($\mathcal{C}_1,\ldots,\mathcal{C}_n$). In set-theoretic notation,

$$\mathcal{D} = \mathcal{G}_1 \cap \ldots \cap \mathcal{G}_m \cap \mathcal{C}_1 \cap \ldots \cap \mathcal{C}_n.$$

Thus, given goals and constraints specified over the action space A, ego would choose the action a^* that maximizes

$$\mathcal{D}(a) = \min\{\mathcal{G}_1(a),\ldots,\mathcal{G}_m(a), \mathcal{C}_1(a),\ldots,\mathcal{C}_n(a)\}.$$

However, in the present procedure, ego chooses actions not to maximize some objective function but to *minimize* logical contradiction. Thus, letting $\mathcal{C}_i(a)$ reflect contradictions between ego's self and actions stemming from norm i, I assume that ego chooses the action a^* (from the feasible set F) that minimizes

$$\mathcal{D}(a) = \max_i\{\mathcal{C}_i(a)\}.$$

In the present model, this decision function becomes

$$\mathcal{D}(\{c,e,t\}) = \max\{\mu_{S\circ M\circ \bar{N}_1}(c), \mu_{S\circ M\circ \bar{N}_2}(e), \mu_{S\circ M\circ \bar{N}_3}(t), \mu_{S\circ M\circ \bar{N}_4}(t)\}$$

for all $\{c,e,t\} \in A$. Equivalently, we might write

$$\mathcal{D}(\{c,e,t\}) = \max\{(\mathbf{s}\circ\mathbf{M}\circ\bar{\mathbf{N}}_1)_c, (\mathbf{s}\circ\mathbf{M}\circ\bar{\mathbf{N}}_2)_e, (\mathbf{s}\circ\mathbf{M}\circ\bar{\mathbf{N}}_3)_t, (\mathbf{s}\circ\mathbf{M}\circ\bar{\mathbf{N}}_4)_t\}$$

where $(\mathbf{s}\circ\mathbf{M}\circ\bar{\mathbf{N}}_i)_j$ denotes element j of the $\mathbf{s}\circ\mathbf{M}\circ\bar{\mathbf{N}}_i$ vector. Again, I assume that ego chooses the action

$$a^* = \operatorname*{argmin}_{a\in F} \mathcal{D}(a).$$[42]

[42] Alternatively, one might place an (inverse) feasibility indicator inside the decision function, so that ego chooses the action

$$a^* = \operatorname*{argmin}_{a\in A} \max\{\mathcal{C}_1(a),\ldots,\mathcal{C}_n(a), 1-\mu_F(a)\},$$

where n is the number of norms. Note that this alternative specification would yield the same optimal action a^* as the specification in the text: infeasible actions ($a\notin F$) would never be chosen since they imply $\mathcal{D}(a) = 1$; feasible actions ($a\in F$) would imply $\mathcal{D}(a) = \max\{\mathcal{C}_1(a),\ldots,\mathcal{C}_n(a)\}$. However, to emphasize the distinction between "physical" constraints (that never can be violated) and "normative" constraints (that are, in practice, often violated), I assume that ego must choose an action a^* contained in the feasible set F.

In the event of a tie (between two or more actions yielding the minimum $\mathcal{D}$(a)), one might invoke various tie-breaking algorithms. For instance, following Yager (1981; see also Ross 1995, ch. 10), we might form a lexicographic preference ordering over actions by comparing first the largest degree of logical inconsistency associated with each action (i.e., $\max_i\{\mathcal{C}_i(a')\}$ for each $a' \in F$), then the second-largest degree of inconsistency, and so on.[43]

To illustrate, suppose again that $e_{max} = 3$. Given the $\mathbf{s}\circ\mathbf{M}\circ\bar{\mathbf{N}}_i$ vectors derived above, the decision function is determined entirely by t:

$$\mathcal{D}(\{c,e,0\}) = \max\{.6,.2,.7,0\} = .7 \text{ for all } c \le e \le 3;$$

$$\mathcal{D}(\{c,e,1\}) = \max\{.6,.2,.6,.6\} = .6 \text{ for all } c \le e \le 3;$$

$$\mathcal{D}(\{0,0,2\}) = \max\{.6,.2,0,.6\} = .6.$$

Applying the tie-breaking algorithm proposed above, ego would choose $a^* = \{0,0,2\}$ because this action implies a lower degree of inconsistency with the norm 3. (That is, $\mathcal{C}_3(\{0,0,2\}) = 0 < \mathcal{C}_3(\{c,e,1\}) = .6$ for all $c \le e \le 3$.) Intuitively, any action {c,e,t} chosen by ego (who possesses the self $S = \{.7,.6,0\}$ and faces the constraint $e_{max} = 3$) must inevitably create some logical inconsistency (given my specification of social norms). However, by choosing to spend a lot of time ($t^* = 2$) with a peer group, ego can at least eliminate any inconsistency induced by norm 3.

Having recognized the potential importance of lexicographic preference orderings over actions, I close this subsection with one final note on the construction of the decision function. As already discussed, matrix composition identifies the strongest chain in a parallel system of propositional chains. Thus, we may rewrite the decision function as

$$\mathcal{D}(a) = \max_i\{\mathcal{C}_i(a)\}$$

$$= \max_i\{\max_{\{j,k\}}\{\min\{\mu_S(j), \mu_M(j,k), \mu_{\bar{N}_i}(k,a_{l(i)})\}\}\}$$

[43] Here is a more precise description of the procedure. For each action $a \in F$, we would list the n $\mathcal{C}(a)$'s in descending order. For convenience, label them $\mathcal{C}^1(a) \ge \mathcal{C}^2(a) \ge \ldots \ge \mathcal{C}^n(a)$. Note that, by construction, $\mathcal{D}(a) = \mathcal{C}^1(a)$. Thus action $a \in a^*$ iff $a \in F$ and $\mathcal{C}^1(a)$ is the smallest $\mathcal{C}^1(a')$ for all $a' \in F$. In the event of a tie (i.e., the set a^* has more than one member), we would choose some action from the set a^{**} where $a \in a^{**}$ iff $a \in a^*$ and $\mathcal{C}^2(a)$ is the smallest $\mathcal{C}^2(a')$ for all $a' \in a^*$. (Given further ties, we would iterate this procedure until we have exhausted all n dimensions available for evaluation.)

where $\{j,k\} \in R \times R$, and $a_{l(i)}$ is the element of the action triple $a = \{c,e,t\}$ associated with norm i. Given that the decision function is equal to a maximum of maxima of propositional chains, one might vary the order of iteration over these max operators without affecting the decision function. In particular, letting "$\wedge$" denote the min operator, we might rewrite the decision function as

$$\begin{aligned}\mathcal{D}(a) &= \max_j\{\max_k\{\max_i\{\mu_S(j) \wedge \mu_M(j,k) \wedge \mu_{\bar{N}_i}(k,a_{l(i)})\}\}\} \\ &= \max_j\{\mu_S(j) \wedge \max_k\{\mu_M(j,k) \wedge \max_i\{\mu_{\bar{N}_i}(k,a_{l(i)})\}\}\}\end{aligned}$$

so that the primary iteration is made over the roles in ego's self (j) rather than norms (i). While this reconstruction of the decision function does not affect its value, it could affect lexicographic preference orderings generated through the tie-breaking algorithm: ego would now consider (for each action $a \in F$) the maximum degree of logical inconsistency associated with each role (rather than norm).

5. DISCUSSION

In this section, I compare and contrast the present framework to some related sociological models and perspectives: previous formalizations of role theory, rational choice theory, and social network analysis. I also discuss fuzzy logic in relation to some alternatives. The section concludes with a brief discussion of empirical implementation. Directions for future research are indicated throughout.

5.1. *Previous Formalizations of Role Theory*

The present framework is not the first formalization of role theory; important previous developments include affect control theory (Heise 1979) and production system models (Fararo and Skvoretz 1984).

Affect control theory (Heise 1979, 1987) addresses brief interaction sequences between pairs of individuals. Each individual begins an interaction with a "definition of the situation" (an assignment of the individuals to a role pair such as parent-child or policeman-criminal) that induces fundamental sentiments (how good/powerful/lively is each role). Each individual also develops transient sentiments that depend on the particular combination of roles and the emergent sequence of behaviors within the interaction. Given these fundamental and transient sentiments, each individual chooses behavior to minimize "deflections" (squared differences between fundamentals and transients).[44]

Production system models (Fararo and Skvoretz 1984; Skvoretz and Fararo 1996) also address brief interaction sequences, though these models focus more on the structure of the interaction than the motivation behind behavior.[45] Originally developed by Newell and Simon (1972) to characterize human decision-making, production systems are ordered sets of if-then rules linking knowledge and action. Adapting this framework, Fararo and Skvoretz (1984) view social institutions (e.g., a restaurant) as sets of interdependent "rolegrams" that specify what type of behavior is required of situational roles (e.g., waitress and customer) conditional on the current knowledge-state (e.g., whether the customer has placed an order). Interaction emerges as individuals repeatedly "scroll through" the sets of rules comprising their respective rolegrams.

The present framework shares some features with each of these approaches. Like affect control theory, it is inspired by an engineering control-systems perspective. In affect control theory, individuals attempt to regulate their own affect (maintaining transient sentiments equal to fundamental sentiments) through their choice of behavior. In the present framework, alters (perhaps unintentionally) regulate ego's behavior (maintaining future actions equal to current actions) through their attributions (which are partially internalized into ego's self). Like production system models, the present framework utilizes if-then rules that link knowledge (of roles and their associated obligations) to action.

However, the present framework differs from previous approaches by addressing a more aggregate (but still "micro") level of human experience. Both affect control theory and production system models address brief interaction sequences that occur at the "micro-micro" or "situational" level. Both approaches assume that individuals adopt single roles on a purely situational basis, ignoring any linkages across situations. In contrast, the present framework ignores the "fine structure" of particular

[44] If interaction proceeds smoothly (i.e., deflections remain small) then the original definitions of the situation will persist. However, if deflections become large then one or both individuals may redefine the situation (adopting a new role assignment with new fundamental sentiments).

[45] See Smith-Lovin (1987:186) for the claim that "production systems show us how to get things done; affect control shows us why we do them" and some suggestions about the unification of these frameworks.

situations, implicitly aggregating over many situations. This aggregation emerges through the assumptions that ego simultaneously holds multiple (transsituational) roles and faces (transsituational) constraints. Indeed, recognizing that these constraints may force ego not to participate in situations associated with some roles in order to participate in situations associated with other roles, the present framework implicitly addresses ego's choice over situations.

Thus the present framework would seem to complement (not replace) previous formalizations of role theory; the appropriate framework depends on the desired (situational or micro) level of analysis. Indeed, we might view situational processes (described by affect control theory or production systems models) as nested inside a slower feedback loop that governs change in the transsituational self (described by the current framework).[46] Incorporating transsituational influences into affect control theory (perhaps through identity modifiers [Averett and Heise 1987]) or production system models (perhaps through simultaneous activation of multiple rolegrams corresponding to both situational and transsituational roles), future research might attempt a formal unification of situation-level and microlevel perspectives.

5.2. *Rational Choice Theory*

Like rational choice theory, the present framework addresses choice under constraint. Indeed, my initial specification of ego's problem—maximize the decision function $\mathcal{D}(a)$ by choosing some action a^* from the feasible set F—closely parallels the canonical rational choice problem in which an individual maximizes a utility function subject to some (budget or time) constraint. Moreover, like the present framework, rational choice models often focus on the micro (rather than situational) level.[47]

[46] This nesting seems consistent with Turner's (1978:1) view that some roles may be "put on and taken off like clothing without lasting personal effect" while other roles "that are grounded in other settings and other stages of the life cycles" are "difficult to put aside when a situation is changed and continue to color the way in which many of the individual's roles are performed."

[47] For instance, a labor economist might adopt a utility maximization model to address an individual's choice between labor and leisure (reflected in the number of hours worked in a given year), but might not attempt to explain hours worked on any particular day (much less the sequence of face-to-face interaction between the individual and coworkers at quitting time).

Given that both approaches may be used to address microlevel choice under constraint, the present framework might be viewed as an alternative to (or perhaps an analog of) rational choice theory. I emphasize two contrasts between the present framework and standard rational choice models. First, the present framework does not merely characterize ego's preferences over actions (through the decision function $\mathcal{D}$(a)), but derives these preferences from more primitive assumptions on the self and social norms. Second, the present framework specifies a particular social-psychological process by which preferences change through time.

Rational choice models introduce preferences (often embodied in a utility function) as a primitive assumption. Because they merely describe (rather than explain) preferences, rational choice models might be married to various (social or psychological or biological) theories of preference formation. The present framework does not introduce the decision function $\mathcal{D}$(a) as a primitive assumption, but maintains that $\mathcal{D}$(a) is generated through logical derivation from (the roles contained in) the self and social norms. Admittedly, this (social-psychological) theory of preference derivation introduces new primitives to be explained: Where does the self come from? Where do social norms come from? But these are questions of "socialization" and "social change" that can be linked to existing sociological literatures. Indeed, while the question of social change is beyond my current scope, the present framework explicitly models the socialization process (by assuming that the self changes as ego internalizes the attributions of alters).[48]

Rational choice models generally presume that preferences are stable, though economists have considered endogenous-preference models in which preferences are formed myopically (Pollak 1970, 1976; von Weizäcker 1971) or rationally (Stigler and Becker 1977; Becker and Murphy 1988). The present framework, encompassing both the link from self to action and the feedback from action to self, might well be labeled an "endogenous-self" model. Because preferences over actions depend on the (current) self, the present framework also constitutes a (myopic)

[48] My specification of this socialization process still leaves open the question: where does the *initial* self come from? Perhaps the obvious answer is that individuals are born with empty self-concepts. Alternatively, anticipating disagreement from sociobiologists, future research might extend the present framework so that some elements of the self (or perhaps partial preference orders) are fixed at birth—hardwired into humans through biological evolution.

endogenous-preference model.[49] However, the present framework differs from previous rational choice models by positing a particular social-psychological process that governs preference change. While Becker and Murphy (1988) endogenize preferences through "consumption capital" functions (mapping current consumption levels into future preferences) that often seem to ignore social context, the present framework draws explicit attention to the process by which the (biased) attributions made by alters gradually induce change in the self (and hence preferences).

A final point emerges by comparing the illustrative model developed in Section 3 to my own previous formalization of *Tally's Corner* within the Beckerian endogenous-preference framework (Montgomery 1994). That paper assumed that ego's altruism toward his family depended on the past level of family consumption (in particular, ego's altruism decreased if he did not provide a socially acceptable level of support). Although comparison of my two models might focus on ego's foresight (in Montgomery 1994) versus ego's myopia (in Section 3) in preference formation, I would emphasize a different point.[50] Namely, while my previous model was motivated with a discussion of roles and norms and logical contradiction (Montgomery 1994:465–67), these concepts are merely implicit in the model itself. In particular, ego's degree of membership in the father role was proxied by his level of altruism; logical contradiction was embedded in a "dissonance" parameter that influences ego's (psychic) cost of not providing for his family.[51]

By failing explicitly to incorporate roles, my previous model (like other rational choice models) becomes difficult to link with relevant sociological research on identity (which emphasizes the social processes by which individuals classify themselves and others into roles) and culture

[49] The degree of rationality (foresight) in preference formation is ultimately an empirical question: when choosing actions, to what extent does ego consider the attributions that alters will make (and the resulting consequences for ego's future self-concept)? Proceeding deductively, future research might suppose that ego chooses actions not simply to "express" her current self, but to regulate her self (maintaining her future self equal to her current self), taking into account the attributions that will be generated by various actions.

[50] The model in Montgomery (1994) might easily be reformulated to assume myopic rather than rational preference formation. Conversely, as suggested in the preceding note, future extensions of the present framework might suppose that ego foresees (and acts to influence) attributions.

[51] Further, while the action "provide for family" is explicitly parameterized (by a socially acceptable level of family support), the norm itself (the mapping from father role to this action) remains implicit: the (psychic) cost of not providing varies directly with ego's altruism.

(which addresses the social process of categorization by which role systems emerge and change). Moreover, by failing to incorporate roles and norms in propositional form, my previous model (like other rational choice models) cannot explicitly incorporate the (possibly biased) logical derivation that often seems to constitute human reasoning about appropriate behavior in the context of social norms. It might be possible to recast the present framework in the "black box" format of other endogenous-preference models—as a process by which current actions a_t influence future preferences $\mathcal{D}_{t+1}$—without any explicit specification of roles or norms or the self. But this paper (with its implied research agenda) stems from my conviction that these vital sociological concepts must be explicit elements in the formal ontology of social systems—not merely superfluous interpretations of preference derivation and change.

5.3. *Social Network Analysis*

The present framework might be linked to social network analysis in two ways. First, recognizing that both perspectives employ similar (graph-theoretic) formalisms, models and techniques developed for network analysis may prove useful in extensions of the present framework. Second, given their complementary focuses on action and structure, the present framework and network analysis might be unified to form a more complete social theory.

Following the convention in fuzzy logic, I have described approximate reasoning using matrix algebra. But approximate reasoning might easily be given an equivalent graph-theoretic representation. In the present application, ego and roles and actions would become sets of nodes; the self and interrole implications and norms would become sets of directed edges (with values reflecting degrees of membership in fuzzy relations).[52] Given this graph-theoretic view of approximate reasoning, logical inferences are

[52] To elaborate, ego's reasoning process would begin with a single node representing ego. This node is connected to the three role nodes (m, f, and w) by directed edges with values given by the vector **s**. Each role node is in turn connected to the other role nodes by directed edges with values given by the matrix **M**. (A loop from a role to itself—corresponding to a diagonal entry of the **M** matrix—always has value 1.0 and might thus be ignored.) Each social norm i connects every role node to every action node in the relevant universe of discourse (C, E, or T) by directed edges with values given by the $\mathbf{N}_i$ matrix. (Note that, if multiple norms address the same set of actions, some role and action nodes will be connected by multiple edges. If we wished to distinguish between these edges, we might color them by norm.) In a similar way, alters' reasoning process could be represented by a graph with directed edges from actions to roles (and between roles).

determined by comparing the strength of various network flows (characterized by max-min composition). Ego's inferences depend on the flows from ego to actions. In particular, my initial specification assumed that ego chooses the action triple {c,e,t} with the highest aggregate inflow. My alternative specification (which identified "negative" flows) assumed that ego chooses the action triple with the lowest maximum inflow. Alters' inferences depend on flows from actions to roles. In particular, my specification assumed that alters set attributions equal to the maximum inflow into each role.

Thus fuzzy logic may be viewed as a "network" theory of reasoning. Although the nodes in this network denote propositions (not individuals) and the edges denote logical (not social) relations, fuzzy logic inevitably uses many of the same formalisms and techniques as social network analysis.[53] Both fuzzy logicians and network analysts have recognized that network flow may be represented in multiple ways by using alternative composition operators. Indeed, many of the composition operators used in fuzzy logic (Ross 1995:210) have already been employed and interpreted by network analysts (Doreian 1974; Peay 1977). Similarly, recognizing that network flows may be aggregated in multiple ways, the various aggregation procedures used (to determine inferences) in fuzzy logic might be compared with various social-network conceptions of range (Burt 1983). Perhaps these formal parallels might convince network analysts both to explore fuzzy logic (since mathematical barriers-to-entry are low) and to consider whether more advanced techniques of network analysis (e.g., blockmodeling [White et al. 1976] or network algebras [Boyd 1991; Pattison 1993]) could find interpretation and application in fuzzy logic.[54]

Beyond the shared formalisms, fuzzy logic and social network analysis would seem to be complements at the metatheoretical level. Social network analysis might be viewed as a set of mathematical techniques for describing and comparing social structures (Pattison 1993) or perhaps (more ambitiously) as an attempt to explain macrolevel structure from properties

[53] Indeed, sociologists might view fuzzy logic as social network analysis come full circle—having returned to Heider's (1946) original theory of cognitive dissonance in which nodes may represent propositions.

[54] Like fuzzy logic, expectation-states theory also adopts an explicit graph-theoretic view of reasoning (e.g., see Berger et al. 1998, especially app. A), although network flows (that drive inferences) are determined by path length rather than max-min composition. Future research might attempt to characterize both fuzzy logic and expectation-states theory as special cases of a more general network theory of reasoning.

of microlevel relations (Boyd 1991). In any case, network analysis does not constitute a complete social theory because it lacks a theory of action (compare Emirbayer and Goodwin 1994). Conversely, while the present framework emphasizes action, it ignores the network structure within which action occurs. These complementary emphases suggest that network analysis and the present framework might be unified to address both structure and action within the same dynamic framework.[55]

As an important first step toward this unification, we might view ego's personal network as a subset of his self-concept. That is, while the present framework presumes that roles are always properties of individuals (e.g., i is an m), future extensions might also permit roles to be relations among individuals (e.g., i is an f to j).[56] Having ignored ego's network, the present framework assumes that alters make a single collective attribution about ego's self. But given a specification of ego's network, future extensions might offer a more faithful formalization of Turner's (1978:13) consensual-frames-of-reference principle which holds that "individuals tend to merge into their persons the roles by which *significant others* identify them" (emphasis added). In the extended framework, different alters might observe different subsets of ego's actions, and thus make different attributions. Ego would weight attributions by the strength of his relation to particular alters; the strength of each relation would itself be determined by past attributions. In this way, extensions of the present endogenous-self framework would also endogenize network formation.

5.4. *Fuzzy Logic and Alternatives*

My dialectic view of the role-person merger (Section 2) might have been operationalized in various ways. While the present framework uses fuzzy logic to model the reasoning processes of ego and alters, future research might attempt to apply alternative logical frameworks. In particular, future research might build upon previous formulations of deontic logic (which,

[55] Though network analysis might alternatively be coupled with rational choice theory (see Montgomery 1996 for one such effort), the present role-theoretic framework seems a more natural complement. Nadel (1957), a cornerstone of the network literature, begins with the conception of a role as a set of behaviors. Moreover, the synthesis of network analysis with (some version of) role theory would seem to be one goal of White (1992).

[56] Indeed, following Boyd (1991), future extensions might specify all roles as relations by adopting the convention that properties (i is an m) are merely relations to oneself (i is an m to i).

to allow reasoning about social norms, extends standard logic to incorporate logical operators that denote permission and obligation).[57]

Fuzzy logic has been criticized by mathematicians and philosophers.[58] However, much of this criticism becomes moot if fuzzy logic is viewed as a positive (descriptive) rather than normative (prescriptive) theory of human reasoning (compare Haack 1996:xi–xii and 230–31).[59] Certainly, as applied by engineers, fuzzy logic is not a proper generalization of classical logic (see notes 20 and 22 for indications). Nevertheless, fuzzy logic remains a useful collection of formalisms for describing reasoning and choice. Reflection on my alternative specifications of ego's problem (Sections 3 and 4) suggests that there are multiple ways to assemble the gears and levers of fuzzy logic—composition operators, implication operators, and choice algorithms—into plausible decision-making machines. While this indeterminacy would disturb logicians who wish to prescribe the (unique) best practice for making inferences, the flexibility of fuzzy logic might be welcomed by role theorists who wish instead to develop a descriptive account of human reasoning in normative settings.

One final direction for future research is suggested by the increasing use in engineering of hybrid neural-fuzzy techniques (Tsoukalas and Uhrig 1997, ch. 14). Especially in the context of expert or control systems, neural networks (which learn directly from training data) and fuzzy systems (which utilize expert knowledge) have complementary strengths. Neural networks adapt more easily (through various learning algorithms). On

[57] Deontic logic is generally formulated as a modal logic (Chellas 1980; Hughes and Cresswell 1996); see Anderson (1962) and von Wright (1963) for role-theoretic applications. More recent research (that might be of particular interest to sociologists) has attempted to ground deontic logic on nonmonotonic logic in order to address the "moral dilemmas" that arise from contradictory norms (Horty 1993, 1994) and to reformulate deontic operators in terms of the preferences (two-place modal operators) of a "superagent" (Huang and Masuch 1995).

[58] E.g., see Haack (1996). However, because Haack identifies fuzzy logic narrowly with Zadeh's (1975) attempt to specify the metalanguage predicates "true" and "false" as fuzzy sets, her discussion of vagueness may be more relevant. That philosophical debate seems to revolve around the following questions. Do there exist useful concepts that cannot be made precise? Do imprecise concepts ever permit valid inference?

[59] The descriptive view of fuzzy logic seems consistent with the usual defense offered by engineers: fuzzy logic *works*. For lists of commercial applications where fuzzy control systems have replaced human operators, see Ross (1995:3) and Tsoukalas and Uhrig (1997:145); see also Kosko's (1992, ch. 9) revealing account of how fuzzy logic might be used to encode the tacit ability of a human operator to back a truck into a loading dock.

the other hand, while the linguistic rules that comprise fuzzy systems may be easily inspected and modified, the internal parameters of neural networks are not readily interpretable. These complementary strengths might suggest the usefulness of hybrid neural-fuzzy systems in which fuzzy rules are encoded into a neural network that then adapts to a local environment and ultimately yields a revised set of fuzzy rules.

Reflection on such neural-fuzzy systems might suggest an alternative approach to situation-level role theory and its unification with higher (micro and macro) levels of role theory. Ethnomethodologists (Suchman 1987) might attack my "rule-based" conception of role theory (and, relatedly, conventional rule-based expert systems) on the grounds that individuals do not act in response to norms (which are merely ex-post accounts of behavior). While I would contend that the ethnomethodological theory of action is itself unclear, that perspective does highlight the tacit nature of much situation-level action not directly governed by a conscious effort to derive appropriate behavior from roles and norms.[60] One potential synthesis of my "rule-based" framework with "account-based" ethnomethodology might assume that (explicit but possibly fuzzy) social norms become encoded within ego as tacit action strategies that gradually adapt to ego's local environment; these tacit strategies can be "retranslated" into fuzzy rules when ego is called upon by alters to rationalize his actions. This proposed synthesis, which clearly suggests a neural-fuzzy specification, would accept the tacit nature of much action (situation level) but also recognize that roles and norms do become explicit both in the conscious reflections and rationalizations of individuals (micro level) and as elements in the larger culture (macro level).[61]

5.5. *Empirical Implementation*

The present paper offers a general modeling framework that permits careful specification and rigorous analysis of role-theoretic explanations. My

[60] The same point might be drawn from Heise's (1979) critique of "inventorial" approaches to role theory. Affect control theory does not assume that individuals store and access inventories of norms. Rather, all relevant information about roles and behaviors is encoded directly into a multidimensional affect space.

[61] Perhaps the key problem in this synthesis (which, in my view, also faces other ethnomethodological theories of action) is to clarify the performance function that governs change in ego's tacit strategies. In particular, (how) does this performance function differ from the stable metapreferences presumed in some endogenous-preference models (Becker and Murphy 1988)?

contribution is thus a new theoretical (not empirical) methodology for role theory. Of course, particular models developed within the present framework might generate empirical predictions (that might be tested against predictions from other models developed within the same framework or some alternative metatheoretical framework). Alternatively, future research might attempt more direct estimation and testing of the framework itself. Aware that the present framework (like all other theoretical research) will ultimately prove valuable only if it can be linked to empirical research, I briefly consider some alternative means of empirical implementation.

Viewing the present framework as a kind of endogenous-preference model, future empirical research might adopt the methodological presuppositions and practices of rational choice theory. Because mental states (preferences) and processes (rationality) are presumed closed to direct empirical inspection, tests of rational choice models focus on predicted relationships between observable choices (e.g., quantity demanded of a particular good) and constraints (e.g., prices and income). For instance, the empirical predictions made by Becker and Murphy (1988) concern the time-path of consumption (of some addictive good) given stable or time-varying prices. Similarly, the predictions of my previous *Tally's Corner* model (Montgomery 1994) concern the time-path of family consumption given ego's labor-market opportunities. Thus a model developed within the present framework (such as the illustrative model in Section 3) might be tested against an alternative (such as Montgomery 1994) by comparing predicted time-paths of choices given time-paths of constraints.[62]

While such tests would permit direct comparison of (endogenous-self) role theory models to (endogenous-preference) rational choice models, exclusive use of that empirical approach would suggest that my emphasis on role-space trajectories and attractors is misplaced: perhaps I should have emphasized the dual problem of deriving trajectories and attractors in *action* space. More fundamentally, exclusive empirical focus on actions and constraints would suggest that my emphasis on roles

[62] Some of the predictions of the present model were discussed above (at the end of Section 3). However, any direct test between my two models is difficult because the substance of ego's choice problem differs markedly between those models. Montgomery (1994) focused solely on ego's tradeoff between own and family consumption; the present model ignores that tradeoff but includes normative conflicts between family consumption, employment, and time spent with the peer group.

and norms is misplaced: why not adopt the simpler "black box" specification of preference formation used in the rational choice literature? Arguably, retention of the present (more elaborate) framework seems warranted only if mental states (ego's degree of membership in roles and subjective understanding of norms) and processes (logical derivation) are presumed open to empirical inspection.

I have portrayed fuzzy logic as a flexible framework for building descriptive models of reasoning and choice. Thus, given empirical measures of (ego's degree of membership in) roles and (ego's perception of) norms, future research might attempt to test between alternative fuzzy-logic specifications of preference derivation.[63] While attempts to operationalize this empirical approach might simply reopen long-standing measurement issues in role theory (see Biddle 1986), it is important to note that one key issue haunting past efforts—the *ambiguity* of roles and norms—is precisely the rationale for using fuzzy sets and relations in measurement. Viewed as a parallel effort to estimate a descriptive model of reasoning and choice, this approach might draw upon ongoing psychological research on biases in logical reasoning (Baron 1994, ch. 9) and reason-based choice (Shafir et al. 1993).[64] Focusing narrowly on ego's reasoning (from roles and norms to actions), this approach might advance past sociological research on role conflict (Sarbin and Allen 1968; Biddle 1986).[65] Focusing on alter's reasoning (from norms and actions to roles), it parallels social-psychological research on (biases in) attribution (Ross 1977; Ross and Nisbett 1991).[66]

[63] In this way, empirical research in role theory would reflect the widespread sociological skepticism about the "revealed preference" methodology of rational choice theory—the skepticism that underlies the recurrent sociological claim that rationality (here logical derivation) is a *variable* not an *assumption*.

[64] Indeed, my contrast between ego's (unbiased) reasoning and alters' (biased) reasoning (see Section 2) might have been motivated by the empirical finding (Lagrenzi et al. 1993) that individuals are better at applying *modus ponens* than *modus tollens*.

[65] Indeed, the present framework helps clear up past confusion about (and conflation of) role ambiguity, role malintegration, role discontinuity, and role overload (see Biddle 1986:83).

[66] Having suggested that future research might attempt to test between alternative specifications of approximate reasoning, other empirical approaches might also prove fruitful. For instance, panel data on (roles in) the self-concept would permit an empirical analysis of role-space trajectories and testing for role-space attractors. While the development of suitable empirical methods remains for future research, I hope that the various empirical approaches identified in this subsection might allay the fear that the present framework cannot possibly be linked to empirical research.

6. CONCLUSION

In this paper, I have attempted to make both conceptual and operational contributions to role theory. At the conceptual level, I have begun to show how role theory may be viewed as a linked collection of dialectic processes. If we accept the (fundamental social-psychological) claim that the self is a social entity, then specification of the self-concept as a set of social roles seems natural. If we accept the (longstanding sociological) view that social norms are behavioral obligations or prohibitions associated with roles, then a logical (propositional) specification of norms seems natural. Moreover, logical derivation (not utility maximization nor probabilistic reasoning) would seem to be the natural process through which individuals make inferences and choices.[67] In short, while the language of rational-choice sociology is decision theory, I contend that role theorists should learn to speak using formal logic.

This dialectic view of role theory might be operationalized in various ways.[68] While future research might well consider alternatives (e.g., various deontic logics), the present paper has applied fuzzy logic. Perhaps the primary benefit of applying this family of logical formalisms is the ability to deal explicitly with the ambiguity inherent in social systems. The self becomes a *fuzzy* set of roles; norms become *fuzzy* relations between roles and actions; inference takes the form of *approximate* reasoning. Moreover, my present formalization of the role-person merger as a fuzzy system yields a (hopefully compelling) graphical representation: the self is a point in role space; the socialization process is a role-space vectorfield; an individual's life course is a trajectory through role space; the individual's long-run self is determined by the norms of the social system.

[67] Thus, when developing descriptive theories of human reasoning and choice, role theorists might incorporate the "logic of appropriateness" over the "logic of consequences" (March 1994); "reason-based" choice over "value-based" choice (Shafir et al. 1993); logical rather than probabilistic specifications of inference (Pearl 1988).

[68] Having called on role theorists to adopt formal logic, I suggest that the proper response is: *which* logic? In recent decades, researchers in philosophy, cognitive science, and computer science (many of whom are motivated by real-world concerns of database management) have proposed many alternative logical formalisms and frameworks; see Rich and Knight (1991) for one helpful overview. In addition to the references already given in note 58, see also the attempt by Devlin and Rosenberg (1993) to formalize an ethnomethodological perspective using situation theory.

REFERENCES

Abraham, Ralph H., and Christopher D. Shaw. 1992. *Dynamics: The Geometry of Behavior*. Redwood City, CA: Addison-Wesley.

Anderson, Alan R. 1962. "Logic, Norms, and Roles." Pp. 11–22 in *Mathematical Methods in Small Group Processes*, edited by Joan H. Criswell et al. Palo Alto, CA: Stanford University Press.

Anderson, Elijah. 1978. *A Place on the Corner*. Chicago, IL: University of Chicago Press.

Averett, C.P., and D.R. Heise. 1987. "Modified Identities." *Journal of Mathematical Sociology* 13:103–32.

Baron, Jonathan. 1994. *Thinking and Deciding*. Cambridge, England: Cambridge University Press.

Becker, Gary S., and Kevin M. Murphy. 1988. "A Theory of Rational Addiction." *Journal of Political Economy* 96:675–700.

Bellman, R.E., and L.A. Zadeh. 1970. "Decision Making in a Fuzzy Environment." *Management Science* 17:141–64.

Berger, Joseph, Cecilia L. Ridgeway, M. Hamit Fisek, and Robert Z. Norman. 1998. "The Legitimation and Delegitimation of Power and Prestige Orders." *American Sociological Review* 63:379–405.

Biddle, B.J. 1986. "Recent Developments in Role Theory." *Annual Review of Sociology* 12:67–92.

Bojadziev, George, and Maria Bojadziev. 1995. *Fuzzy Sets, Fuzzy Logic, Applications*. London: World Scientific.

Boyd, John Paul. 1991. *Social Semigroups: A Unified Theory of Scaling and Blockmodelling as Applied to Social Networks*. Fairfax, VA: George Mason University Press.

Brewka, Gerhard, Jurgen Dix, and Kurt Konolige. 1997. *Non-Monotonic Reasoning: An Overview*. Stanford, CA: Center for the Study of Language and Information.

Burt, Ronald S. 1983. "Range." Pp. 176–94 in *Applied Network Analysis*, edited by Ronald S. Burt and Michael J. Minor. Beverly Hills, CA: Sage.

Chellas, Brian F. 1980. *Modal Logic*. Cambridge, England: Cambridge University Press.

Cooley, Charles H. 1983 [1902]. *Human Nature and the Social Order*. New Brunswick, NJ: Transaction Publishers.

Devlin, Keith, and Duska Rosenberg. 1993. "Situation Theory and Cooperative Action." Pp. 213–64 in *Situation Theory and Its Applications*, Vol. 3, edited by Peter Aczel, David Isreal, Yasuhiro Katagiri, and Stanley Peters. Stanford, CA: Center for the Study of Language and Information.

Doreian, P. 1974. "On the Connectivity of Social Networks." *Journal of Mathematical Sociology* 3:245–58.

Drazin, P.G. 1992. *Nonlinear Systems*. Cambridge, England: Cambridge University Press.

Elster, Jon. 1978. *Logic and Society*. New York: Wiley.

Emirbayer, Mustafa, and Jeff Goodwin. 1994. "Network Analysis, Culture, and the Problem of Agency." *American Journal of Sociology* 99:1411–54.

Fararo, Thomas J. 1989. *The Meaning of General Theoretical Sociology*. Cambridge, England: Cambridge University Press.

Fararo, Thomas J., and John Skvoretz. 1984. "Institutions as Production Systems." *Journal of Mathematical Sociology* 10:117–81.

Feller, William. 1968. *An Introduction to Probability Theory and Its Applications*. New York: Wiley.

Fiske, Susan T., and Shelley E. Taylor. 1991. *Social Cognition*. New York: McGraw-Hill.

Haack, Susan. 1996. *Deviant Logic, Fuzzy Logic*. Chicago, IL: University of Chicago Press.

Hage, Per, and Frank Harary. 1983. *Structural Models in Anthropology*. Cambridge, England: Cambridge University Press.

Hannan, Michael T. 1998. "Rethinking Age Dependence in Organizational Mortality: Logical Formalizations." *American Journal of Sociology* 104:126–64.

Hannerz, Ulf. 1969. *Soulside: Inquiries into Ghetto Culture and Community*. New York: Columbia University Press.

Heider, Fritz. 1946. "Attitudes and Cognitive Organization." *Journal of Psychology* 21:107–12.

Heise, David. 1979. *Understanding Events*. Cambridge, England: Cambridge University Press.

———. 1987. "Affect Control Theory: Concepts and Model." *Journal of Mathematical Sociology* 13:1–33.

Horty, John F. 1993. "Deontic Logic as Founded on Nonmonotonic Logic." *Annals of Mathematics and Artificial Intelligence* 9:69–91.

———. 1994. "Moral Dilemmas and Nonmonotonic Logic." *Journal of Philosophical Logic* 23:35–65.

Huang, Zhisheng, and Michael Masuch. 1995. "The Logic of Permission and Obligation in the Framework of ALX.3: How to Avoid the Paradoxes of Deontic Logics." *Logique & Analyse* 149:55–74.

Hughes, G. E., and M. J. Cresswell. 1996. *A New Introduction to Modal Logic*. London: Routledge.

Kim, Ki Hang, and Fred William Roush. 1980. *Mathematics for Social Scientists*. New York: Elsevier North Holland.

Kosko, Bart. 1992. *Neural Networks and Fuzzy Systems*. Englewood Cliffs, NJ: Prentice-Hall.

———. 1994. *Fuzzy Thinking*. London: Flamingo.

Lagrenzi, P., V. Girotto, and P. N. Johnson-Laird. 1993. "Focussing in Reasoning and Decision Making." *Cognition* 49:37–66.

Lemmon, E.J. 1965. *Beginning Logic*. London: Chapman and Hall.

Lewis, Oscar. 1966. "The Culture of Poverty." *Scientific American* 215:19–25.

Liebow, Elliot. 1967. *Tally's Corner*. Boston: Little, Brown.

Mamdani, E. H. 1976. "Advances in Linguistic Synthesis of Fuzzy Controllers." *International Journal of Man-Machine Studies* 8:669–78.

March, James G. 1994. *A Primer on Decision Making*. New York: Free Press.

Masuch, Michael, and Zhisheng Huang. 1996. "A Case Study in Logical Deconstruction: Formalizing J. D. Thompson's *Organizations in Action* in a Multi-Agent Action Logic." *Computational and Mathematical Organization Theory* 2:71–114.

Mead, George H. 1934. *Mind, Self, and Society*. Chicago, IL: University of Chicago Press.
Montgomery, James D. 1994. "Revisiting Tally's Corner: Mainstream Norms, Cognitive Dissonance, and Underclass Behavior." *Rationality and Society* 6:462–88.
———. 1996. "The Structure of Social Exchange Networks: A Game-Theoretic Reformulation of Blau's Model." Pp. 193–225 in *Sociological Methodology 1996*, edited by Adrian E. Raftery. Cambridge, MA: Blackwell Publishers.
———. 1998. "Toward a Role-Theoretic Conception of Embeddedness." *Journal of Mathematical Sociology* 104:92–125.
Nadel, S.F. 1957. *The Theory of Social Structure*. London: Cohen and West.
Newell, Alan, and Herbert A. Simon. 1972. *Human Problem Solving*. Englewood Cliffs, NJ: Prentice-Hall.
Patterson, James T. 1980. *America's Struggle Against Poverty, 1900–1980*. Cambridge, MA: Harvard University Press.
Pattison, Philippa. 1993. *Algebraic Models for Social Networks*. Cambridge, England: Cambridge University Press.
Pearl, Judea. 1988. *Probabilistic Reasoning in Intelligent Systems*. Palo Alto, CA: Morgan Kaufmann.
Peay, Edmund R. 1977. "Matrix Operations and the Properties of Networks and Directed Graphs." *Journal of Mathematical Psychology* 15:89–101.
Péli, Gábor, Jeroen Bruggeman, Michael Masuch, and Breanndán Ó Nualláin. 1994. "A Logical Approach to Formalizing Organizational Ecology." *American Sociological Review* 59:571–93.
Pollak, Robert A. 1970. "Habit Formation and Dynamic Demand Functions." *Journal of Political Economy* 78:745–63.
———. 1976. "Habit Formation and Long-Run Utility Functions." *Journal of Economic Theory* 13:272–97.
Rich, Elaine, and Kevin Knight. 1991. *Artificial Intelligence*, 2nd ed. London: McGraw-Hill.
Ross, Lee. 1977. "The Intuitive Psychologist and His Shortcomings: Distortions in the Attribution Process." Pp. 173–220 in *Advances in Experimental Social Psychology*, edited by L. Berkowitz. Orlando, FL: Academic Press.
Ross, Lee, and R. Nisbett. 1991. *The Person and the Situation*. New York: McGraw-Hill.
Ross, Timothy J. 1995. *Fuzzy Logic with Engineering Applications*. New York: McGraw-Hill.
Sarbin, Theodore R., and Vernon L. Allen. 1968. "Role Theory." Pp. 488–567 in *The Handbook of Social Psychology*, 2nd ed., vol. 1, edited by Gardner Lindzey and Elliott Aronson, Reading, MA: Addison-Wesley.
Shafir, Eldar, Itamar Simonson, and Amos Tversky. 1993. "Reason-based Choice." *Cognition* 49:11–36.
Skvoretz, John, and Thomas J. Fararo. 1996. "Generating Symbolic Interaction: Production System Models." *Sociological Methods and Research* 25:60–102.
Smith-Lovin, Lynn. 1987. "Affect Control Theory: An Assessment." *Journal of Mathematical Sociology* 13:171–92.
Stigler, George J., and Gary S. Becker. 1977. "De Gustibus Non Est Disputandum." *American Economic Review* 67:76–90.
Stryker, Sheldon, and Anne Statham. 1985. "Symbolic Interaction and Role Theory."

Pp. 311–78 in *The Handbook of Social Psychology*, 3rd ed., Vol. 1, edited by Gardner Lindzey and Elliot Aronson. New York: Random House.

Suchman, Lucy A. 1987. *Plans and Situated Actions*. Cambridge, England: Cambridge University Press.

Tsoukalas, Lefteri H., and Robert E. Uhrig. 1997. *Fuzzy and Neural Approaches in Engineering*. New York: Wiley.

Turner, Ralph H. 1978. "The Role and the Person." *American Journal of Sociology* 84:1–23.

———. 1990. "Role Change." *Annual Review of Sociology* 16:87–110.

Vallacher, Robin R., and Andrzej Nowak, eds. 1994. *Dynamical Systems in Social Psychology*. San Diego: Academic Press.

von Weizäcker, Carl Christian. 1971. "Notes on Endogenous Change of Tastes." *Journal of Economic Theory* 3:345–72.

von Wright, G. H. 1963. *Norm and Action: A Logical Inquiry*. London: Routledge and Kegan Paul.

White, Harrison C. 1992. *Identity and Control: A Structural Theory of Social Action*. Princeton, NJ: Princeton University Press.

White, Harrison C., Scott A. Boorman, and Ronald L. Breiger. 1976. "Social Structure from Multiple Networks: I. Blockmodels of Roles and Positions." *American Journal of Sociology* 81:730–80.

Yager, R. 1981. "A New Methodology for Ordinal Multiobjective Decisions Based on Fuzzy Sets." *Decision Science* 12:589–600.

Zadeh, Lotfi A. 1965. "Fuzzy Sets." *Information and Control* 8:388–53.

———. 1975. "Calculus of Fuzzy Restrictions." Pp. 1–39 in *Fuzzy Sets and Their Applications to Cognitive and Decision Processes*, edited by Lotfi A. Zaheh, King-Sun Fu, Kokichi Tanaka, and Masamichi Shimura. New York: Academic Press.

NAME INDEX

SUBJECT INDEX